Business
as a
System of Power

T0296041

Business
as a
System of Power

Robert A. Brady

With a new introduction by
Douglas Dowd

Transaction Publishers
New Brunswick (U.S.A.) and London (U.K.)

New material this edition copyright © 2001 by Transaction Publishers, New Brunswick, New Jersey. Originally published in 1943 by Columbia University Press, New York.

This book is printed on acid-free paper that meets the American National Standard for Permanence of Paper for Printed Library Materials.

Library of Congress Catalog Number: 99-087783
ISBN: 0-7658-0682-7 (paper)
Printed in the United States of America

Library of Congress Cataloging-in-Publication Data

Brady, Robert A. (Robert Alexander), 1901-
  Business as a system of power / by Robert A. Brady; with a new introduction by Douglas Dowd.
    p.cm.
  Originally published: New York: Columbia University Press, 1943.
  Includes bibliographical references and index.
  ISBN: 0-7658-0682-7 (paper : alk. paper)
    1. Industries. 2. Trade associations. 3. Democracy. I. Title.
HD71 .B7 2000
338.9—dc21

99-087783

To

WESLEY CLAIR MITCHELL

who, without knowing it, has had much
to do with the writing of this book

CONTENTS

INTRODUCTION TO THE
TRANSACTION EDITION[1]

R OBERT A. BRADY WAS BORN in 1901 into a hard-working farm
family in Marysville, Washington—on the social and physical
edge of the United States. Between then and his early death in
1963 Brady forged a career of scholarship quite extraordinary
for an economist, even in an era when economists' scope of knowledge was considerably broader than it is now. His competence
extended through and beyond economics into engineering, the
physical sciences, history, and literature, and he was at ease in
several languages.

By the time Brady entered Oregon's Reed College the works
of Thorstein Veblen (1857–1929) were widely discussed, both
critically and favorably. Brady was much influenced by Veblen,
whom he came to know during the 1920s; he always acknowledged that influence in his own far-ranging books and essays,
even though he often differed significantly from Veblen in style,
scope, and conclusions.

The backgrounds of Brady and Veblen were quite similar in
some respects and, in others, strikingly different. Both were born
on farms (Veblen in Wisconsin), but in families with wildly divergent social and economic characteristics: Veblen's father was a
well-to-do and cultivated immigrant Norwegian who was on the
frontier of scientific farming. Two in Veblen's family became
prominent academics, Thorstein in economics, nephew Oswald
in mathematics.

Brady's father, in shocking contrast, was one of numberless
thousands of "boughten" white children sold into de facto sla-
very by their families after the Civil War—in his case at the age of
four, for fifteen dollars. He was purchased by a Midwestern farmer,
was variously abused—forcibly denied any education, his teeth

brutally removed to be sold when he was six—and worked as a slave until he managed to escape at the age of sixteen. The consequences of that ordeal shadowed the elder Brady's entire life and, as well, those of his seven children.[2]

In addition to the general similarity of Brady's and Veblen's scholarly interests and accomplishments, there was a basic commonality in their sociopolitical positions: both embraced industrialism but were sharply critical of its evolution within the capitalist framework; both deplored nationalism, organized religion, all forms of despotism, chicanery, media hype, and puritanical obsessions; both were what may be seen as a special U.S. creed of "radical populism"—which, however, they saw as having diverse forms of socialism as the desired goal. Veblen's works suggest some kind of highly decentralized (what the British came to call) "guild socialism". Brady, who was insistent on the need for democratic economic planning, envisioned a larger role for the state.[3]

Among Veblen's many books, those most influential for Brady's own work were *The Theory of Business Enterprise* (1904), *The Instinct of Workmanship* (1914), *Imperial Germany and the Industrial Revolution* (1915), and *Absentee Ownership: Business Enterprise in Recent Times* (1923). These works wererepresented most clearly in Brady's *The Rationalization Movement in German Industry* (1933), *The Spirit and Structure of German Fascism* (1937), *Business as a System of Power* (1943), and *Organization, Automation, and Society: The Scientific Revolution in Industry* (1961).

All of those works, as well as others, whether by Veblen or Brady, shared the following arguments: 1) the ineluctable scramble of business for always more concentrated economic power; 2) the constant tendency for that power, both in its accumulation and in its use, to spread inexorably from the economic to the political and cultural spheres; 3) the creation and adoption of nationalistic and other dangerous irrationalities (such as racism) to enhance support for business power (in whatever guise) and diminish the possibilities of competing power centers (such as labor); 4) the possibilities and imperatives of modern technology, which 5) required for their beneficial realization fully democratic societies wherein, among other matters, economic decisions would be made in terms of socioeconomic rather than business criteria.

In these and other analytical areas, one of Veblen's many pithy aphorisms of contrast serves just as well for Brady: "Profits is a business proposition, livelihood is not."[4]

The generally common interests of Veblen and Brady were matched by a generally common analytical focus. Both were radically anti-capitalist; although both were well versed in Marxian economic theory and in the historical and then current realities of Europe, they differed importantly from Marx. As suggested above, their focus was on the insatiable appetite of business for *socioeconomic power*, with its initial source the control over the means of life.

Of course Marx also took ownership and control of the means of production as the source of capital's power over both workers *and* the state—"The executive of the modern state is but a committee for managing the common affairs of the whole bourgeoisie";[5] so it was appropriate to make the core of his analysis "Accumulation! Accumulation! That is Moses and the Prophets!"

In their differences with Marx, Veblen and Brady were also differentiated from European critics of capitalism; they became, instead, what I have termed above "radical populists" or "Made in the U.S.A."

Of the many factors distinguishing Brady and Veblen from Marx and his European followers were not only the numerous historical contrasts between the United States and all other societies but, as well, the many decades separating Marx's era from their own. Veblen began to write fifty years after Marx, Brady seventy-five years later. In those intervals, industrial capitalism had changed in many and critical ways. Until very late in the nineteenth century, not even the formal elements of political democracy existed in Britain, and even less so on the Continent. And Britain was, of course, the model for Marx's capitalism.

Veblen and Brady, by contrast, lived and functioned in the United States at a time when political democracy—whatever its limitations then or subsequently—was in full swing. Marx's era was also one of capital shortage; in such conditions, the means to capitalist ends were considerably simpler than in any portion of this century: the concentration on accumulation was both necessary and sufficient.

The twentieth century, in both of its halves, commenced and
and remained utterly different: 1) in the first half, there was either
too much capital or, what is saying much the same thing, inadequate
markets, making capital accumulation increasingly difficult and rare;
2) capitalism's new lease on life after World War II was made possible only by massive qualitative changes in all realms impinging on
the socioeconomic process—economic, political, cultural, military,
political, and geographic—all of them interdependently stimulated
or required by the historically novel setting of a "cold war."

Thus, throughout this century, if business were to advance or
even to protect its always-abiding interests in capital accumulation—and with whatever degrees of reluctance or enthusiasm—
it became necessary to extend its powers continuously into political and sociocultural institutions—directly or indirectly.

That this was so as regards the state had become obvious in the
early years of this century, not just because by then the state was
becoming multi-functional but because at the same time and for
overlapping reasons, workers were organizing always more effectively. It was more than electioneering rhetoric when, in 1912,
presidential candidate Woodrow Wilson observed that "as government becomes always more important, it becomes always more
important to control the government." Not many years earlier,
Washington D.C. had been a sleepy southern town.

The very title of Brady's *Business as a System of Power* was em-
blematic of the sociopolitical sea change that had occurred since
the nineteenth century. It may be believed that Brady's initial
impulse to undertake this book was occasioned by his substantial
studies of interwar Germany. He was of course very much at home
with the realities of the U.S. economy, and had *Business* been
concerned only with the United States it would still have been an
important study. However, what gave *Business* its special qualities
and strength in 1943 (and still today) is that it comprehended
the functional similarities of the business systems of the leading
industrial capitalist nations of the interwar period: Britain, France,
Germany, Italy, Japan, and the United States.

A sense of what is to come announces itself in the early pages
of Part 1. After noting that his is a comparative study of the attempts of those six nations to expand business controls within

their societies, Brady remarks that "at the outset of such an effort one is struck by four extremely interesting facts":

> First, the transformations undergone by business organizations in the totalitarian countries are fully consonant with, and may be considered the logical outgrowths of, previous trends in structure, policies, and controls within the business world itself.
>
> Second, along every significant line the parallelisms in the evolution of business centralization within the several national systems, including those within countries still functioning on a liberal-capitalistic basis, are so close as to make them appear the common product of a single plan.
>
> Third, all business policies have been increasingly discussed and formulated in the face of widespread ... popular opposition, ... which more and more challenges the traditional business view of the proper objectives and responsibilities of economic leadership. . . .
>
> And finally, the implications of power in such widespreading business controls, together with the popular challenge to business leaders, cause all economic issues to take on a political meaning, and thereby cause the role of the government to grow in importance in a sort of geometric ratio. (pp. 5-7)

Part 2 is a detailed study of business attitudes, behavior, and politics of six nations during the interwar years. For those whose consciousness was formed in the expanding and buoyant economic years of the half century now ending, the descriptions of the means and ends of business in the leading industrial capitalist nations in those two decades might well seem fanciful, despite Brady's meticulous documentation.

They were of course the most tumultuous years in history. Business—among others, of course—was enduring unprecedented and substantial socioeconomic stresses, and it responded desperately. Italy, Germany, and Japan became explicitly fascist, with much support and little dissent from the business community; France took much the same path and, as Brady shows, France was close to arriving there before the German occupation. Of the six nations, only Britain and the United States remained political democracies. The whys and wherefores of those developments are fully described and analyzed in *Business*.

There have of course also been "stresses" in the second half of this century; but they have been minor in the major nations, if often substantial in many of the weaker societies. Beginning in the 1970s, socioeconomic stresses reappeared, though in ways necessarily different both in nature and impact from the interwar period. The first intimations of trouble took hold in the "stagflation crisis" of the 1970s. Since then, although there has been what has been dubbed "the corporate counterattack"[6]—to rollback social legislation and union power—the response has been but a pale glimmering of interwar business behavior. That has been true not only because the difficulties that took hold in the 1970s were modest compared with the interwar period, but that they did so in a world of substantially different institutions.

If—or as many have come to believe, when—a serious global economic crisis were to occur, what now seems fanciful could soon be seen as considerably less so. It is more than a mere possibility that the first stage of such a crisis was edging its way over the economic horizon with the onset of "the Asian flu" in 1997. With the appearance of developing weaknesses in the economies of Britain, Italy, Germany, and France in 1999, and the deepening of Japan's now decade-long recession, it seems more likely than not that the "flu" could become a global pneumonia. Brady's warnings of 1943, albeit with substantial alteration, thus have more than historical interest.

All the more so is that the case when one considers Part 3 of *Business as a System of Power.* Its three chapters summarize the means and ends of the economic, social, and political policies pursued by business in between the two world wars. In all three of the policy areas the differences between that past and any future crisis are likely to be more striking than their similarities. Setting aside that the ugly developments of the interwar period would not have been seen as possible, let alone probable, before World War I,[7] it remains necessary to add that in its very different ways, our world is also precariously placed. Whether the focus is narrowly economic, social, political, or ecological, and whether national or global, the years ahead cannot be viewed as being more stable than unstable.

There are no workable blueprints that tell us how to move from a dangerous to a safe society, whether as regards social or ecological tensions, nor did Brady seek to construct one. But, in *Business as a System of Power* (as well as in others of his writings), he did show us in a compelling and clear analysis just how unsafe society was; whatever the outward appearances, it may be no less so today.

Brady's work was finished as the 1960s began. So much has changed since then as to make today's society seem another world entirely. If anything, however, there is less reason for complacency today than forty years ago, however little there may have been then.

In addition to potential economic crises and ongoing extant social tensions—not least those heightened by ethnic, racial, and religious tensions—there are few areas of the world today unmarked by other serious conflicts, whether in the Middle East, the Balkans, much of Africa and Latin America, many parts of Asia or, not without relevance, the urban areas of all too many of the rich nations.

The background against which all that turbulence is being played out, and directly or indirectly aggravating them, is an existing calamity whose looming dangers stand out starkly. And, it may be added, that would have heightened Veblen's scorn and Brady's rage, concerned so much as both were with waste and inefficiency. As both actual and potential, national and global production have risen to undreamed of heights in recent decades, in those same decades more than three-quarters of a *billion* people have come to be subject to famine, and 2 billion suffer from malnutrition (from which 40,000 children die every day).[8] Meanwhile, the world spends roughly 1 *trillion* dollars yearly on the military; meanwhile, producers and nations struggle to find ways to deal with excess capacities in industry and agriculture, in virtually everything; meanwhile, also, 10 to 15 percent of the world's most comfortable inhabitants flit from shop to shop, dithering over what to buy next.

All this has a moral connotation that neither Veblen nor Brady would have made much of; but both would have pointed to how irrational and dangerous it is for a world to produce peoples with such clashing areas of striving, a very large group because it has too little, a much smaller group because it has too much.

And it is in the United States, the richest and most powerful nation in all of history, where these bitter contrasts are most vivid— as they were in Britain in Disraeli's time, "two nations, between whom there is no intercourse and no sympathy: who are as ignorant of each other's habits, thought and feelings, as if they were dwellers in different zones, or inhabitants of different planets." In such a world, the counsel of a Brady never loses its vitality.

DOUGLAS DOWD

San Francisco, CA
March, 1999

Notes

1.   Much of what follows was put forth earlier in my essay "Against Decadence: The Work of Robert A. Brady (1901–63)," in *Journal of Economic Issues* (December, 1994). My indebtedness to Brady's daughters Joan and Judith was substantial for that essay, and I wish to note it once more here.

2.   The "boughten children" were seen as "indentured servants." But the latter were normally obligated by themselves for a period of 4-7 years; these children were sold and "indentured" until the age of 21—an age few reached without serious damage, if indeed they survived. The story of Brady's father (and much more) is at the center of a brilliantly written and horrifying novel by Joan Brady (Robert's daughter), *Theory of War* (New York: Knopf, 1993). In her "Author's Note," she says simply "my grandfather was a slave. . . . This so scarred him that no one who came near him afterwards could escape the effects of it; four of his seven children—including my father— ended up as suicides." It is of more than passing interest that Brady's purchaser was the Norris family; their son, two years older than the Brady boy, was George W. Norris, who became the Republican senator from Nebraska— and central for two landmarks of the New Deal, the Tennessee Valley Authority and the Norris-La Guardia (labor relations) Act.

3.   For Veblen's views, never made fully explicit, see some of his essays in *The Engineers and the Price System* (New York: Viking, 1947); for Brady, see his *Organization, Automation, and Society* (Berkeley: Univ. of California Press, 1961).

4.   *The Theory of Business Enterprise*, p. 276.

5.   From the *Communist Manifesto*.

6.   By economic historian Richard Du Boff, in his *Accumulation & Power* (Armonk, NY: M.E. Sharpe, 1989), Chapter 7.

7.   Except, perhaps, for Veblen, and for the appropriate reasons. In his "The Opportunity of Japan" (1915) and his extended remarks on Germany in "The Socialist Economics of Karl Marx," (1908), he anticipated the move toward a militarized society that would combine the advantages of the maintenance (in Japan) or revival (in Germany) of "medieval" attitudes of obedience and servility with the economic prowess of modern industry. Veblen saw the working class of Japan as being coerced into giving up their

efforts to democratize Japan, and the already well-organized working class of Germany as being seduced by nationalism to the same end. The first essay may be found in Leon Ardzrooni (ed.), *Essays in Our Changing Order* (New York: Viking, 1983), and the second in *The Place of Science in Modern Civilization* (New York: B.W. Huebsch, 1919).

8.   The data are put out regularly by UNICEF and in the annual United Nations Development Report. These figures were for 1986; they have worsened since.

FOREWORD

MEN HAVE ALWAYS EXPERIENCED difficulty in perceiving the thrust of deeper tendencies beneath the surface phenomena of their day. Particularly when long-established institutional systems have been breaking up under them have they tended to mistake symptom for cause and to greet predictions of major change with incredulity and aversion. In the main, they wrestle with obvious immediacies in familiar terms; for the rest, the deeper tendencies, they prefer to wait and see. If such a policy has seemed to be not without some justification in more leisurely eras of change, it is today nothing less than disastrous. For we are living through one of the great climactic eras of history, a major faulting of the institutional crust. A symptom of the extent of current change is the extreme ideological confusion. Fascist monopoly capitalism adopts "National Socialism"; organized industry opposes organized labor in the name of "democracy"; and ideological opposites fight side by side for goals that sound alike only because they are left vague. In such a time, when men and their most cherished concerns are being dragged headlong at the heels of confused events, the one chance for constructive recovery of control lies in the diagnosis of underlying causes.

In this book Dr. Brady cuts through to the central problem disrupting our world, the most dangerous issue democracy faces. This problem is not basically created by Adolf Hitler and the Axis nations, but by the organized economic power backing the Hitlers in nation after nation over the industrial world as a device for shoring up for yet a while longer a disintegrating economic system. And while this war against the immediate Axis Hitlers must be fought and won as a necessary step in the reëstablishment of a democratic world, we citizens of the United States and of other democratic nations would better learn, and quickly, to focus our strategy on the fact that the war is an episode in the world-wide counter-revolution against democracy; for, win, lose, or draw in the military war, democracy will be lost unless it also wins, even as it fights the Axis nations, its internal political conflict.

This is a book about power and the organization of power around the logic of technology as operated under capitalism. The characteristic thing about democracy is its diffusion of power among the people. That men have recurrently had to have recourse to revolutions in order to assert such a pattern of power attests the inveterate presence within society of a contrary tendency. Power is no less "political" for being labeled "economic" power; for politics is but the science of "who gets what, when, and how." Alexander Hamilton advocated and Jefferson opposed the effort of clotted economic power to substitute concentrated minority class power for diffused power. Lincoln referred to this same tendency when he wrote in 1860, "Soberly, it is now no child's play to save the principles of Jefferson from total overthrow in this nation"; and he went on to speak of "the miners and sappers of returning despotism" engaged in undercutting democracy. The preponderant weight of economic power in the Constitutional Convention, while conceding the outward forms of political democracy, went on at once to curb the exercise of the very power it had just granted; it crippled the force of democratic power at the source by parceling up this power by a marvelously dexterous system of barriers to its expression. Thus political equality under the ballot was granted on the unstated but factually double-locked assumption that the people must refrain from seeking the extension of that equality to the economic sphere. In short, the attempted harmonious marriage of democracy to capitalism doomed genuinely popular control from the start. And all down through our national life the continuance of the union has depended upon the unstated condition that the dominant member, capital, continue to provide returns to all elements in democratic society sufficient to disguise the underlying conflict in interests. A crisis within the economic relations of capitalism was bound to precipitate a crisis in the democratic political system.

Democracy in the era of economic liberalism has viewed power as a thing to be feared, rather than used; and this disposition, coupled with the checks on democratic action written into the Constitution, has prompted American democracy to state the problem of power negatively. It has been casual, to the point of recklessness, about the positive development of its own authority. Formally, democracy has held all the aces. But actually, as Laski has pointed out, "The disproportion in America between the actual economic control and the formal political power is almost fantastic." Despite intermittent guerilla warfare between state power and private economic power through all our national life, democracy has slurred over the challenge to its very existence inherent in growing economic power. This has been due to a number of factors. (1) The fact that the issue between the two types of power has been so heavily cloaked under the sectional issue between the agrarian and the Eastern industrial states has diverted attention from the fact that capitalist economic power constitutes a direct, continuous, and fundamental threat to the whole structure of democratic authority everywhere and always. (2) The appearance of the Industrial Revolution simultaneously with political democracy distracted men's attention from the perennially unfinished task of building democracy. Equipped with a new and marvelously growing technology and with a raw continent beckoning to be exploited, Americans turned their attention all down through the nineteenth century to the grand adventure of getting rich. Democracy was taken for granted as substantially achieved, or at most requiring only to be defended. And a naïve and dangerous popular faith has grown, notably since the Civil War, that democracy and capitalist enterprise are two aspects of the same thing, so that the progress manifestly occurring in industry must also be happening in the democratic political system. Since democracy itself thus failed to throw constantly new goals ahead to catch the imagination and to evoke the energy of its citizens, men thus deprived of anything bigger to work for have in the main vindicated the cynical view that they are motivated only by selfish personal interests. Under such a distorted view of democracy, in which the state and society are nothing and the individual everything, democracy has become increasingly identified with the protection of one's personal affairs; and this has steadily sapped its vitality. (3) Because this "American way" has worked so seemingly opulently, and because of man's need in the rough and tumble of an increasingly insecure world to feel immutable security somehow back of him, American citizens, preoccupied with everything but the affairs of democracy, have increasingly imputed to the Constitution, the central symbol of American democracy, an extravagant finality. If this great and mysterious It were but defended, democracy remained unchallenged.

In such an environment, democracy has been largely tolerant of the businessman, for the most part encouraging him with a lavish hand; for upon his restless enterprise the public welfare was conceived to rest. The "trust busting" of the turn of the century was a protest against what seemed to be excesses in an otherwise normal system, not a protest against the system itself. Even in recent decades, as business has grown in power until it has become a jostling giant, democracy has largely failed to recognize its political significance. The world was large and its wealth seemingly unlimited, and if business was growing bigger and more noisily insistent, this was viewed as but a surface manifestation of rugged growth. Down to the First World War abroad, and until 1929 in the United States, what businessmen did was regarded as primarily their own business. Since the fruit of their activities slopped over in taxes, wages, and dividends, it was manifestly contributing to general welfare.

But this nominal division of powers could not be maintained within the structure of capitalist nationalism. As industrialization has spread over the world and competition has increased, the reciprocal relation between state power and economic power has become more apparent. The fundamental import of what has been happening at a quickening tempo since the Russian Revolution of 1917 is the abandonment of the liberal fiction of the separateness of these two kinds of power. Organized business enterprise is less and less willing to tolerate checks on its activities by the state; more and more it needs the state as active ally; and the national state, in turn, having delivered itself over by accepting the definition of its welfare as synonymous with the welfare of its business system, needs increasingly the utmost of aggressive efficiency from its businessmen. Business is in politics and the state is in business. The state political apparatus can tolerate only the most efficient management of the economic system, since it depends directly upon the latter for national power in foreign relations; whereas the economy must have the political power to extend control, as the Nazis have demonstrated, to the regulation of the social sphere, "not to gratify lower-class maudlinness or rapacity but to secure national concord and efficiency" as an essential aid to foreign economic competition. The result is an unmistakable trend toward the monolithic power structure of the totalitarian state.

And the public does not know what to do about this merging of powers up aloft over its head. As business has organized and has begun to state cogently and lavishly the case for its version of such an "ordered society," the popular challenge expressed earlier in the campaign to curb bigness by governmental action has become confused and blunted. Big business has carefully disseminated to the little man at the grass roots enthusiasm and pride as an American in the superefficiency of the marvelous assembly lines and other paraphernalia of giant technology that produces his automobiles and other daily conveniences. The little man is puzzled, hypnotized into inaction: if he is not to oppose *bigness* itself, the bigness of Henry Ford, Du Pont, and the other great corporations that makes these characteristically American things possible, what *is* he to oppose about big business? The technique of dazzling, confusing, and dividing the opposition, used by Hitler, has been skillfully practiced by the propagandists for big business.

The rapidly spreading web of interindustry organization of this business power is the immediate focus of Dr. Brady's book. We live in an era in which only organization counts; values and causes with unorganized or only vaguely organized backing were never so impotent. The rapidity of current change creates the need for quick decisions, which puts the organized minority that knows what it wants at a thumping advantage over the scattered and wistful majority. In fact, it is able, as the Nazis have demonstrated, to exploit majority confusions ruthlessly in the name of majority values to minority ends.

One of the most striking conclusions from Dr. Brady's book concerns the similarity in type and function of the organization of business interests from nation to nation, despite seemingly widely dissimilar national backgrounds. This is due primarily to the inner common tendencies within capitalist-controlled technology wherever it operates. But it is also due in part to the fact that men operating across the world from each other learn organizational and other tricks of their trade as rapidly as these appear. Major changes

in the way men live and work together under industrial conditions
no longer happen in one industry or òne country and then spread
at a pace to be measured in decades or generations. Inventions have
shrunk physical space and organization has diminished social space.
World competition sees to it that a profitable technical or organizational device runs around the world of organized interest before
common folk in the country of origin are generally aware that it
has been developed.

Social organization around functional concerns is normal to human beings. Western liberalism, imputing freedom and rationality
to the individual, washed its hands of the problem of securing positive organization; it proceeded on the assumption that, wherever
organization was socially desirable, men would recognize the need
and forthwith organize themselves. Such a theory not only misread
human nature but it failed to take account of the momentum developed within such a cultural complex as machine technology
owned and exploited within a legally buttressed system of private
property rights. Liberal democracy has never dared face the fact
that industrial capitalism is an intensely coercive form of organization of society that cumulatively constrains men and all of their
institutions to work the will of the minority who hold and wield
economic power; and that this relentless warping of men's lives and
forms of association becomes less and less the result of voluntary
decisions by "bad" or "good" men and more and more an impersonal web of coercions dictated by the need to keep "the system"
running. These coercions cumulate themselves to ends that even
the organizing leaders of big business may fail to foresee, as step
by step they grapple with the next immediate issue, and the next,
and the next. Fantastic as it may sound, this course may end by the
business leaders of the United States coming to feel, in the welter
of their hurrying perplexities, that survival depends on precisely
the kind of thing Germany's big business wants: the liquidation of
labor and other popular dissent at home, and a "peace" more vin-
dicative than the Versailles Treaty, that will seek to stabilize an
Anglo-American feudal monopoly control over the entire world.

Liberal democracy likewise never solved the problem of bigness;
but it alternately fought and condoned it in a confusion of inconsistent policies. A cultural system drenched with the artisan spirit

of small enterprise found difficulty in accepting the facts that modern machinery demands integration and that productive enterprise, released from making a pair of shoes for a known local customer and set to making standard goods for an impersonal and theoretically unlimited "market," likewise demands organization. Hence the recurrent efforts to curb bigness. But both bigness and monopoly are normal antecedents to the stage of planned provision for the needs of society which we are now entering, and there is no longer any point in attacking either. The only relevant questions today are: Who controls these productive facilities, and to what ends? and How effectively are they organized to achieve these ends? Or, stated in another way: Will democratic political power absorb and use economic resources, bigness and all, to serve its ends, or will big economic power take over state power?

The modern phase of business as a system of organized power began with the spread of the corporate organization of industry after the 1860's. The world of 1870 did not speculate much about the grip which corporate business was to have on the lives of all of us a half-century later. Corporate organization, like the monopolies it made possible, was viewed as the exception, unadapted to general business. The precise significance of Dr. Brady's book is that he takes this same organizational tendency within industrial society—now become the rule rather than the exception and moved along to its contemporary stage of organized inter-monopoly control—and shows us where the logic of such a centrally organized system of power is carrying us. For synchronized monopoly directed by a peak all-industry strategy board is but corporate business come of age. The difference between the early and the mature stages is that, whereas corporate organization completed the taking of the instruments of production out of the hands of the laborer and strengthened economic power in its challenge to democratic political power, the mature stage Dr. Brady describes is moving on to wrest even the formal political means of curbing economic power from the hands of the citizens of democracy. Corporate organization pocketed production; its giant offspring is pocketing the nation, including the entire lives of its citizens. And organized business is extending this anti-democratic web of power in the name of the people's own values, with billboards proclaiming "What's Good for Industry Is Good for Your Family," and deftly selling itself to a harassed people as "trustees," "guardians," "the people's managers" of the public interest.

The large identities in problem and in organizational form to meet these problems in nation after nation suggest with startling emphasis that we in the United States are caught in the same major coercions that industrial capitalist nations everywhere face. We, too, have no choice as to whether economic and state power shall be merged; for there will be no survival for nations that seek to perpetuate the economic wastes and frictions and the social anarchy entailed in the operation of state power and economic power as rivals. The sheer fact of the emergence of the phenomenon of effectively planned nations has, because of the logic of organization inherent in modern technology, outmoded at a stroke the old system under which all our American national life has been lived. In the United States, the present stage of organized, centralized business power, already reaching out in control of schools, media of communication, public opinion, and government itself, provides more than a broad hint of the direction events will take, if present tendencies remain unchecked. In England, longer in the war than ourselves and closer to the choice that must be made, the same power tendencies are at work, despite optimistic reports of surface democratic manifestations. As this is written, the London *New Statesman and Nation* for August 15, 1942, carries a review of a book by an English businessman, N. E. H. Davenport. "He shows, in effect," says the review, "that what has happened is that the vested interests of monopoly capitalism have, for all practical purposes, taken over the government of the country. Behind the facade of political democracy they are preparing the economic foundations of the corporate State; and, to no small extent, they are being aided and abetted in this task by the powerful trade unions. . . . [Mr. Davenport] has made it clear beyond discussion that unless we are able very soon to persuade or compel the Prime Minister to swift and profound changes in his economic policy, we shall defeat Hitler only to be delivered into the hands of the same type of men for whom a Hitler is a necessary instrument."

In this really desperate predicament, American democracy is unprepared fully to assert itself. We are organizing—belatedly—to fight a war for "democracy," but we are rendered gullible by our traditions as regards the precise thing for which to fight. We speak vaguely of "the Four Freedoms," and yet we do not go on to give these war aims, at home and abroad, the full-blooded, realistic content so essential if men are really to be quickened to fight for democracy. Such muting of democratic objectives creates the blurred confusion which can provide the perfect setting for the strong men who know what they want. Born as a nation coincidentally with the upsurge of the Industrial Revolution, situated in a rich continent which we have built up with the bodies of cheap foreign labor, protected by the accident of location during the years of our fumbling growth, we have through all our national life been borne forward by a favoring tail wind. This past we view, quite characteristically, not as a stroke of luck but as the vindication of the superior rightness of "the American way"; and this makes for complacency. Growing out of this is our blindness to any way of conceiving our national future other than in terms of the simple extension of our expansive past. Our national naïveté about organization is disastrous in the present crisis. We are called "a nation of joiners," but the individual still holds the focus of our national imagination. With all the flotsam and jetsam of our "joining," we have little popular belief in or experience of the hard-bitten type of relentless organization for power ends; and where we see it, for instance, in the Tammany type of politics, we deplore it even as we condone it as a special case and a somehow necessary evil. Of all the Western industrial nations, we are the least class-stratified psychologically and the only one without an active labor party or its equivalent in our national political life. And, again, this is not because "the American way" is fundamentally different, but primarily because the American ideology as regards capitalism is less sophisticated than is that of any other Western nation.

Thus our traditions conspire to make us unable to read the meanings behind the organization Dr. Brady describes. We are opaque to the political import of this massing of business power, and we still insist on regarding it as primarily a concern only of the businessmen. Meanwhile, the lawyers with their convenient conception of the role of the law, the public-relations men, the press, and all the other pliant agents of organized business go busily about on cat

feet as they spread the net and tighten the noose for those so abundantly able to make it "worth their while." Burnham's plausible
thesis of the "managerial revolution" has been seized upon by business, and a powerful medium like *Fortune* proclaims itself in its
new editorial policy as the organ "for the managers of America."
But behind the fiction of the "manager class" so conveniently steri-
lized from the taint of special interest stands the same old power.
"The voice is Jacob's voice, but the hands are the hands of Esau."

If the American rank and file—the upwards of four fifths of the
nation who are working-class and small-business folk—are thus
illiterate in the language of contemporary power, the case is almost
as bad with those experts, the professional social scientists, whom
society supports because they profess to know about men's institutions. It is no accident that, as Dr. Brady points out, a world of
scientists who comb their fields for important problems for research
have left the problem of the power organization and politics of big
business so largely unexplored. For the most part, contemporary
social scientists still exhibit toward the changing business world the
encouraging moral optimism of Alfred Marshall. Nor are we helped
by the fact that the crucial science of economics derives its data
within the assumptions and concepts of a system conceived not in
terms of such things as "power" but of blander processes such as
the automatic balancing of the market.

American public opinion tends to reject out of hand any answer
to the question "Where are we going?" that is not couched in the
familiar optimistic terms. As we fight the present war, involving
an unparalleled tangle of ideological inconsistencies, the popular
mood encouraged by government and sedulously sponsored by business is to ignore controversial questions and to concentrate on winning the war. But the First World War gave interindustry coördination of big business rapid acceleration; post-war conditions gave
it its opportunity and successful foreign precedents; and the management of the present war has been taken over by representatives
of big business. And this time they may be in Washington for keeps.
We shall emerge from this war well on our way to having a permanently planned and managed economy; and if business controls
the goals of that planning, that will mean management also, from
top to bottom and from center to circumference, of all relevant so-

cial and cultural life. The fresh, growing shoots of new life in our American culture will either be destroyed or ruthlessly grafted to the main trunk.

The thing we do not realize, or are prevented from realizing, is that we are building the structure and accompanying animus of the post-war world by the manner in which we fight the war. The already half-accepted formula that "You can't fight *this* war democratically" is both factually incorrect and a one-way ticket to American fascism. If democracy is suspended now, it will not reappear at the peace conference. If during the war we avoid the development of genuine democratic organization and participation, if we curtail the partial organization of labor we now have instead of moving forward to its thoroughgoing democratic extension, we can know for certain fact that democratic people's organizations will be similarly frustrated after the war. Both during the war and after, the issue is identical: Who controls, and to what ends? An answer to that question has been preparing in the organization Dr. Brady describes, and it is crystallizing in the staffing and manner of operation of current wartime controls in Washington.

As things stand, the fight is not an equal one. On the one side is abundant good will but lack of organization and channels of communication, some suspicion of the way business is fencing in the war for itself, divided counsels in organized labor and middle-class suspicion of labor, large confusion as to the issues, and a tendency to trust that "they" in Washington will somehow bring us through the war and then everything will be all right again. On the other side, effective organization and the crisis nature of the present, requiring quick decisions and encouraging decision in terms of blunt short-run objectives, favor those who seek to exploit the war to make the United States safe for big business. The *de facto* power of big business is reflected in the fact that the Government itself is, for the most part, timid and afraid of what big business will do if the war is not made "worth its while."

One stout weapon remains in the hands of the little people at the grass roots of democracy: no one dares to challenge in frontal attack the basic democratic thesis. (If an American version of fascism comes, it will have to come disguised in the full outward trappings of democracy.) The people can seize this remaining weapon and use it offensively and defensively as the price for their participation step by step in the war effort. We live in a heroic time. And democracy will either throw off its lethargy and rise insistently to the stature of the times—or it will cease to exist.

ROBERT S. LYND

New York City
October, 1942

ACKNOWLEDGMENTS

THIS BOOK is the first direct product of an extensive and continuing study of the rise of bureaucratic centralism which was begun in 1934 with the aid of a generous grant from the Carnegie Corporation. The original subsidy, which underwrote basic travel and research expenses, was supplemented by a more recent grant which makes possible prompt publication of this book by the Columbia University Press. I am deeply grateful not only for the financial assistance given by the Foundation, but also for the keen and sustained interest of Dr. Frederick Keppel and his associates in the work as it has been developed.

So much assistance has been given me in the research, writing and final preparation for publication that I cannot hope to catalogue my full indebtedness without fear of serious omissions. Special mention should be made, however, of the assistance given by several experts in the chapters dealing with the development of the "peak associations" in the various countries examined: Dr. Franz Neumann on the German material; Dr. Carl Schmidt on the Italian; Dr. Louis Launay and Mr. Robert Valeur on the French; Dr. William Taylor and Mr. Harry Oshima on the Japanese; and Major Leonard Urwick on the British; and various officials of the LaFollette Committee and the Anti-Trust Division of the Department of Justice on the American. I am further indebted to Dr. Neumann for his reading of the entire manuscript.

In the later stages of the work, I gained immeasurably from an infinity of suggestions and criticisms, major and minor, contributed by Professor Robert Lynd; from the laborious task of checking sources performed by Mr. and Mrs. Joseph Phillips; and from the assistance of Mr. Maynard Gertler, who, at considerable expense of time and effort, has checked detail with the editorial staff of the Columbia University Press from beginning to end. Special mention should also be made of the staff of the Columbia University Press, who have managed somehow to turn the otherwise harrowing task of preparing a book for publication into a pleasant and profitable experience for the author.

I wish also to thank the authors and publishers cited for permission to quote from their works. For permission to reproduce, with minor alterations, material which previously appeared as articles in their pages, I am indebted to the following: *Pacific Affairs*, September, 1940 (for Chapter III); the *Political Science Quarterly*, June–December, 1941 (for Chapters VII and IX); and the *Journal of Political Economy*, February, 1942 (for Chapter I).

Finally, I wish to acknowledge with thanks the countless aids of my most severe and relentless critic, Mildred Edie.

Whatever merits the book may possess are largely traceable to sources such as these; the faults, I need scarcely add, are mine alone.

ROBERT A. BRADY

Berkeley, Calif.
July 15, 1942

Introduction

EFFORTS TO ORGANIZE BUSINESS
FOR POLITICAL ACTION

ATTEMPTS to unify business on an ever more comprehensive basis
are inevitable. For how else is it possible to cope with the administrative and managerial problems of an industrial technology
which has for decades past been moving toward such a policy?

Intuitively, the most unsophisticated know this part of the story.
The breakfast table draws its supplies from the most distant lands.
The factory soaks up materials from a continent and sets the finished products flowing along well-grooved channels to the ends of
the earth. Finely meshed networks of transportation, communication, and energy bind the whole more closely and rigorously together with each passing day. Within these spreading networks,
industrial technology, in an infinity of small ways—hither and yon,
endlessly, restlessly, ceaselessly—weaves tighter and more exact-
ingly the multifarious interdependencies which engineers, step by
step, wring from the master patterns of the unfolding natural-
science "web of reason." Integration, coördination, planning, these
are the very root and marrow, the essence and the spirit of the industrial system as it is being developed in our times. In these respects changes are unidirectional, additive, cumulative. From them
there is no turning back. And, as the bitterly fought issues of the
Second World War—a "total war" which pits entire economic
systems against each other—have made abundantly plain, the end
is not yet.

POLICY AT THE CROSSROADS

Moving with this trend, however consciously or intuitively,
businessmen all over the world are engaged in weaving parallel

webs of control. As the separate strands are extended, a point is reached at which, willy-nilly, a choice of direction is forced upon the businessman. One way leads to the shaking off of all popular restraints on such cumulative powers and to shaping the contours and determining the content of economic policies pregnant with far-reaching political, social, and cultural implications. This is the totalitarian road. Organized business in Germany, Italy, Japan, and France has chosen to move in this direction, and has already found that the choice once made is both irrevocable and fraught with dangerous consequences. For it seems that, for better or for worse, what businessmen have taken for the agent of social catharsis is no less than a modernized version of Hobbes's *Leviathan*, whose self-appointed monarchs have learned from the inspired pages of *The Prince* only a *Realpolitik* of survival; a *Realpolitik* which may as readily demolish as resurrect any given structure of preëxisting special-interest controls, including—through the precarious fortunes of subsequent wars, revolutions, or internal paralysis—those of the business interests which fathered, with money, ideas, and leaders, the original coup d'état.

The contrasting choice is to force the growth of a sense of responsibility to democratic institutions, not by transmuting arbitrary controls into series of patriarchal relationships, however mellowed and benevolently postured, but by steadily widening the latitude for direct public participation in the formulation of economic policies affecting the public interests. How, is not for us to say. But clearly this is the alternative which faces highly örganized business in England, the United States, and other scattered countries still moving within the orbit of the liberal-capitalistic system. Here, just as in the totalitarian countries before the fateful decisions were made, business must choose. If it hesitates, choice will be thrust upon it. On the record no further compromise is possible except a compromise moving definitely in one direction or the other. For sovereign power is indivisible, and a house cannot long remain divided against itself.

Considered solely from the point of view of vested interests, this choice is not an easy one for organized business to make. It is difficult not only because one route has thus far led to successive and politically dangerous disasters while the alternative entails a democratization reaching to the very roots of the ideology and the institutional sanctions upon which the business system rests as a whole, but also because organized business, however widely it may have cast its webs of influence and however swiftly its leaders may be centralizing authority through machinery of their own or others' devising, still has great difficulty in finding its collective mind. Some businesses are big; some little. Some are interested in contraction, others in expansion; some in local markets, others in national and international markets. Commodities, businesses, trades compete with each other long after conditions of partial or complete monopoly have been effected in restricted areas. For widely varying reasons some favor dictatorships, while others—particularly small businesses—can survive only in a democratic world. Within this newer business world, as often as elsewhere, what is one man's meat may well be another man's poison.

Thus even when organized business may have found some traces of collective mind, it faces the greatest difficulty in expressing a collective will, in focusing effort on the articulation of an internally coherent business program, in giving membership a sense of direction through promotion of a common social-psychological outlook, and in formulating for the doubtful a common set of simple and realizable goals. Yet, faced with the larger decisions which the trend of national and world affairs have placed before it, without these things business will everywhere be reduced to programmatic futility, and its centralized direction may well find itself without the wit at the critical moment to make even those half-hearted compromises urged upon it—as a condition to survival on any workable version of the time-honored principles of "muddling through"— by its own more vocal bellwether prophets such as Rathenau and Filene.

This is what happened in France, where organized business, unable to reconcile itself to further extension of democratic controls, sold its birthright for a condition of permanent vassalage to a foc sworn to destroy not business, but France. In the conquered territories, German firms have taken over the assets of resident concerns by right of conquest, not through "business as usual." [1] And by the

---

[1] As shown, for example in the history of the Hermann Göring Works—modern equivalent of the Stinnes empire—collected out of regrouped former governmental

same token, if Britain is conquered one cannot expect the Nazi principle of *Britannia delenda est* to be softened on behalf of the Federation of British Industries merely because the guiding figures in the *Reichswirtschaftskammer* learned their first economic lessons from the schoolteachers of Manchester. If German business succeeds in supplying the arms to, and financing the efforts of, a victorious Third Reich, its normal assumption will be that "to the victor belongs the spoils," an assumption followed by the British, in their turn, in South Africa and India. When a country is conquered, neither the business community as a whole nor any single individual within the inner business-control sancta can be sure of survival.

In the struggle for control over business power, small business is everywhere losing out.[2] Amongst the giants, whoever will not play according to the transformed rules will, upon becoming truly recalcitrant, be expelled by methods which partake more and more of the spirit of the purge.[3] If we can draw any certain lesson from events of the recent past it is surely this, that organized business in one national system will show no mercy to organized business in

---

industrial properties, as well as concerns taken over in conquered territories, and miscellaneous private enterprises. For further details see pp. 49–50, following. See also current issues of the London *Economist* for data on French, Belgian, Norwegian, and Rumanian firms taken over by German interests following conquest. Nearly every leading German banking, industrial, commercial, and shipping company has shared in the booty to some extent.

[2] See data submitted by Willard Thorp on business failures, in the Prologue of the TNEC Hearings (see note 10, below) data presented in the Census of Distribution (1935), VI, 11; TNEC Monograph No. 17, *Problems of Small Business;* and data submitted below in chapters on compulsory amalgamation schemes in England, Germany, Italy, and Japan. The small become enrolled in control apparatus dominated by the large, shift into highly localized markets or the unprofitable fringes (such as credit and durable goods as against cash and carry, where the risks are higher and the gains through financing are secured and siphoned off by finance companies and the banks), become "sub-contractors" to the large, exist on sufferance for strategic reasons in facing regulatory authorities, submit to legislation and administrative controls which are the product of organized large-scale business pressure. See J. R. Sprague, *High Pressure* (New York, 1938).

[3] What of Thyssen? everybody asks. But also, what of the Jews, what of Polish businessmen when the Germans took over, what of Skoda, what of the Lorraine ore fields, what of the rights of foreign corporations and stockholders? What of "chiselers" and "sellers-below-cost" in NRA, of perpetrators of "Unfair Trade Practices"? What of the fact that the Codes and the FTC Fair Trade Practice agreements are typically designed to catch the small-scale violator of business "codes" drawn primarily by the large, even though it be the latter which enjoy the almost exclusive attention of the Anti-Trust Division?

another national system, once conflicts of interest have forced matters to the arbitraments of war. The delegation of the Federation of British Industries in Manchukuo failed once it became clear that Japan was able to consolidate its military victory, just as did a like attempt on the part of the same organization on the day following the British catastrophe at Munich.[4]

The underlying principles are not new. They are clearly in keeping with those long familiar to students of "trust and combination" *Realpolitik* in the domestic arena, and to those who have followed the clash of economic imperialism throughout the period leading up to the two World Wars on the larger field of action. The principal differences which contrast the contemporary with the past are found only in the size and compactness of current organization and in the scale on which the issues are now drawn. There is no difference in the issues themselves.

PARALLELS IN THE EVOLUTION OF BUSINESS CONTROLS

Thus a comparative study of attempts to expand business controls within the several capitalistic systems becomes a prime necessity for both business and the public. At the outset of such an effort, one is struck by four extremely interesting facts. First, the transformations undergone by business organization in those countries which have revamped their national systems along totalitarian lines are fully consonant with, and may be considered the logical outgrowths of, previous trends in structure, policies, and controls within the business world itself. Second, along every significant line the parallelisms in the evolution of business centralization within the several national systems, including those within countries still functioning on a liberal-capitalistic basis, are so close as to make them appear the common product of a single plan. Third, all business policies have been increasingly discussed and formulated in

---

[4] The FBI delegation was in Manchukuo during the investigations of the Lytton Commission engaged in negotiations with Japanese interests. They were unsuccessful here, and the Japanese subsequently pushed them out of north and central China as well. During the Munich negotiations which led to the downfall of Czechoslovakia, a committee of the Federation of British Industries was holding pourparlers with the Reichsgruppe Industrie which called for dividing European and world markets between British and German interests through a series of widely expanded cartel controls.

the face of widespread—in many respects very highly organized and always potentially threatening—popular opposition, whose interests have been coming into conflict with those of organized business in a way which more and more challenges the traditional business view of the proper objectives and the responsibilities of economic leadership as such. And finally, the implications of power in such wide-spreading business controls, together with the popular challenge to business leaders, cause all economic issues to take on a political meaning, and thereby cause the role of the government to grow in importance in a sort of geometric ratio.

It does not follow from the first of these facts that "totalitarianism" was the inevitable result of previous trends in business organization within the Axis states, but only that it was inescapable, because those trends were unmodified when circumstances of an eventually revolutionary character forced quick decision within strategically placed business circles committed to no further compromises with democratic government. It does not follow from the second fact that there was actually such a plan. The reverse is true. But it does follow that there were common sets of forces operating through greatly varying historical environments, with many factors (such as the level of industrial development and the nature of business organization at the time of rapid adoption of industrial and business methods) [5] differently timed, blended, juxtaposed, or set in conflict, which shaped and posed the issues in similar ways. And from the third and fourth, only this follows, that the issues everywhere come to rest not on whether the government was or is to be the coördinator, for that is now truly inescapable, but on whether the government will be able to coördinate and plan economic activities toward popular ends, responsible directly therein to democratic institutions, or toward the specialized interests of self-assertive and authoritarian minority groups.

From these considerations the special question necessarily arises, does capitalist civilization anywhere show any signs of being able or willing to plan means and unify ends on a national scale according to a workable formula that is still consonant with democratic institutions? We well know what happened in the totalitarian countries where organized business underwrote the antidemocratic re-

[5] See, in particular, the chapters on Germany, Italy, and Japan.

action. Can different results be expected elsewhere? Everyone concerned with the present dramatic crisis in world history would like to see this question resolved. Opinions, in reply, already differ as deeply and fundamentally as the status and social philosophies of those who give answer. This much is certain, the attempt—sometimes made consciously, but more often in groping fashion—to cope with the problem in some manner or other is being made in every major capitalistic country in the world. Business is becoming aware of the range of larger issues, is organizing to meet and resolve them, and its collective efforts to these ends are widening out on an ever more comprehensive scale.

And as it gathers together its forces, it comes everywhere to think politically, begins to come to grips at a thousand and one points with the "social question" in all its bewildering manifestations. So proceeding, organized business has more and more found itself compelled at least to make the attempt to evolve new "social philosophies," which will meet the more fundamental challenges dividing its own members in the preferred reaches of the social pyramid and at the same time meet those other challenges thrown at it by the leaders of the vast popular ranks becoming increasingly conscious of their own specific and often opposing interests.

In accomplishing this aim, can business still hope to retain its control over the inner sancta where the fundamental economic decisions are made? And if it succeeds in any marked degree in so holding on, will the political and social controls evolved be reconcilable with continuation of a democratic way of life? These are the fundamental, the critical questions of our times.

LACUNAE IN THE HISTORICAL LITERATURE

Many of the steps by which these issues have been pushed to the fore, and also the history of business methods evolved to meet them, have still to be traced. Most important of all the numerous gaps in the literature, which has laid bare one or more facets of the problems here posed, is that dealing with the specific forms of organization established by business for the dual purpose of unifying within its own ranks while presenting a common front to all opposition groups. This lack in the literature is the *raison d'être* of this study, which in itself can scarcely hope to give more than a sketch of a vast terrain that urgently requires careful mapping and systematic investigation.

What has been generally missed by scholars interested in such matters is that these forms of organization, regardless of the initial purposes of their sponsors, rarely confine themselves for long to strictly "economic" matters. As a general rule, the bigger and more comprehensive trade associations and their federational or "peak associations" (*Spitzenverbände* as they are known in the German literature [6]) become, the more clearly do social and political policies edge to the fore. Economic problems thus come to be quickly intertwined with these other issues, and the trade association begins to take on an entirely new cast of thought and to hew a line in keeping with newly transformed political directives.

So it is that, if the growth in the relative importance of giant corporations is properly termed "concentration of economic power," expansion of trade-association networks means "mobilization of the entire business community." If the former is defined as "trustification," [7] then the latter implies "unification" or "synchronization." [8] If the former carries with it growing resort to "monopoly practices," the latter calls for increasing "political and social awareness."

The two, of course, are not independent phenomena. As the following pages will show they are related in time, in origin and processes of growth, in the logic of circumstances which bind them to each other as historical developments, and in the compulsions they exert for an ever and cumulative widening of governmental regulation and control. Herein lies the larger significance of each—an importance that transcends by far the consequences of the two taken separately and by themselves.

Appreciation of the precise nature and the real meaning of such interdependence has been retarded by a curious shortcoming in the body of current economic and political literature. That the two have long existed side by side is now generally recognized. That the larger corporations and dominant business groups have taken an

---

[6] See pp. 29–36 for a description of the pre-Nazi *Spitzenverbände*.

[7] See Joseph Schumpeter, *Business Cycles* (2 vols., New York, 1939).

[8] A summary history of the National Association of Manufacturers is entitled, "The Nation's Industry Synchronized," which implies a conception of functions one step beyond mere "unification."

active, and more recently (since the depression of the '30s) a leading, position in the trade associations has been taken for granted.
But the trade association has appeared to be, in the main, relatively
unimportant in the formulation and promotion of business policy
as a whole. The result has been comparative neglect. A neglect,
incidentally, so pronounced that one refers with difficulty to a
single outstanding study of any one trade association, or any single
line of trade-association policy in the entire economic literature of
the last decade.[9]

Thus, while "concentration of economic power" has become
sufficiently important to merit the entire attention of one of our
most noteworthy recent governmental investigations,[10] and has become the subject matter of a vast and swiftly proliferating technical
literature on forms of "monopoly" [11] and "trust problems," the
trade association, the intercorporate "institute," and the chamber
of commerce have been almost entirely neglected by the learned
fraternities. With but minor exceptions—and then only with reference to antitrust proceedings, problems of "civil liberties" or discussions of general "association activities"—they have largely escaped the dragnet of official inquiry as well.[12]

Yet sixty years after the beginning of the so-called "trust movement" in the United States, the Department of Commerce found

[9] In American literature there is only one outstanding study of the phenomenon
in general, and that, *Employers' Associations in the United States*, by Clarence E.
Bonnett, was published in New York in 1922. Even this excellent survey related only
to the labor angle of a few highly specialized (at that time) employer associations.

[10] "Investigation of Concentration of Economic Power," made pursuant to Public
Resolution No. 113, 75th Congress, "Authorizing and directing a select committee
to make a full and complete study and investigation with respect to the concentration of economic power in, and financial control over, production and distribution
of goods and services." Hereafter the investigation and its findings will be referred
to as TNEC Hearings.

[11] By the term "monopoly" I mean, in the present connection, all those various
forms and practices which give some degree or other of power over the conditions
and terms of doing business which reach upon the direct limits of corporate control.
See Chapter VII.

[12] See the various volumes of the Senate Committee on Education and Labor ("La
Follette Committee") dealing with the National Association of Manufacturers, the
National Metal Trades Association, the Associated Industries of Cleveland, etc. Hereafter I shall refer to these materials as La Follette Committee Reports. The National
Resources Committee, in its recent publication *The Structure of the American Economy* (Washington, D.C., 1939), devotes slightly less than two pages in a 76-page discussion of "The Organization of Economic Activity" to all trade associations and
chambers of commerce.

that "The 'Key' factor in the NRA program is America's 3,500 larger [State and National Trade Associations], and the over 10,000 local Trade Associations, Chambers of Commerce, etc." [13] The 1931 edition of *Commercial and Industrial Organizations of the United States* [14] lists 19,000 organizations, "made up of 2,634 [15] interstate, national and international, 3,050 state and territorial, and 13,625 local organizations." Even this listing has since been found to be incomplete. Almost the entirety of this swiftly growing business network has been established since 1900, and probably three-fourths of it since the World War.

In 1870 there were not more than 40 chambers of commerce in the United States. Sixty years later, there were an estimated 3,000. These are set up on a local, county, state, or national basis. "Basic Membership" of all such chambers of commerce has recently been estimated to be a million or more. [16]

Equally rapid have been developments abroad. A list given out by the German Economic Ministry in 1930 showed some 2,272 national, district, and local associations affiliated with the Central Committee of German Employers' Associations (Zentralausschuss der Unternehmerverbände). [17] Even this list does not appear to be complete. In addition to these, an expert has estimated that Germany possessed in 1930 some 2,100 cartels, a type of organization intermediate between the trade association and the combination, [18] in the manufacturing industries of that country alone. [19]

The changes brought about by the Nazis in Germany meant

13 "High Lights of the NRA, Chart 3," statement issued July 10, 1934, by the American Trade Association Executives, and prepared by the Trade Association Section of the Marketing Research and Service Division of the Bureau of Foreign and Domestic Commerce, U.S. Department of Commerce.

14 Issued by the Bureau of Foreign and Domestic Commerce, U.S. Department of Commerce, 1931.

15 Of which 2,381 are strictly commercial and business when all trade union, scientific, engineering, and professional organizations (253 in number) are excluded from the reckoning.

16 See *American Chambers of Commerce*, by Kenneth Sturgess (New York, 1915), and "Local Chambers of Commerce, Their Origin and Purpose," issued by the Commercial Organization Department of the Chamber of Commerce of the U.S. (Washington, D.C., undated).

17 *Jahrbuch der Berufsverbände im deutschen Reiche*, (1930), p. 43.

18 The cartel is more like the early American "pool"; it has legally recognized contractual standing. More recently cartel functions have been taken over by many trade associations, particularly the American. See pp. 211, 244.

19 Horst Wagenführ, *Kartelle in Deutschland* (Nürnberg, 1931), p. xiii.

streamlining, not abolition, of this elaborate machinery. A like generalization holds for Italy, where under four strictly business associations out of a total of nine Fascist Confederations there are to be found 91 separate associational groupings.[20]

Although comprehensive data on England, France, and Japan are more difficult to obtain, the same trends are observable. And, once again, we find that almost all of this associational machinery is of comparatively recent vintage. Possibly, as with the United States, three-fourths of it is postwar. In Japan most of it appeared after the early '30s. This holds for cartels, both national and international, as well as for trade associations and chambers of commerce.

Of all these multifarious associations, only the cartels have been examined with any considerable care; even here there is a general lack of critical works on individual cartels except in a few highly especialized fields (iron, steel, coal, and potash) and it is becoming increasingly difficult to distinguish between cartel and normal trade-association functions. In the comprehensive survey of "The Economic and Social History of the World War" published under the auspices of the Carnegie Endowment for International Peace,[21] there is scarcely a mention of even the more important of these organizations, although again it was the conditions of wartime which provided the major stimuli to their formation and expansion. The reports of the British "Committee on Industry and Trade" (Balfour Committee),[22] published in the later twenties, make only side and quite incidental references to an occasional few. Nor do the monumental reports of the German Committee of Inquiry,[23] concluded but a short while before the Nazi government assumed power, take this organizational mushroom growth more seriously. As indicated, the TNEC devotes but one very superficial monograph to the trade association,[24] and

[20] See Fascist Era, Year XVII (published by the Fascist Confederation of Industrialists), pp. 207–12.

[21] Running into several hundred monographs, brochures, and abridgments of one sort or another, and including every country a party to the World War on either side.

[22] Seven volumes, with a "Final Report" published in 1929.

[23] Ausschuss zur Untersuchung der Erzeugungs- und Absatzbedingungen der deutschen Wirtschaft (Enqueteausschuss), begun in 1926, completed in 1931, and running well over a hundred volumes.

[24] No. 18, Trade Association Survey. "Superficial" because based solely on answers to questionnaires voluntarily filled out by 1,311 trade-association executives who

in other scattered cases makes only side reference to the subject.[25] But for the most part its writers miss the real significance of NRA and ignore all the mass of data collected through the efforts of the Anti-Trust Division under the leadership of Thurman Arnold.[26] In only one restricted discussion does it really come to grips with the political powers of the "peak association" at all.[27]

This general neglect becomes all the more astonishing when the growth of trade-association networks is related to two other factors. First is the correlative growth in the preponderance of the "peak association." Influenced largely by experience with more or less vigorous wartime controls, in their postwar expansion trade-association networks began slowly but cumulatively to show certain definite characteristics which marked them off definitely from prewar types. They ceased growing like Topsy, and began more and more to expand systematically, with an eye to ever more comprehensive coverage; in an orderly fashion they began to take up each link in a chain of related problems of guidance and control, and to submit increasingly to centralized direction. Before the war, "peak associations" were largely unimportant or wholly lacking, and those in existence only occasionally came to the forefront of attention.[28] After the war, they sprang up everywhere, and shortly began to serve as centralized, coördinating, business-policy boards for vast segments of the several national economies.

In the second place, though here the timing varies greatly from

naturally would not and did not answer significant questions relating to the exercise of cartel-like functions, though the listings of activities given in Table 25, p. 373, might have caused its authors to take notice that the Anti-Trust Division has found these associations almost everywhere exercising such functions.

[25] No. 34, *Control of Unfair Competitive Practices through Trade Practice Conference Procedure of the Federal Trade Commission*, a rather bad whitewash of the FTC; No. 35, *Large Scale Organization in the Food Industries;* No. 39, *Control of the Petroleum Industry by Major Oil Companies* (section on the American Petroleum Company); and No. 43, *The Motion Picture Industry—A Pattern of Control* (section on the Motion Picture Producers and Distributors of America).

[26] See almost any of the several dozen indictments of the Anti-Trust Division issued from the beginning of 1939, particularly those relating to the food, construction, metals, and machinery industries and to patent pooling. See also numerous speeches of Assistant Attorney General Thurman W. Arnold, and his *Bottlenecks of Business* (New York, 1940).

[27] No. 26, *Economic Power and Political Pressures.*

[28] They were most highly developed in Germany, but were still largely in germinal form. In manufacturing, centralized peak associations were found in England, the United States, Switzerland and a number of other smaller manufacturing countries. None of any importance were to be found in France, Italy, and Japan.

one country to the next, the rise of peak associations has been generally paced by the movement of the business giants to the centers of the spreading webs of control. In Germany, and to a lesser extent in England, the two tendencies went pretty much hand in hand. The same was true also of Japan, though here both tendencies appeared very late. In the United States the latter was not clearly evidenced until the advent of NRA. But by the late thirties, the industrial and financial giants had practically without exception moved into the citadels of peak-association power all over the world.

These two tendencies take on an added significance when they are paired with two other well-known developments within the business world of the corporate giants. One is the fact that through a multitude of familiar devices (interlocking directorates, patent-pooling and other cartel-like agreements, holding companies, intercorporate ownership of securities) [29] the ties that bind the giants together have long been growing so close, so mutually reinforcing that within, and to a certain extent amongst, the several capitalistic countries they have come as a whole to take on the characteristics of unified, more or less compact, and internally homogeneous groups.[30] And the other is the fact that, within the several corporate segments of this almost consanguineous community of interests, *de facto* control has gradually been narrowed down until it is now typically held by very small, almost entirely self-perpetuating and largely non-owner directorial and managerial cliques.[31]

[29] See TNEC Monograph No. 9, *Taxation of Corporate Enterprise*, Chapters III and IV.

[30] Of particular interest in this connection, aside from those cited in footnote 31, below, is a series of studies published at intervals by *Die Wirtschaftkurve* (a monthly publication of the Frankfurter Zeitung) after the stabilization (1924) of national and international intercorporate affiliations of various British, French, American, German, Belgian, and other combines. See the "Electronics Chart of the Sound Picture Industry of the World," reproduced by H. A. Toulmin in *Trade Agreements and the Anti-Trust Laws* (Cincinnati, 1937); Robert Liefmann, *Beteiligunge und Finanzierungs Gesellschaften* (Jena, 1921); and the TNEC Monograph No. 36, *Reports of the Federal Trade Commission on the Natural Gas, Gas Pipe, Agricultural Implement, Machinery, and Motor Vehicle Industries.*

[31] Adolph A. Berle, Jr., and Gardiner C. Means, *The Modern Corporation and Private Property* (New York, 1933); National Resources Committee, *The Structure of American Economy;* Robert A. Gordon, "Ownership by Management and Control Groups in the Large Corporation," *Quarterly Journal of Economics*, May, 1938; TNEC Monograph No. 11, *Bureaucracy and Trusteeship in Large Corporations*, Part I.

Any reader who will stop for a moment and attempt to think through the implications of these several developments when related to each other in such a fashion will see at once that trade associations suddenly take on a new and almost spectacular significance. So considered in this new light they become at once power entities which may in some cases have the indefiniteness of a *Herrenklub,*[32] and in others the potency of states within states—particularly when viewed as monopoly-minded forces, with a political turn of interest, thus strategically grouped together into centralized nationwide peak associations. But either case shows that everywhere and in every land, business has been "going political" as rapidly as it masses power.

The careful and systematic studies required as a basis for searching through the full historical and practical implications of this new massing of organized economic power have nowhere been made. Numerous individuals, including President Roosevelt [33] and some of his leading subordinates,[34] have shown some real appreciation of

[32] A club—similar in social cross-section in some respects to the famous New York Union League Club—of Junker potentates, landlords, industrialists, and military figures who met at fairly regular intervals in a down-town Berlin hotel throughout the post-war interval, and who were largely responsible, via the ministrations of von Papen, Hugenberg and others, for the original compromises and subsidies which led directly to the Nazi assumption of power.

[33] "Unhappy events abroad have retaught us two simple truths about the liberty of a democratic people. . . . The first truth is that the liberty of a democracy is not safe if the people tolerate the growth of private power to a point where it becomes stronger than their democratic state itself. That, in its essence, is fascism—ownership of a government by an individual, by a group, or by any other controlling private power." Message from The President of the United States, Transmitting Recommendations Relative to the Strengthening and Enforcement of Anti-Trust Laws, Senate Document 173, 75th Congress, 3d Session.

[34] "Lest the people learn the lesson of history the dark powers of concentrated wealth choose in each new struggle a new name for themselves, avoiding the old names that carry the historic smell of tyranny. Tyrant, Satrap, Pharaoh, Caesar, Emperor, Czar, and Kaiser have left their sulphurous trail across the pages of history. Today in Europe they have new names. In America we call the lesser rulers Business Leaders and Corporation Lawyers, the great ones are simply kings—oil kings, match kings, soap kings—hundreds of them. The great Overlord who will draw them all together into a perfect plutocratic dictatorship has not yet appeared. But there are portents in the heavens which betoken his opportunity." Willis J. Ballinger, Director of Studies and Economic Advisor to the Federal Trade Commission, at the opening of hearings before the Temporary National Economic Committee. Again, "The best way to bring home the final results of these pressures is by the concrete example of Germany. Germany, of course, has developed within fifteen years from an industrial autocracy into a dictatorship. Most people are under the impression that the power of Hitler was the result of his demagogic blandishments and appeals to the mob. This incorrect diagnosis has been responsible for most of the bad guesses

the range of issues involved and the size of the stakes in play. But for the most part discussion has run in terms of vague defense or innuendo on the one hand, or a mere superficial glossing over on the other.[35]

The following survey cannot possibly hope to span the gap—it is a far greater void than any one student can hope to bridge—but it may possibly point the way to some more fruitful research to follow.

THE METHOD OF APPROACH

The selections made for the following chapters have been guided by two main considerations. First, and at the risk of sacrificing at a good many points desirable accumulative detail, the plan has been to obtain as wide a cross-section of variations on the major pattern as possible.

England, great industrial pioneer, contrasts with Japan, a late arrival amongst the major capitalistic powers. England as center of the vast British Empire contrasts with the minuscular empire of Mussolini's Italy. Some of the great capitalistic powers never really threw off feudal and autocratic carry-overs from their respective pasts; others, such as the United States, have little memory of these institutions at all. Laissez-faire doctrines and the ideals of free competition long dominated both political and economic thinking in England, France, and the United States, but never made much headway in Germany or Japan.

A second consideration was the selection of the field of manufacturing. The reasons for this choice were several: manufacturing is itself the very heart and soul of the industrial system; singly it is

about German economy since Hitler came into power. Actually *Hitler holds his power through the final and inevitable development of the uncontrolled tendency to combine in restraint of trade.*" Thurman Arnold, address before the Denver Bar Association, May 15, 1939 (mimeographed release, Dept. of Justice), italics mine. Or, again, "Germany presents the logical end of the process of cartelization. From 1923 to 1935 cartelization grew in Germany until finally that nation was so organized that everyone had to belong either to a squad, a regiment or a brigade in order to survive. The names given to these squads, regiments or brigades were cartels, trade associations, unions, and trusts. Such a distribution system could not adjust its prices. It needed a general with quasi-military authority who could order the workers to work and the mills to produce. Hitler named himself that general. Had it not been Hitler it would have been someone else." Arnold, in an address before the American Bar Association, July 10, 1939.

[35] As in TNEC Monographs No. 7, *Measurement of the Social Performance of Business* and No. 11, *Bureaucracy and Trusteeship in Large Corporations.*

the major force making for change in the structure of economic relationships; the conflicts of interests are more clearly visualized and more readily focused in this field; the "peak associations" among manufacturers typically came first, or coming later, quickly assumed a position of commanding leadership; [36] the literature, though largely fugitive, is nevertheless more plentiful than for comparable organizations in other fields of business activity. In general it may be said that whichever way the manufacturing peak association goes, so will go not only the trade association and cartel network of each country as a whole but also all of their various interlocking peak associations.

In each case the plan has been, after first briefly following through the historical development of the peak association, to sketch in broad outlines the peculiarities of national institutions, social backgrounds, and political characteristics which conditioned, at each significant step, the functions, membership coverage, structure, and policies of the association. In all cases, particular attention has been paid to relationships with labor and the government. In order to bring certain comparisons and contrasts even more sharply to mind it was decided to separate the countries which have gone over formally to the totalitarian bloc from those which are still moving within the orbit of the liberal-capitalistic system. It is particularly important to note, in this connection, that the so-called principle of "self-government in business"—and some variation on the expression is employed in all countries which have developed peak associations, the better to coördinate networks of business organization—is not abandoned with the transition from a "liberal" to a "totalitarian" basis. In both systems it is now quite generally accepted as unavoidable that large and increasing measures of governmental regulation must be extended over the economic system as a whole. But what appears in the first as a defensive measure to slow the process down, appears in the second as a tech-

---

36 Others in the United States are: retailing, The American Retail Federation; banking, American Bankers Association; railroads, American Railway Association; power, Edison Electrical Institute. None of these compares even remotely in importance with the National Association of Manufacturers, and most of them are affiliated directly or indirectly with that organization. The only rival body is the Chamber of Commerce of the United States, which the NAM helped to found, and whose functions are in turn largely those determined by its manufacturing members—typically belonging also to the NAM. This picture is duplicated in most countries in the world.

nique of formal decentralization of administration, coupled with what may be a more or less flexible method of delegating authority from on top.

How authority is so centralized and delegated in the two cases depends greatly upon the nature of the policies guiding the inner groups which are vested with power to formulate policy. The better to bring out these points and to underline what seem on present evidence the long-run implications of policies now guiding decisions, the bulk of the discussion of policy has been siphoned away from each of the more descriptive historical sketches in Parts I and II, and is brought together in the three concluding chapters, dealing respectively with economic, social, and political issues. Every effort has been made in these chapters to condense the discussion to the utmost in the hope that the more provocative and far-reaching issues will thereby stand more clearly outlined, and that, so standing in view, they may stimulate discussion and criticism from every possible angle.

Part I

THE EVOLUTION OF MANUFACTUR-
ING PEAK ASSOCIATIONS IN THE
TOTALITARIAN BLOC

Chapter I

THE NEW ORDER FOR GERMAN INDUSTRY

THE BATTLES of Poland, France, the Balkans, and Russia have been object lessons in the techniques of "lightning war". Complete mechanization on the one hand and full coordination of air, land, and naval forces on the other have proven an irresistible combination against allied military strategists whose tactics have been still largely grounded in the obsolete methods of "fixed position" combat. But equally irresistible in a closely related field has been another Nazi innovation—that of the fullest possible coordination of propaganda, diplomacy, and economic power. To date, this latter coordination has developed a striking power equal in paralyzing effect to that of the military forces; its actual conquests have reaped material gains for the Third Reich which exceed far beyond anything the latter has had to offer, even in the major theater of war.

The separate elements in both cases are in no important sense of the term new. What is new is the fact that each element has been rationally exploited to the fullest possible extent, and at the same time all elements have been combined into a program which has been not only centrally directed but also dominated by a limited series of internally coherent objectives. While synchronization amongst the military branches is grounded in the works of Scharnhorst, von Moltke, von Schlieffen, von Hofman and their compatriots, the new synthesis is more boldly conceived, action is deployed on a far greater scale, and the services are coordinated on an infinitely more meticulous and finely detailed basis. Similarly, synchronization of the nonmilitary machinery traces back to such as von Treitschke, Bismarck, the elder Krupp, Stinnes, von Moellen-

Chapter I

THE NEW ORDER FOR GERMAN INDUSTRY

THE BATTLES of Poland, France, the Balkans, and Russia have been object lessons in the techniques of "lightning war." Complete mechanization on the one hand and full coördination of air, land, and naval forces on the other have proven an irresistible combination against allied military strategists whose tactics have been still largely grounded in the obsolete methods of "fixed position" combat. But equally irresistible in a closely related field has been another Nazi innovation—that of the fullest possible coördination of propaganda, diplomacy, and economic power. To date, this latter coördination has developed a striking power equal in paralyzing effect to that of the military forces; its actual conquests have reaped material gains for the Third Reich which extend far beyond anything the latter has had to offer, even in the major theater of war.

The separate elements in both cases are in no important sense of the term new. What is new is the fact that each element has been rationally exploited to the fullest possible extent, and at the same time all elements have been combined into a program which has been not only centrally directed but also dominated by a limited series of internally coherent objectives. While synchronization amongst the military branches is grounded in the works of Scharnhorst, von Moltke, von Schlieffen, von Hoffman and their compatriots, the new synthesis is more boldly conceived, action is deployed on a far greater scale, and the services are coördinated on an infinitely more meticulous and finely detailed basis. Similarly, synchronization of the nonmilitary machinery traces back to such as von Treitschke, Bismarck, the elder Krupp, Stinnes, von Moellendorf and Walther Rathenau. But, in order to be properly understood, the new synthesis must be compared simultaneously with the spiritual imperialism of the Catholic Church, the political imperialism of the Roman Empire, the psychoanalytic imperialism suggested by Le Bon, and the economic imperialism of the greatest of all British empire builders, Cecil Rhodes.

In a sense, the objectives of the Nazi program for a "new order in Europe" are self-evident. Clearly military and nonmilitary programs are now but different facets of a dynamically expansionist imperial state which has effected a third line of coördination, that of domestic and foreign policy. And so, as a program for imperial coördination of European (and possibly both African and other) peoples on a continental basis, it represents a logical unfolding from earlier Germanic models for fusing the Germanies into a compact and militarily omnicompetent state. The Hohenstaufens, Frederick the Great, Friedrich List, Bismarck, the late Kaiser would all have understood the driving forces that lie behind the Hitlerian juggernaut.

Whether world domination be the eventual aim or not, there can now be no question that the Nazi conquerors are thinking of at least something like a modern European equivalent of the old Roman Empire. In this picture, a nucleus of compact, more or less "racially" and culturally homogeneous peoples stand at the center of an imperial system which is surrounded on every side by subject nations which, powerless to resist, may yet be simultaneously "enslaved" and allowed some degree of "provincial" self-government. On the outer fringes of these provincial areas, the expanding lines of conquest—always seeking but never finding "natural frontiers" —soon force division of the world into great competing, hostile, and continent-wide imperial systems. Within each such major system every effort will be made, step by step with the advance of conquest, to weave the whole ever more closely together by construction of the most modern transportation, communications, power, industrial, trade, and military networks. And the pattern of control fitted over "great-space economy" will necessarily be that of a militarized hierarchy of imperial command and subordination.

If so much may be predicted from analysis of past trends and present developments, what then becomes of the capitalistic system? Will it disappear? Is it even now on its way out? Or is the transmutation of form and content one which is also in line with past developments in the structure, organization, functioning, and larger objectives of monopoly-oriented German business enterprise?

GENESIS OF GERMAN IMPERIAL CAPITALISM

Taproots for all the immensely elaborated organizational networks that characterize twentieth century Germany are found in Bismarck's imperial system. Under his capable hands, industrial capitalism underwent a sort of forced-draft growth within the confines of a modernized cameralism, in its turn greatly modified in many respects by important feudal carry-overs. The whole of the elaborate and amazingly efficient bureaucracy, inherited directly from the days of Frederick the Great and the systems of Kammern, was placed at the disposal of plans which visualized a swift catching-up and rapid overreaching of the industrial rivals of Imperial Germany. To this end the recalcitrant landed aristocracy were bribed, beaten into line, or deliberately fused with favored industrial, shipping, and commercial circles, with the inevitable result that the stigmata of special privilege were transferred wholesale to the new fields of upper class interest. And, on the other extreme the radicalized proletariat were numbed into submission by a combination of social security concessions—Bismarck's adaptation of *Realpolitik* to the "social question" which succeeded in robbing Lassalle of all independent initiative—and superpatriotic romanticism which appeared to gear labor's fortunes inescapably to those of the expanding state apparatus.[1]

[1] Within the Social Democratic theory, there existed a not unimportant social imperialist trend which was definitely anti-English; it was based on the belief that imperialist expansion would benefit the German worker and would act as a grave-digger of capitalism. This trend is represented by Lensch, Schippel, Cunow, and Parvus, and later by August Winnig. A fuller discussion of this matter is contained in Franz Neumann's *Behemoth* (1942), pp. 210–15 (to this excellent study the present author owes much). Again it is interesting to note that much of Bismarck's social legislation was taken over in large part from the programs of the Social Catholics led by Baron von Ketteler—his bitterest opponents in his ill-fated Kulturkampf (the Nazis have succeeded here where Bismarck failed). This program led ultimately to the great papal encyclical on "The Condition of Labor" (*Rerum Novarum*) (1891) and indirectly to *Quadragesimo Anno* (1931). The *Rerum Novarum* launched a movement which contributed greatly to the success of Italian Fascism (see pp. 62-66, below), while the *Quadragesimo Anno* provided the direct inspiration for the cor-

Coming onto the industrial stage comparatively late,[2] under such auspices, and with England as the principal rival,[3] there was little tendency to comply with the tenets of competition or laissez faire. Some speculation on, followed by half-hearted experimentation with, the advantages of the Manchestrian system had, of course, taken place. For a short period of time during the sixties and the seventies ideas imported from England seemed to be gaining ground. But this *Blütezeit* of laissez faire was brought to a close with the famous Bismarck tariff of 1879. Germany thus returned to more familiar ways. These ways—from the romanticism of an Adam Mueller and the rationalized protectionism of a Friedrich List—her theoreticians had assured Germany were fitting and proper in the face of economic conditions and in the perspectives of future need.[4]

All the important institutional seeds[5] of contemporary Ger-

porate state of the ill-starred Schuschnigg. A circular of the Federation of Austrian Industries (undated, but apparently of 1934) traces the new "vocational reorganization" to the "Constitution of May 1, 1934," which was based on *Quadragesimo Anno* and which "starts out with the inviolate right of private property, and then confronts individuality of property with the socialistic conception, that is, individual property in relationship to the welfare of the whole."

[2] Thorstein Veblen, in his *Imperial Germany and the Industrial Revolution* (New York, 1915), has attempted to show how great an advantage this late arrival was for the unrestricted taking over and full expansion of the techniques of mass production. See, in particular, pp. 174–210.

[3] How very seriously this rivalry was taken by the British has been shown by Ross J. S. Hoffman, in his penetrating study, *Great Britain and the German Trade Rivalry, 1875–1914* (Philadelphia, 1933). The major themes of modern German imperialism are the hatred of England and anti-Marxism. This dual hatred forged the various groups of the ruling cliques together for imperialist expansion. See Neumann, *op. cit.*, pp. 193–210.

[4] Political parties and trade unions in the direct Marxian tradition were in the main satisfied to let combination take its course. They were convinced that the ultimates in such centralized control were the prelude to the socialist state of the future. Such was the idea underlying the Socialization Law of March 23, 1919, in which the Social Democratic government actually undertook to help along the process of capitalist consolidation. See, in particular, Elisabeth Schalldach, *Rationalisierungsmassnahmen der Nachinflationszeit im Urteil der deutschen freien Gewerkschaften* (Jena, 1930) and Fritz Tarnow, *Warum arm sein?* (Berlin, 1929).

[5] (a) *Autarkie:* employing rationalized techniques in manipulation of protective tariff schedules, special shipping subsidies and expert bounties; promoting the idea of self-sufficiency in foodstuffs and industrial raw materials—"Buy German." (b) The concept of *Grossraumwirtschaft*, coupied to *Lebensraum*, or that of a balanced imperial system having complementary and adequate raw materials, industrial and financial resources, population homogeneity in proper relation to "inferior" and "colonial" subject populations, and cultural unity. Neumann, *op. cit.*, pp. 171–83, has an extended discussion of *Lebensraum*. (c) A social system of graded hierarchy and worth,

many were sown in this final rejection of Manchester. And, amongst these, an almost completely free field was opened to every conceivable type of monopoly, quasi-monopoly, or monopoly-oriented device which did not clearly militate against the felt needs of the state. No important bars were placed against combinations in general or in any field. Not until 1923, with the passage of the famous law against "the abuse of economic power," [6] was any legislation placed on the statute books which could effectively check the more obvious abuses of collusive action on the part of the cartels. In the main, the state laid a premium on fusion, organization, compacts, agreements, communities of interest. If at any point the state stepped into the picture, it was primarily to protect one collusively organized section of the business world against the overwhelming power of another collusively organized section, or to act as an ally, a promoter, a guardian, or a partner of some particular type of central economic control apparatus. The result has been a proliferation of organizational activity without parallel in modern times. A few data will illustrate the point and show how far concentration of control had gone by the time the Nazis took over.

COMBINATIONS AND MONOPOLY GROUPINGS.[7]

Coal
(a) Ten companies produced 68.98 percent of total output and employed 67.88 percent of all labor.

---

led by the cultural elite (Treitzchke, Nietszche, Houston Stewart Chamberlain) which is the predecessor to the idea of the *Ständestaat* (see R. W. Darré, leader of the National Food Estate (*Reichsnährstand*), *Neuadel aus Blut und Boden* (Munich, 1939) or Andreas Pfenning, "Das Eliten-Problem in seiner Bedeutung für den Kulturbereich der Wirtschaft," *Zeitschrift für die gesamte Staatswissenschaft* (1939), Vol. 99, Part IV. (d) An internal "harmony" of all interests and classes, in which the concessions of Bismarck to the trade unions are as father to the conceptions which underlie the Nazi Labor Front. (e) An exclusion of influences, secular or ecclesiastical, which detract from such internal unity, in which Bismarck's Kulturkampf serves as prototype for persecutions of "alien" Jewish and Catholic influences. (f) The complementary external face to internal unity and harmony is "totalitarianism" in war and peace.

[6] See the summary of the jurist, Rudolf Callman, *Das deutsche Kartellrecht* (Berlin, 1934).

[7] All data, unless otherside indicated, are given as of the last more or less "prosperous" year, 1929. Even such data serve only as indication of a general movement which it is next to impossible to summarize in simplified terms. As Levy has well said, "The industrial organisation represented by cartels and trusts can hardly be elucidated by statistics." Hermann Levy, *Industrial Germany, a Study of Its Monopoly Organisations and Their Control by the State* (Cambridge, England, 1935), p. 15.

Three companies produced 37.93 percent of total output, and employed 37.22 percent of all labor.

(b) Under law the coal industry was divided into ten producing districts, each of which was governed by a special coal syndicate, and made subordinate to a national coal association and the federal coal council.[8]

Steel and Iron

(a) Three concerns produced 68.8 percent of all pig iron; one concern produced 50 percent.

Four concerns produced 68.3 percent of all crude steel; one concern produced 43 percent.[9]

(b) One concern, the United Steel Works, held the following cartel quotas: pig iron, 38.445; crude steel, 38.298; "A"-Products, 40.023; bar iron, 30.724; band iron, inland and foreign, 38.955; thick sheet, 39.742; rolled wire, 29.161; wire, 22.224; pipe, 50.613.

Electro-technical (manufacture of electrical machinery and goods) 1.9 percent of all firms employed 66.1 percent of all persons. Two firms, A E G and Siemens-Halske-Siemens-Schuckert, completely dominated both "heavy" and "light" current fields.

Electric power

"Two-thirds of the current production and delivery of all German public electrical enterprises (concerns producing power for sale to third parties) are concentrated in the hands of seven concerns." Two companies delivered over 40 percent of the total power consumed in 1929–30.[10]

Chemicals

One company, the vast I.G. Farbenindustrie A.G., owned 35 percent of all invested capital and employed over one-third of all employees.[11]

---

[8] The second largest of these three companies was owned by the Prussian state. It produced 8.15 percent of the total output, employed 6.72 percent of the labor, and owned 17.21 percent of the known coal reserves. The "forced cartels" or coal syndicates included three governing the lignite industry. Later a *Gaskokssyndikat* was organized and attached thereto. Under the law, private industry, modified only by the interest of the Prussian *fiskus* as owner and mine operator, regulated itself with a semblance of quasi-legal authority to enforce its decisions—the Social Democratic version of what came subsequently to be known as the principle of "self-management" (*Selbstverwaltung*) in business.

[9] This one concern, the Vereinigte Stahlwerke, was likewise a heavy producer of machinery, the largest producer of coal, the largest participant in *Ruhrgas* (largest long-distance gas supply system in Germany) and an extensive producer of power, chemicals, fertilizer, etc.

[10] These two largest concerns were known as "mixed enterprises," being owned jointly by private interests, the Reich, various states, and local city and communal groups. Both of them, in turn, were tied in with coal, lignite, gas producing, and other groups.

[11] These percentages greatly underestimate the relative importance of the I.G. at that time. Including partially or completely owned and controlled subsidiaries, its

Potash

A closed syndicate ("forced cartel") governed the entire industry, as in coal. Four of the leading 9 concerns were organized in the Kalibleck, controlling about 77 percent of the industry's quotas.[12]

Shipping

Two companies, the Hamburg-Amerika and the North German Lloyd, almost completely dominated all overseas shipping.[13]

Industrial cartels.—According to estimates made by different experts, there were four cartels in Germany in 1865. Thereafter occurred the following spectacular growth in numbers: 1875, 8; 1887, 70; 1890, 117; 1900, 300; 1911, 600; 1922, 1,000; 1925, 1,500; [14] 1930, 2,100.[15] Data collected by the Cartel Bureau of the National Federation of German Industry for the year 1926 listed 1,543 cartels to which its various subsidiary special trade and industry groups belonged. They were distributed as follows: [16]

Milling	15	optics	56
Iron making	73	Metalware	78
Smelting and semi-manufactures	17	Wood	44
Machine industry	147	Leather	46
Iron, steam boiler, and apparatus	48	Stone and earth	30
Railway car construction	1	Building industry	36
Motor vehicles and wheels	8	Ceramics	10
Iron and steel ware	234	Glass industries	20
Electric manufacturers, fine mechanical equipment and		Chemical industries	91
		Oil and fats	36
		Paper	107
		Textiles	201

relative size was pretty close to twice that of the figures given. It has since grown relative much more important in the whole structure of the Nazi economic system.

[12] The balance was similarly organized. Control was so complete that prices, production, plant capacity, markets, conditions and terms of delivery, patents, etc., could be and at times actually were controlled lock, stock, and barrel.

[13] Before the Nazis came into power these two were fused in a community of interest which had become for all practical purposes as rigid as formal amalgamation. To the above figures might be added data on banking (where control was centralized in the four "D" banks), forwarding (particularly in Berlin and Hamburg), department and retail store trade (Karstadt's, Leonard Tietz, Wertheim), etc.

[14] An official government estimate for 1925 placed the figure at 2,500, but it appears to have included many nonindustrial cartels and similar organizations. See Wagenführ, *Kartelle,* p. xiii.

[15] *Idem.* The estimate excludes "cartels and cartel-similar organizations in agriculture, banking, exchanges, transportation, insurance and the free professions."

[16] *Ibid.,* p. xiv.

Clothing	71	Food and luxuries	49
Brewing, malting, and mill-		Shipping and forwarding ...	4
ing	97	Total	1543
Sugar and foodstuffs	24		

According to an estimate of the German Business Cycle Institute all raw and semimanufactured goods produced within Germany and about half of all finished industrial goods were in 1938 bound by monopoly or by cartel agreements. See Neumann, *op. cit.*, p. 291.

Trade associations, federations, and business coördinating groups.[17]—So numerous and so varied in details of organization and functions are the pre-Nazi trade and industrial associations that statistical summary is next to impossible. Some idea of the level of development may be had by reference to the membership rolls of the Central Committee of German Employers' Associations. This body was made up of industrial, trade, and financial associations, organized on a national, regional, and local basis. Counting all these together, there were 2,272 associations within 14 central business associations,[18] in turn divided into 8 groups.[19] Even this listing is incomplete, and the web of business organization not included under the Central Committee seems at some points to have been very extensive.[20]

In any of these fields or in respect to any of this organizational machinery it is equally impossible to summarize neatly (1) the limits of power within, amongst or between monopoly or semi-monopoly groupings, (2) the degree to which the various

[17] It will help to clarify the following discussion if certain distinctions are kept in mind: (1) cartels, syndicates, and the like are organizations for the *control of production and commodity markets;* (2) employers' associations are organizations for *control of the labor market;* and (3) central federations of trade associations are political pressure groups (*Standesverbände*) or organizations for the *control of public opinion and the government.* A scheme of the various types of business organization in the Weimar Republic is found in Neumann, *op. cit.*, pp. 238, 239.

[18] Respectively, the National Committee of German Agriculture, National Federation of German Industry, Federation of German Employers' Associations, National Association of German Handicrafts, National Association of German Transportation, Employers' Association for the German Newspaper Industry, Hansa League for Trade, Commerce and Industry, Central Federation of German Retail Trade, National Association of German Wholesale and Overseas Trade, League of Wholesale Employers Associations, National Association of Bank Managements, Central Association of German Bank and Banking Trades, National Association of Private Insurance, Employers' Association of German Insurance Enterprises.

[19] Respectively, Agriculture, Industry, Handicrafts, Transportation, Miscellaneous, Commerce, Banking, and Insurance.

[20] For a list of associations not affiliated directly or indirectly with the Central Committee, see Wagenführ, *op. cit.*, p. 1, footnote 1.

trades and employers' associations were able to centralize and to enforce policy decisions, (3) the areas in which a large measure of "free competition" was still to be found, or (4) the exact nature of governmental control, regulation, or participation, federal, state, or local. One is safe in concluding only that in general the centralizing trends were uniform, unbroken, mutually reinforcing, and additive. Cumulatively they promoted monopoly powers, centralized policy determination, and necessitated an interlacing of governmental and business authorities until by the advent of the Nazis little more than systematization and streamlining were required for inauguration of the much heralded "corporative economy."

The most important, by all odds, of these German business-coördinating, political pressure groups was the National Federation of German Industry (Reichsverband der deutschen Industrie—RDI), to which the present National Industry Group is the Nazified successor. The National Federation of German Industry was, in its turn, a postwar fusion of two predecessor organizations, the Central Association of German Industrialists, founded in 1879,[21] and the Industrial Alliance, dating from 1895. The history of its origin and growth, from more or less haphazard first beginnings of the present all-inclusive and highly streamlined, industrial policy-control network, shows a logical unfolding of the possibilities inherent in a large-scale industrial capitalism, when morganatically wedded to a powerful centralized state which is dominated by consciously expansionist imperial ambitions. Important as is the history of the evolution of the National Industry Group in and of itself, its larger significance is found in the fact that its historical antecedents were dominated by forces typical and symptomatic of this fusion in the whole of German national life.

EVOLUTION OF THE NATIONAL FEDERATION OF GERMAN INDUSTRY

The history of the two predecessor organizations is marked by partial conflict, absorbing at times the bulk of associational energy,

---

[21] *Handwörterbuch der Staatswissenschaft* (Jena, 1928), 4th ed. VIII, p. 502. This date checks likewise with data given out by the Reichsverband der deutschen Industrie. Wagenführ, however, fails in his extraordinarily comprehensive compendium to mention this date at all; I have been unable to account for the discrepancy.

and by occasional coöperation. Though representing divergent interests at many points, their respective histories brought them into increasingly closer contact with one another. Preliminary attempts at partial or complete fusion before the First World War made but little headway.[22] The exigencies of war economy brought them formally together for the first time (1914) in the War Committee of German Industry. In 1918 this gave way to the German Industrial Council, which was in turn superseded by the National Federation of German Industry.

The Central Association of German Industrialists represented the first enduring coagulation of any large block of industrial interests in Germany. Excepting only the short-lived Central Federation of German Industrialists (Zentralverband deutschen Industrieller), organized in 1856, there had been prior to 1879, no grouping which could be said to represent any considerable block of raw materials and manufacturing interests *per se*. The Handelstag, or Convention of Commerce, founded in 1862 as a central coordinating institution for some 160 Chambers of Commerce in Germany, was not set up so as to serve the specialized needs of any broad line of business activity. This the Central Association attempted to do.

Its origin is commonly attributed to concern over the protective tariff. By and large the association seemed to be in favor of relatively moderate tariff schedules, but at the same time was definitely opposed to any outright surrender to the Franco-British free trade system.[23] This position was strengthened during the decade of the seventies by virtue of changed international positions following the Franco-Prussian War,[24] and by the altered domestic situation

[22] One effort which led to the Interessengemeinschaft der zentralen Industriellenverbände (Community of Interests of the Central Industrial Associations), 1906-8, seems to have enjoyed little popularity.

[23] More or less formally inaugurated with the Anglo-French Treaty of Commerce in 1860. The Germans followed with tariff-lowering "most favored nation" treaties negotiated with Italy in 1863, Switzerland in 1864, Norway, the Hanse Towns, Spain and the Netherlands in 1865, Austria in 1866, Portugal in 1867. Following the Austro-Prussian War in 1866, the terms of the tariff agreement between the two countries were extended to all other countries with whom special agreements had already been made. The Bismarck tariff represented a complete reversal of this trend.

[24] The phenomenal recovery of French industry following the War of 1870 and the payments of reparations to the Germans was paralleled by a correspondingly sharp setback, assuming almost catastrophic proportions within the course of the next three years, in Germany.

resulting from the great world-wide depression of 1873 and the subsequent beginning of a long period of decline in world price levels.

How important a role was played by the Central Association in the inauguration of the new protective policies ushered in by the Bismarck tariff of 1879 is a matter of dispute. But at any rate, the Association's principal interest seems at the very outset to have centered primarily in various forms of protective tariff legislation. From tariffs the outlook seems quickly to have expanded to include legislation touching upon a steadily widening range of economic problems.

These activities quickly brought the Central Association into conflict with other interests, especially the chemical industry. It was accused of promoting the welfare of the heavy—apparently quite largely raw materials—industrial field to the disadvantage of the finished goods field. Despite emphatic denials to the contrary, the Central Association was soon faced with organization of rival interests in the form of the Central Bureau for the Preparation of Trade Agreements (Zentralstelle für Vorbereitung von Handelsverträgen), established with headquarters in Berlin in 1879. This association seems to have met with but indifferent success, and thus to have been superseded entirely in 1895 by the much more comprehensive and better organized Industrial Alliance (Bund der Industriellen).

The purpose of the Industrial Alliance appears to have been twofold. On the one hand it was to represent the interests of the finishing goods industries, which had been more or less neglected, if not openly opposed, by the Central Association. On the other hand, it was apparently hoped that coöperative relationships could readily be established between the two organizations on behalf of common industrial interests.[25] Some at least expected either that the Alliance would absorb the Central Association or that the two would at some time in the future be fused into a single body.

Whatever the founders' expectations, the Industrial Alliance,

25 "The Bund was organized in 1895 as the result of a demand for an organization representing the interests of manufacturers of finished products, and also 'because it seemed desirable to find a liberal and general basis for the joint representation of commerce and industry as a counterpoise to the Agricultural Alliance.'" *American Industries* (Feb. 15, 1903), p. 3.

thanks to comprehensive membership basis,[26] low dues, and vigorous leadership, quickly became the leading industrial organization in Germany. Dedicated to "protection of the common interests of German industry as well as coöperation in all questions affecting it," the Alliance proceeded to the formation of legislative pressure blocs and the promotion of a comprehensive member service supplemented by a general public relations propaganda campaign.

Though friction with the Central Association of German Industrialists rendered fruitless many attempts to achieve a "united front," the exigencies of war ultimately compelled what the efforts of peacetimes could not achieve. As indicated above, the first real united industrial front came with the establishment of the governmentally regulated war Committee of German Industry. Further experience with the German Industrial Council paved the way for eventual union, achieved immediately following the revolutionary interlude,[27] in the establishment of the National Federation of German Industry (Reichsverband der deutschen Industrie —RDI).

The new organization swiftly grew to a position of commanding importance in the organizational fabric of German industry. The Federation brought together "445 national, 58 regional, and 70 local associations, 1,363 individual members, and 70 Chambers of Industry and Commerce." [28] Via such memberships, cartel affiliations increased from some 300 around 1922 to more than 1,500 during the middle twenties. As organized in 1931, members of the Federation were divided into 19 divisions, subdivided into 32 functional groups (Fachgruppen), in turn made up of 889 national, regional, and local trade associations and chambers of commerce and industry.[29]

Spectacular as the growth indicated by such figures may appear, they fail to give any clear idea of how comprehensive and all in-

[26] Membership was open to the following: manufacturing concerns in any field, independent engineers and chemists, industrial associations, leagues and federations. A special category of "extraordinary members" need only have German residence.

[27] During the revolutionary interlude a preliminary form of what under the Nazis became the Labor Front was evolved; this was known as the "Works Committee of Industrial Employers and Employees of Germany."

[28] Wagenführ, op. cit., p. 2.

[29] Jahrbuch der Berufsverbände im deutchen Reiche, pp. 46–48.

clusive this organizational meshwork had become by the early thirties. A couple of illustrations will suffice. Group 10 of the Federation of German Industry is designated Machine Building. It included the following organizations: [30]

Federation of German Machine Building Associations
Federation of German Machine Tool Manufacturers
German Cutting and Stamping Machinery Association
Federation of German Wood-Working Machine Manufacturers
Association of Textiles Machine Makers
Federation of German Agricultural Machine Industries
German Locomotive Alliance
Federation of German Steam-Driven Machine Producers
Federation of Pump and Pump-Machinery Makers
Special Federation of Gauge and Auxiliary Machinery
Federation of Elevator Makers
Association of German Railway Car Builders
Paper-Making Machinery Federation
Association of German Printing Machinery Producers
Brewery Machinery Association
Federation of German Milling Machinery Makers
Association of Crusher and Dressing Mill Machinery Producers
Association of German Armature Industries
Federation of German Appliance Making Industries
(76 Additional Associations)

Largest and most important of these is the Federation of German Machine Building Associations (Verein der deutschen Maschinenbau Anstalten—VDMA). Not only is it the largest, but it is in turn a central association of the machine-building industry which includes the bulk of all firms producing machinery in Germany as well as most of the other associations in the machine-producing field such as those listed above. Founded in 1892 with 29 concerns employing 13,000 workers, by 1930 it included some 1,424 firms, employing 359,000 workers. If one adds to those, members of some 81 affiliated special trade associations, the VDMA in that year represented 2,150 firms employing 450,000 workers, or around 80 percent of all producers of machinery in Germany.[31]

The VDMA in turn divided its members into 13 "functional or trade groups" (Fachverbände), each made up of one or more "spe-

30 *Ibid.,* p. 47.
31 Exclusive of repair shops and firms having less than 25 workers. Wagenführ, *op. cit.,* p. 113.

cial" or trade associations. The central office of the VDMA served in three distinct capacities. As organizer, it set as its task (1) "promotion of the organic federation of German industry in special associations of individual trades and groups of trades"; (2) the performance of a wide range of service functions on behalf of membership, a service ranging from such things as the supply of routine information and the setting of uniform cost-accounting methods to promotion of cartels and the exercise of political pressures; [32] and (3), the working out of special agreements and liaison activities with other similarly organized industries.[33]

The special or trade groups joined to the VDMA were organized along lines similar to the parent or central association. Through this machinery there was created a vast, inclusive, and tremendously efficient apparatus for centralizing information relating to every facet of technical, commercial, and political questions of every member directly or indirectly associated with the VDMA. In many respects members were free to accept or reject any portion of the services or the advice given on most points where interests were joined. But the history of the organization likewise shows that to an increasing extent agreements were leading to legally enforceable compacts (cartel agreements and intercartel compacts such as the Avi-Abkommen) at the same time that the roots of the network

[32] According to Wagenführ, *op. cit.,* p. 115, the work of the central office is divided as follows: I. Special problems of economic science, cartel problems, publications, editorship of the economic sections of the journal, *Maschinenbau;* II. Trade agreements, Tariff relations with foreign markets and competitive conditions abroad; III. German import tariffs; a) general questions and raw materials duties, b) duties on machinery; IV. Raw materials supply for the machine industry; V. Problems of transportation; VI. Taxes, special imposts, the Young Plan; VII. Banking and credit problems, corditions of payment, questions of the internal market; VIII. Legal questions, delivery terms, protection of legal rights; IX: a) Exhibitions and fairs (General Machine and Appliance Making in Leipzig), advertising, b) information on sources of customer demand, VDMA address book; X. Technical-economic questions (inclusive of information on work materials, accident prevention, standards, professional training; XI. Cost accounting and book-balancing, economical conduct of business, specialization; XII. Insurance questions, insurance office of the machine industry; XIII. Organization of the Machine industry, in particular the establishment of special trade associations; XIV. Statistics.

[33] These include special agreements with the iron-producing industry, the cast-iron consuming association, the electro-technical industry, etc. Especially interesting is the so-called Avi Abkommen, or Avi-agreement, concluded between the steel industry and the machine-tool industry; it called for special reductions in the price of steel used for machinery intended for export.

were reaching down through the entire structure of the industry.

While the VDMA is not directly typical of more than the better-organized of the member groups of the National Federation, still the basic trends exemplified in its history are coherent with those shaping the organizational patterns of the less well coördinated industries. And the speed with which the network was reaching downwards from the large industries to the small, and outwards to include issues affecting the entire range of business, was truly phenomenal.

A second illustration relates to the functional division of labor between the Federation of German Industry and its sister organization, the Federation of German Employers' Associations (Vereinigung der deutschen Arbeitgeberverbände), one of the member groups of the Central Committee of German Employers' Association mentioned above. But while the latter organization was a loose, more or less paper proposition, the Federation of German Employers' Associations was a compact, well-organized body tied in directly with the membership of the National Federation of German Industry, made up almost entirely of manufacturing enterprises belonging to the RDI, fully conscious of the role assigned it, and fully prepared to coöperate with the RDI, to the full extent of its ability.[34]

First organized in 1913 as a federation of some 61 national employers' associations possessing some 249 subsidiary (mostly regional and local) associations, it grew by 1929 to include 180 Main or National employers' associations (*Hauptverbände*) having 2,900 subsidiary associations. By this time the division of labor with the RDI was fairly clear-cut and complete; the employers' association took care of all labor issues and the RDI of all more or less strictly economic and commercial problems. Each in its appropriate sphere constituted a well-nigh all-inclusive body in the industrial life of Germany as a whole. But while functionally separated, the two bodies appear to have worked in the closest harmony with each other. Policy direction, however, rested with the RDI. Though made up of the same basic membership ranks, crucial decisions

---

[34] The Federation of German Employers' Associations and the RDI were, by their charters, committed to collaboration. See Neumann, *op. cit.*, pp. 236, 237.

affecting both bodies naturally gravitated into the hands of the RDI, for the simple reason that specifically business interests determined the position on labor, social issues, and the law.

It would be possible to continue tracing the organizational ramifications of the RDI almost indefinitely, and to show how its influence was dominant in most of the leading municipal and regional chambers of commerce and industry, how its officers swayed the whole of the elaborate machinery set up for the purpose of rationalizing industrial and commercial processes under the auspices of the National Board for Economy and Efficiency (Reichskuratorium für Wirtschaftlichkeit),[35] and how its influence cumulatively permeated the rapidly expanding system of semigovernmental corporations, control boards, and advisory offices established during the Social Democratic interlude. Yet such a pursuit would serve only to fill in details which would not at any important point seriously alter the larger picture as given.

It was this system which under the Nazi regime was made over into the still more highly centralized National Industry Group.

THE NATIONAL INDUSTRY GROUP
(Reichsgruppe Industrie)

The enabling law for the Preparation of the Organic Reconstruction of Germany's Economic System (February 27, 1934) was designed to "serve the purpose of eliminating the excessive organization of German business hitherto prevailing, with its resulting inactivity, as well as the obstruction and disturbances caused by the rivalry of individual organizations. It is planned to carry out a comprehensive, strict, and uniform organization of all parts of industry." [36] In effect the law cleared the way for the following: (1) extension of the organizational network to include all business, major and minor, throughout the entire Reich, membership now being made compulsory; (2) elimination of duplication, overlapping, and working to cross-purposes within the main lines of policy

---

[35] This is true even though the National Board was supported by direct governmental subsidies. Subsidiary to it were The National Board for Agricultural Technique, The German Standards Committee, The National Committee for Conditions and Terms of Delivery, The Committee for Economical Production, The Committee for Economical Management. Each of these, in turn, were central coördinating bodies for all activities in the entire Reich, falling into their respective bailiwicks.

[36] *News in Brief*, II, No. 5 (March 15, 1934), p. 2.

formulation and control; (3) vesting power to compel some degree of compliance in semi-autonomous "self-governing" bodies possessing at least semilegal authority.

Under the new arrangement the National Federation of German Industry became, as the National Industry Group, one of seven National Groups [37] dovetailed into the National Economic Chamber, and placed directly under the National Economic Minister. The transformation did not mean that all the old machinery was necessarily scrapped. For example, none of the leading national, regional, or local trade associations or central associations such as the VDMA were abolished.[38] They might remain, much as before, as group pressure agencies, but with this provision, that all firms in each respective industry, member of the trade association or not, must belong to the appropriate division or subdivision of one of the National Groups. Contrariwise, all the functionally separated employers' associations were liquidated simultaneously with the dissolution of the trade unions, and the two sets of interests were fused together in the National Labor Front. The Groups—as with their predecessor bodies—were left with strictly business and technical problems on their hands.

Just how the National Industry Group has been fitted into the new control structure can be simply explained. At the top of the control pyramid brought together under The Minister of Economics is the National Economic Chamber, "organized along two main lines, *functional* and *regional*. The first is a purely vertical division, including all enterprises and business associations falling into any trade or industrial group. There are six of these altogether. Each of the *National* Groups is in turn subdivided into, first, *Economic*, and then into Trade Groups (*Fachgruppe*) and Subtrade Groups (*Fachuntergruppe*).[39] In the single case of the National Industry Group there was an intermediate step between

[37] The others were Commerce, Banking, Insurance, Handicrafts, Power [and tourist industry]. Excepting only power, these groups parallel the appropriate divisions of the Central Committee of German Employers' Associations, the only previously existing central policy-coördinating body for all German economic activity. See Robert A. Brady, *The Spirit and Structure of German Fascism* (New York, 1937), pp. 296–311.

[38] Whether or not this generalization includes the National Federation of German Industry itself I have been unable to determine. Competent authorities seem uncertain, and though it seems a point simple to check, I have thus far been unable to do so.

[39] See Neumann, *op. cit.*, pp. 242, 243.

the Economic and the National Groups, known as 'Main Groups.' " [40] The division into Main Groups was, however, abolished about 1938.

Taking all the National Groups together, we find a total of approximately 43 Economic Groups, 393 Functional Groups, and 6 national transportation groups directly under the minister of transportation. The overwhelming importance of the National Industry Group in this arrangement is shown by the fact that 28 in the first and 222 in the second of the group classifications fell into its bailiwick.

The regional organization brings all groups, national, trade or "functional," resident in each of 14 provinces into 23 Provincial Economic Chambers.[41] Each of these regional Chambers has powers parallel with those of the National Economic Chamber.[42] This is true also of the regional divisions of the several classes of Groups in relation to their respective national organizations.

Avoiding further detail so far as possible, the picture presented by the new realignment of German economic organization can be summarized as follows: (1) The old trade associations, business

[40] *Ibid*, p. 300. There were seven of these main groups: (1) Mining, Iron and other metal Ore Production; (2) Machine-Building, Technical, Optical, and Fine Mechanical Industries; (3) Iron, Plate, and Metal Wares; (4) Stone and Earth, Wood, Building, Glass, and Ceramics Industries; (5) Chemicals, Technical Oils and Fats, Paper and Paper-Making; (6) Leather, Textiles and Clothing; (7) Food Products Industries.

[41] These are as follows:

Economic Province	Headquarters of Chamber
East Prussia	Königsberg
Silesia	Breslau
Brandenburg	Berlin
Romerania	Stettin
North Marx	Hamburg
Lower Saxony	Bremen and Hanover
Westphalia	Dortmund and Dusseldorf
Rhineland	Cologne
Hessia	Frankfort-on-Main
Central Germany	Magdeburg and Weimar
Saxony	Dresden
South-West Germany	Karlsruhe and Stuttgart
Bavaria	Munich
Saar	Saarbrücken

There are five more in Austria and Sudetenland.

[42] The function of the provincial economic chambers are even wider than those of the National Economic Chamber. They are also clearing offices (*Ausgleichstellen*) for the distribution of public contracts among businessmen domiciled in their territory. See Neumann, *op. cit.*, p. 245.

federations, alliances, etc. excepting in some cases only the peak or central associations (*Spitzenverbände*)—exist much as before. But whether membership still remains voluntary is not certain. The trade association may properly be regarded as a policy-initiating, or policy-promoting body. (2) Much as under the American NRA, when trade associations were in large part transformed into Code authorities without losing their independent status, so the German business associations are organized into Groups. Membership in the appropriate Group, however, is compulsory for both members and non-members of trade associations. The functions of the Group are to discuss, coördinate, and execute policies in the control of price and raw materials and in the distribution of orders and the supervision of cartels.

(3) The Group arrangement represents a minor alteration in the preëxisting system of groups or divisions of the various national and central coördinating machinery (*Spitzenverbände*), of which the National Federation of German Industry was typical. (4) Cartels whose policies were largely coördinated through the Cartel Bureau (*Kartelstelle*) of the National Federation of German Industry are now coördinated through the machinery of the National Industry Group.[43] The same holds for cartels in fields of business brought into the other coördinate Groups of Commerce, Banking, and the like. (5) Power is vested in both the National Economic Chamber and in the various Provincial Economic Chambers to make decisions in accordance with various types of enabling legislation. This power is derived from the Minister of Economics (*Reichswirtschaftsminister*) and is at least semilegal in effect. This hierarchy then provides the policy-enforcing or policy-executing machinery of German business.

THE CENTRALIZATION OF POWER TO DETERMINE POLICY WITHIN THE NEW NETWORK

It may be observed at the outset that the leitmotiv of the Nazi organizational plan is complete centralization of power to determine policy in all cases, with respect to all activities, and with regard to all phases or aspects of policy.[44] This complete antithesis of

---

[43] On the relation between groups and cartels (which is critical) see the reform edict of the minister of economics of Nov. 12, 1936, in Neumann, *op. cit.*, p. 272.

[44] Thus, since May, 1942, all labor issues are united in the federal Trustees of

democratic organization is commonly called "Fascist Totalitarianism," and is said to rest upon three basic principles: The Leader Principle, the Authority Principle, and the Total Principle. In effect these mean simply that all society, all occupations, all businesses are organized into all-inclusive hierarchies of control and governed in such a way that (a) all competencies are appointed from above and held at the discretion of each superior office in the hierarchy, that (b) all duties and all responsibilities are set from above, and that (c) each superior authority reserves the right at will to extend control to every phase and facet of the activities of each inferior body or grouping.

What this means to the economic organization of the country in practice may be readily shown.

1. An increasing number of combines or corporations are or have become partnerships (Otto Wolff), or *Kommanditgesellschaften* (wherein one partner is fully liable while the other is restricted to his—or their—shares, as in the case of Friedrich Flick since 1937); in other words they are limited liability companies.[45]

2. Within the individual units, the power of the management as against (a) labor, (b) stockholders, and (c) the general public has been immensely enhanced. (a) Within factory walls the manager or his delegate is recognized by law to be the "Leader," and the employees to be his "Followers." His formal power ranges over all activities of and all relations with labor on the job.[46] (b) The law which limits dividend disbursements to 6 percent, when coupled to the *de facto* practice of coöptative recruitment of directorial and managerial ranks and the *de jure* "leadership" principle, in effect

---

Labor, under the Ministry of Labor (headed by Fritz Sauckel), the much vaunted labor front being merely an "educational"—terrorizing—agency. All business issues are centralized in the National Economic Chamber, all agriculture in the National Food Estate, all cultural activities in the National Chamber of Culture, all provincial government in the Reich, all local government in the Communal Thing (*Gemeindetag*), all executive, legislative and judicial authority in the Führer.

45 The reasons are as follows: a) because of internal financing, the appeal to the capital market is less important; b) the three above-mentioned forms are not subject to publicity.

46 Subject only to the superior competent authority of the Labor Trustees, the employer under law has the right and the power to determine (1) hours, rest pauses, etc., (2) time, amounts, and nature of payment, (3) basis of calculation—day, hourly, or piecework—of wages, (4) nature, amounts and method of collection of fines, (5) termination of employment (except as limi.ed by statutory rules), and (6) "The utilization of remuneration forfeited by the unlawful termination of an employment."

transfers the run of the stockholders into a class of "rentiers," deprived of all power to participate in policy formulation on any important issue. (c) And, finally, the new regime encourages the extension and exercise of cartels and cartel-like controls in which there is no effective public representation whatsoever.[47] Here is the *ultima ratio* of the process described by Berle and Means as the "splitting of the property atom." [48]

3. The big concerns have been encouraged to become bigger. Amalgamations, combinations, have been promoted rather than retarded in practically all fields. Particularly noteworthy are the expansion of such firms as the Dye Trust (I.G. Farbenindustrie A.G.), which has become almost a complete monopoly in several of the more important heavy and light chemical lines; the Krupp armament works, which has taken over much of the giant Skoda plants in former Czechoslovakia; and the great new Hermann Göringwerke, which has taken over portions of the Thyssen interests and leading Austrian iron and steel works. But the same tendency is found in shipping, local and river transport,[49] and many of the light industries—notably textiles.

4. Much the same holds for cartels. As Professor Pribram has pointed out, despite "repeated official declarations intended to discourage the spread of monopolist tendencies . . . up to the present the cartelization movement seems to have held the upper hand over any admonitions to the contrary." [50] Under the new laws promulgated early in the Nazi regime (in particular that of July 15, 1933) the number of cartels, the range of policies brought under

[47] That is, no direct representatives of consumers, coöperative organizations, workers, or any other affected portion of the public.

[48] *De facto* there is next to nothing to distinguish the average German stockholder (that is, the typical small stockholder, unless included for one reason or another in the small "inside" directorial or managerial circles) under the new regime from the typical French "rentier" class or the holder of German government bonds.

[49] Not only have amalgamations been encouraged within these fields—e. g., the formal fusion of the North German Lloyd and the Hamburg Amerika line—but there has also occurred a good deal of intraservice fusion, notably between rail and terminal trucking facilities, and between river and canal fleets and land transportation. An excellent and very compact summary of the concentration movement under the Nazi regime is given by Dr. Günter Keiser, "Der jungste Konzentrationsprozess," *Die Wirtschaftskurve*, II (1939), 136–56, 214–34. See also Maxine Yaple Sweezy, "Distribution of Wealth and Income under the Nazis," *Review of Economic Statistics*, XXI (Nov., 1939), 178–84. For additional material on the growth of combines see Neumann, *op. cit.*, pp. 288–92.

[50] Karl Pribram, *Cartel Problems* (Washington, D.C., 1935), pp. 262–63.

cartel controls, and the rigidity of the controls have all increased markedly. Compulsory features have been added in many cases, requiring membership of hitherto outside firms, facilitating the establishment of compulsory selling syndicates and greatly expanding control over such things as plant capacity, pricing policies, cost-accounting methods, etc.

An appraisal of the speed with which cartel activities have grown [51] is greatly complicated by the practice followed under the Nazis of blanketing entire industries with cartel-like controls of one sort or another, the specific purposes of which may vary a good deal from case to case, but which make it next to impossible in many instances to tell where cartel policies end and governmental controls begin. All cartel price-control measures are, for example, under the control of a National Price Commissioner, who bases his decisions in almost every case on the advice and the proposals of the groups as coördinated by the National Economic Chamber.[52] In a general way it may be said that the Nazi government has operated so as to universalize the cartel type of controls over the whole of the German national system in much the way that Colbert attempted to expand guild controls over the whole of the economic life of the *ancien régime*.[53]

[51] E. g., "According to a report published by the German Institute for Business Cycle Research (in its *Wochenbericht* of Dec. 6, 1933), between July and November, 1933, about 30 cartels were reorganized, mainly by the inclusion of outsiders; and about 40 lines of industry changed from free competition to various systems of market control." *Ibid.*, p. 263.

[52] See the discussion in Neumann, *op. cit.*, pp. 307–9.

[53] "Specifically this means *legal authority* to do a number of things: control investment, whether by establishment of new plants or expansion of old; control borrowing on the market or increase in capital by self-financing; fix prices, quotas, and penalties; protect small enterprises, etc. Under these authorities, for example, construction of new plants was forbidden in the chalk industry. For differing period of time, production was limited and new *plant construction* was forbidden in the following industries: jute-weaving, paper and pulp, textile goods, cement and hollow glass, cigar and cigar-boxes, high tension electric cable, zinc-rolled products, clocks and watches (with the exception of wrist-watches), nitrogen, superphosphates, stone objects and materials, peat moss, radio, smoking tobacco, horseshoes, hosiery dyeing, rubber tires, white lead, red oxide of lead, litharge, white zinc, lithopone, staining and earth dyes, pressed and rolled lead products, tubing, and insulation in a number of cases, notably in such industries as cement, hollow glass, zinc-rolling, paper, paper cartons, and stone objects. In the smoking-tobacco industry measures were taken to protect small producers by preventing expansion of the large." Brady, *The Spirit and Structure of German Fascism*, pp. 340–41. See also various issues of *News in Brief;* Heinz Mullenseifen, *Von der Kartellpolitik zur Marktordnung und Preisüberwachung* (Berlin, 1935); and *Marktordnungsgrundsätze der Reichsgruppe Industrie* (undated).

But while some of these measures are designed specifically to defend the interests of small business, nevertheless, in the main, the cartels may be regarded as "self-governing bodies" typically dominated by the large concerns.[54] Consequently the expansion of the cartel apparatus serves—in contradistinction to the pre-Nazi condition in many respects—to enhance the power of the great combines by rounding out and supplementing the controls which they require for the full instrumentation of their monopolistic interests; their power is subject to check only by the regulatory power of the government.

5. Correlative with the outward expansion of the business organization network through the Groups to include all industrial, commercial, and financial activity in the Reich has gone a reshaping of lines of control into a definite hierarchical pattern, which gathers together all effective power to determine and enforce decisions and center them in the upper reaches of the pyramid. Within the central offices the following facts determine the typical location of policy-determining power; (a) the center of gravity in the National Economic Chamber unquestionably resides in the membership of the National Industry Group;[55] (b) the center of gravity in the National Industry Group with equal certainty is located in the heavy industries; (c) the heavy industries are led in every significant respect by the giant combines. These facts must be coupled to the rule that the intent and effect of the changed conditions in the general economic system at large is to (d) formalize and universalize the coöptative principle in the recruiting of executive staffs. Keeping in mind, then, that the hierarchical principle of

[54] "The class that has fared the worst (under the Nazis) so far is the middle class —officials, small shopkeepers and artisans—who were Hitler's first enthusiastic followers. . . . The shopkeeper, who hoped to get rich from the elimination of Jewish competition, has been forced to absorb the difference between increased wholesale and fixed retail prices, and small artisans are being crowded to the wall for lack of raw materials. . . . 34.7 per cent of 375,741 retailers net less than 125 marks a month (fifty dollars at official exchange rates), which is considerably less than a skilled worker receives. As a result there is a great dying off of independent middle-class enterprise. . . . German industry is undergoing a process of concentration which tends to concentrate industrial control into a few mammoth concerns." New York *Times,* Sept. 3, 1937. See the discussion in Neumann, *op. cit.,* p. 274, and on the elimination of small businesses, *ibid.,* pp. 263–65, 282–84.

[55] This can be shown in a number of ways; by reference to leading officers, by identity of policies initiated and carried through; by the dominance of the heavy industries in rearmament, war, and reëmployment programs, etc. The analyses of the personnel have been made by Neumann, *op. cit.,* pp. 388–92.

organization in Germany (1) identifies at each point of delegation executive with judicial and legislative powers, and (2) traces all authority from the top down (all responsibility from the bottom up), it will be seen that the net effect is—subject only to governmental check— [56] to locate economic hegemony in the closely-knit managements of the large combines in the heavy industries.[57]

6. The specific doctrinal content of the propaganda fed out to all parties of interest through the media available to the new control apparatus is in many respects indistinguishable in basic assumptions, its view of human nature and society, its criteria of truth and falsehood, its social valuations, and its leading appeals and arguments from that which has been long characteristic of the "welfare capitalism" of such huge industrial combines as the Dye Trust, Krupp, Siemens and Halske-Siemens-Schuckert, and the A.E.G. The main differences are twofold. In the first place, propaganda directed to different interest groups—labor, the general public, farmers, and others—has been integrated, coördinated, and in large part centralized. And in the second place, the propaganda has been generalized to cover the whole of the German business system.

Thus the Nazis have provided means for achieving the ultimates in the tendencies underlying the organizational efforts which preceded their entrance onto the scene. The pattern of control common to all large-scale business enterprise is here expanded so as to encompass the entire range of economic activities, and to regiment and direct all parties of interest throughout the entire country. This hierarchical pattern—coupled with the concept of occupationally and functionally self-contained, all-inclusive, definitely circumscribed, and centrally directed trade and group categories which are ranged in a graduated order of power, duties, and importance so as to include the activities of all Germany—constitutes the essence of the "Corporate State." [58]

---

[56] See chapters VIII and IX.

[57] Excepting, in part only, agriculture, transportation, and handicrafts.

[58] " 'Corporativism' is chiefly preoccupied with securing a smooth and undisturbed function of Capitalism by bringing about, in each branch of industrial production, a benevolent harmonization, a renunciation of class-war, between owners' associations and workers' syndicates." Aurel Kolnai, *The War against the West* (New York, 1939), p. 325. This is a half-truth which underestimates the importance of the "corporative" idea for other purposes. Added to Kolnai's statement is the idea of more

"STATUS CAPITALISM" AND THE STATE

At no point is there so much confusion and difference of opinion on the National Socialist system as in the nature of the relationship between the state and capitalistic enterprise. Detailed knowledge of the facts in and of themselves do not make the picture any easier to summarize for the uninformed reader. Certainly a great deal of capitalistic enterprise has been and is being liquidated in whole or in part. Many of the more important entrepreneurial activities and powers have been curtailed or eliminated entirely. Many fields of economic activity have been wholly preëmpted by the government, and the network of controls emanating from the leading offices of the state reach into every nook and cranny of the nation's economic life.

Three additional developments make the picture doubly difficult to interpret properly. First, the Nazi propaganda itself is ostensibly, and in many respects emphatically, anticapitalistic. The Nazis claim, in fact, to have abolished capitalism entirely, and to have established in its place a pre-Romanic system in which property rights held in fee simple are transmuted into the equivalent of the "fixed family inheritance," and where the content and quality of inheritance rights are (ultimately) fixed by the state to correspond with a hierarchically arranged system of social or class gradations— in turn founded upon occupational differentiations as determined by bio-social inheritance factors. This idea they refer to as the *Ständestaat*—literally a State of Estates, or of classes, or Social-economic Castes.[59]

Secondly—and perhaps more important—the infiltration of controls exercised from central headquarters, state or private, effects a metamorphosis in the very nature of the problems at stake. Problems of monopoly controls, becoming politicized as an incidence to the wielding of coercive authority, are necessarily handled with a view to many factors other than mere price and marketing advan-

or less self-contained, employer-controlled, hierarchically arranged, occupational categories which serve for modern industrialism in much the same way the medieval guilds did for handicraft societies. See Chapter VIII and see also Neumann, *op. cit.*, pp. 228–38, "The Myth of the Corporate State."

[59] See, e. g., Kolnai's discussion of the writings of Hans Blüher, Houston Stewart Chamberlain, Nietzsche, and others, particularly Chapters I, II, III, VII, and VIII.

tage. Only the historically untutored, or politically and philo-sophically naïve could suppose that the power phase of coördinated monopoly controls would be handled in terms of "duopoly," "oli-gopoly," "imperfect competition," and the like.[60] The proper terms of reference are those associated with what Weber refers to as *Bürokratie, Patrimonialismus, Patriarchalismus,* and *Feudalis-mus.*[61]

And finally, the outbreak of the Second World War has placed Göring's much publicized Four Year Plan (*Vierjahresplan*) in the limelight, seeming thereby, to call for recalculation of all the varia-ble factors in an already overly confused picture. This complication is doubly baffling for the simple reason that it is so very difficult to learn much about the Four Year Plan—or, indeed, to learn whether there is even the substance of anything more than a comprehensive plan of military conquest at all.

Without entering very far into the issues involved at this point, it is possible to clarify the picture—even in the absence of much needed evidence at points—by recalling to the reader's mind that the Nazi state is made up not of one single central controlling bureaucracy, but of at least four such bureaucracies; these are, re-spectively, the civil service, the army, the party, and the economic. While differing from each other in points of view and interest in many places, these four bureaucracies are not separate and inde-pendent, but interlaced and interdependent. Civil and criminal law, and the whole of the legislative, executive, judicial and ad-ministrative machinery of the Third Reich have been centralized, unified,[62] and brought into line with the basic hierarchical pattern of the *Ständestaat.* Into this fabric has been introduced the Nazi party bureaucracy; it is at present almost impossible to determine

[60] Irrespective of the logical or formal merits of such works as Edward Chamber-lain's *The Theory of Monopolistic Competition* (Cambridge, Mass., 1933) or Joan Robinson's *The Economics of Imperfect Competition* (London, 1933), writers on eco-nomics have committed the fatal error of supposing that the simple hedonism and the circumspect marginalism of competitive equilibrium analysis could be trans-posed or merely modified by monopoly forms. The maximizing of profits rests in-creasingly on entirely different influences, powers, and factors than they are led to suppose. And even this objective may be so fundamentally altered by accretions to power, and by compromise with other desiderata of control, as to be almost entirely incompatible with the presumptive model behavior these authors are led to assume for their genus *homo monopolisticus.*

[61] Max Weber, *Grundriss der Sozialökonomik* (1925), in particular, pp. 650–753.

[62] See Karl Loewenstein, "Law in the Third Reich," *Yale Law Journal,* XLV (March, 1936), 779–815.

where one begins and the other ends.[63] The Nazification of the army, following the removal of von Fritsch and the old guard just before the invasion of Poland, served to fuse this rapidly expanding bureaucracy jointly with the state apparatus and the Nazi party. The organization of the National Economic Chamber, and its correlative labor, agricultural, and cultural "estates," [64] completes the picture by dovetailing with the other hierarchies at a thousand and one points, personalities, machinery, competencies, and functions.

The net product of this four-way fusion has been referred to by people interested in the economic angle as "status capitalism," meaning a monopolistically organized, militaristically minded, hierarchically graduated and "feudalistically" directed [65] autocracy in which the upper social reaches, after having made the necessary compromises with the *nouveaux puissant* demagogery of platform and political tract, band together to constitute a governing class within a state expanded on a footing highly reminiscent of Plato's microcosmic model, the Sparta of Lycurgus. It is in this setting that the concept of the "Junker" has come to the fore again.[66] For the term "Junker" has been generalized to mean not merely the old landed aristocracy of the Prussian Marches, but something more nearly like the term "Tory" in England [67]—literally, a "nature-determined" and self-contained "ruling class." [68]

[63] This holds, for example, with the whole of the Party Tribunal system, which has been incorporated into the regular legal machinery of Germany (Loewenstein, *op. cit.*). An even more striking example is the incorporation of the NSBO (National Socialist Business Cell Organization) directly into the Labor Front. Similar examples could be multiplied almost indefinitely.

[64] Analogous to the National Economic Chamber (which includes all economic activities and interests in Germany, transportation alone excluded), are the National Food Estate, which comprehends all agricultural activities and interests, the National Chamber of Culture, responsible for the whole "cultural" program, and the Federal Trustees of Labor (under the Ministry of Labor), the coördinating body for the interests and activities of labor.

[65] Meaning, specifically, a suzerain relationship with each competency held "in fief" on a pseudo-contractual basis, fixed in custom, and resting upon means for insuring throughout the social pyramid fixity of social station, fixity of occupation. and ultimately a high degree of fixity of residence.

[66] See Karl Brandt, "Junkers to the Fore Again," *Foreign Affairs*, XIV (Oct., 1935), 120–34. Brandt, of course, means more than is implied above. Actually, he finds a steady and cumulative infiltration of the old Junker ranks into the civil, military, economic, and party ranks—many of them in leading positions.

[67] In fact, this is exactly what the Nazis (before the outbreak of war with England) defined the word "Tory" to mean. It is no accident that the top-flight finishing schools for Nazi party leaders reserve for their graduates the honorary title of "Junker."

[68] Actually, as in Plato's famous illustration of the metals and in Pareto's concep-

Whereas in a feudal society the economic resources of the baronry were rooted in agricultural holdings, in the adapted capitalism of the Third Reich the gigantic strength of the new "Junker class" is drawn from industrial, commercial, and financial properties. And to the extent that the feudal nature of the economic relationships in medieval society was not compromised by virtue of the fact that the nobility possessed legal, civil, and military rights in addition to the economic, so also this new fusion called "Fascist Totalitarianism" is no less an expression of monopoly controls simply because similar elements are mixed into the "Junker" social composition.[69]

In fact, a carefully reasoned analysis of the past developments summarized in this chapter will show not only that the Nazi state grew by fairly normal processes out of the evolution of capitalistic forms in Germany, but also that the bureaucratic fusions traced out above are not only consistent with, but absolutely essential to, a continuation of such previous lines of growth. Without them, capitalism in Germany unquestionably could not long have survived under any circumstances. With them, it may be enabled to endure for a considerable period of time in the future.

From the standpoint of practical propaganda, it seemed advantageous to Nazi officialdom to describe this new arrangement as noncapitalistic, or even anticapitalistic. The "profit motive," it is said, no longer dominates business decisions. In its place has come "service to the community." This is, of course, exactly what is meant by the American authors, Mooney and Reiley, when they lay down the dictum on behalf of highly organized American business that the real function of capitalism is to make "profits through service, profit in this sense meaning the compensatory material gain or reward obtained through service." [70] It reflects a point of view which is consonant with that expressed in the famous "You and Industry" series of the National Association of Manufacturers.

tion of the "circulating elite," provisions are made for especially gifted outside-of-the-ruling-class recruits to rise to the top. These are regarded, however, primarily as sport cases—exceptions to the rule.

[69] Of course, it may be correctly upheld that this analogy with feudalism is unhappy, because feudalism is opposed to bureaucratization and contains the essential element of personal relationship. Nevertheless, it would seem to illuminate the nature of the property holdings and spheres of economic control in the Third Reich.

[70] James D. Mooney and Alan C. Reiley, *Onward Industry!* (New York, 1931), p. 342.

In making "business responsible to the community" through the revamped control network of the "'new social order," the Nazi leaders profess to be promoting "self-government" or "self-management" in industry. It is also interesting to note that much of the time spent by officials in German central business offices has to do with what they term problems of "fair trade practices," "fair prices," rules against "selling below cost," and the like.[71]

Now an inevitable corollary of making such a system of business "self-management" work is the possession of the necessary power to punish offenders. It was on this particular rock that the price and production control measures of NRA were rent asunder. The Nazis have made no such mistake. That many concerns would be liquidated when the central control apparatus possessed the necessary power to force "free riders" into line was inevitable. This accounts for many of the cases of forced liquidation of small concerns. But even the large and giant enterprise is not necessarily exempt from the laws of its own making, for the simple reason that domestication of warfare does not necessarily do away with the basis of conflict. It may, however, change a good many of the rules. Thus many of the largest businessmen in Germany were forced to hand over their properties to competitors because they were Jews. And Thyssen, of the heavy industries, apparently chose to play a lone hand and got caught in a combine which he was unable to overcome. Like Schacht, at the critical point he played with the wrong crowd of "insiders," and, as has happened to many unsuccessful promoters in American business (Fisk, Drew, Gould), was forced out.[72]

---

[71] See in particular *Marktordnungsgrundsätze der Reichsgruppe Industrie*, a primer of rules for "regulating the market" according to the new "fair trade practice rules."

[72] Insull, Mitchell, and Whitney are in a different class only because they were caught via regulatory machinery which the business community either assented to, or, opposing, had had forced on them by political forces which held that only through such controls could the business community, and with it the capitalistic system, be saved from the disaster its own malpractices were bringing down upon it. Numerous observers have found in the spectacular rise of the Hermann Göring Works proof of an inherent Nazi tendency towards "Socialization." Nothing could be farther from the truth, as the party-approved *Berliner Tageblatt*, Dec. 2, 1938 ("Vom Wachstum des 'Reichswerke'-Konzerns") has pointed out at some length. Kurt Lachmann in "The Hermann Göring Works," *Social Research* (Feb., 1941), pp. 24–40, finds the company a new version of the postwar Stinnes or Haniel groups, and a type of "industrial empire building" which bears a close "resemblance to the amassing of lands and fortunes by the feudal lords of the seventeenth century." The analogy is intrigu-

None of these considerations are inconsistent with the point made that, under the Nazis, previous trends in the evolution of centralized business control were carried on, with the principal difference residing in the facts that under the new regime they could be brought to their logical conclusions more swiftly, more ruthlessly, and more rationally than theretofore, and that all economic issues must now be openly decided in a political frame of reference.

But how far has the war altered the picture? Under the decree of October 26, 1936, giving Field Marshall Hermann Göring dicta-

---

ing, but actually the combination represents a somewhat "privitized" regrouping of industrial properties previously owned by the Reich, Prussia, various municipalities, properties taken over from the governments of conquered Austria (e. g., Steyr-Daimler-Puch A.G., Maschinen- und Waggon-Fabrik A.G. Simmering, and Donau-Dampt-Shiffahrts-Gesellschaft) Czechoslovakia (e. g., Skoda), Poland, Roumania (most important of which is the Reshitza iron works), Norway, and—more recently—Belgian, Dutch, and French concerns.

German banks and "the industrialists" participated in the founding and expansion of the combination, though to what extent is unknown. It is significant, however, that the primary purpose of the new industrial complex—leaving aside liquidation of Göring's private debts—was the exploitation of low-grade domestic iron ores at government expense, for delivery to Krupp, Vereinigte Stahlwerke, and others, as raw steel for fulfilling armament contracts with fixed but generous profit allowances. Its subsequent expansion into a unified vertical combination and the regrouping of its holdings along functional lines (1) mining and smelting, (2) munitions and machine building, (3) shipping on rivers and canals, is entirely in keeping with past practices of German industrial concentration. Private control is greater, and private interests are served more clearly, under the new regrouping than was the case of the properties before they were brought together in the new combination. It is very difficult, if not at present entirely impossible, to evaluate the status of other such public or semi-public corporate enterprises. Neumann, op. cit., pp. 298–304, interprets the Göring set-up as a party combine with heavy-industry participation. Figures are produced in this book.

The Labor Front now does the biggest travel business in the world. Ley recently announced plans for the mass production of cheap farm tractors to be produced, apparently, along lines similar to the Labor Front-financed "Peoples Car" plant at Fallersleben (now producing tanks). The Labor Front has also taken over some 9,000 consumer coöperatives in Germany, and is also, through the Labor Front Bank (which collects around 500,000,000 marks annually in dues), possessor of one of the largest European banking systems (Business Week, March 15, 1941, p. 96). On the Labor Front combine, see Neumann, op. cit., p. 304.

Göring, Funk (head of the Reichsbank) and other leading Nazi officials have also organized a continental-wide oil trust, capitalized at $32,000,000. PM (March 4), 1941. On the Continental Oil Corporation, see Neumann, op. cit., pp. 276–77, 356–68, 396–98.

Certain only is this, that (a) these trusts are privately directed by Nazi officials acting in collaboration with private interests for non-democratic purposes, and (b) that they are being organized on an European-wide basis. See Albert T. Lauterbach, "German Plans for a New Economic Order in Europe," in Germany's Challenge to America's Defense (Planning Pamphlet No. 4 of the National Economic and Social Planning Association).

torial power to carry through the Second Four Year Plan, all economic activities in Germany were brought into six special groups:

(1) Production of German Raw Materials and Semi-Manufactures
(2) Allocation of Raw Materials
(3) Employment of Labor
(4) Agricultural Production
(5) Price Policies
(6) Foreign Exchange Supply.

On July 13, 1937, section (2) was dissolved, and there was created in its place two divisions, those of Foreign Trade and of Iron and Steel Utilization. Since that date the plan has apparently undergone many—and possibly in some respects far-reaching—changes. Its general purpose called for exhaustive detail on the present and potential resources of the Reich, and for ways and means of mobilizing these to the fullest extent and with the maximum speed. An observer, present in Germany during the elaboration of the various phases of the Plan, details the functions of the new machinery as follows: [73]

1. Supply of detailed information for achieving production potentials, including data on working conditions. Envisaged were: possible elimination of dual and overlapping capacities; amalgamation and coordination of plants and enterprises, mainly in an effort to save on transport and distribution costs; a report was made on how far labor hours could be increased, based on the fact that there were no new or unemployed workers to be absorbed; detailed data on obsolescence, which had already made itself prominent in mining and the steel industry (having become very much worse since 1937, particularly in the railroad industry). Particular emphasis was placed upon the development of synthetic or *Ersatz* industries.
2. The direction of the maximum of the available potential into military uses. A final and amazing estimate was made of just how far consumption—and more important—production of capital equipment for home use could be cut so that arms and exports would benefit.
3. Estimates of various national costs and subsidies involved in the use of admittedly poorer raw materials and minerals which exist at home, when substituted for better materials imported from abroad. Particular attention was paid to iron and lumber, but re-use of old materials also received a good deal of attention.

---

[73] The author of these remarks, anonymous for obvious reasons, was in an unusually fortunate position for observation of the whole plan as it was unfolded from 1936 on. His summary checks in the main with every bit of evidence I have been able to obtain from other sources.

4. The financial end of operations: for the first year it was planned
   that 80 percent of the costs involved would be carried by private industry, of which 30 percent was to be based on existing assets, and
   50 percent handled through new financing (stocks and bonds): banks
   would supply 8 percent and the government 12 percent by subsidy.
5. A detailed plan for possible markets abroad, and a statement of why
   Germany was having difficulties in foreign markets (mostly attribu-
   table to lowered qualities).
6. Unified control by staff under the direction of Field Marshall Hermann Göring.

Great as these and subsequent changes have been, yet the Second
Four Year Plan seems clearly, and in all leading particulars, to
have been directly in line with the First Four Year Plan. Although
the earlier plan (1932–36) had as its declared objective the abolition of unemployment and the creation of German self-sufficiency,
it was during this period that all the important Nazi social, economic and legal organizations were established, the basic new price
and marketing controls elaborated, the foundations for remili-
tarization laid and the task of rearming actually begun. The Second
Four Year Plan (1936–40) bridged the gap between a militarized
peace and full belligerent status, but involved little more than
further elaboration and strengthening of previous machinery, together with a more deliberate reorientation of all efforts toward the
impending war. The Third Four Year Plan (sometimes referred to
as the Second Four Year Plan in the Nazi literature) looks towards
the dual objectives of still more complete coördination of civil and
belligerent control efforts on the one hand, and towards the reorganization of occupied territories with a view to the "organic" incorporation into the imperial network of the German dominated
"new order in Europe" on the other.

Thus the Four Year Plans have followed a fairly consistent pattern from the beginning. Tracing what little may be learned about
them from their inception, it seems that there is little, at bottom,
to distinguish them from other war plans of the First World War,
particularly those of Hohenzollern Germany, except the much
higher levels of organization and control and the greatly expanded
perspectives of imperial aggression. So far as industrial and business
organization is concerned, practically every significant idea elaborated in the new system is to be found, at least in germinal form,

in the Central Purchasing Corporation (Zentraleinkaufsgesellschaft —ZEG) and the series of semi-autonomous "mixed" control committees and compulsory syndicates which dominated the war control measures in Germany from 1915 on through to the cessation of hostilities.[74]

The Four Year Plans appear thus as straight-line development from these predecessor plans. Both anticipated the whole of economic activity coördinated to the needs of the war, with separate all-inclusive planning and control bodies for each important trade, industry, or functional activity (e. g., price control), and with all these dovetailed through an appropriate machinery. The First World War supplied experimental results on a big scale. Marshal Göring is bringing all the isolated strands together on a new and more comprehensive basis. Now business leaders are sitting down with governmental officials, military chieftains, and imperial party leaders, and are working out policies governing all economic activities in the entire Reich.

But the larger significance of these business-government relationships is found in the fact that during the between-wars interlude there was no fundamental departure from the basic organizational patterns of the World War. Many of the forced syndicates, notably those in coal, lignite, and potash, continued in force. The war stepped up the speed of cartelization tremendously, but the postwar period carried on the process. The "mixed" corporations, some of which sprang into existence during the war, continued to dot the economic landscape, particularly in the fields of power, gas, coal, iron and steel, and shipping. War-type price controls, production controls, internal and external market allocations, pooling of patents, technical innovations such as standardization and typification (of assembled products) were not given up. Rigidity of control was in many respects relaxed, and there was certainly a marked decline in the role of the government and the military.

Yet certain leading ideas remained, first of a completely coördinated economic system, based upon the full "coöperative" participation of the upper business baronry in politico-economic decisions; this was in turn to be divided into all-inclusive "self-

[74] See "Kriegswirtschaftslehre und Kriegswirtschaftspolitik," *Handworterbuch der Staatswissenschaft* (4th ed., Jena, 1928), V, 984-1022.

governing" trade and industrial central policy-controlling bodies, which should be endowed with legal or quasi-legal power to enforce decisions in the name of the state, and which, finally, would be guaranteed successful results through an elaborate system of governmental subsidies, allowances, and guarantees. In the interlude of peace, business leaders had acquired the habit of looking back at the experience of the war as the training ground and the germinal source of ideas for the coördinative efforts which time and circumstance were persuading them to extend to the outermost reaches of the German economic system.

At the critical juncture the Nazi solution, with its abolition of trade unions and its wholesale destruction of democratic institutions, seemed a necessary and logical fulfillment of these processes of growth. Therefore, though not without some occasional misgivings, German business leaders embraced it. Now they face the prospect of being able to expand their private economic empires, by the aid, advice, and consent of the new German-dominated totalitarian system which they expect shortly to extend to the outermost bounds of Europe and Africa, upon a continental and intercontinental basis.

How far such expansion will mean further modification of part capitalistic forms of organization remains to be seen. Regimentation through the instrumentality of the state will doubtless continue, but there is as yet no reason for believing that it will depart far from the present principles of "self-government in business" [75] which did so much to bring the regimentation on. But it is impor-

[75] The wartime control of industry rests today: a) with the general deputies under the Four Year Plan, primarily concerned with nationalization (now coördinated by Wilhelm Fanger, president of the Mannesman combine and leader of the national group industry); b) with the *Reichsstellen* for raw-material allocation. The *Reichsstellen* are now merely raw-material allocation offices; however, they are slowly being dissolved and their functions taken over by the existing cartels or by newly created cartels (coal and cellulose, wool and steel). See *Economist*, April 4, 1942 (radio broadcast from Germany); c) with the national Price Commissioner; d) with the general commissioner for labor supply; e) with the Reichsbank (for capital issues); f) with the Wehrwirtschaft (*Rüstungsamt*) of the Supreme Command of the Armed Forces, which is represented especially in the combing-out commission for the adequate distribution of labor; g) with the National Economic Chamber; h) the supreme authority is vested in the ministerial council for the defense of the nation. This has i) delegated a large part of its authority to the minister of economics, W. Funk, as general commissioner for economic affairs. See Neumann, *op. cit.*, p. 252, and the scheme, p. 253.

tant to note that given this principle fused with the companion Nazi ideology of class and racial predation it follows from extension of the old patterns over the new terrain that *Wirtschaft* and *Krieg* become but two internally related phases of the many faceted and inherently expansionist *Herrenstaat*.

Chapter II

THE FASCIST SYSTEM OF
COLLATERAL SYNDICATES

THE ROLE and significance of the Fascist Confederation of Industries is inextricably bound up with the development of Fascism and the unfolding of its appropriate institutional expression, the Corporate State. This is true because, at bottom, it is not only fair but also entirely accurate to speak of Fascism as a "revolution from the right," or, more simply, as "counterrevolution." [1] And in counterrevolution the forces centered around the more compactly organized, possessing classes must of necessity choose the issues and shape—with whatever compromises the *Realpolitik* of *Domination* may enforce—the course of future events.

But why should such vigorous and sweeping counterrevolutionary action occur first in Italy, one of the least industrialized amongst the capitalistic states? There is an interesting historical analogy here with the contemporary situation in Russia, which helps to throw the Italian situation at the end of the war into sharp relief. In Fascism capitalistic institutions were able to triumph; in Communism they faced defeat. Yet both Italy and Russia were among the "weakest links" in the chain of capitalist nations. In each case, at a critical point the pendulum seems barely to have swung the way it did. It is probably not too far from the truth to say that had Russia not turned Socialist in 1917 it would have adopted some form of "Fascism," and had Italy in 1922 not fallen unexpectedly to the Fascists it would have become a Socialist state (though the "March on Rome" came after the high tide of postwar revolutionary Socialism).

[1] See Carl Schmidt, *The Plough and the Sword* (New York, 1938), Chapter III, "Counterrevolution."

Both countries were primarily agricultural.[2] In both, rural life was characterized by deep contrasts between vast estates owned by politically powerful and immensely wealthy families on the one hand, and an overwhelming majority of more or less propertyless, poverty-stricken, ignorant, and repressed peasantry on the other. In both, important feudal carry-overs survived intact down to the outbreak of the World War. In neither had Parliamentary institutions or the first grudging concessions to popular sovereignty seriously affected the vast proportion of the population. Both were still political patchworks, and in neither had largely borrowed, nationalistic sentiments penetrated far beneath the thin upper layers of class-conscious jingoism.[3]

In both, the level of industrialization was, comparatively speaking, low, and what industrial nuclei had developed were highly localized. Of these, most were foreign transplantations, representing primarily English, French, and German capital. What local capital was involved in each case came largely from the great landowning families, with which rising industrial, trading, and finance capital was, consequently, closely associated from the beginning.[4] Industrialization came comparatively late, and in both cases, once begun, the pace of growth and development was unusually swift. At a time when industrial technique of its own momentum was be-

[2] See the summary given in Robert Michels, *Italien von Heute* (Leipzig, 1930), pp. 19–20, of Bakunin's description of Italian social classes in 1870. It needs only minor alterations to be held valid for Italy of 1914 or 1940.

[3] "Before the World War Italian nationalism was the concern of a group of snobbish writers rather than of serious thinkers. Every effort was made to adapt the philosophy of the German imperialist Treitschke, or that of French prototypes such as Maurras and Barrès, to Italian conditions." William Ebenstein, *Fascist Italy* (New York, 1939), p. 4. "The state has been dominated by classes. But now we begin to conceive of the state as an emanation of the entire nation. The state is the active organ of the entire nation, for the entire nation." E. Corradini (founder of the Nationalist Association) *Il volere d'Italia* (Naples, 1911), p. 175. The lack at that time of any deeply felt national or articulate and cohesive social ideologies among the two peoples goes far to explain why, of all the soldiers fighting in the World War, the Italians and the Russians were equally and by all odds the worst. The slaughter of the Masurian Lakes was paralleled by the demoralizing catastrophe of Caporetto —a catastrophe which appears to have been repeated in but slightly different form on the plains below the Guadarramas during the Spanish Civil War.

[4] The more important and more highly organized *latifondi* were located in the rich Po Valley. At the two ends of the Valley are to be found the more important industrial and commercial centers of Italy. The great landowners constituted the social and economic aristocracy in the great cities where industrial undertakings first struck root. From the same closely knit social circles came the leadership for the great employers' associations in both agriculture and industry.

coming large-scale, and capitalism of its own native driving power was resorting everywhere to monopoly devices, this forced-draft growth tended at once to sharpen the social cleavages and to strengthen and unify the forces of antidemocratic reaction. By the "accidents of history" monopoly forms of capitalism, mercantilistic sentiments, and feudal social institutions were in both immediately juxtaposed.

In Russia proletarian forces won the throw of the die; in Italy, property. For the spread of the Socialist-Communist state Russia lacked industrialism; for the dominance of capitalist institutions and controls Italy lacked a widespread business system. Russia undertook to solve her problem by a backward step into NEP, in order to lead more easily into the industrialization program of the Socialist Five Year Plan. Italy devised the Corporate System.[5] And the Corporate System is to be understood as that morganatic alliance between organized, Italian, patrimonial capitalism and the type of feudal controls long advocated by the Papacy, from which it was hoped to find at once an end to class war and full defense of the existing social-economic *status quo*.

ANTECEDENTS OF THE CORPORATE STATE

Without dipping farther into the historical background than is necessary to make clear the component elements out of which this apparently novel "experiment" was compounded, attention may be focused on three factors of unique importance; [6] (a) the "social program" of the Catholic hierarchy; (b) the rise and peculiar composition of the pre-Fascist labor movement; and (c) the strategic power of the closely coöperating central associations of industry and agriculture.

The social program of the Catholic hierarchy.—This was evolved as means for counteracting the rise of class-conscious trade unions dominated by left wing and materialistic—in particular by Marx-

---

[5] The essence of the Fascist corporate system is found in hierarchical implementation of patrimonial class domination by monopolistically oriented and compactly organized vested-interest groups.

[6] The "Nationalist" movement, though important, can be ignored for our present purposes. Like Fascism, which it preceded, it was not in itself a causal or contributory force, but the result of such force. Nor was its strength, as expressed in numbers or influence, of much importance.

ian—social philosophies. It may be divided into three phases: from the first third of the 19th century to the delivery of the Papal Encyclical *Rerum Novarum* in 1891; from *Rerum Novarum* to the inauguration of the Fascist system in 1922; after the Papal Encyclical in commemoration of *Rerum Novarum*, delivered in 1931 and known as *Quadragesimo Anno*.[7] Beginning, in the first phase, as a general criticism of conditions created out of the capitalistic milieu, the papal position had shifted until by 1931 it not only formally endorsed Mussolini's fascism *per se*, but also recommended the formula as a panacea for all other industrial countries as well.

In the first phase, Catholic writers took their place among various proponents who hoped to solve the issues of class conflict and industrialism by recourse to doctrines inspired by Christianity.[8] Le Play, the French engineer, hoped to transform the employer into a benevolent master who would care for his workmen as father to his children. Protestant writers such as Kingsley, Carlyle, and Ruskin wanted something less patriarchal, but saw in various forms of class collaboration good Tory means for turning the lion of industrial capitalism into the lamb of social harmony. The leading Catholic writers, however, went straight to the Middle Ages—the period in which the Church dominated the whole of European society—for their inspiration.

Under one form or another a series of Catholic spokesmen [9] advocated recrudescence of the medieval conception of a corporatively organized society. Many of these initial expositions were the work of French émigrés returning to the homeland following the Treaty of Vienna in 1815 and the inauguration of the Holy Alliance. On the

[7] The intervening period, 1922 to 1931, might, in turn, be divided into two intervals: a period of partial and at times bitter conflict between church and state reaching from the inauguration of Fascism to the Lateran Accord in 1929; and from the Lateran Accord, which recognized Catholicism as the official religion in return for Papal support of Fascist leadership in the upbuilding of the new Roman Empire, to recommendation of corporate ideas by the papacy as the solution of the "Social question" in general. Most notable of its successes has been the "clerical fascism" of the ill-starred Austrian totalitarians, Dollfuss and Schuschnigg, and the system of General Franco which emerged from the Spanish Civil War.

[8] See "Doctrines Inspired by Christianity," in C. Gide and C. Rist, *History of Economic Doctrines*, pp. 483–514.

[9] An early representative of these was Philip Buchez, *Essai d'un traité complet de philosophie, du point de vue du catholicisme et du progrès* (Paris, 1838–40), and Abbé de Lamennais, *La Question du travail* (1848).

other wing a few were highly reminiscent of the social-communism advocated so vehemently by the early church fathers,[10] since they appeared in large part as attacks on the institution of private property and in defense of workers' rights to a fair wage and a decent standard of living. But Catholic writers of a more "practical" turn of mind advocated simply mixed or collateral syndicates in which the principles of hierarchy would dominate and the employer would play the role of "leader" or "master" to his flock. The model was the Church,[11] and "the corporations which would be set up under the aegis of religion would aim at making all their members contented with their lot, patient in toil, and disposed to lead a tranquil, happy life." [12]

Though never entirely free of important schismatic differences, the Social-Catholic movement maintained almost from the beginning a fairly coherent reform program. Prior to the revolutionary upheavals of 1848 it was predominantly antiliberal, generally opposing both laissez faire and free competition on the grounds that the doctrines of the Physiocrats and the early French liberals on the one hand and the socially irresponsible practices of certain traders and manufacturers on the other largely accounted for the French Revolution, its tempestuous aftermath, the rise of anticlericalism, and the spread of class antagonisms. The "free thinking" bourgeoisie were distrusted almost as much as the popular democracy for which it appeared inevitably to prepare the way.[13]

The events of 1848 convinced Catholic thinkers that socialism, as the residuary legatee of liberal and democratic doctrines, was the

10 Such as Tertullian, St. Ambrose, St. Cyprian, Gregory of Nazianze. See the program of Vicomte de Villeneuve-Bargemont as outlined by Thomas Parker Moon, *The Labor Problem and the Social Catholic Movement in France* (New York, 1921), pp. 19–25. See also Paul K. Crosser, *Ideologies and American Labor*, New York, 1941.

11 "The corporation is simply the model of the Church. Just as for the Church all the faithful are equal in the sight of God, so here. But equality ends there. For the rest of it is a hierarchy." Quoted by Gide and Rist, *op. cit.*, p. 500, from Segur-Lamoignon, *L'Association catholique*, July 13, 1894.

12 Gide and Rist, *loc. cit.*, quoted from the Encyclical of Leo XII, December 28, 1878, called *Quod Apostolici.*

13 Veuillot, a clerical journalist, was opposed to the "free thinking bourgeoisie" but held that, while misery must be destroyed, "poverty is a divine institution" and charity the true social science. He proposed a Holy Roman Democracy to parallel the Holy Roman Empire; the latter, of course, was to lead the former by authoritative principles and both were to be hierarchically directed from above. The Confederation of Italian Industries was later to refer to its own program, patterned along these lines, as "authoritarian democracy." Moon, *op. cit.*, p. 30.

greatest of all the Church's enemies. Moderates like Melun and Le Play lost out, and, under the stimulus of the official patronage of Napoleon the Third, the movement began to take more definite shape around three leading objectives; first, to overcome the radicalization of the working classes through an ideological conquest of the "workers' souls"; second, to transform the employer from a hardhearted profit seeker into an aristocratic and paternal "leader" of his men; and third, to revive the medieval guild or corporate form of organization.

The first objective called for universal indoctrination with official Catholic Christianity, the second for various forms of benevolent social legislation, and the third for integral or mixed syndicalism. Under Count Albert De Mun and Count La Tour du Pin, these three phases were forged into an effective political program which was shortly taken up abroad—particularly in Germany under the leadership of Baron Wilhelm Emmanuel von Ketteler—and which soon received official papal blessing.

Industrial organization, De Mun held, should take the form of "the Catholic Guild, which is neither a trade-union, nor a tribunal of arbitration, but a center of Christian activity where the interest of the profession is superior to private interest, where antagonism between capitalist and workingman gives way to patronage exercised in a Christian spirit and freely accepted. . . . It is always the same thought: limit competition, associate common interests, impose upon the employer the duty of patronage, uplift labor and the condition of the laborer." [14]

Contemporaneously with De Mun's agitation (in the seventies and eighties), a great deal of interest in programs for class collaboration was aroused by the "experiment" of the French spinning firm of Harmel at Val-des-Bois. In the words of a very sympathetic observer, the "Christian Guild" of the Harmels was evolved as follows:

The simple principle of union by itself was considered inadequate; it tended to create labor-unions hostile to capital and bent on class warfare. The principle of democratic control of industry would logically lead to the elimination of the employer. The principle of capitalistic paternalism, if taken alone, was inadequate because it failed to awaken any vital response among the workingmen. The Harmels attempted to

---

[14] *Ibid.*, pp. 99–100.

make a Christian synthesis of these principles. In the first place, the workers were permitted, nay encouraged, to form various associations—a men's club, a woman's association, a girls' society, a mutual benefit society. Democratic control was practiced in the management of these associations, and was represented by elected shop-committees, but was not carried to the extreme. The Guild Board, an elective council of workingmen, was consulted on such questions as shop-management and wage-schedules, but had no sovereign authority in these matters; the policy of the employers was to act with democratic advice and consent, but not to abdicate their authority. The third principle, paternalism, received expression in manifold efforts on the part of the employers to promote the material and moral welfare of the workingmen, to foster and guide even the institutions controlled by the workers. The paternal influence may be seen in the fact that one of the employers acted as chairman of the Guild Board, and the supervision of general guild interests was entrusted to a committee composed of the members of the firm, the chaplain, the school-director, and representatives of the various workingmen's associations. In this fashion the three principles of association, democratic control, and capitalist paternalism were combined and balanced in a complex organism consisting of first, employers, second, the general committee of employers and representatives of the workingmen's institutions, third the workingmen's Guild Board, fourth, shop committees, fifth, various economic, social and religious associations among the work-people.[15]

Here is a précis not only for much of the social legislation that was to follow, but also for the more benevolent type of company union as well as the more violently counterrevolutionary Fascist syndicates of the Mussolini regime. Gone completely was the attitude of hostility toward capitalist and employer wherever he could be persuaded to add to his entrepreneurial functions those of father and leader to his employees. And also, by the same token, gone completely was the hostility to labor organization wherever workers could be gathered into associations, governed and directed by employer interests from above in a fixed hierarchy of command and subordination and deliberately modeled after the pattern of the Universal Church.

Until late in the century the papacy had paid relatively little attention to the Social-Catholic movement. The general idea, of course, of universal guild organization under the benevolent supervision of the Church has never been abandoned. From time to time

15 *Ibid.*, pp. 114–15.

references had been made to guilds in various papal utterances, such as, for example, *Humanum genus* in 1854, *Quod Apostolici muneris* in 1878, and *Aeterni Patris* in 1879. But it was with the encyclical letter of Pope Leo XIII on "The Condition of Labor" (*Rerum Novarum*) in 1891 that recrudescence of the corporate organization of society became the official doctrine. The Encyclical was directed specifically at the Socialists, and in condemning their social doctrines Leo XIII saw fit for the first time to commit the Church to full support of capitalistic institutions. Social inequality, private ownership of the means of production, free competition, laissez faire, the accumulation of great wealth, and the rest, were justified as "just" and according to 'the "laws of nature." Conversely, "class war" was declared "irrational," since "in a state it is ordained by nature that these two classes (the rich and the poor) should exist in harmony and agreement." The employer was to treat his labor "justly" and render him that which was due. The multitudes must, he said, be kept "within the line of duty." Organization along lines of medieval guilds provided at once the ideal solution for social conflict, an offset for the greed of the poor, and a solvent for the cupidity of the rich.[16]

Various Catholic Social-Action groups took up the new program with great enthusiasm. Shortly, some of these groups began to look forward to the "corporative reorganization of society" [17] as a whole. All masters and men were to be organized, preferably, in mixed syndicates, consisting of both employers and labor, or *collateral* syndicates, in which the two groups would be organized separately for purposes of group collaboration.[18] The state was not to interfere

[16] See in particular, *Rerum Novarum*, paragraphs 53 to 65, inclusive, reproduced in full in Henry George, *The Condition of Labor, an Open Letter to Pope Leo XIII* (New York, 1891), pp. 121–57.

[17] "We must direct all our private initiative and concentrate public attention upon this one reform—the corporative reorganization of society." Cited by Gide and Rist, *History of Economic Doctrines*, p. 497, from *Programme de l'oeuvre des cercles ouvriers*, April, 1894.

[18] "In 1894 the Congress of Catholic Circles which met at Rheims declared that, 'without minimizing the difficulties which stand in the way of extending the mixed *syndicats*, the formation of such *syndicats* must be our chief aim.' In 1904, Father Rutten, one of the leaders of the Belgian Catholic Syndical movement, in a report on the syndicalist movement writes as follows: 'We do not despair of the mixed *syndicat*, which in theory we certainly think is nearest perfection. But we must not blind ourselves to facts, and whether we will or no we have to admit that at the present moment the mixed *syndicat* in ninety industries out of every hundred seems

with such autonomous associations except to see that they were duly protected and did not use their pooled strength to the detriment of the general community. They were, in short, to be self-governing associations for the promotion of class collaboration.[19]

In the subsequent period of organization, the idea of collateral syndicates, sometimes referred to as "integral syndicalism," definitely gained the upper hand. It is interesting to note that this idea was taken over unaltered to form the basis of the Fascist system of organization by social-economic categories.

The early years of Fascist rule found Mussolini and the Pope frequently at swords' points. But just as accession to power stilled the former's lingering radicalism, so the immense ideological strength of the latter amongst the mass of the Italian peasantry coupled to the expansive power of the papal hierarchy blunted the anticlerical edge of Fascist propaganda. In the Lateran Accord of 1929 Fascism adopted the papacy on condition that the papacy concede popular allegiance to the objectives of Fascism and the State and Empire in which those objectives were embodied.[20]

It was hardly to be expected that the Accord, widely acclaimed as it was, would settle all the issues at dispute. *Quadragesimo Anno* was condemned by many Fascists for some of its implied criticisms of their system. But in the main the document possesses historical significance primarily for its wholesale acceptance of the tenets underlying the Fascist social program.

"Harmony between ranks in society" now became the dominant theme: "Now this is the primary duty of the state and of all good citizens," the Pontiff declared, "to abolish conflict between classes with divergent interests, and thus foster and promote harmony between the various ranks of society." [21] Instrumental to this objective "must be therefore the reëstablishment of vocational groups,"

---

quite Utopian.' " Gide and Rist, *op. cit.,* pp. 76, 498, quoted from Duchesne, *Syndicats ouvriers belges* (1906).

19 This early statement of the principle becomes explicable when it is recalled that *Rerum Novarum* was directed against Socialism as much for its apotheosis of the power of the state in opposition to private capitalism as for its support of heretical social and moral principles.

20 For the text of the Lateran Accord, see Walter C. Langsam and J. M. Eagan, *Documents and Readings in the History of Europe Since 1918* (Chicago, 1939), pp. 557–66.

21 All quotations are from copy of the text reproduced in Langsam and Eagan, *op. cit.,* pp. 567–72.

for "as nature induces those who dwell in close proximity to unite into municipalities, so those who practice the same trade or professions, economic or otherwise, combine into vocational groups."

While such organization of social-economic categories is to be "autonomous," Pius definitely rejected "free competition" and the past "errors of the 'Individualistic' school" as "the true guiding principles of economics." They had their place, to be sure, but "it is very necessary that economic affairs be once more subjected to and governed by a true and effective guiding principle." This the state is alone competent to determine, and in taking notice of "special syndical and corporative organization . . . inaugurated . . . within recent times," the Encyclical declares that "little reflection is required to perceive the advantages of the institution [Fascist institution] thus summarily described: [22] peaceful collaboration of the classes, repression of Socialist organizations and efforts, the moderating influence of a special ministry." Fixity of status and occupation, the outlawing of strikes and lockouts, and the location of the ultimate powers of umpire and reconciliation in a theologically acceptable totalitarian state assured to His Holiness that "social harmony" and "class collaboration" of which Leo XIII had dreamed forty years before.

There was some bitter [23] to be taken with the sweet, but in the

[22] "The state here grants legal recognition to the syndicate or union, and thereby confers on it some of the features of a monopoly, for in virtue of this recognition, it alone can represent respectively workingmen and employers, and it alone can conclude labor contracts and labor agreements. Affiliation to the syndicate is optional for everyone; but in this sense only can the syndical organization be said to be free, since the contribution to the union and other special taxes are obligatory for all who belong to a given branch, whether workingmen or employers, and the labor-contracts drawn up by the legal syndicate are likewise obligatory. It is true that it has been authoritatively declared that the legal syndicate does not exclude the existence of unrecognized trade associations.

"The corporations are composed of representatives of the unions of workingmen and employers of the same trade or profession, and as true and genuine organs and institutions of the state, they direct and coördinate the activities of the unions in all matters of common interest." *Quadragesimo Anno*, Langsam, *op. cit.*, p. 569. This language is practically identical with that employed in the official propaganda ministry of the Fascist party. Cf. *The Law of April 21, 1927*, known as the Labour Charter, reproduced in Langsam, *op. cit.*, pp. 519–25.

[23] In particular that "concentration of power" which "has led to a threefold struggle for domination" for power within the dictatorship, for control over the state, and amongst the states, which leads to war. Also, "the intermingling and scandalous confusing of the duties and offices of civil authority and of economics" which not only degrades "the majesty of the state" but leads to "economic imperialism." *Quadragesimo Anno, loc. cit.*

light of subsequent events it would appear that the rapprochement between the papacy and the New Roman Empire has been growing steadily closer.[24] Even the Axis accord does not seem to be wholly unwelcome in papal circles.[25]

The composition of the pre-Fascist labor movement.—There is no need here to recapitulate the voluminous expository and argumentative literature on this phase of the Italian corporate-state background.[26] It will suffice to indicate in rough outline a few of the peculiarities of the Italian labor movement which made it so readily and generally adaptable to the type of controls which the organized "right" sought, under Fascism, to place on it.

1. Though of comparatively recent origin, the labor movement in Italy had begun to form central federations and confederations early in its history. There was practically no such thing as a labor movement in any part of the country before 1874. Yet by 1890 first efforts were already being made to federate. After a number of reverses, these efforts had succeeded, at the outbreak of the war, in bringing the vast bulk of organized labor into three great confederations: The General Confederation of Labor (CGL), with about 321,000 members; the Catholic Italian Confederation of Labor (CIL), with around 103,000 members; and the Italian Syndicalist Association (USI), with some 100,000 members.[27] By 1920, after a period of decline during the war, membership had risen until the CGL and the CIL were able to claim a membership of 2,150,000 and 1,205,447, respectively. This represents not only an unusually high level of

[24] In the Abyssinian venture it was commonly believed that the papacy lent its financial support, and in the Spanish Civil War it allied itself openly on Il Duce's side.

[25] The new totalitarian system in process of formation in France appears to enjoy papal blessing. Only belatedly, and then only under considerable pressure, was reproof for the utterances of Father Coughlin forthcoming.

[26] To mention but a few, favorable summaries are given in the semi-official volume by Fausto Pitigliani (now in exile), *The Italian Corporative State* (London, 1933); Michael T. Florinsky, *Fascism and National Socialism* (New York, 1936); Benito Mussolini, *The Corporate State* (Florence, 1936); various publications (in mimeograph) of the Italian Library of Information; and Michels, *Italien von Heute*. Critical summaries are found in Ebenstein, *Fascist Italy*; Gaetano Salvemini, *Under the Axe of Fascism* (New York, 1936); George Seldes, *Sawdust Caesar* (New York, 1935); and Carl T. Schmidt, *The Corporate State in Action* (New York, 1939).

[27] I find no two authorities who agree on these figures. The data for the CGL and the USI are taken from *Freedom of Association* (Series A, No. 31, International Labor Office, Geneva), IV, 4–5. The figures for the CIL are from Wladimir Woytinsky, *Die Welt in Zahlen* (Berlin, 1926), II, 123.

unionization, but also an unusually high degree of centralized direction. On this footing trade unionism loomed large.

2. Membership was drawn primarily from agricultural and handicraft labor. Data taken from official sources,[28] showed 453,000 industrial workers belonging to trade unions in 1912 for 408,000 agricultural workers. Subsequent years did not greatly alter the picture.[29] Even as late as 1921 probably not more than one-third of organized Italian labor could be classified as "industrial."[30] The strength of the labor movement, in other words, was much less than it appeared to be. The reasons were as follows:

(a) The movement was widely scattered geographically, and the typical unit was small, localized, provincial, and more or less independent and self-contained.

(b) Organized agricultural labor was property minded: its principal grievance was the perpetuation of the system of *métayage*, and its members were neither very conscious of their own class nor conscious of having a great deal in common with the industrial workers.

(c) The position of the large number of handicraft and shop employees was not greatly different. Their lingering feudal attachments and partially articulated middle-class sentiments made them at best poor and unreliable partners in a militant, class-conscious struggle for political power.[31]

3. A third and even more fatal weakness in the Italian labor movement was centered in more or less irreconcilable doctrinal differ-

[28] Woytinsky, *op. cit.*, II, 124; cited from *Annuario Statistico Italiano*, Series 2, VII (1917–18), 330.

[29] The war years were an exception; there was then a tendency for agricultural members to increase over industrial membership, indicating a relatively heavier war draft on the latter group.

[30] Even the most militant and class-conscious of the central associations, the CGL, had 294,000 out of 1,206,000 members listed as attached to agriculture. In addition, many other crafts, e. g., the bulk of those listed as textile workers (78,000 in 1921) should really be called agricultural laborers. For another viewpoint on agricultural workers and trade unionism in Italy consult the writings of Ignazio Silone, who has developed the subject in detail and who takes a somewhat different position.

[31] The number included in this category must have been numerically more important than Woytinsky's figures indicate. It is possible that when due allowance is made for those listed under industrial categories who worked as handicraftsmen the number would be as large or larger than those properly classed as industrial workers. In addition, close to 100,000 workers were employed in governmental or semigovernmental (railways, post and telegraph, etc.) activities and who were, consequently, at least partially controlled by governmental authorities under civil-service regulations.

ences. The largest of the three more important general groups, the General Confederation of Labor, was led, perhaps more clearly than any other continental trade-union group, by politically minded socialists of the more orthodox (not revisionist, as in Germany) school. The second largest group, the Italian Confederation of Labor, followed the line laid down by *Rerum Novarum* and was, consequently, in the main quite hostile to the CGL. Its mixed-syndicates program bears a very close resemblance to the "company union" in the United States, and its alternative, integral syndicates, was erected on the substitute foundation of organized "class collaboration." The third group, the Italian Syndicalist Association, followed a mixture of ideas adapted from Bakunin, the anarchist, and from theorists of the Sorel persuasion. Their position was similar in a number of respects to the anarchist trade unions of Barcelona as shown in the early stages of the Spanish Civil War. They favored, in the main, economic as against political action, and they had a tendency to be very militant upon an insubstantial organizational structure—that is, they submitted badly to group discipline and the centralization of authority.

Thus, while Italian labor movement was simultaneously numerically imposing, fired in at least two camps with revolutionary doctrines, and sufficiently centralized to be able to move rapidly on occasion, it was hampered because (a) it was compounded of largely dissentient occupational groupings of widely varying sense of group solidarity, political education, and social attachments, and (b) it was split into three groups, which differed from one another on objectives and methods. To this should be added the fact that at the critical moment, during the postwar period before the coming of the Fascists, leadership was complicated by two additional difficulties: on the one hand, militant leaders were divided between the more violent, Sorelian syndicalist type (of which Mussolini was an outstanding example) and the Marxists; and, on the other hand, the Marxists were split between those who had devoted and still wished to dedicate the bulk of their energies to the gaining of political privileges for labor, and those who were prepared to face a distinctly revolutionary situation with a revolutionary program of action.[32]

[32] Even amongst these latter, there was no clear realization of the revolutionary possibilities of the years 1920–22 until it was too late. Palme Dutt in *Fascism and*

It is not necessary here to trace again [33] the results of this posture of affairs on the labor side during the period of occupation of the factories and the spread of general-strike tactics in the two years preceding the political triumph of Fascism. Suffice it to say that the unions then came so close to complete triumph that the organized opposition was determined to strike at the root of the matter by destroying for all time all power of independent union initiative and that they found in Fascism an acceptable formula for translating intent into action. And the Fascists in turn, with ambivalent éclat, evolved this program by deftly fusing Sorelian ideas, happily bereft of all revolutionary sentiment, with catholic integral syndicalism as evolved by the CIL—but now sheared from its popular moorings.

The Central Employers' Associations.—The employers' association movement in Italy likewise possessed three peculiarities which, in combination, go far towards explaining the early adoption of such a relatively mature employer's solution of their labor problems. In the first place, alongside of—and in some respects preceding—industrial organization came organization of agricultural employers, dominated by the feudal-minded and closely knit owners of the great *latifondi*. In the second place, both associations, while working very closely together on many matters, never divided their interests in political and economic affairs from their interests in social and labor matters. And thirdly, dominant influence among industrial employers was held by groups both highly localized in the industrial north and operating on a (relatively) large scale in new, swiftly growing, and technologically modern industries.

Under the first point, it is interesting to note that organization of agricultural employers was started by and grew to exercise great influence under the owners of the spreading *latifondi* in the Po

---

Social Revolution (London, 1934), p. 96, quotes Serrati, from whom most followers of the Leninist persuasion hoped a great deal, as declaring at a subsequent Congress of the Communist International that "Our fault is that we never sufficiently prepared ourselves for the events that have overtaken us. . . . Today we believe it essential to abandon the democratic illusion, and to create a combative, active, and audacious Party." Additional aspects of the problem were the impact of Bolshevism, the growth of the Maximalist movement and the corresponding confusion.

[33] See, in particular, the very pro-Fascist book by Pietro Gorgolini (with a foreword by Mussolini), *The Fascist Movement in Italian Life* (London, 1923), and the very anti-Fascist book by Angelo Rossi, *The Rise of Italian Fascism* (London, 1938).

Valley. As the movement spread to other parts of Italy, it stimulated organization of small farmer holdings around a variety of social and economic objectives. But, from the beginning, the leadership of the great landowners of the north (together with an increasing pressure towards federation and unification) tended to repress interests and objectives in conflict with their own.

The General Confederation of Agriculture was finally brought into existence in 1911 as a coördinating body for all Italian agricultural-employer interests, but, although its membership was said to be around 700,000 landed proprietors, its program was centered largely around the single-minded defense of the system of *métayage* [34]—a system not unlike the recently much publicized. sharecropper relationship of the American South. [35] What this indicated, of course, was first that the vast bulk of the Italian agricultural population—and Italy is primarily a rural country even today [36]—was made up of laborers and tenant farmers [37] and that ownership of land was highly concentrated. [38] And secondly, that the social rela-

[34] At its first congress the Confederation "defined its guiding rules" as follows: "That all the affiliated associations should support and extend the system of *métayage*, as being the most effective instrument for creating a stable social basis for agricultural progress and for the economic and moral improvement of the workers themselves, and that, while observing in the drafting of the economic clauses of such contracts [with organized agricultural workers] a liberal and modern spirit, they should defend the necessity for safeguarding the technical direction of the owner against the efforts of any who may seek, whether by the limitation of this power or by insisting on the substitution of farming leases for contracts of *métayage*, to withdraw the administration of rural undertakings from the hands of those technical experts who have done good service to the cause of agricultural progress and production. . . . That the principle of co-partnership should be extended even to the class of occasional workers and to that of workers with fixed wages." Quoted in ILO, *Freedom of Association*, IV, 8.

[35] "Métayage, a system of land tenure in Western Europe and also in the United States, in which the farmer pays a certain proportion (generally half) of the produce to the owner (as rent), the owner generally furnishing the stock and seed or a part thereof." Murray, *New English Dictionary*.

[36] "The economic life of Italy is basically rural. . . . The total gainfully occupied population of ten and more years of age is 17,262,521; 8,083,332 are occupied in agriculture. The total population of the country in 1931 was 41,176,671, of which number nearly 48 percent was comprised in families whose head was employed in agriculture. . . . Data for any of the last thirty or forty years would not give a substantially different picture of the economic structure of the rural population." Schmidt, *The Plough and the Sword*, pp. 1, 10.

[37] "According to the occupational census of 1931, roughly 8,000,000 persons over the age of 10 are engaged in agriculture. Of this number about 3,000,000 are classed as 'operating owners,' 900,000 as 'cash-tenants,' 1,700,000 as 'share-tenants,' 2,500,000 as 'wage-workers,' and 27,000 as 'managers.' " *Idem*.

[38] "The 3,800,000 dwarf and small holdings comprise but 32.7 percent of all the

tionship between the possessing and the landless classes was of a distinctly feudal stamp.

This feudal stamp was not lost when the great Po Valley estates went over to modern forms of highly mechanized industrial agriculture during and following the war. Relationships between master and men continued in much the same atmosphere as before, with the main difference that the latter had lost whatever social claims they had once possessed, and that the former, much as in the case of large-scale agriculture on the American Pacific Coast, had been freed of certain more or less compelling obligations assumed under the technically more primitive arrangement. That is to say, the mood, the social outlook, the plans and programs of the leading figures in the General Confederation of Agriculture were of the patronal, patrimonial, feudal stamp.

Not until after the war did employer interests in the industrial field succeed in attaining the level of central organization achieved by agricultural employers in 1911. Earlier efforts had been made from time to time, the last preceding attempt in 1910 having, even at that late date, proved premature.[39] In 1920 the General Confederation of Italian Industry was organized as a central policy-forming body for some one hundred member bodies,

divided among federal organizations [of which twenty-five were national] and local organizations and was made up of two sections:
(a) The Economic Section, which protected all kinds of industrial interests and set up as its aim the defense of those interests by means of direct co-operation in the drafting of laws and also by supporting the interests of its members against the state;
(b) The Trade Union Section, which studied and solved problems connected with the relationships between industrialists and the staff dependent on them, and also problems connected with social legislation.[40]

All commentators agree that the Confederation was a highly organized institution, exercising "a powerful influence on the whole

---

farm land in the country, whereas the 400,000 large farms control 67.3 percent thereof. These figures evince the extreme concentration of land ownership in relatively few hands." *Ibid.*, p. 13.

[39] A parallel attempt made in that year to form the Association of Italian Joint Stock Companies (Associazone fra le Societa Italiana per Acione) was more successful. It maintained an independent existence through the war, and was instrumental in the accouchement of the Confederation of Italian Industry. See Pitigliani, *The Italian Corporative State*, pp. 144–45.

[40] ILO, *Freedom of Association*, IV, 9.

of national life" from the day of its inception. As with its agricultural counterpart, it united in a single body both social (primarily antilabor) and economic interests. Headquarters were maintained at Milan, the leading industrial city of north Italy, which, being located in the center of the upper Po Valley, brought them into immediate juxtaposition with the Agricultural Confederation. And the leading figures in the Confederation were the captains in command of that impressive network of large-scale industrial enterprises which were concentrated in that area.

Not only did the big industrialists lead in the inner councils of the Confederation, but the establishments over which they held control fell largely, and in some respects entirely, in the general classification of the "new" industries which had arisen out of chemical and engineering research after the turn of the century. Italy was a comparatively late industrial arrival, and she lacked, furthermore, material resources for the large-scale development of many of the older industries. The newer industries required large initial outlays in scientific research and experimental development; their capital needs were heavy and, once launched, they were closely protected under patent and similar monopoly controls.

Within the northern Italian manufacturing nucleus the most important industries were heavy chemicals, machines, textiles, and engineering. Most of the big concerns, such as Snia Viscosa in rayon, Fiat and Isotta Fraschini in automobiles and allied lines, Ercole Marelli and Pirelli in electrical manufacturing, Breda in railroad equipment, and the giant Montecatini in the chemicals, ordnance and metal field, date either from immediately before the First World War, or rose to importance during and immediately after that catastrophe.[41] Most of them were financed in whole or in part

[41] Snia Viscosa: founded July 18, 1917, headquarters and larger plants at Milan, capital in 1938, 525,000,000 lire; Fiat: founded in 1906, headquarters in Milan (automobiles, diesel engines, parts, railroad stock, airplanes and engines, etc.), capital in 1939, 400,000,000 lire, employed 54,000 workmen; Montecatini: founded in 1888, headquarters in Milan (copper, pyrites, sulphur, fertilizers, dyes, varnishes, rayon, aluminum, pharmaceutica, etc.), capital in 1938, 1,300,000,000 lire; Ercole Marelli: successor in 1920 to parent company founded 1891, headquarters in Milan (electrical equipment, motors, generators, pumps, etc.), capital in 1938, 80,000,000 lire; Isotta Fraschini: headquarters in Milan (steel, automobiles, engineering, ordnance, bronze, aluminum, magnesium, etc.), capital in 1938, 120,000,000 lire· Pirelli: founded in 1920, headquarters in Milan (electrical cables, automobile tires, etc.), capital in 1938, 263,981,500 lire, 20,400 employees; Breda: successor in 1899 to parent company or-

by foreign capital,[42] catered directly or in large part to a demand dominated by the rapidly expanding transportation, communication, and power networks which were of at least a semipublic character on the one hand, or sold directly to the various governmental bodies concerned with public construction and war needs on the other. All of these factors made not only for large scale development, but also for expansion on a monopolistic or semimonopolistic footing from the very beginning.[48]

Under auspices such as these—and it cannot be too strongly emphasized that in Italian industrial councils the great preponderance of power and influence lay in these circles—the natural, normal, matter-of-course attitude of the leadership of the General Confederation of Italian industries should have been monopoly-oriented in all economic affairs, and patronal or feudal in all social matters. That is to say, the exigencies of background and organization were such as to cause complete accord with the General Confederation of Agriculture (most conservative and reactionary and at the same time most highly developed of agricultural employer associations anywhere in the world) in the normal course of peacetime events. How much more logical then, that, given the recent, vivid experience with the autocratic controls of war-time, they should face a new emergency with the mood, the outlook, and the will to improvise the necessary weapons for consolidating a common front of employer interests against the threat of revolutionary action from below.

---

ganized in 1850, headquarters in Milan (steam and electric locomotives, railroad rolling stock, ships, airplanes, etc.) capital in 1938, 127,800,000 lire, 17,073 employees.

[42] There were, in addition, a good many important, wholly foreign owned, subsidiaries, such as the Societa Generale Italiana Viscosa (capital in 1938 of 75,000,000 lire, and wholly owned by the British firm, General Rayon Ltd.) and the branch systems of Ford and General Motors. Most of these concerns have branches and affiliates scattered all over Europe, and corporate holdings, spheres of influence, etc., interlace with other foreign holdings until it is practically impossible at any one point to unravel the skein.

[43] A situation arose, in other words, not greatly unlike that which W. Sombart traces at such length in Der Moderne Kapitalismus (Leipzig, 1902), I, Part II, through the early mercantilistic and cameralistic phases of capitalism, when the army and public authorities dominated so many of the leading supply industries. Added to this is the point Veblen has argued so cogently for Germany—in his Imperial Germany and the Industrial Revolution (New York, 1915)—that the borrowing country borrows the latest, most advanced techniques of production and marketing. The Italians borrowed from abroad large-scale production methods and monopoly forms of organization.

Not, of course, that there is any direct proof that the General Confederation of Italian Industries singly or in association with other employer bodies did actually "think up" the Fascist state. Nor, even, that there was uniform agreement within these circles on just exactly what and how to face the critical situation that arose in the postwar confusion.[44] But that they did find in Fascism something which they could support and from which they could derive great advantages to themselves there is no longer any question whatsoever. For present purposes, the significant fact is that the organizational structure, spun after much trial and error under the Fascist regime, is a straight-line development from that which had been evolved out of these employer circles in the past, and that the system which followed the March on Rome was coherent not only with former growth trends, but also with the attitudes and ideologies which had become dominant in organized Italian business.

The Corporate State.—Again it is not necessary to recapitulate in detail the numerous, and for present purposes, largely accurate summaries that have been made of the machinery of the corporate state, or the steps by which this machinery has been brought to its current state of development. The system is not yet complete, enthusiastic proponents avow, and is not likely to reach that state for a long time to come, if ever. Many of them like to stress that it is of the very nature of Fascist institutions that these neither do nor can achieve settled and permanent forms, since they are devised as flexible instruments to encourage growth and change and not as glove-fits for a static condition.

It may be in point, however, to indicate briefly a few of the features of the new system which make it appear not so new or out of line with recognizable trends abroad. In its most recent annual publication, the Fascist Confederation of Industrialists, successor in 1926 to the General Confederation of Italian Industry discussed above, speaks of the new system as a "guild economy," this being, they say, "the nearest English equivalent to the Italian 'corpora-

---

[44] There were conflicts at numerous points between organized industry and agriculture, between heavy and light industry, between industrial and financial interests. See Daniel Guérin, *Fascism and Big Business* (New York, 1939), for a discussion (very inadequate) of the conflict of interests between the Banca Commerciale Italiana, representing light industry, and the Banca Italiana di Sconto, representing heavy industry, in the early days of the Fascist dictatorship. See also Rossi, *The Rise of Italian Fascism.*

zione.' " And they cite a dictionary definition of the word "guild" which terms it "a corporation or association of persons engaged in kindred pursuits for mutual protection and aid." If then, you "extend this definition to a whole nation of producers . . . you have a fairly adequate conception of Italian guild economy." [45]

"An Outline Study" of "The Organization of Production and the Syndical Corporative System," especially prepared for the American public by the official New York representative of the Italian propaganda ministry, makes much the same point. Finding a "general identity of motive and a somewhat similar process of development among all associations of producers from the dawn of history down to our modern age," the writer, significantly enough, traces the rise of ideas and elements leading to and incorporated in Italian Fascism from most ancient times through associations fixed in social status, occupationally circumscribed, self-contained, and exclusive, and making for "harmony" in society. The associations succeed in this by virtue of the subjection of their members to a regime of class stratification, characterized by relative vertical immobility, and rigorously controlled from above by a self-appointed and coöptative "elite." Governance proceeds via the instrumentalities of hierarchical privilege and prerogative provided by the political apparatus and is exercised "authoritatively" (antidemocratically) over such occupationally organized servile and semiservile strata below.[46]

Direct precedents are traced to the Papal Encyclicals of *Rerum Novarum* and *Quadragesimo Anno,* to the earlier organizations of labor and capital which preceded these, and to the model of D'Annunzio's "10 corporations of producers"; in its turn, D'Annunzio's model was adapted from the *Quadragesimo Anno,* in terms of the "integral syndicalism" advocated by the *Rerum Novarum.*

[45] *Fascist Era, Year XVII,* p. 33.
[46] China: "Corporative life has always been the cornerstone of the static civilization of China." Its universal system of "organized groups of producers" was on a "voluntary," "caste" footing which "combined Church, school, court and town-hall of occidental communities" and which was characterized by "absence of sharp friction between the employer and the employee." India: "Division of labor has also been the keystone of society" practicing "rigid separation of groups from a social and religious standpoint." Egypt: had a "system of organized and coördinated labor" with "privileged classes" and "state controlled corporations," etc. The Near East, ancient Rome and the medieval guilds: the latter are termed "functional democracies," an idea which may have led to the description of Fascism by the engaging expression "authoritarian democracy." See *The Organization of Production and the*

In the evolution of Fascist corporative ideas, the exact role of the Fiume programs, known as the "Carta del Quarnaro," is not clear. Announced in a burst of lyric enthusiasm as the Constitution of the Free State of Fiume by the poet Gabriele D'Annunzio, September 8, 1920, it proposed to do away with all past parliamentary institutions and the old state bureaucracy and to substitute for the "citizen" the "producer." All former state functions were to be decentralized and managed by ten compulsory but "autonomous" (self-governed) corporations of producers, divided along parallel lines by employer and employee interests and grouped according to major occupational interests.[47] Property was not to be abolished but capitalists were to become "wise leaders seeking to further the interests of their company"[48] according to the principle that the "sole

---

Syndical Corporative System (Italian Library of Information, New York, 1941), and *Fascist Era*, p. 32.

[47] According to Article 19 of the Carta del Quarnaro, the corporations or guilds were to be constituted as follows:

"In the first guild are enrolled the salaried workmen in industry, agriculture, commerce, and transportation; and the artisans and small proprietors who perform their own rural task or who have a few casual helpers.

"The second Guild comprises the technical and executive staff of every private industrial and rural establishment, excluding the proprietors themselves.

"In the third are enrolled all those attached to commercial establishments, who are not strictly workmen; and in this too joint-proprietors are excluded.

"The fourth Guild unites the promoters of industry, agriculture, commerce, and transportation, provided they are not merely proprietors, but according to the spirit of the new laws, wise leaders seeking to further the interests of their company.

"The fifth is composed of all public, communal, and civil employees of all ranks.

"The sixth comprises the intellect of the land: the young student body and its instructors; teachers in the public school and students in the higher institutions, sculptors, painters, decorators, architects, musicians, and all those who carry on the fine arts, scenic arts, and decorative arts.

"In the seventh are enrolled all those who practice professions of their own choice which have not been included in the preceding classifications.

"The eighth is composed of coöperative societies in production, labor consumption, whether industrial or agricultural; and only the executives of these same societies can be represented.

"The ninth comprises all sea-faring people.

"The tenth has neither art, nor number, nor title. Its coming is expected like that of the tenth Muse. It is reserved to the mysterious forces of the people consecrated to the unknown genius, to the apparition of the new man, to the ideal transfiguration of labor and time, to the complete liberation of the spirit over pain and agony, over blood and sweat. It is represented, in the civic sanctuary, by a burning torch upon which is inscribed an old Tuscan work of the time of Communes, a remarkable allusion to a spiritualized form of human labor: Fatica Senza Fatica [Toil without Toil]." From a mimeographed translation in the library of the Casa Italiana, Columbia University.

[48] *Idem.*

lawful claim to dominion over any means of production and exchange is labor. Labor alone is master of the thing made most advantageous and more profitable to general economy." [49] The state was not to intervene in the internal life of the corporations so long as relations within and amongst the corporations were felicitous and peaceful.

Two fundamental ideas underlie the Fascist redaction of ideas borrowed from these sources. First is the conception that readers of an historical turn of mind will recall underlay the attempt of Colbert, the great French mercantilist, to smash feudal localization and trade restrictions by (a) generalizing the structure of guild controls so that they would not serve as barriers between different sections of the country, but would become coextensive with the national domain, and by (b) endowing such expanded trade organizations, either as a whole or segmentally by concerns or groups, with mercantilistic prerogatives of regulated self-governance and monopolistic privilege. [50] For the medieval guilds in the Colbertian effort, substitute the preceding organizations of business and labor in the Fascist system. The Fascist systematization of the whole of the machinery taken over along definite model and hierarchical lines is thus seen to represent peculiarities of organizational procedure, and not differences of theory.

In the second place, the Fascist innovations centered around the plan to expand the structure of controls of the legal business corporation to the whole of the associations and federations with which such corporations were associated; this was to be done, however, without at the same time endowing the parallel organizations of labor with power to counteract the expanded controls—which, of course, would have defeated the main purpose. Under the old regime, the individual corporation possessed, wherever it was free to act as it desired, a system of rigorous and thoroughly despotic controls over policy formation and execution. Outside of the individual corporation and amongst corporations of like business interests, power shaded off into a loose penumbra of more or less unenforceable "communities of interests." The Fascists sought to substitute in place of the penumbra the more compact, "dense,"

49 *Ibid.*, Article 9.
50 See Eli Heckscher, *Mercantilism* (London, 1935).

and imperative regime of command and subordination of the business corporation.

This regime was to relate to the whole range of economic and social issues which concerned the conduct of economic activity. It had to do, in other words, with prices, production, markets, cost systems, plant expansion, taxation, subsidies and subventions, tariffs, and the rest, as well as with labor problems. But if extension of the characteristic internal regime of the business corporation to the whole of each trade or industry or "category" or "cycle of production," was to be carried through, what was to become of the trade unions? Were these, in compliance with the first conception, to be expanded parallel with the employers' associations? And if so, how reconcile the new set-up with the second conception?

The answer was found in taking the form of the first and the essence of the second. More simply, the powers of the business corporation were expanded to cover the entire industry, and the trade unions, now deprived of all power of independent action, were forthwith expanded into all-exclusive bodies under the authority of a central administration, which was sympathetic with and closely allied in aims, programs, and point of view with the business interests—if it was not at times and places, as some critics aver, wholly dominated by these interests.

However, the structure of the system devised over the intervening years has, in ways but slightly different from the mechanism of the Hitlerian variant, shown that the attempt to carry through some such a program of coördinated, definitive and all-inclusive class controls, presents but a limited series of organizational alternatives. Hierarchy is of the essence of its structure. Authority comes from the top down in all things, and responsibility from the bottom up. Coverage is of necessity "totalitarian" [51] that is, over all persons in all sections of the country and in all their activities.

There are five major bureaucracies to be coördinated in the new system: those of the economic world, the army, the Church, the civil service, and the Fascist party. Coördination—which may and probably does mean to a considerable degree social-economic fusion through marriage, group associations, and other devices, in

[51] See Chapter VIII, below.

the upper reaches of the hierarchy—required the following modifications and compromises:

(1) all occupational or economic groupings in whatever field are organized in all-inclusive categories directed by policies coherent with the interests of, if not actually formulated in detail by, the great leaders of industry, commerce, finance, and agriculture;

(2) the relationships among these are militarized according to the pattern known in management literature as "military organization," and are enforced by a coördinated military and policy system;

(3) the Church undertakes to inculcate in both "leader" and "led" a mood of satisfaction and contentment with the pastor ("trustee of God")-to-his-flock relationship and with the supersession of transcendental over materialistic biases and values;

(4) all relationships are formulized by and through an all-pervading bureaucracy, which circumscribes rounds of duties and responsibilities, in the performance of which—as interpreted by superior officers in the hierarchy—it is vested with state authority;

(5) the Fascist Party sees to it that these various phases of coördinated class domination are fused by moving them along the path of imperial expansion, a path kept open by a cumulatively enlivened nationalistic sentiment and the imminent danger of war.

The resultant structure of control, so far as it bears on the subject matter of the present study, is less complex than it appears at first. The main outlines are simple. Four "principles" are said to dominate: organization by occupational, or trade "categories"; organization by regions; organization by social position; and organization by hierarchy.

(1) Occupational categories mean exactly what they imply—the basis of segregation is the more or less clearly delineated trade, industrial, or occupational zones. These are called syndicates.

(2) Some 13,464 in number, the syndicates are in turn grouped (a) into provincial and interprovincial Unions, of which there may be [52] some 882 altogether, and (b) into national category federations, of which there are 150 all told.

[52] "May be," since there is a provincial Union in each of 98 provinces (including four for Libya) for each of the 8 "main branches of activity" only if, however, these activities are to be found in each province. Since it appears that such a provincial Union is established wherever there is to be found more than one local organization,

(3) The "integral syndicalism" principle calls for all-inclusive parallel employer and employee organizations all the way down the line, except that (a) the basis of category division need not be exactly the same, that is, the labor category may be broader or narrower than the corresponding employer category [53] and consequently the number of categories may be larger or smaller, and (b) the arts and professions fall more or less entirely outside the employer-employee bifurcation.

(4) Finally, the hierarchical principle holds throughout, and in three general aspects. (a) Structurally, proceeding from the local, syndical, employer or employee interest, with but local, syndical, employer or employee power and authority, on up through the provincial and interprovincial Unions on the one hand, and the national Federations, Confederations of Federations, and the National Council of Corporations on the other. This part of the Italian system is strikingly like the system devised by the Nazis and outlined in Chapter I. (b) As between the employer and the worker categories, it would appear from all the available evidence that employer interests definitely hold the upper hand, and that through this rather complicated machinery, the rule which makes the employer *Herr im Hause* within the factory relationship likewise holds in the social field. The model here, as previously pointed out, was Catholic "integral syndicalism," and Salvemini is unquestionably correct in comparing these directly with "company unions." [54] (c) Authority throughout the entire pyramid stems from the top, with the head of the government (Mussolini) in theory the fountainhead of all delegated offices and competencies. The system, in short, is entirely and exclusively coöptative at the top; from that point downwards it is appointive with tenure, du-

---

there must be the number indicated unless such economic provinces (without more than one) are to be found in Italy, which is improbable. I have been unable to learn anything whatsoever about the number or the functions of the "Interprovincial Unions."

[53] Thus, there are 5,826 workers' "Local Syndical Associations" for 6,595 in the employer classification. In the next layer, there are 32 National Federations for the former to 96 for the latter. There are equal numbers of National Confederations (4 each), and the principle of "equal representation" holds for the National Council of Corporations, though the basis of classifications bears no necessary relationship to that obtaining below.

[54] Salvemini, *Under the Axe of Fascism*, Chapter VII, "Company Unions, Nazi Unions, and Fascist Unions."

ties, and responsibilities subject to instantaneous alteration in any fashion whatsoever from on top—which means, of course, no recourse whatever, from below, grounded in substantive rights.[55]

Legal authority begins in theory with the National Federations (Juridical Associations of the "First Degree") and expands in power and influence upwards through the Confederations (Juridical Associations of the "Second Degree") and the National Council of Corporations; it comes to a head in the sovereign Chamber of Fasces and Corporations. All powers and authorities derive from this fountainhead. But the fountainhead is—as all such human institutions are—in turn, controlled by dominant pressure groups. Who are they?

Several analyses have been made of the social composition of the inner controlling groups.[56] All of them reach the common conclusion that the leading personalities are those associated with the great landowning, industrial, commercial, and financial houses and associations on the one hand, and the central leadership of the closely allied, socially compact, and self-perpetuating military, clerical, civil service, and party hierarchies on the other. Who, or what particular group, at any given time holds the upper hand can only be determined by independent analysis of the interplay of facts, forces, and personalities on each separate occasion. But it is beyond dispute that the net result, judged in the light of all the available facts, is coherent with the interests, the points of view, the lines of growth inherent in monopoly-oriented, capitalistic enterprise, thus transmuted through acquisition of political power into a regime of exclusive privilege and patrimonial command.

Finally, it may be noted that there are not lacking Fascist theoreticians able to find that these conditions are not only coherent with, but absolutely indispensable for the realization of, the economic

[55] Except as guaranteed in the Labor Charter and in various decrees. These, however, come entirely from on top, and are revocable at will—which is to say that they exist on tolerance and thus, in event of any point of dispute with the hierarchy of command, ultimately not at all. Most of the "labor leaders" are actually not laborers, being typically of "middle, class" origins. In any event, they must be Fascist party members, they are appointed upon recommendation of Fascist party selected panels through the Fascist party hierarchy, and they owe no responsibility whatsoever to the syndicates which they do not represent but command.

[56] See Salvemini, op. cit., pp. 43–49, Ebenstein, Fascist Italy, Schmidt, The Plough and the Sword, and Louis R. Franck, Les Etapes de l'économie fasciste italienne (Paris, 1939), pp. 43–45.

equilibrium which constitutes the long sought good of free competition. As argued, for example, by Amoroso, one of the leading Fascist academicians, the conditions which, under the regime of free competition, fix the point of equilibrium in the determination of wages are identical with those laid down in the Charter of Labor.

Why, then, is the Charter of Labor and the intervention of the state, required, one may ask! As summarized by an Italian student of corporative economy in the graduate school at Columbia University, Giorgio Pelligrini, the answer of Amoroso and his compatriots would run about as follows:

Ideal conditions of free competition cannot be realized in the present (unregulated) economic organization. It is true that free competition brings about economic equilibrium; it is true that economic equilibrium is the result of a sound economy; it is true that this sound economy improves the welfare of all classes; but there is to be found in present society no such thing as free competition. Liberalism, which pretends to be the champion of free competition, in reality brings about the division of society into two groups—the bourgeoisie and the proletariat —and strengthens the first against the second. Socialism, which pretends to cure the evil, in reality destroys free competition directly, and with it economic equilibrium and thereby sound economy. Corporativism, instead, with the institution of organs whose sole aim is the elimination of all the influences contrary to a stable economic equilibrium, brings about the ideal conditions for the free play of economic forces, and, therefore, is the only sound economy.

If, as the Fascist Confederation of Industries comments, the confessedly antidemocratic principles of Fascist political regimentation may be termed "authoritarian democracy," perhaps the view of Amoroso may properly be captioned "regimented free competition"! It is doubtful if, under the new National Socialist guidance, Fascist logicians will be encouraged to resort further to many dubious circumlocutions. *Verbundene Wirtschaft* goes better with the institution of the lock-step in word as well as deed.

Chapter III

JAPAN: KOKUTAI AND THE "CO-PROSPERITY SPHERE"

"THE ECONOMIC WORLD needs a guiding hand to direct its diverse energies," explained Mr. Ogura, head of the immense Sumitomo interests upon his appointment by ex-premier Konoye as "economic dictator of Japan." Expected, as reported in American newspapers, "to become a sort of Japanese Knudsen," flanked at will by a " 'brain trust' . . . not of bureaucrats, but of business men" [1] of his own choosing, Ogura was vested with the powers of a supreme economic coördinator, in what has been described as "a complete corporative State built into the existing constitutional structure of Japan." While one organ of state policy, the Supreme Cultural Council, is to see that "all people will think only reformed thoughts," Mr. Ogura is to draw on all his business experience in order that the principle, "the public service first," may be supported naturally through continuation by the Supreme Economic Council of control over Japanese industry under the system of "private enterprise." [2]

JAPAN'S PECULIAR INSTITUTIONAL MACHINERY

However strange this may sound to Western ears—and it is not so strange now as it would have seemed a short time ago—it represents in principle nothing essentially new for the Japanese. Control over business policies has always been highly centralized in the Island Kingdom, and that centralization is traceable, genetically, to environmental forces almost the complete inverse of those fostering similar movements in the United States and England. Tap-

[1] New York *Times*, April 1, 1941.
[2] Hugh Byas, "Japan's Fascist March," New York *Times*, Dec. 15, 1940.

roots for centralization in these latter were struck in periods formally committed to unmitigated free competition and laissez faire. But in Japan, feudalistic carry-overs, mercantilistic practices, and monopoly-oriented capitalism have from the beginning stood side by side.

Throughout the period of the Meiji Restoration, the setting for the rise of Capitalism has been predominantly patriarchal, antidemocratic, antiliberal, anti-laissez faire, and those superficial concessions to Western *petit-bourgois* economic and political institutions, which on occasion faintly leavened the modern era, have, particularly in the light of more recent events, served only the more heavily to underscore the fact.[3] The principle of *Kokutai*—"the state body corporate"—carried over from ancient times has, under an economics dominated by large-scale governmentally fostered, industrial capitalism, served to knit seemingly disparate elements of old and new into an efficient and generically totalitarian state. Current lines of development are converging swiftly and unmistakably to create a national system similar at bottom to that advocated by lawgivers of the Axis Powers, although the system does not approach full articulation in the best approved authoritarian manner.

Thus business enterprise in Japan has, from the earliest days, unfolded its activities in an atmosphere largely, and at times wholly, dominated by principles, controls, and social philosophies which are internally coherent with what we in the Western world have come more recently to identify as *Fascism*. The oriental symbolism, in keeping with a deep and tenacious past, is more heavily blooded with the naïve chivalric pietism of a society still organized on lines

[3] How superficial were the changes wrought in the social, political, and economic life of Japan by the "Enlightenment" (period of the Meiji Restoration) is nowhere better illustrated than in a series of articles, remarkable for their complete candor, contributed by various Japanese professors to a special Japanese edition of *Weltwirtschaftliches Archiv*, Vol. XLVI, July, 1937. All the social legislation—even Parliamentary forms of election and representation—are treated very much as was Bismarck's famous social legislation of the '80s, as authoritative reforms, concessions, and tactics, and not as evidence of either conversion of the Japanese people to democratic-liberal principles, or as moves occasioned by fear of popular antagonism from the submerged ranks at the bottom of the social pyramid. It is worth recalling, in this connection, that what the Japanese did copy along these lines was not taken in the main from England or the United States, but from Imperial Germany. See also Thorstein Veblen, "The Opportunity of Japan," in *Essays in Our Changing Order* (New York, 1934).

of status, and with the simpler patriarchal or familial charisma of its characteristic emperor and ancestor worship. *Tenno* (the emperor), for example, is at once father, ruler, and high priest in a patently theocratic state still governed by rules of honorific etiquette and graduated subservience. But if this renders the task of domination in a caste-minded society far easier for the oriental *Führer* than for his Western counterparts, it is largely because in Japan industrial, commercial, and financial capitalism has been absorbed into the old social system without seriously and for long challenging or greatly modifying the preceding structure of controls.

It is especially necessary to emphasize this point now, for there exists a common disposition to look upon more recent developments in Japan as either a complete reversal of policies dominant since the latter half of the nineteenth century,[4] or as the product of a somewhat vaguely conceived military coup d'état. Neither, of course, is correct. The answer to the former is that Japan borrowed freely, adopted and adapted at need, but that she did not, with the decline of the Shogunate and formal repudiation of feudal controls, fundamentally alter at any significant point the nature or functioning of her hierarchical social order, and that as a result of this lack of change the new order represents somewhat less than a straight-line, but still a consistent, development from the pre-Meiji, pre-Perry times. And the answer to the latter is that militarism, far from being antagonistic to either the new or the old, was actually part and parcel of both. In the hands of the Choshu and

[4] See H. G. Moulton and J. Ko, *Japan, an Economic and Financial Appraisal* (Washington, D.C., 1931), where the Restoration is regarded as a sharp and complete break with the past. Professor Saburo Shiomi refers to the occasion, "When Japan broke away from feudalism in 1848" and a few pages later on tells how "the old patriarchal conception of the family as a complete social and economic unit has been incorporated in the guild system." "Aufbau der Industriewirtschaft and Technischer Fortschritt in Japan," *Weltwirtschaftliches Archiv*, XLVI (July, 1937), 118–56. The "outward forms of feudalism," Professor Allen points out, were "gone for ever" with the crushing of the Satsuma rebellion in 1877. But he quotes a Japanese writer who appraises the significance of what was "set up in its stead" as "a bureaucracy that retained the spirit of the Shogunate. It is not too much to say that the political and social institutions of the new Japan were only another expression of the Tokugawa system." To which Professor Allen adds, "The main result of the Restoration was, in fact, the substitution of what came to be called the Sat-Cho group for Tokugawa. It was a change of governors rather than a change in the system of government." G. C. Allen, *Modern Japan and Its Problems* (London, 1928), pp. 62, 64.

Satsuma clans, the military order was so clearly shaped as a phase of the peculiar expansionist dynamism of totalitarian ideology, interests, and process, that the one is unthinkable in the absence of the other. In Japan, because of this continuity with the past, the identification of the old social order and the new economic and political forms of business ramification and military expansion is made more easily and more painlessly than was the case even in the Nazified streamlining of Prussianized Germany.

Not, of course, that there is or has been absence of conflict of interests and ideologies in contemporary Japan. Far from it. How bitter the internecine warfare has been between military and naval branches of the armed services, between civil administration and military juntas, between small business, labor and peasantry on the one hand and the huge and omnivorous combines on the other, or even amongst these latter themselves, it is extremely difficult, at least on the evidence available to foreigners, to say. It appears not only that such cleavages do exist, but also that they have been at times far-reaching and sanguinary. But they have never been sufficiently deep or fundamental to alter seriously the structure of Japanese society nor the sanctions upon which its castelike hierarchical controls rest.

The social framework of this system represents a fusion of feudalism and the concept of the patriarchally governed, absolute state. Stigmata of feudalism are to be found in connection with a peculiar social-occupational gradation on the one hand and a system of guild and guild-like associational groupings on the other. Some of the latter—such as various trade unions and coöperative societies—were for a period of time during the twenties more or less "free" of constraints exercised from above. During the thirties, however, and especially with the outbreak of war on the Asiatic mainland, such partial freedoms have been gradually worn away until, to all intents and purposes, freedom of association in the liberal-democratic sense no longer exists. With minor exceptions, all occupational categories in industry, trade, and agriculture are organized into more or less all-inclusive unions, associations, federations, and guilds. But behind all such associational forms is a backdrop which represents a blend of the feudal spirit of "servile solidarity" and the patriarchal norms of an "autonomous co-optative bureaucracy." [5]

At the gravitational center of this somewhat confusing mesh-work of partially modernized clans, guilds, military cliques, family dominated bureaucracies and businesses, on the one hand, and hierarchically graduated occupational strata, classifications, "cor-porations" and federations, on the other, stands the omnicompetent tutelary and administrative authority of the state—a state in both theory and practice more absolute than those of the European "age of the benevolent despots." In the Japanese symbolism, this power comes to focus in the person of the Emperor who, in addition to being supreme head of the lay state and commander-in-chief of the armed forces, is also the ceremonial director of the official religion of *Shinto*. Via *Shinto*—in itself a sort of combined system of social etiquette and personal ethic pieced together from Buddhism, Con-fucianism, Taoism, and other elements of adapted belief and rules of status—the Imperial House becomes the recognized symbol of the dominance of the family and patriarchal system of Japan.[6]

Thus the Imperial House stands for the principle of *Bushido*, or the ethic and practice of the spirit of complaisant subordination to the universal rules of status which becomes complete only with un-questioning acceptance by the mass of the population of the atti-tudes, the duties, and the compulsions expressed in "the state of being willing and ready to die at any moment at the bidding of a recognized superior." *Bushido*, writes an ardent proponent, "is the result of the feudal ages—entirely governed and thoroughly

[5] Veblen, *Essays in Our Changing Order*.

[6] "History records that all manner of foreign ideas have, from time to time, flooded the nation, but standing like a sun, about which these new ideas found their proper and subordinate place, has, through long ages, stood the Imperial House. Indeed no foreign idea—Buddhism, Christianity, Democracy, Socialism,—may survive in this country and find root in the consciousness of the Japanese unless it subordinates it-self to that undefinable yet all-pervasive soul element of the Yamato race, which stands crystallized and symbolized in the person and tradition of His Imperial Maj-esty. For deep in our race is rooted a reverence for the Emperor as the descendant of the very gods to whom we owe our being. Indeed, even to speak the words 'Tenno Heika' or 'Shison' conveys to us a very solemn and deep impression and stirs to depths our profoundest emotions. To explain or rationalize this attitude is un-necessary; it is fact and true because it exists." Quoted from the Japan *Times* in Professor Taid O'Conroy, *The Menace of Japan* (New York, 1934), p. 71. See also Uichi Iwasaki, *The Working Forces in Japanese Politics* (New York, 1921).

permeated by sovereign authority and humble obedience."[7]

While *Bushido*, as the principle underlying the etiquette of a past age of feudal knighthood, has been greatly undermined during the modern era,[8] it has apparently been quite easy to translate its ancient sanctions into modern terms. Throughout the Japanese literature dedicated to preservation and strengthening of the *status quo* runs the language borrowed from *Bushido*: "loyalty," "honor," "obedience," "sacrifice," "duty," "humility," "unity," "harmony," "patriotism," "authority," and similar terms. These are the terms, and the blending underneath them is in line with the ideas and points of view, of course, which are typical of Fascist ideology in Europe. They express the habitual turn of mind of a caste-ordered society, well-schooled in the techniques required to divert, canalize, and control popular strivings from below. Their utility to the central authorities in the promotion of imperial expansion abroad and the structures of autocratically governed self-sufficiency at home are entirely obvious.

The ease of transition from the old to the new has been further facilitated by the fact that the interlude between the Meiji restoration and the consolidation of the current system did not see the rise of sufficiently powerful antagonistic popular movements to shake the transmuted structure of traditional class control. There was, to repeat, no real "liberal period" but rather a time of blending of inherited social biases with altered interest groupings. But the incubus of the past was too heavy and the period of time before the new lines of autocratic control became clear was too short for labor unions, farmer groups, consumers' coöperatives,[9] or even the more general and confused liberal middle-class parties, to strike deep roots.

- [7] Professor Yasuma Takata, "Kulturelle und geistige Voraussetzungen für Japans Aufstieg." *Weltwirtschaftliches Archiv*, XLVI (July, 1937), 1–13.

[8] See *Bushido, the Soul of Japan* (Philadelphia, 1900), written by Inazo Nitobe of the Imperial University, who translates the term to mean "Military Knights' Ways" or "Precepts of Knighthood." Bushido is not, however, to be compared with the humane chivalry of the Arthurian legend; it represents, on the contrary, "the essential readiness of the warrior to lay down his life in battle since he regarded life as a transitory gift the enjoyment of which, like the blossom of the cherry tree, was necessarily of short duration." London *Times*, March 18, 1942.

[9] Coöperatives were very extensive in the countryside and actively fostered by numerous government agencies (federal and local). But all were carefully controlled and have functioned in the manner of mutual-aid societies to relieve the monotony and poverty of the agrarian way of life.

Thus the new Japanese totalitarianism has been easier to achieve than in any other major industrial-capitalistic country. More than that, it has provided an environment which not only enormously facilitates the centralization of policy-forming power in business, but also identifies immediately the feudal and patriarchal-minded hierarchies of business with the political and military bureaucracies. Japanese capitalism, in short, has been in large part and from its very beginning an upstart phase—but part and parcel, nevertheless—of the Japanese political and social system of status—a system on the economic side, in a word, of *status-minded monopoly capitalism.* Its closest historical parallel is probably the system forecast in the *Kameralism* of Frederick the Great; in contemporary times its approximates the patterns of Nazi Germany.

At the center of the system on the economic side stand the great state-encouraged, monopolistically-oriented, and patriarchally-governed family enterprises known as the *Zaibatsu.* Around, and in large part directly subservient to, these are the lesser enterprises, business and agricultural federations, handicraft guilds, colonial development corporations, "mixed enterprises" and other forms of economic organization and control.

THE *ZAIBATSU:* AT THE CENTER OF THE WEB OF CONTROL

The numbers of the *Zaibatsu* are limited, but they differ with the sources quoted. G. C. Allen [10] and Neil Skene Smith [11] refer to the "Big 4." The *Japan-Manchoukuo Year Book* [12] (semiofficial) refers to the "Big 3," the "Big 8," and the "Big 14." The first seems to be the more commonly accepted number, since generically the term *Zaibatsu* means "money cliques," and "of these, four are outstanding—namely, Mitsui, Mitsubishi, Sumitomo, and Yasuda." More loosely the term is applied to large-scale business combinations in general.[13]

[10] G. C. Allen, "The Concentration of Economic Control in Japan," *Economic Journal,* XLVII (June, 1937), 271–86.
[11] Neil Skene Smith, "Japan's Business Families," *The Economist,* June 18, 1938, pp. 651–56.
[12] See in particular the 1938 issue dealing with Konzerns of Japan.
[13] Such as Okura, "concerned chiefly with trading, mining, textiles and motor-transport; Asano with cement, mining, iron and steel and heavy engineering; Kuhara with heavy engineering, chemicals, mining and aquatic products; Ogawa-Tanaka

The dominating role of the "Big 4" is without adequate parallel in any other major capitalist country. Smith cites estimates which "have suggested that sums equal to 60 per cent of the 21,000 million yen (£2,100 millions, at par) invested in all Japanese joint-stock companies are controlled by these concerns; and that Mitsui alone accounts for 5,000 millions yen (£500 millions), or nearly 25 per cent of the total." [14] Adding to the "Big 4" the banking interests of the Shibusawa and Kawasaki concerns, the six groups held in 1938 57 percent of all funds deposited in banks, trust companies, life, marine, fire, and accident insurance companies [15]—a figure, by the way, which contrasts with an estimated 45 percent equivalent for 1929.

Their range of interests extends to all the modern industries of Japan and to some of the traditional trades also. Shipping, shipbuilding, foreign trade, warehousing, colonial enterprise, engineering, metal manufacture, mining, textiles, and sugar- and flour-milling all fall within their sphere. . . . A glance at a few of the leading trades will show the extent to which the concentration of control over industry and trade has been achieved. For this purpose we may confine ourselves to Mitsui, Mitsubishi and Sumitomo. These three control about half the copper production and nearly the same proportion of the coal output, and Mitsui Bussan (the trading company of Mitsui) alone deals in about one-third of the coal marketed in Japan. More than half of the tonnage of merchant ships is owned by them. Of the steamers building in 1936 55 per cent of the gross tonnage was being constructed in yards belonging to Mitsui and Mitsubishi. The Oji Company controlled by Mitsui has about 75 per cent of the capacity of the paper industry and Mitsubishi owns the greater part of the remainder. These two firms possess 70 per cent of the flour-milling capacity and practically all the

---

with chemicals; Kawasaki with banking, insurance, rayon and shipbuilding; Shibasawa with banking, shipbuilding and engineering; Furukawa with copper-mining and refining and electrical plant; Mori with chemicals and electric-power generation." Allen, "The Concentration of Economic Control in Japan," p. 272.

14 Smith, "Japan's Business Families."

15 The shares of the Big Six and the Big Four respectively in the following were, in 1938: Bank Deposits, 59% and 40%; Property in Trust by Trust Companies, 68% and 66%; reserves of life insurance companies, 28% and 20%; and reserves of marine, fire, and accident insurance companies, 82% and 73%. Again, recent war years have seen a huge expansion of the Zaibatsu. This can be seen by comparing the data of the 1940 (p. 1140) and 1941 (p. 1134) issues of the *Japan-Manchoukuo Year Book*. From June, 1939, to June, 1940, the estimated worth of companies controlled by the *Zaibatsu* jumped from 1,857 million yen to 2,368 million yen for Mitsui, 1,745 million yen to 2,050 million yen for Mitsubishi, 1,712 million yen to 2,390 for Mangyo, 624 million yen to 1,330 for Sumitomo, and 484 million yen to 540 for Yasuda.

sugar-refining mills. Much of the chemical industry is in their hands, including the bulk of the ammonium-sulphate and artificial fertiliser production. Mitsubishi dominates the aircraft industry, and through its control over the Asahi Glass Company monopolises the sheet-glass output. About half of the goods in warehouses are in those owned by the three great *Zaibatsu*, who also conduct about one-third of the foreign trade. Mitsui Bussan alone is responsible for nearly one-fifth of this trade; it imports a quarter of the raw wool used in Japan, and about the same proportion of the raw-silk exports passes through its hands. Toyo Menkwa, another Mitsui concern, until recently handled one-third of the raw cotton imports and one-fifth of the exports of cotton textiles. Most of the enterprises which have been founded to develop the raw material resources of the colonies, Manchukuo, China, and the South Sea countries have been established by the *Zaibatsu;* for instance, much of the Manchurian soyabean trade is conducted by them or their subsidiaries. The great cotton-spinning industry is less dependent upon the *Zaibatsu* than are the other large-scale trades. Yet even here Mitsui has interests in Kanegafuchi Boseki, and Mitsubishi in Fuji Gasu Boseki, which are among the six largest companies in the country; while Mitsui, through its subsidiary, Toyo Menkwa, has control over several smaller concerns. Mitsubishi controls much of the canned-fish trade, one of the three large brewery companies in Japan and one of the two large foreign-style confectionery manufacturing companies. The *Zaibatsu* are predominant in the heavy engineering industry. Their interests extend to woollen textiles, rayon, cement and petrol-refining and dealing. In all the new industries as they have appeared the *Zaibatsu* have usually taken the initiative. At present Sumitomo is developing the aluminum industry, and Mitsui the hydrogenation process.[16]

Such data take on added significance when it is realized that the *Zaibatsu* "are pre-eminent at once in finance and also in industry and commerce." In this respect, Japanese industrial development is similar to that of Germany, where the interdependence between banking and industry has been extremely close from the very beginning. Yet the degree of control over both fields is not only more closely held in Japan than in Germany, but the fact that in Japan, as in no other country of the world, the general public puts its money into savings accounts as fixed deposits rather than into industrial securities tends still further to enhance the importance of this interlinkage. "The small producers," Allen points out, "who in the aggregate are responsible for the larger proportion of the output of consumable goods, are financed by merchants, who, in

16 Allen, "The Concentration of Economic Control in Japan," pp. 276, 277, 278.

turn, obtain the bulk of their resources from the great banks. Those who control the financial institutions can, therefore, play a dominant part in the development of industry." [17] In this manner not only have many small firms come under the influence of the "Big 4," but also several of the other large concerns such as Okura, Asano, and the chemical properties of Nobuteru Mori.

"One can scarcely go into any corner of the Japanese Empire," writes Chamberlain, "without finding one of the big capitalist combines firmly entrenched and skimming the cream of whatever profits are to be made." [18] How wide-spread this "skimming" process has become can readily be visualized by the curious able to examine carefully the chart of the holdings and affiliations of the house of Mitsui reproduced in the *Japan-Manchoukuo Year Book* for 1938.

The importance of the *Zaibatsu* is further enhanced by the fact that the expansion of their interests and controls has been accompanied by a general trend towards concentration throughout all phases of Japanese economic life, as shown by the following data: [19]

	1909	1913	1918	1923	1927	1933
Total number of companies	11,549	15,406	23,028	32,089	38,516	71,196
Number of big companies (with capital of over 5 million yen)	38	59	293	589	687	713
Proportion of big companies to total (in percent)	0.3	0.4	1.3	1.8	1.8	1.0
Paid-up capital of all companies (million yen)	1,367	1,983	4,707	10,194	12,634	14,547
Paid-up capital of big companies (capital over 5 million yen)	495	755	2,523	6,227	8,113	9,264
Proportion of capital of big companies to total capital (in percent)	36.2	38.1	53.6	61.1	64.2	63.7

---

[17] *Ibid.*, p. 275.

[18] W. H. Chamberlin, *Japan over Asia* (Boston, 1937), p. 228.

[19] Data from *Résumé statistique de l'empire du Japon* (Tokyo, 1912), p. 108; *ibid.* (1924), p. 72; *ibid.* (1930), p. 46; *ibid.* (1934), p. 44; *ibid.* (1936), pp. 46–47. According to an investigation by the Industrial Bank of Japan, quoted in the *Osaka Mainichi and Tokyo Nichi Nichi* (English), July 26, 1941:

	No. of mergers	Am't of capital involved (in yen)
1st half of 1940	69	1,802,353,000
2nd " " "	143	2,093,143,000
1st " " 1941	172	3,024,770,000

The Bank gives the following reasons for the increase:

Built up around and led by the *Zaibatsu*, the large aggregations of capital represent a degree of actual concentration far greater than the superficial data of corporate holdings of the giant concerns would seem to indicate. No important policy of state, it is safe to say, is likely to be realized unless it has the active or tacit approval of the great houses that stand at the gravitational center of this swiftly growing concentration movement.

The *Zaibatsu*, in turn, are closely held family systems, controlled through the device of family owned holding companies. Again the case of Mitsui, largest and oldest of the *Zaibatsu*, may be taken as typical. The House of Mitsui consists of eleven affiliated Mitsui families,[20] all offshoots of the founder, Sokubei Mitsui. The head of each family is a member of the Family Council, and only family heads may vote at Council meetings. The head of the main Mitsui family is *ipso facto* head of the Council. The other ten families have a strict and traditional family rank and status. The Council is governed through a Family Constitution, first drawn up in 1722 by the third Mitsui, and revised and brought up to date in 1900. The full text of the 1900 Constitution has never been published, for many passages are held as strict family secrets. It is known that there are 10 chapters and over 100 articles. Of the Constitution, Russell[21] remarks, "In no other large business institution in the

---

"1. The Government has advised companies in financial difficulties to carry out merger.

2. With the kaleidoscopic change in the world situation many companies were obliged to effect amalgamation due to the difficulty in obtaining raw materials.

3. From the viewpoint of enterprise rationalization financial organs have advised industrial companies to effect mergers."

[20] Oland D. Russell, *The House of Mitsui* (Boston, 1939), p. 4, quotes a Japanese authority, Shumpei Kanda, who in 1937 estimated the fortunes of the eleven family heads as follows:

Baron Takakimi	450,000,000 Yen
Takahisa	170,000,000 "
Geneyemon	200,000,000 "
Baron Takakiyo	230,000,000 "
Baron Toshitaro	150,000,000 "
Takanaga	140,000,000 "
Takamoto	60,000,000 "
Morinosuke	80,000,000 "
Takaakira	60,000,000 "
Benzo	60,000,000 "
Takateru	35,000,000 "
Total wealth	1,635,000,000 "

[21] *Ibid.*, p. 23.

world is the power and unity of family so firmly entrenched and safe-guarded as in the House of Mitsui through this rare document."

So fundamental is the pattern of Mitsui in the family systems of the gigantic Japanese combines that it is worth quoting Russell's summary of this remarkable document somewhat at length: [22]

Chapter One specifies the six main families and five branch families by name, and prescribes that branch families may not be elevated to the status of main families, nor may any future branch families be admitted to the Council.

It is characteristic of the spirit of the document that Chapter Two expressly defines the duties of the family members before there is any mention of the rights and prerogatives of these members. In this chapter are laid down these principal points:

1. Members of the family shall respect the rules prescribed by the founder, associate with each other as brothers, coöperate in all things, work together to enhance the prosperity of the House and to consolidate the foundations of each family.
2. Dispense with excessive luxury and practice simplicity and economy in living.
3. When of proper age, sons and daughters of the eleven families shall study in good institutions of learning.
4. No debts shall be incurred by members of the Family nor shall any one member guarantee the loans of others.
5. All special actions require the consent of the Family Council.
6. The Family Heads shall observe the various contracts and indentures in transacting their various businesses, shall take turns in inspecting the business conditions of each of the firms and establishments of the House of Mitsui, shall submit reports to the Council, shall call the Council whenever it is found that any officer of any firm of the House of Mitsui is undertaking or attempting to undertake dangerous plans, or if he is found committing some wrong so as promptly to adopt means of dealing with the offender and set about rectification or prevention of similar acts.

Chapter Three outlines the prerogatives and duties of the Family Council, voting rights, and general agenda of Council meetings. The second article of the chapter gives to the Council the right of "distribution of profits, earmarking of reserves, budgeting of expenses and payments of the various firms of the House, and distribution of property in case any of the companies of the House should be dissolved." Actually these details are handled in general by the *Mitsui Gomei Kaisha*, but the Family Council acts as sanctioning body.

22 *Ibid.*, pp. 20–23.

The Fourth Article of the chapter specifies that the Council shall determine the household budgets of each of the eleven members of the family; and this is religiously followed, even to the extent of "entertainment allowance."

Chapter Four concerns marriage, adoption, and regulations about collateral branches. It has never been published in detail.

Strict rules are provided in Chapter Five for clamping a heavy hand on "those members of the House who misconduct themselves or who squander money or property." It is a matter of record that these regulations rarely have been invoked.

Chapter Six is the original Sixth Precept of the Founder's Constitution, and is characteristic not only of the spirit of the entire document but a three-hundred-year-old Mitsui Principle. It specifies that "Retirement shall never be permitted unless it is unavoidable," and includes a maxim of Hachirobei: "The lifework of a man lasts as long as he lives; therefore do not, without reason, seek the luxury and ease of retirement." The rest of the chapter deals with inheritances in the event of compulsory retirement.

Chapter Seven details the duties of the directors of the Mitsui firms and lays down a code, mostly secret, "to assure perfect contact among them so as to obviate friction."

Chapter Eight is held in extreme secrecy. Only family members and the higher directors of the business organization know its provisions. In general, it sets strict limits to various capitalizations, specifies common property and the property of each family. It details the handling of reserve funds, classified as "common reserves, preparatory reserves, extra reserves, outlay reserves and descendant reserves." The descendant reserves are set aside whenever a son or daughter is born into any of the families.

Contractual safeguards among family members are dealt with in Chapter Nine, which asserts that "Violation of rules or contracts by any member of the main and branch families is punished by reprimand, disciplining, and more severe methods under the Civil Code, if necessary. It is evidence enough of the strength of the Constitution as a force of law on the family members to observe that the Mitsuis have never gone into civil court against each other.

The final chapter provides for necessary supplementary rules and amendments with the provision that "Should there be changes in the law of the land which makes the foregoing Constitution of the House of Mitsui infringe them, changes shall be made in the Constitution, but in such a way as not to lose the spirit of the original Constitution."

No better illustration could be given of the completely patriarchal character of the system of the *Zaibatsu* than this. Only the mechanism of control, the holding company, is modern. All the

Zaibatsu "have a pyramidal structure, with a holding company at the top controlling the main operating companies and the 'side-line' concerns. Each of these two classes of company has numerous subsidiaries, which frequently, in turn, have small companies largely dependent upon them." However, actual day-by-day administration is, G. C. Allen tells us, "largely in the hands of one or more distinguished 'Banto' (literally 'head watchman') such as Nanjo of Mitsui, Ishikawa of Sumitomo, Kozo Mori of Yasuda and, until recently, Toyotaro Yuki of Sumitomo." [23] The Banto may be, in fact typically are, "adopted" into the familial structure and come to be completely identified—not infrequently through marriage alliances—with the family hierarchy of the House.

It is, perhaps, superfluous to add that the governing relationships in these hierarchies of command and subordination bear throughout the patriarchal-feudal stamp. Frequent dissatisfaction has been expressed with such paternalism by executive staffs [24] and, of course, by labor whenever and wherever it has had any opportunity to organize. But in those places which have been kept antiseptic to all forms of disaffection, staffs may still properly

be designated as vassals of the entrepreneur, and are ready even to make sacrifices for his honor. Another aspect of this feudal attitude is the tendency to lay great stress on the esteem and standing of the enterprise. The Japanese is not content merely to draw his salary; he wants to be active in the correct way, in the correct place, and wherever possible in an outstanding, universally respected undertaking.[25]

This is in keeping with *Bushido,* and may, naturally, have at times its better side.[26] Yet, challenged at any point by the growth of

23 "The Concentration of Economic Control in Japan." Allen's point is well taken here, except that Mori is connected with Sumitomo and Yuki, with Yasuda.

24 Particularly with the deepening of the depression. Criticism by the younger army officers, becoming keen during the early 1930s, seems to have accelerated such dissatisfaction amongst the younger staff members of the "Big 4," who felt especially resentful over their low chances of promotion. The resultant change in policy, called "slewing-around"—donation of funds to national social organization, some "slowing up of the tendency of big business to monopolize all branches of trade," etc.—does not seem seriously nor at any point to have altered the picture.

25 Emil Lederer and Emy Lederer-Seidler, *Japan in Transition* (New Haven, Conn. 1938), p. 187.

26 "The great entrepreneurs take it for granted that through bad times as well as good they will carry at least their clerks, and if at all possible their workers; in case of dismissal there is a moral claim to a six months' bonus. Everywhere, in both public and private service, the bonus plays a great role—further evidencing the persistence of feudal, patriarchal habits of thought. Service is to be rewarded not only

antagonistic liberal-left mass movements, it has led to coördinated and comprehensive measures not only for suppressing independent political parties, labor unions,[27] and other such popular organizations, but also to systematic methods for the totalitarian extirpation of "dangerous thoughts"; this is accomplished by "thought control" [28] in restraint of "ideational offenders," and is effectuated through such programs as the "National Spirit Mobilization" of the "National Harmonizing Society." [29] The Supreme Cultural Council represents the final step in this direction.[30]

SUPPLEMENTARY AND PERIPHERAL WEBS OF CONTROL

The influence of the *Zaibatsu* reaches far beyond the fingertips of corporate control. Mention has already been made of the power they are enabled to wield over other large concerns through their control over credit, and their ability to manipulate markets, prices, and the framework of law so as to bring small concerns into a position of economic dependence upon them. Most small industrial establishments, Allen remarks in another connection,[31] are dominated by merchant employers, who finance the producers, co-

with the expected payment but also with a voluntary gift (of course as determined by customary law, but still with overtones of the gift) and wherever possible generously. The employer has a number of other obligations, as, for example, gifts to the clerks in case of a wedding or the birth of a child, and long excursions, paid for and participated in by the employer." *Ibid*, p. 188.

27 Not including, of course, many types of superpatriotic and vigilante or semi-vigilante Fascist-type organizations. For a description of these, see O. Tanin and E. Yohan, *Militarism and Fascism in Japan* (London, 1934).

28 An interesting summary of these efforts is given in an article by Hugh Byas in the Magazine section of the New York *Times*, April 18, 1937, called "Japan's Censors Aspire to 'Thought Control.' "

29 Bibliography Section, *Public Opinion Quarterly*, July, 1938, p. 528 (based on an article in *Contemporary Japan*, Sept., 1937, written by Moriyama Takeichiro and entitled, "Rescuing Radicals by Law"): "By a high administrator of the 'Law for the Protection and Observation of Ideational Offenders effective since November 20, 1936, which is intended to rehabilitate both the mental and the material life of such offenders in order that they may be converted from radical doctrine and restored as loyal and useful members of society.' 'The zeal, paternal feeling, and devotion with which those who apply the law are thus serving the nation, have an important bearing upon the reform of the existing order which is a watchword of the nation today.' Twenty-two such Homes for Protection and Observation are said to exist in Japan, to afford 'ideational offenders' an opportunity to 'resume their studies.'" See also the discussion, "Organ for Spiritual Drive Favored," in the *Japan Times and Mail* Aug. 3, 1938.

30 Byas, "Japan's Censors."

31 G. C. Allen, *Japan; the Hungry Guest* (London, 1938), p. 103.

ordinate their activities, and market the finished goods." "Generally speaking," writes a Japanese authority,[32]

small industries have no economic independence in regard to the sale of their manufactures. They do not constitute perfect independent units in the market of competitive transactions as contrasted with large-scale capitalistic enterprise. . . . Most small industries are so circumstanced as to be obliged to enter into business relations with large business interests in order to secure the sale of their manufactures. Partly because of the financial necessity of entering into such business relations and partly because of the fact that the purchasers of their manufactures are limited in number, small industries have little free choice in the marketing of their goods. That is to say, most small industries exist in subordination to influential capitalists, who perform the role of customers in the sale of their manufactures. It is no exaggeration to say that in the present-day market organizations, they are entirely dependent on powerful capitalistic concerns for their existence.

Recent war manoeuvers seem to have further heightened this condition of dependence. An article in the *Mitsubishi Monthly Circular* (November, 1938), appraising the significance of the Sino-Japanese war for small enterprises, found that two tendencies stood out: (1) an even greater dependence of these small establishments upon their functions as subcontractors to large enterprises; (2) enforced and compulsory enrollment of small establishments into Industrial Associations, of which 1,200 new associations, or more than 54 percent of the total number now in existence were organized in the first year of hostilities, 1937–38. These associations have served as a sort of "national grid" for the distribution and allocation of raw materials, and have been instrumental in establishing the type of rules and regulations for self-organization and group discipline which accord with the *Kokutai* principle. While many of these associations appear to have been initially motivated by hostility to the *Zaibatsu*,[33] there can be no question but that in the main they are subservient to the larger course of events subject to the manipulation of, and the definitive controls mapped out by, the giants.

[32] I. Otsuka, "Characteristic Features of Japanese Small Industries and Policies for Their Development," *Kyoto University Economic Review*, Oct., 1939, pp. 22–23.

[33] This seems to be the case with many of the more recently established handicraft and merchant guilds, and the *Zaibatsu* appear to have been for a time pretty much disturbed by criticisms emanating from such sources. But the emergencies and

Centered around the *Zaibatsu* is a far-flung system of closely interlocking cartel and syndicate controls. The coal cartel, established in 1921, attempts to regulate prices, set production quotas, and the like, for the entire Japanese industry. A sales syndicate for the raw-iron industry, established in the same year, includes all island and Japanese-controlled Korean and Manchurian producers. The cement industry is organized into three overlapping cartel groupings, the Japanese Portland Cement Producers, founded in 1900, the Japanese Portland ˙Association, founded in 1910, and the Japanese Cement Consortium, organized in 1924. Amongst the three, controls cover technical innovations, advertising, conditions and terms of. delivery, establishment of production quotas, and so on. A community of interest binds together the leading paper producers (85 percent of the paper, and 90 percent of the pulp in 1929). A series of cartel-like associations governs the cotton, silk, and other textile industries of Japan.[34]

The strength of the *Zaibatsu* in the cartel system is indicated by their percentages of production volume, or of total capacity, in various of the more powerful cartel groupings (1936): [35]

Industry and Leading Zaibatsu	Percentage of Output or Capacity
Steel materials—Japan Steel (owned by the government plus important *Zaibatsu*)	65
Pig iron—Japan Steel	74
Coal—Mitsubishi	31
Copper—Mitsubishi	31
Shipbuilding—Mitsubishi	16
Alloys—Mitsubishi, Japan Steel	41
Cement—Mitsubishi, Mitsui	44
Paper—Mitsui	84
Flour—Mitsui, Mitsubishi	99
Sugar—Mitsui, Mitsubishi	43
Shipping Tonnage—Mitsubishi, Sumitomo	55

exigencies of wartime seem, for the time being at least, to have stilled such opposition.

[34] Most of the above was taken from Karl Hahn, *Die Industrielisierung Japans* (Giessen, 1932), pp. 126–27.

[35] *Fortune*, Special Japan Issue, Sept., 1936, p. 136. See also *Japanese Trade and Industry*, published by the Mitsubishi Economic Research Bureau, Tokyo (New York, 1936), pp. 114–29.

In addition to the cartel structure, there exists a series of central "peak associations," so clearly dominated by the *Zaibatsu* and the large concerns grouped around and dependent upon them as to resemble more closely clubs or fraternities than actual trade associations. While there is, for foreign observers, no way whatsoever of now gauging their relative importance, they show tendencies quite similar to those underlying the growth and expansion of comparable organizations abroad:

Almost all economic organizations in Japan have developed after the World War. Excepting chambers of commerce and industry, they have no legal basis, but as Governmental control of the national economy becomes stricter, the part played by these organizations is necessarily of greater importance. The most representative organizations, the members of which include all branches of the national economy are the Japan Chamber of Commerce and Industry, Nippon Kogyo Club, Nippon Keizai Renmeikwai, and Zensanren.[36]

The first of these, the Chamber of Commerce and Industry of Japan,[37] originated in 1928 under legislative sanction as the legally competent and officially recognized central federation of all the chambers of commerce and industry in Japan Proper, "organized according to the Law and the judicial persons and organizations in Chosen (Korea), Taiwan (Formosa), Karafuto (Japanese Saghalien), Kwantung Province and abroad, authorized by the Minister of Commerce and Industry." [38] It was successor to the Associated Chamber of Commerce of Japan, organized in October, 1892, under authority of a "Chamber of Commerce Ordinance" promulgated in 1890 when "chambers of commerce became official organizations of merchants and industrialists." [39]

The nature of this quasi-governmental body has been described by an official representative as follows: [40]

[36] *Monthly Circular,* issued by Mitsubishi Economic Research Bureau, Dec., 1937, written in response to query by the author.

[37] These appear to have been modeled after the pattern of the German Chamber of Commerce and Industry, rather than after the type dominant in the United States and England, and thus to carry much greater weight with their constituencies than is the case in these latter countries.

[38] From a typed summary prepared by the Assistant Secretary of the Japan Chamber of Commerce and Industry, Tokyo, Japan, in reply to direct questions by the author.

[39] Mitsubishi Economic Research Bureau, *Monthly Circular,* Dec., 1937.

[40] Summary, cited in footnote 38 above.

The work of the chamber is conducted by a president and two vice-presidents elected every four years in the general meeting of the member chambers [41] held once a year. The standing committee, consisting of representatives of 16 chambers of commerce and industry representing industrial centers in Japan, meets monthly in place of convoking the general meeting. Of course, an extraordinary general meeting can be called when urgency is required. Twelve councils are commissioned from the leading businessmen and the erudities [sic] as the consultative organ.

The functions of the Chamber are, among others, to make representation to the proper authorities in relation to commercial and industrial questions, to consider and execute the matters presented by the chambers and other business organizations, to issue reports and statistical information on commercial and industrial conditions, to organize and supervise commercial or industrial bodies, and to attend to business pertaining to the International Chamber of Commerce and the International Labor Conference. Assistance can also be rendered by performing the settlement by arbitration of disputes arising out of trade, commerce and manufacture, and by issuing certificates on this and other matters connected with trade, commerce and manufactures, such as the origin of goods, market price, and so on. Naturally the object of the Chamber is to promote and protect the trade, commerce and industry of Japan and it is specially interested to act as the intermediary between foreign merchants and the commercial and industrial communities in Japan.

Power here would seem (1) to relate primarily to the general supply of information, general guidance, and general supervision, of member policies on problems of broad economic interest; (2) to possess some degree of officially granted authority in the exercise of its legally defined prerogatives; (3) to be centered in the hands of representatives of the chambers of commerce and industry resident in the great industrial cities; and (4) through relatively small membership in these latter, to be readily subject to the control of the giant concerns clustered around the *Zaibatsu*.

The Nippon Kogyo Club (Industrial Club of Japan) is another World War baby. Having been established in 1917, it "exclusively represents the interests of large industries which developed during the World War, and thus constitutes a private organization of large

[41] "When the Chamber of Commerce and Industry of Japan was organized, the number of the member chambers of commerce and industry was only 80. The number has gradually increased, numbering at present 149, including 108 in Japan Proper, 4 in Karafuto, 13 in Chosen, 1 in Kwantung Province, 11 in Manchukuo, 5 in China, 4 in the United States, 2 in India and 1 in South America." *Idem.*

industrialists." [42] In other words, it is a sort of "Union League Club" of the *Zaibatsu* circles, having for its objects, "to facilitate intimate intercourse among its members, . . . to investigate economic policies from the standpoint of large industries . . . [to promote] the harmonization of the interests of capital and labor, and . . . [to serve as] the representative organization for Japanese industry in intercourse with foreign businessmen."

Stimulated by problems of the great postwar depression to expand its functions further, the Nippon Kogyo Club took the lead in forming two other organizations, Nippon Keizai Renmeikwai (The Japan Economic Federation) in 1922 and Zenkoku Sangyo Dantai Rengokai (Zensanren—National Federation of Industrialists) in 1931. The former was established ostensibly as a "branch of the International Chamber of Commerce." In reality it appears to serve as a compact coördinating body of a limited number of national business organizations, dominated in turn by a few of the giant concerns, and devoted primarily to the formulation of economic policies for the Japanese business community as a whole: [43]

Members of this economic organization include 30 organizations, 216 judicial persons, and 427 individual businessmen. The managing organs are the General Meeting, councilors meeting, directions (sic), resident directors, resident committee and councillors. The resident committee is an organ to the chairman (sic), and is elected by the chairman among resident directors, directors and councillors. The work carried on by this organization is as follows: (1) Facilitating intercourse among businessmen, (2) Formation of an economic policy representative of businessmen, by investigation on the part of its own board and by outside experts, (3) Representing Japanese business in relations with foreign economic organizations.[44]

"Besides being the headquarters of the Japanese National Committee for the International Chamber of Commerce, since its inception, the Federation now possesses within its organization, the Japanese American Trade Council, the Japan-British Trade Committee, and, quite recently, the Japan-Italian Trade Committee . . . The Federation is rendering manifold services to the Government in the formulation and execution of important national eco-

[42] *Monthly Circular.*   [43] *Idem.*
[44] See also the "constitution" of the Japan Economic Federation, dated April, 1937 (obtainable in English).

nomic policics. Its position may well be compared with that of the Federation of British Industries in London and of the United States Chamber of Commerce in Washington, D.C." [45] Presided over by the eminent Baron Seinosuke Goh,[46] the Federation is at least a blueprint for full and complete coördination of the economic, financial, and commercial policies of the island empire.

Zenkoku Sangyo Dantai Rengokai performs a like function in the labor field for a parallel cross-section of the upper reaches of Japanese big business. "The main objective of this association is similar to that of employers association [sic], protecting the employers' interests against attack from the labor movement. It is composed of five local associations—Kwanto, Kwansai, Middle, West, and North—and these local bodies entertain relations with chambers of commerce and industry, and manufacturers' associations." [47]

In 1937 a supreme effort was made to bring together all centralized employers' and business confederations "which would concentrate all the interests of businessmen" vis-à-vis the government. Thus was called into being on September 27, 1937, the Nippon Keizai Dantai Renmei (The Japanese League of Economic Organizations) under the joint auspices of the Japan Economic Federations, the National Federation of Industrialists, and the Japan Chamber of Commerce and Industry. Representatives were sent by individual organizations as follows:

Japan Chamber of Commerce and Industry   9
Japan Economic Federation   8

[45] *East Asia Economic News*, published by the Japan Economic Federation, Aug., 1939.

[46] "His career as a businessman began in 1898 when he became the president of the Nippon Transportation Company. He became successively or concurrently the head of innumerable corporations, such as the Imperial Commercial Bank, the Tokyo Stock Exchange, the Nippon Iron Manufacturing Company and the Tokyo Electric Light Company. He has been the president of the Chamber of Commerce and Industry of Japan, and is the vice-president of the Society for International Cultural Relations." Since becoming President of the Federation, "Baron Goh became the head of the Organizing Committee of the two big national corporations, the North China Exploitation Company and the Central China Development Company, which have been established in accordance with the fixed policy of the Japanese Government." *East Asia Economic News*, July, 1939.

[47] *Monthly Circular*. "In view of the history . . . it is clear that the Federation was organized to present a united front of capitalists against the labor class." *Trans-Pacific* (weekly), May, 1940, p. 11.

National Federation of Industrialists   6
Tokyo and Osaka Clearing Houses   4
Trust Company Association   2
Life Insurance Company Association   2
National Association of Local Bankers   2

Nine commissions were established, "six of which were to specialize on control over commodities such as textile raw materials, fuels, metals including iron and steel, rubber and hides, lumber, and paper respectively. One commission will investigate price problem [sic] while another will supervise the supply of labor and technicians. The last commission will supervise industrial finance." [48]

Apparently the new organization has worked very closely with the government, constituting as it does, a sort of private "National Defense Council" for business enterprise. With the possible exception of the National Association of Local Bankers, every one of the member peak or central associations is directly or indirectly dominated by the *Zaibatsu*.

Schematically, it would be hard to imagine a much higher degree of policy-determining power than is indicated by the combination of the *Zaibatsu* and its concentric cartel and federational machinery. The hierarchy of business control seems well-nigh complete. Even further importance is lent by the closeness of the tie binding the system, almost from the start and from center to circumference, with the government.

ZAIBATSU AND KOKKA NO TAME

As with the great eighteenth-century European mercantilistic states in their times, Japan's entrance onto the world stage witnessed a deliberate and systematic dovetailing of the power requirements of army and navy, the *Realpolitik* of imperial expansion, and the swiftly unfolding needs of monopoly-oriented industrial, commercial, and financial capitalism. That the state should take the lead was both natural and inevitable.

With a view to the speediest possible modernization of her industrial apparatus, the state established up-to-date factories and workshops, and promoted by every means at its disposal the expansion of national industries. Many of the thriving industries of

[48] *Idem.*

present-day Japan—arsenals, chemical works, iron and steel plants, cotton spinning, power-loom weaving, silk filatures, shipbuilding, railways, paper mills, glass works, type-casting, the manufacture of safety matches, coke, gas, bricks—may be traced back to the initiative, encouragement, and guidance of the Meiji Government. The state also established trade and industrial schools, seamen's training institutes, and imported foreign technicians and advisors—as early as 1875 more than 500 foreign experts were so employed. On the financial side the state loaned mechanical equipment or capital to private entrepreneurs at low rates of interest, or granted outright large subsidies for the creation of mills and factories, foundries and dockyards. *Kokka no tame,* "for the state," was the term used to encourage industrialism. A competent foreign investigator, commenting on these practices, writes: [49]

The part played by the government cannot be overemphasized. Japanese industry of the present day owes its state of development primarily to the efforts of a highly paternalistic central government.

In the period 1867–83, the state assumed direct responsibility for the industrial and financial development of Japan. Increasingly thereafter it endeavored to withdraw from direct participation in the industries aided as soon as possible, and turned its holdings over to private companies.[50]

In some cases (railroads, communications, iron and steel, dockyards) this policy has not been entirely feasible, and the state has continued as an active agent in manufacturing.[51] Private capitalistic enterprise, however, developed apace, and the close association of state and private capitalism has continued in unbroken sequence to the present day. The granting of subsidies, for example, has become so firmly entrenched as an integral part of governmental

[49] John Orchard and Dorothy Orchard, *Japan's Economic Position* (New York, 1930), p. 90. See also, Moulton, *Japan,* in particular Chapter XVII, "The Government in Relation to Economic Enterprise."

[50] The extent to which this disposal of government properties stimulated private enterprise may be shown by the case of the Miike coal mines in Kyushu. In 1886 the government sold these mines to the Mitsui family for 4,550,000 yen. "Within a year the Mitsuis not only had recovered the 4,550,000 yen but made a handsome profit. One conservative estimate is that the mine has averaged 3,000,000 tons a year at ten yen a ton for fifty years. On the basis of thirty percent clear net profits, the Mitsuis in a half-century have realized 450,000,000 yen on a 4,550,000-yen investment." Russell, *The House of Mitsui,* pp. 223–24.

[51] See Hahn, *Die Industrielisierung Japans,* pp. 104–7.

policy that it not only persists but has been expanded and generalized until its influence spreads throughout the major industries
of the country. The government not only extends such aid to infant
industries, but also to practically all the older industries whether
experiencing tangible difficulties or not.[52] Throughout the twentieth century an expanding system of autarchic aids, direct and
indirect, has been elaborated on the subsidies model; accordingly,
tariffs, import quotas, export bounties, currency depreciation and
manipulation, foreign-exchange controls, not to speak of an increasing monopolization of colonial trade resulted in the creation
of the Yen-bloc.

While the state has not only encouraged industrial growth but
also directed it along particular channels, it has not seriously interfered with the conduct nor the private profits of the dominating
business concerns. "Japanese large-scale industry," the Lederers
write,[53]

has taken on the character of modern enterprise without having gone
through a period of transition from feudalism. In its origins the patronage of the State was of decisive importance. . . . Frequently the State
intervened to assist families in danger of bankruptcy, supporting them
by credit grants, perhaps even through many years. The greater the
name and the closer its connection with politically influential parties
the more securely could the firm count on being tided over periods of
heavy losses. Small people, however, families without connections, were
lost if they could not make their own way.[54]

It would be a mistake, however, to conclude that such intimate
relationships between government and business enterprise are
merely of the order of "growing pains" involved in "catching up"
by forced draft methods. To be sure, "Mercantilism was introduced
at the beginning of the Meiji Era and it is still the ruling force at

[52] Cf. Herbert M. Bratter, "The Role of Subsidies in Japan's Economic Development," IV (May, 1931), 377–93.
[53] *Japan in Transition*, pp. 238–39.
[54] Even the emergence of a war economy in Japan since 1937 and the institution
of some severe restrictive measures has not interfered with profit-making opportunities. The *Oriental Economist* index for the profit rate of joint stock companies shows
a sustained average of about 20% per annum for 1937 and 1938, and it is noted that
the war influences on the profit rate are "so negligible that the general condition may
be regarded as stationary." *Oriental Economist*, Supplement, "Japan Prepares for
Continental Construction," Oct., 1939; see also *ibid.*, Supplement for 1939–40, p. 30,
and the issue of Oct., 1941, pp. 509–10.

the present time.".[55] Yet so to summarize present trends is to greatly oversimplify the story. What is being accomplished is the gradual rounding out of a highly coördinated Fascist-type of totalitarian economy dominated by an ideology which a Japanese authority declares to be increasingly that of the army bureaucracy: "nationalistic, expansionist, anti-capitalistic, anti-individualistic, antifactional, anti-communistic, and socialistic."[56]

Even the phraseology here is almost identical with the customary Nazi and Fascist propaganda offerings. The *Oriental Economist* terms the system

State Capitalism. . . . Japan married socialism to capitalism and its offspring was state capitalism. The term is an arbitrary one for want of a better. It means the people, through the state, put up part of the money for some important national enterprise, and private capital the rest, usually about half and half. The state restrains capital, and capital spurs the state. The one gives the national interest with a check on profit, and a sharing by the people as a whole. The other restrains such weaknesses as bureaucracy and nepotism. State capitalism is the nexus.[57]

It is significant that the writer of these lines is thinking directly and specifically of great "mixed" enterprises (owned partly by government and partly by private interests). There are a number of these, and the pattern of control seems to be gaining steadily in both official and business favor. Mention has already been made of the great Japan Iron and Steel Company, which produces about half of the total Japanese output, and which under most recent plans is owned about half and half by governmental and by private interests. But on a similar plane a whole series of new colonial, transportation, and communication works are being developed.

[55] Professor Eijiro Kawai, "Neue politische Kräfte des wirtschaftlichen Aufbaucs," *Weltwirtschaftliches Archiv*, XLVI (July, 1937), 62–78.

[56] Chitoshi Yanaga, "Recent Trends in Japanese Political Thought," *Pacific Affairs*, June, 1940. The author adds, somewhat quaintly, "Japanese ideas are at once radical and conservative." "Anti-capitalistic," of course, means, "anti-liberal," anti-free-competition, and anti-laissez faire. But in no other sense. Other Japanese writers refer to the new order more simply as "Japanese National Socialism."

[57] George Gorman, "Japan's Three Principles," *Oriental Economist*, March, 1940. The expression "state capitalism" is unfortunate, since it suggests (a) ownership by the state and (b) pursuit of nonproperty ends. Neither is borne out by the facts. State ownership is supplementary and additional to private capital; there is no sign of desire to expropriate private interests, and the results of government activity redound to the advantage of ruling-class circles and private business enterprise. See pp. 113–19, following.

The model here has been the semigovernmental South Manchurian Railway.[58] Others are the new China Federal Reserve Bank,[59] the North China Development Company,[60] and the Central China Development Company.[61] Industrial enterprises taken over or newly established in the conquered territories are being handled in a similar fashion, when they are not included directly in the interest radii of the "development companies." [62] Thus the army has brought in Y. Aikawa, now allied to the *Zaibatsu*, to take over the Showa Steel Company. Recent schemes for a national electric power grid comparable to the British Central Electricity Board are being laid out on a similar basis. The newly formed International Electric Communication Company [63] is being governed much as

[58] Capital 800,000,000 ¥ (yen); assets valued (1936) at 2,000,000,000 ¥. "Controls nearly all the railways in Manchuria, North China and part of Korea, and is comparable, in many ways, with the Canadian Pacific, the Trans-Siberian and other great lines . . . it has developed most of Manchuria's coal, iron and gold mining, gas, electricity, and water supplies, docks, engineering works, modern hotels and newspapers." Smith, "Japan's Business Families." Since December, 1937, a great proportion of South Manchurian Railway's property in the heavy industries has been transferred to the Manchurian Industrial Development Corporation, headed by Y. Aikawa. The M.I.D.C.'s capital of 450,000,000 yen is contributed equally by the Manchukuo Government and the Japan Industry Company, one of the smaller *Zaibatsu*. See *Japan-Manchoukuo Year Book*, 1940, pp. 860–66, for a description of the M.I.D.C.

[59] Capital 50,000,000 ¥; half provided by the Yokohama Specie Bank, the Industrial Bank of Japan, and the Bank of Korea; balance by various Chinese banks.

[60] Capital, 350,000,000 ¥, one half contributed by the Japanese government.

[61] Capital (*Oriental Economist*, May, 1940) 173,000,000 ¥, owned about half and half by government and private business interests. Its operations include salt, mining, textiles, fishing, railroad, housing projects and properties.

[62] Under these schemes, Japan was divided into nine regional blocs with a monopoly distribution company in each bloc. These schemes went into operation on April 1, 1942.

There are other "mixed enterprises" which are mainly syndicates. These are the Japan Rice Co., capital 30,000,000 ¥, Japan Fertilizer Co., capital 50,000,000 ¥, and the Japan Coal Co., capital 50,000,000 ¥. In each case, the government contributes half of the capital, besides passing out many forms of subsidies. All three have complete monopoly over the buying and selling of the commodity concerned. Another group of "mixed companies" is concerned chiefly with the development of mining. These are: Imperial Fuel Development Co., capital 20,000,000 ¥, Japan Gold Production Co., capital 20,000,000 ¥, and the Imperial Mining Development Co., capital 30,000,000 ¥. Half of the capital is contributed by the state. Colonial and transportation development companies not mentioned previously are: South Seas Transportation Co., Japan Transportation Co., capital 20,900,000 ¥, Korea and Manchoukuo Development Co., 8,000,000 ¥, Formosa Development Co., 18,000,000 ¥. South Seas Development Co., 15,300,000 ¥, and the Manchuria Development Co., 33,300,000 ¥.

[63] The new company "is a national policy communication company which came into being through the consolidation of the former Nippon Wireless Telegraph Com-

though it were a "mixed enterprise," even though the direct government participation in ownership seems to be of minor importance.

Such data but barely scratch the surface, for they fail clearly to indicate the wide ramifications of a network of enterprises of a trust-like character which the Japanese have been swiftly elaborating throughout the entirety of their newly acquired "autonomous circle of common prosperity" in "Greater East Asia." Within Japan proper, reorganization schemes are being announced almost daily which combine entire industries into single or closely coördinated trusts. Since the beginning of 1941, reorganization schemes have been announced for such widely varying trades and industries as electric light bulbs (for export), oil, silk, spinning (ten management enterprises coördinated by a single policy administering body), deep-sea fisheries, and automobiles.[64] These are paralleled by a mushroom growth of similar Japanese dominated private trusts in Korea, Manchukuo, North China, and the South Sea areas. Many of these are deliberately organized as central and all-inclusive trusts for the whole of Japanese dominated territories. Thus the East Asia Shipping Company has been recently "entrusted" with "the task" of organizing shipping with the mainland, and Dai-Nippon Airways with the spinning of a centrally directed Far Eastern air traffic system.[65]

---

pany and the International Telephone Company under the terms of a special law." It is to handle all wireless telegraphic and a part of the cable telegraphic traffic of Japan and the Japanese empire, and is aimed at "uniform control, completion and development of the international communication network of Japan." *Oriental Economist*, July, 1940.

[64] In 1941, the following reorganizations were completed: 77 cotton spinning companies were merged into blocs, leaving only 14 companies; 37 woolen companies were reduced to 8. Similar steps were taken for other textile companies like silk and rayon. See the annual report of Mr. S. Tsuda, president of the Cotton Spinners' Association, *Oriental Economist* (August, 1941), p. 423. As for the other industries, nine leading packing firms were merged into one; 27 machine tool firms formed the Nisshin Machine Industry Co.; six canning companies formed the Toyo Can Manufacturing Co., 960 glass firms reduced to 50. Those industries in the process of reorganization in the fall of 1941 and probably completed now are: Portland cement, 23 firms reduced to 5 or 6, imitation leather, 16 firms into 4, marine leather, 19 into 1, oil, 14 into 6, municipal transportation, unification of companies in each city, woolen yarn wholesaling, 200 dealers into 24 blocs with one firm in each, tanning, 800 into 30 or 40 blocs, soap manufacturing, 500 into 50 blocs. Cf. *Osaka Mainichi and Tokyo Nichi Nichi* from August to October, 1941, inclusive.

[65] Toshio Narasaki, "Oriental Great Economic Circle and Transportation Policy," *East Asia Economic News*, Jan., 1941.

The "co-prosperity sphere" has been variously described. One Japanese writer outlines this oriental equivalent of the Nazi "new order in Europe" in the following terms: [66]

The Oriental Great Economic Circle signifies the economic circle comprising Manchoukuo, China, the Netherlands Indies, French Indo-China, Thailand and British Malaya under the leadership of Japan. The areas belonging to this circle should strive to bring about a complementary existence with free exchange of commodities, performing at the same time their shares in the productive activities. In such an economic circle, it is natural that the country the most advanced in the fields of culture, economy, industry and technical arts should take the lead of other nations, and in the Orient this duty of leadership devolves without question upon Japan.[67]

Parallel with these developments, the government has taken an increasingly active hand in the process of forced cartellization, establishment of compulsory price and marketing control, and various other forms of regulation which serves to promote the centralization of economic policy-forming power. Under the Bureau for Industrial Regulation, established in 1930, for example, the Ministry of Trade and Industry may declare any "consolidation" to be a regular cartel organized *by itself* "with the definite purpose of promoting industrial economy," if approved by more than half of the potential membership. And, "if more than two-thirds of the members of the cartel agree to the provisions agreed upon, they may petition for a contract and the Ministry can make such a contract with them." [68] The Bureau's powers in theory, even under the original enabling act, range over the entire field of industrial organization and policy:

[66] *Idem.*

[67] A frank version of the above general aims is expressed by Mr. Masatsune Ogura, Finance Minister in Konoye's third cabinet, in a series of articles, "How to Fight Economic War" in the *Osaka Mainichi and Tokyo Nichi Nichi* (English), Aug. 2–3, 1941: "Nippon can specialize in heavy industries and China in light industries to advantage. The products of these two countries can supply not only the co-prosperity sphere but all the world as well. The Greater East Asia Co-prosperity Sphere affords an ideal market for our manufactured goods. Hundreds of millions of East Asiatics are our potential customers. . . . If we should succeed in settling the emergency and in bringing about expansion, whatever financial burden we may have shouldered will bring returns many times over."

[68] Professor Masamachi Royama, "Die wirtschaftsrechtliche Struktur als Grundlage des japanischen Wirtschaftsaufschwungs," *Weltwirtschaftliches Archiv*, XLVI (July, 1937), 79–92.

The first department (or division) handles supervision and checking of industrial transactions, carries out scientific research and administers any financial reform required to achieve special improvements. The second division supervises the standardization of industrial products, the uniformity of manufacturing processes, and the propaganda advertising of home products. Thus all different forms of industrial production are checked, supervised, and virtually controlled by these two departments.[69]

Other governmental coördinating activities extend and deepen the web of official control. The Bureau of Economic Resources, established in 1928, "has jurisdiction over all plans that deal with regulation and disposition of raw materials and both human and material economic resources."[70] The Bureau of Supervision or General Board of Control, organized in 1935, is a sort of central "Kontrollamt" of the entire national economic system, subject to the direct authority of the Cabinet.[71] How far such control may go can be seen in the field of agriculture, where a wide-ranging network of regulation covers practically the entirety of the Japanese agricultural system, including its economic interests at all levels of production and marketing. The model here is the Rice Law, passed in 1921 and subsequently altered and greatly reinforced by a number of amendments. In its current form it is probably the most rigid, all-inclusive, and totalitarian law relating to any major agricultural industry anywhere in the world.[72]

The final step taken in this direction is reflected in the establishment of the Supreme Economic Council, charged with the task of coördinating "total agricultural associations, total vocational and industrial associations and 'free enterprise units' which will continue to exist outside the corporate bodies." Under leadership of the government, "plans for an empire industrial federation" made

[69] *Ibid.*   [70] *Ibid.*   [71] *Ibid.*

[72] Dr. Shiroshi Nasu, "Ziele und Ausrichtung der japanischen Agrarpolitik in der Gegenwart," *Weltwirtschaftliches Archiv*, XLVI, 157–84. According to this authority "the total agricultural debt rose from 750 million yen in 1911 to 4600 million yen in 1929" and by this latter date approximately 30 percent of all Japanese farmers were insolvent and unable to pay their debts. The effect of the various price and marketing and agricultural control laws seem not to have been the liquidation of this growing mass of agricultural indebtedness, but rather to have cumulatively pressed the poverty-stricken peasant layers into a straightjacket reminiscent of the Procrustean pattern of the German Reichsbauerngesetz—or law of compulsory entailment. See also the sketch of "the agricultural reorganization movement in the *Monthly Circular* of the Mitsubishi Economic Research Bureau, March, 1941, p. 11.

up of "leaders representing the steel, coal, electricity, shipping, and cotton industries" was approved as the agency to work with the government in order to implement these plans. The new federation seems to be practically coextensive with the existing Japan Economic Federation (it may actually be that body!). The dominating principles were said to be "public service first," abandonment of "liberalistic profitseeking" and "spontaneous and autonomous formulation of economic policy." The suspicion that "the government wishes business men to have the management of the nation's economic affairs" [73] (authoritative self-government in business) seems to have been fully justified with the announcement that Mr. Ogura, head of Sumitomo (third largest of the *Zaibatsu*), was to be made the Imperial "Japanese Knudsen." [74]

In addition to the expansion of this meticulously exacting regulatory network, the government has not hesitated under the emergency of war to wipe practically out of existence large sections of the business system. Most noteworthy here is the policy which has come to be known in the Japanese patois as *Butsudo* (a contraction of the Japanese words meaning "mobilization of commodities"), which was gradually inaugurated after the middle thirties. On the surface *Butsudo* is a system of war rationing which places special emphasis upon the power of the government to prohibit the manufacture or sale of any commodity in any fashion it may see fit and to canalize productive capacity as the exigencies of a wartime economy may determine.

Actually, it vests in the government power to build up or undo entire branches of industry in either war or peace. Under *Butsudo*, for example, the domestic sale of cottons has been almost entirely eliminated.[75] Various strictly nonessential foodstuffs can be sold only in limited amounts. Its net effect has been not only to bring

[73] Byas, "Japan's Censors." "Under intensifying wartime conditions, the situation has changed quite perceptibly. Government authority has steadily increased and the Government and a special group of officials connected with the big moneyed interests have come to have much say in the economic scheme of the nation. With the progress of the planned economy, these officials are likely to play greater and greater parts in concert with the various industrial and business 'gauleiters' or district leaders, who are moving up to become fuehrers. These rising men are also leaders of their respective cartels." Hirose Higuchi, *Japan Times Weekly and Trans-Pacific*, March 27, 1941, p. 458.

[74] "Mr. Ikeda, the former executive head of the great Mitsui corporation, . . . is now attached to the Emperor as one of his personal consultants." Hugh Byas, *The Japanese Enemy, His Power and His Vulnerability* (New York, 1942), p. 33.

[75] *Manchester Guardian*, July 20, 1938.

about a considerable dislocation of industry and a great deal of occupational unemployment, but also to force many concerns either to suspend operations or to go out of business entirely. By the early part of 1939 some 9,793 establishments employing 68,273 persons were suspended, and some 1,709 establishments employing 6,223 were openly liquidated.[76] Most of these businesses were small scale; many of them were simply handicraft shops.

Yet even *Butsudo* does not run counter to the general picture outlined above. Quite the contrary. It merely represents the logical fulfillment of the partnership between business and government which has characterized the evolution of capitalistic institutions in Japan from the very beginning. In it is revealed the determination to coördinate in a national fashion the entirety of economic activity on behalf of the volatile will and vaulting ambitions of the new social-economic hierarchy.

The elements here are not greatly dissimilar to those noted for other totalitarian systems of the general Fascist type.

1. The *Zaibatsu*, the monopolistically-oriented enterprises centered around them, and the extensive network of trade associations, chambers of commerce, cartels, and similar bodies of which they are the acknowledged leaders, constitute an elaborate, semilegal hierarchy of graduated economic power. The smaller businesses, handicraft establishments, and the various other layers of the "professional" middle classes thus exist within a sort of all-inclusive "corporate" regime;. their organization by occupational categories guarantees them something of the order of a stable living according to customary standards, providing they do not conflict with such policies as *Butsudo*.

2. This hierarchy works very closely with the civil and administrative bureaucracy of the state. In fact it is probably not too far from the truth to refer to the gradually consolidating economic bureaucracy as the economic aspect of the state bureaucracy. This constitutes the Japanese version of "National Socialism, which is inclined to regard anti-capitalism as separate from socialism and thus associate state-absolutism with socialism." [77] Capitalism, in

---

[76] Isoshi Asahi, *The Economic Strength of Japan* (Tokyo, 1939). Principally affected were the textiles, leather, rubber, and iron and steel industries.

[77] "National Socialism is a combination of state-absolutism, which has always been a sheet-anchor to Japanese political thought, and Socialism. . . . Japanese National Socialism opposes two important theories of Marxism: (1) it rejects the theory of

this context, is interpreted to be "competitive" and "unregulated" in terms of the "well-being of the state."

3. The military is becoming increasingly part and parcel of the same control pyramid. At times, as in the beginning of the Manchurian and Chinese "affairs," the army has been able to take independent action. But under the regime dominated by the cliques centered around Matsuoka, internal conflicts seemed to be largely smoothed out, and that close community of interests which has always held the military and imperial-nationalistic interests together in Japan once again asserted itself.[78]

Japan has really remained a military nation in spite of all the constitutional contributions of western democracy. . . . The Key to the development and expansion of Japanese industry until Japan became established as a major industrial power was increasing militarism. . . . The Administrators and commissioners, the large-scale corporations of the Railroad Company of South Manchuria, and Mitsui and Mitsubishi, the Yasuda and Sumitomo, and other organizations down to the small rice growers and industrial workers and minor craftsmen . . . are all well aware of the numerous factors that control Japan's economic status. In spite of all internal conflicting interests and social differences, all classes of Japan's population are concerned in but one important matter: *Japan must progress and she must be successful.*[79]

---

the decline of state-control; and (2) it rejects the theory of the rise of internationalism. . . . National Socialism appealed to the mass of the Japanese because state-absolutism still exercises its original and traditional influence in Japan." Kawai, "Neue politische Kräfte des wirtschaftlichen Aufbaues."

[78] The Tojo-Terauchi-Suğiyama clique in control of the army at the present time is close to the *Zaibatsu.* The Terauchi family has been close to the Mitsuis since the first World War days when the elder Terauchi was Prime Minister, while Tojo is intimate with the Mitsubishi. One paper calls Tojo the "most conservative of the army clique."

Commenting on the New Economic Structure Law of 1941, Joseph Newman, New York *Herald-Tribune* correspondent in Tokyo and one of the ablest journalists on Japan, declares in a recent book, *Goodbye Japan* (New York, 1942), p. 199: "The power, however, was left largely in the hands of big business, whose representatives in the offices of Finance Ministry and Commerce and Industry Ministry applied the law in such a way that the big-business clans grew stronger, a larger part of the middle class was liquidated, and workers and peasants were able to buy less goods with their money than ever before. The business clans were permitted to continue their 'voluntary regimentation,' through their independent industrial cartels. They not only were given bigger orders than before by the militarists but also a guarantee of seven percent profit on their iron and steel output as well as subsidies to encourage production. The government announcement of subsidies for big business was made by the president of the Iron and Steel Control Association, who was privately connected with Mitsui, Mitsubishi and other leading business clans."

[79] Johannes B. Kraus, "Wirtschaftsgesinnung und völkisch-politische Grundbedin-

4. And finally, the psychopathic, ideological, propaganda cement which holds the *Kokutai* amalgam together is the fused power of *Shinto* and *Bushido*. In a very interesting doctrinal glorification of the Japanese way, Ginjiro Fujihara, quotes with warm approval the words of Lothrop Stoddard: [80]

Present-day Japan is thus stung to action by the sharpest of life's instincts—that of self-preservation. Now add to this primeval urge a burning faith in 'Great Japan' and the peculiar excellence of the Yamato Race; add to that again the Bushido code glorifying self-sacrifice and welcoming heroic death, and we can realize the fierce longing in Japanese hearts to cut the Gordian knot of their difficulties and hew out a great destiny with the Samurai sword.

Or, as Dr. Kraus, a very sympathetic observer, puts the matter somewhat more dryly, "Japan's secret is that she knows how to control her economic system through the ethics of Samurai or 'Samurai Geist.' " [81]

The final step here has been already taken with the *de facto* dissolution of all the old parties and the emergence of a fully totalitarian "single-party state." The new Fascist party, deliberately modeled after those of Italy and Germany, is still somewhat vague in outline. It is known as the "Association for Assisting the Throne" (AAT), which is in charge of the "National Movement for Assisting the Throne" (NMAT), and was at its inception, *ex officio*, directed by the former premier, Prince Fumimaro Konoye. Launched officially on October 12, 1940, it appears to be conceived as an official government body.[82] A "Parliamentary Bureau . . . has for

---

gungen als Voraussetzungen des japanischen Industrielisierungsprozessen," *Weltwirtschaftliches Archiv*, XLVI (July, 1937), pp. 45–61.

[80] Ginjiro Fujihara (also written Fujiwara) *The Spirit of Japanese Industry* (Tokyo, 1936, pp. 118–19. For over a quarter of a century ex-Minister of Commerce Fujihara was chief executive of the Oiji Paper Company, a gigantic paper monopoly controlled by Mitsui interests, and formerly associated directly with Mitsui in a number of important positions. Fujihara was also a member of the House of Peers.

[81] Kraus, *op. cit.*

[82] "The Coöperation Council [of the A.A.T.] is an organ through which the will of the people is conveyed to the Administration and vice versa, and is, thus vastly more than an advisory organ of the Government. The Central Coöperation Council is in Tokyo and there are district coöperation councils of the prefectures, cities, and towns and villages. The membership of the Central Coöperation Council is composed, besides representatives of the prefectural coöperation councils, of persons recommended by the heads of the district A.A.T., from among members of various public bodies and of the prefectural assemblies and government officials, to be approved by the President." *East Asia Economic News*, Feb., 1941.

its object to ensure the satisfactory functioning of Parliament, for which purpose the political parties of the past were dissolved to form a unitary whole in the A.A.T. Other departments, including those for the direction of national life, propaganda works, and planning, have already commenced activities for the development of the National Movement." [83] Its central motive is held to be that "of the moral ideal of a harmonious, complementary development of the peoples of East Asia and for the establishment of a new world order." [84]

Paralleling this "constructive" action has gone dissolution not only of all the old political parties, but also of all the various democratic and trade-union organizations. In the place of the labor unions has come an organization apparently modeled directly after the Nazi Labor Front.[85] And in the place of the other associations there has sprung up a bewildering array of authoritatively led youth, patriotic, and other organizations of a completely totalitarian stamp.

Economic policy-forming powers became highly centralized with the passage of the New Economic Structure Law in August, 1941. This law called for the establishment of all-inclusive cartels, called control associations, in each of the following industries: iron and steel, coal, chemical, cement, machine tools, nonferrous metals, foreign trade, foodstuff, medicine, shipping, shipbuilding, and

[83] In the reorganization of 1941, the Parliamentary and Planning bureaus were abolished.

[84] *East Asia Economic News*, Dec., 1940.

[85] "The first meeting of the All-Japan Convention of Patriotic Trade Unions (Aihoku Rodo Kumiai Zenkoku Konwakwai), which was organized in April, 1936, by the union of all patriotic or nationalistic trade unions with reactionary ideas in general politics, was held at Tokyo on September 27, 1936." It placed itself in full opposition to the Japan Trade Union Council (the central federation of regular Japanese Trade unions). Its platform planks called for: (1) "Propagation of the Japanese Spirit," (2) "Institution of a Law for the Control of Industry and Labor," (3) "Demand for the Establishment of an Industry and Labor Council," (4) "A thorough Industrial Service for the Country," (5) "Nationalization of a Labor Festival peculiar to Japan," (6) "Unity of the War Front of Labourers and Farmers." It "denounced present social and democratic thought as being mere imitation of the West and contrary to Japan's national constitution, and upheld a reorganization of all trade unions in the spirit of love for the country in the true Japanese spirit." Foreign Affairs Association of Japan, Tokyo, *Japan Year Book*, 1938–39, p. 773. Another Patriotic Industrial Association (Sangyo Hokuku Kai) was established in 1938 and shortly received government support. *Japan Year Book*, 1939–40, p. 723. From these beginnings the final step seems to have been recently taken with the announcement of the formation of an all inclusive labor organization.

land transportation. The control association will embrace all the firms, semiofficial, "mixed" companies, trade associations, and existing cartels and will possess complete control of production and distribution in the industry concerned. The president of the control association will act in the capacity of a "Fuehrer" of the industry.

He has full authority to appoint or dismiss the vice-president, chief director, directors, councillors and other officials of the association and may also dismiss any director or directors, with the permission of the competent Minister, of a member company or organization, when he considers that their deeds are harmful to the conduct of the affairs of the association. The business of the association in regard to materials, funds and labor required for production equipment will thus be operated under the guidance and direction of the president. Products of the industry concerned are not permitted to be sold without his consent.[86]

If the need arises, a supreme central organ embracing all these control associations will be set up.

Commenting on the control associations in the New Structure plans, the London *Economist* (July 12, 1941), declared: "The scheme, when it emerged, was so emasculated that public corporations which had been planned were now nothing but private cartels under another name." Up to December, 1941, three control associations were established: in the iron and steel, coal, and shipping industries. Hachisaburo Hirao, head of the Iron and Steel Manufacturers' Federation, and for forty years the able managing director of the Mitsubishi subsidiary, Tokyo Marine and Fire Insurance Co., became president of the Iron and Steel Control Association. The Federation of Coal Mine Owners' Association dissolved and emerged as the Coal Control Association, with the president of the former, Kenjiro Matsumoto, becoming the president of the latter organization. Mr. Matsumoto is also a director of the Mitsui Trust Co. In November, 1940, the Central Shipping Federation, headed by Noboru Ohtani, for many years the president of Mitsubishi's huge Nippon Yusen Kaisha, changed its name to the Central Marine Transportation Control Association. A year later, the latter was reorganized into the present Shipping Control Association with Mr. Ohtani as the president.[87]

86 *Oriental Economist*, Sept., 1941, p. 460.
87 The correctness of the London *Economist's* comments is also shown in the case

With the Association for Assisting the Throne serving as the supreme ideological coördinator for both the Supreme Economic Council and the Supreme Cultural Council and as official bearer of the doctrinal position allied to *Shinto, Bushido,* and the fanatical worship of *Amaterasu-O-Mikami* (sun goddess, the legendary ancestress of the imperial house), the means will stand at hand for the final fusing together of the upper reaches of the existing hierarchies into a caste-like state. Close alliance among the cliques, intermarriage,[88] and similar fusions had already gone far towards smoothing the road before the appearance of the single party state.[89] And that state is a symbiosis clearly dominated by an econ-

of the particular control associations which were in the process of establishment when the U.S.–Japanese war broke out. Thus the *Osaka Mainichi and Tokyo Nichi Nichi* (English) of Sept. 24, 1941, declares: "it has become certain that the association (Nippon Warehouse Association) will be designated as a control association," with Shinzo Mihashi, president of Mitsubishi Warehouse Co. and the Nippon Warehouse Association becoming the president of the control association. The trade-control association seems likely to be headed by Ginjiro Fujihara (see footnote 80, above).

[88] It has not been possible to check the following, but the picture it submits seems highly probable in view of subsequent developments: "All the big monopolist concerns maintain very close personal contacts with the Court, the high bureaucracy, the high nobility, government circles, and with the leaders of the two big political parties (the Seiyukai and the Minseito).

"Thus, the Japanese Emperor is personally interested in the Mitsubishi concern. One of the daughters of Iwasaki (head of the concern) married the late leader of the Minseito Party, Kato; another married the Minister of Foreign Affairs in the last Minseito government, Shidehara: and a third married the Minister of Finance in the same government, Inouye, who was assassinated in 1932. One of the principals of the Mitsui concern, Fujiwara Ginjiro [see footnote 80 above], is a member of the House of Peers; another, Yamamoto Jotaro, is a prominent leader of the Seyukai Party.

"One of the most prominent feudal aristocrats, Prince Saionji (the last member of the Genro), is a brother of the founder of the Sumitomo concern, and an uncle of its present owner.

"Of the Yasuda concern, Takahashi Koreikiyo is one of the leaders of the Seiyukai; Mori Hirozo is chairman of the Government Bank of Taiwan and Shijo Takahide was formerly Minister of Commerce and Industry." E. Varga and L. Mendelsohn, *New Data for V. I. Lenin's "Imperialism: the Highest Stage of Capitalism"* (New York, 1938), pp. 105, 107.

[89] Speaking of the growth of the single-party idea, a correspondent, M. B. Thresher, in a recent issue of *Oriental Affairs* (July, 1940) writes, "Mr. Chuji Machida, President of the majority party, the Minseito, made his endorsement of the plan dependent on the acceptance by Prince Konoye of the leadership of the projected party. Prince Konoye, true to form, raised objections to assuming the post, the principal one being that he was President of the Privy Council. His resignation of this office on June 24th is naturally taken to indicate that the stage is now set for the establishment of a single party under his leadership." Simultaneously, conversations with the Axis powers took on a more serious tone: "On June 22nd, the Parliamentary League for Attainment of the Objectives of the Sacred Campaign (the Chinese cam-

omy in which policy-forming powers are so centralized and held that it may most appropriately be described on its economic side as a regime of monopoly-organized *status*—not *state*—capitalism.

---

paign), addressed to Hitler a copy of a resolution expressing their admiration for the great achievements of the Reich, and their hope that it would go on to destroy Jewish control of the World. The Social Mass Party issued a statement about the same time urging the Government to strengthen the Axis and cease negotiating with Britain and the U.S.A." The fruits of this shift are already apparent today: in the formation of the Supreme Economic and Supreme Cultural Councils, in NMAT and the establishment of AAT, in the appointment of Mr. Ogura to the position of an "economic dictator." The group centered around Matsuoka, himself closely allied to the *Zaibatsu*, has come to the fore with what appears to be at once an effective single-party and a greater empire formula. The anti-Comintern Pact has been followed by the Berlin-Rome-Tokyo pact. With the opening of the Burma road the adventure in Indo-China and the general *Drang nach Suden* the country is stripping for action in a major war. The last vestiges of parliamentary forms of government and popular participation are rapidly being liquidated. The militarily omnicompetent, economically coördinated, politically streamlined, inherently expansionist, patriarchally guided, oriental variant of totalitarian status capitalism emerges.

Chapter IV

FRANCE: THROUGH DOUBLE DEFEAT
TO VICHY'S "NEW ORDER"

THE Confédération Générale du Patronat Français (CGPF) represents almost the ultimate in expression of that "inherent tendency to combine and form ever larger business units"[1] which goes back beyond the earliest days of the industrial system into France's earlier and all-embracing system of medieval guilds. Though not a "combination" itself in the ordinary technical usage of that term, it has nevertheless clearly arisen as a by-product of the concentration movement and, before its recent dissolution,[2] the expansion of its functions had been halted but a single pace short of the establishment of a "corporative system" structurally coextensive with national and imperial frontiers. There is some evidence that under the most recent Pétain regime the last step has already been taken. If so, the pattern of control evolved over the past decades is now in process of being fully rounded out and France stands in the ante-room of a formally Fascist-type state.

Whether this last is yet true or not[3] does not greatly matter. What is significant is the fact that such a transition, in full keeping— structurally, functionally, and in terms of social outlook—with past lines of development in the evolution of employers' central policy-forming bodies in France, could be made without seriously upsetting any institutions, conventions, or interests except those opposed to the advance of groups who stand to gain from inaugu-

[1] William F. Ogburn and William Jaffé, *Social and Economic Studies of Post-War France* (New York, 1929), p. 552.

[2] The Confederation was formally dissolved shortly after the German victory; this, it appears, was a preliminary to general reorganization of French economic life consonant with past trends but more clearly patterned after the German (rather than the Italian) totalitarian model than was previously the case.

[3] See pp. 145–49.

ration of the "corporate state." That this could be true of a country but yesterday still so imbued with the popular ideas and democratic values transmuted from the French Revolution is of far greater moment than that these ideas and values should have been, even temporarily, submerged. For it would then clearly demonstrate that "Fascism" was not so much imposed by a militarily victorious totalitarian power from without, as that it had been evolved through more or less "normal" processes from within, by elements which found in the war an auspicious occasion for thus consolidating a power which had been gravely threatened in recent times (by the "Popular Front" movement), and which they now hoped at long last to be able, through control over the political machinery, fully to wield. What these "normal" processes are remains to be seen.

ORIGINS: A PERIOD OF "FREEDOM OF ASSOCIATION"

The CGPF, as it stood at the moment of its dissolution, was the product of a thorough reorganization in 1936 following the conclusion of the famous Matignon Agreement between its predecessor organization, the General Confederation of French Production (Confédération Générale de la Production Française), and the General Confederation of Labor (Confédération Générale du Travail—CGT). This predecessor body was, like similar organizations in England and Germany, a "war baby," having been "called into existence" in 1919 by M. Clémentel,[4] Minister of Commerce, to aid in the reorganization of French economic life after the First World War.

Behind this latest attempt at the creation of a vast and all-inclusive syndical organization of industry lay a long period of experimentation with less comprehensive forms. And these, paradoxically, first took root in the midst of a swiftly proliferating meshwork of local, occupational, and regional employer associations at a time when France, far more completely than any other modern industrial country, was formally and legally committed to absolute prohibition of all forms of association whatsoever. Under the famous Le Chapelier law of 1791, an attempt was made to wipe out all vestiges of guild organization, but in so doing a prohibition

---

[4] René P. Duchemin, *Organisation syndicale patronale en France* (Paris, 1940), p. 1.

was laid on every conceivable type of private association designed in any manner to promote common interests, whether of laborers, employers, or any other special interest group.[5]

Legal freedom from this interdict first came with the promulgation of the Act of March 21, 1884, "respecting the foundation of industrial associations," a law subsequently widened and generalized by an act passed July 1, 1901.[6] In the meantime, however, the prohibition did not seem to have seriously hampered, or even greatly to have slowed down, the formation of employers' associations. Nor did it entirely prevent the formation of workers' organizations, though clearly the history of enforcement under the interdict shows that the act was designed more to prevent the rise of workers' organizations than to inhibit expression of employer solidarity.[7] "By 1881 there were in Paris alone 130 employers' associations, with 15,000 members, and 150 workers' organizations, with 60,000 members, while 350 workers' organizations were in existence in the province."[8]

It is interesting to note, in passing, that the central issue involved in passage of the new laws was not mere "freedom of associations." Whereas Le Chapelier desired to prohibit private associations as such, in 1884 debate turned only on the matter of whether membership should be voluntary and free, or compulsory and "corporate." This was because in the earlier period all associations were regarded as "corporate" *per se,* or as direct carry-overs of

[5] Noteworthy are the two following sections of the Act:
Section 1. Since the abolition of all forms of corporations in the same grade or occupation is one of the bases of the constitution, it is forbidden to recreate such corporations under any pretext whatever.
Section 2. Citizens of the same grade or occupation, and workers or journeymen in any art or craft, may not, when assembled together, appoint a president, a secretary or an alderman, keep a register, enact decisions or establish any regulations concerning what they call their common interests. Quoted in *Freedom of Association* (International Labor Office, Geneva, 1927), II, 90.

[6] Laws passed in 1849 and again in 1864 considerably modified the unfair incidence and severe penalties formerly imposed under the Le Chapelier law.

[7] "Statistics show that while legal penalties were seldom imposed upon employers, workers organizations, including those of the most harmless character, were ruthlessly suppressed. . . . During the reign of Louis Philippe the relative proportion of prosecutions was as follows: one employers' association for eight workers', 40 percent of the employers were acquitted as against 5 per cent of the workers." II.O, *Freedom of Association,* II, 93.

[8] *Ibid.,* p. 98.

specialized feudal privileges. Passed in 1791 in the early days of the French Revolution, the law of Le Chapelier expressed the desire of the rising commercial, trading, and industrial classes to be rid of that vast, cramping network of guild and feudal restrictions which Colbert had attempted to liquidate by nationalizing, and Turgot had hoped to sweep away entirely.

Once on the statute books, the law proved of special value in preventing the rise of labor organizations (since these were held to be inherently of a "corporative" character); but it did not wholly prohibit various forms of commercial and employer collusion (since the employers still lacked any real sentiment for all-inclusive group action). By the decade of the eighties, however, sentiment in business circles for the principles of "free competition" and "laissez faire" was being rapidly undermined in France as elsewhere. To employers it then became desirable to remove the formal prohibitions on employer associations. They wished to enjoy powers of association of at least a semicorporate character, while adhering to the principle of "freedom of association" as a basis on which to deny the comprehensive demands which organized labor might see fit to make, if vested with power to compel all workers to join and to bargain collectively for entire industries. Once the level of organization in employer groups had itself approached such limits, agitation for a reversal of the 1884 formula began to appear, and we find a return to the organizational pattern of pre-Le Chapelier France.[9]

So to state the case, however, is apt to be slightly misleading, since it tends to gloss over certain facts of unique importance to an understanding of the peculiar susceptibility of France to "corporate" forms of organization. French production is still primarily small scale, specialized, in many respects highly localized, and—by comparison with England, Germany, and the United States—relatively free of large-scale trusts and combinations.[10] This fact might be expected to discourage corporate ideas. Yet even before large-

---

[9] See pp. 127 ff.

[10] It might be more accurate to state that both factors exist in France. A large number of small and middle-sized businesses as well as high concentration can be found. Examples of large-scale trusts are as follows: iron and steel industry; chemical industry; machine building; production of electric power; fuel production.

scale concentration began to make much headway in France, the main discussion in economic organization turned directly on that issue.

The answer to this paradox seems to lie in the fact that France, somewhat similarly to Germany and Japan (and in sharp contra-distinction to England and the United States), never really got wholly rid of medieval guild "corporate" forms of organization at all.[11] Nowhere else is the gap between *de jure* and *de facto* (prior to the law of 1884) so great as in France. During this period, local, regional, and in many cases national associations of handicrafts-men, trading and commercial interests, and workmen—frequently disguised under the form of various friendly and benefit societies—continued to exist. Such associations not only continued to exist but were strongly influenced throughout by codes of conduct, methods of working together, organizational biases, and a sense of quasi-professional group solidarity strongly reminiscent of, if not—as was frequently the case—directly traceable to, medieval times.

The relatively small-scale nature of French economic activity proved, consequently, rather a strength than a weakness in taking advantage of the forms of organization allowed when the ban was raised in 1884. More than that, for many industries, and in many rather peculiar ways, the trade association became not a secondary but a primary form of organization, quickly assuming functions and representing interests, and even, in some cases, communities of interest, comparable to those of the cartels, trade associations, and semifraternal associations (such as Kiwanis and Rotary). This was true even when the trade association had relatively little power, since the prevailing conception of its function was such as to make it useful along all these lines, whenever the occasion should arise.

It is, thus, not surprising that the passage of the laws of 1884 and 1901 should be paralleled by rapid spread of the associational net-work. An American observer in 1916 wrote that he found "in France . . . nearly 5,000 employers' associations, having a mem-bership of over 400,000; and about as many commercial associa-tions, with an equal membership." These were in turn "in a manner regulated by law and joined by affiliation into member associa-

---

[11] This is true mainly of the handicrafts. The trade associations of industry and commerce are nineteenth-century children.

tions, which in turn are joined into the principal or controlling organization with headquarters in Paris, and all working with very great success for the interests of French industry and commerce." [12]

The tendency to draw separate organizations together into federations evidenced itself at an early date. The first "Federation of Industrial Associations (Chambre syndicale) known under the name of the *Groupe de la Saint-Chapelle*" was organized in 1821 by the Carpentry Association. "The year 1858 saw the beginnings, on similar lines to the Saint-Chapelle Groupe, of the National Union of Commerce and Industry, which by 1869 included 55 industrial associations representing industries other than the building trade." [13] In 1859 the first effort was made to bring all existing associations into a national confederation by the formation of the National Union of Commerce and Industry. Others followed in short order.

The Central Committee of Trade Associations (1867) was intended to provide a central organization to include both the building trades and the National Union. The Commercial and Industrial Alliance (1896) in its rules provided for specialized committees, and marks a higher degree of development. Finally, the Federation of French Manufacturers and Merchants, founded in 1903, provided for the institution of regional committees and delegates from the various departments, and endeavored to group its members in sections, but without taking the goods manufactured as the basis of classification. [14]

The object of the first national federations was clear: "to make sure that they were not unions only of certain professions (trades, industries) but of all employers" the better to speak on behalf of "collective interests" of French employers as a whole. [15] According to the survey of the International Labour Office this interest was

[12] In a speech delivered by Mr. D. E. Felt, Vice-President of the Illinois Manufacturers' Association, and reproduced in *American Industries*, June, 1916, p. 15, it was argued, "In Germany and in France, organization of manufacturers is compulsory. In France, there must be at least one for each department, and the law imposes upon them the duty of advising the Government and the legislators on all industrial and commercial matters. They are, in part, supported by a tax." I have been unable to find any support for the assertion that the associations referred to enjoyed any direct government authority or support whatsoever.

[13] ILO, *Freedom of Association*, II, 92.

[14] "Employers' Organisations in France," *International Labour Review*, July, 1927, pp. 50–77.

[15] See, in particular, Etienne Villey, *L'Organisation professionnelle des employeurs dans l'industrie française* (Paris, 1923).

pursued through three distinct phases of development after 1884. The first was a "preparatory period" (1884–1900) characterized primarily by educational efforts designed to create among employers "an atmosphere of mutual confidence" and to encourage "measures calculated to promote useful but restricted coöperation between industrial establishments." This was followed by a period of "defensive tactics," in which they proceeded to take measures against the "possible results of the development of social legislation," against "international competition," and against the rising power of the trade unions, particularly the CGT (Confédération Générale du Travail).[16]

The results of this second period were enormously to increase membership in the "primary employers' associations, the membership of which doubled between 1900 and 1908, and to give more life and force to the unions and federations of associations." But even more significantly, "a general plan or organization . . . for each branch of production and inter-trade agreements arose and prepared the way for an all-inclusive concentration." [17]

The third phase was ushered in by the World War. This period the International Labor Office refers to as "the phase of action," and the action developed on the initiative of the government:

During hostilities the State had the monopoly of the markets; being the sole client giving orders it was in the position to insist on concentration. In order to intensify production and to impart flexibility unto the running of the establishments it brought about the formation in each branch of industry of powerful central organizations or syndicates which linked up the individual establishments.[18]

French war organization had the effect of spreading out organizational networks so as to include in some fashion or other nearly the whole of the business system, while at the same time vesting the association, for all practical purposes, with the powers of semi-autonomous, compulsory cartels. With the end of the war, governmental pressures along these lines were not greatly relaxed. Conversations running throughout 1918 led in 1919 to the demand of M. Clementel that special efforts be made to draw together the heads of this vast associational apparatus into a single centralized

16 ILO, *Freedom of Association*, II, 102–3.
17 *Ibid.*, p. 103.   18 *Ibid.*, p. 104.

body, able to speak with an authoritative voice for all French industry on all matters relating to business and national interest. The result was the founding in 1919 of the Confédération générale de la Production Française (CGPF).

In the words of M. Duchemin, President and leading spokesman of the CGPF from 1925 to 1936, the purpose of the CGPF was

to enable the Department of Commerce, through the creation of a vast syndical organization, formed on the demand of government but rigorously independent of it, to possess at all times the information and knowledge of trends which seemed indispensable to it in resolving innumerable economic problems as they arose, and to take the necessary steps on behalf of the national welfare.[19]

The purpose was simply and clearly to provide,[20]

in a word, our country with a federative organization similar to those which exist at the present time in a number of foreign countries, such as,
The Federation of German Industries
The Federation of British Industries
The United States Chamber of Commerce [21]
The Central Union of Swiss Employers' Associations
The Central Industrial Committee of Belgium.

Through such a body, the employers and the Minister of Commerce hoped to develop among industrialists "the habit of working in common, of reconciling their various conflicts, and of evolving means for harmonious development of their productive operations." [22] Here, then, is the French redaction of the formula, "self-government in business": all-inclusive organization of industry into private and centralized associations, functioning with, but entirely independent of, formal government control, in order to pool business information, agree on common lines of business policy, and work towards common business ends.

FROM 1919 TO THE MATIGNON AGREEMENT

"The new confederation has for its object to assemble and bind together all the innumerable associations [*syndicats*] scattered over the entire national territory." [23] Its method was to organize con-

---

[19] Duchemin, *Organisation syndicale*, p. 2.   [20] *Ibid.*
[21] The proper comparison here, of course, is with the National Association of Manufacturers, not the United States Chamber of Commerce.
[22] Duchemin, *loc. cit.*   [23] *Ibid.*, p. 3.

stituent association in groups, and then to develop and expand the
work of the groups in all directions. Collective action was to be
coextensive with range of business interests:

There is not a single question, whether it be documentary or technical,
fiscal or relating to customs tariffs, economic or social, whether relating
to the organization of production or concerted lock-outs, whether dealing with a common wages policy or strike-breaking measures, which is
not thoroughly studied by the special departments of the organizations,
or which does not provide an opportunity for direct negotiations with
the authorities.[24]

The manner of grouping industries together was designed to
facilitate to the utmost such promotion of collective interests. The
initial plan (July 4, 1919) divided industry into 21 groups. After
the modification of October, 1919, these appeared as follows:

1. Processing of Agricultural Products
2. Foodstuffs Industries
3. Public Works; Construction; Housing
4. Quarrying; Ceramics; Glass-works
5. Leather and Hides
6. Textile Industries (Production)
7. Clothing and Related Industries
8. Chemical Industries
9. Mining Industries
10. Heavy Metallurgy
11. Light Metallurgy
12. Building: Mechanical, Metallurgical, Electrical
13. Engineering; Copper Smithing; Foundries
14. Electricity; Public Lighting; Tramways
15. Maritime Industries; Transport
16. Aeronautics; Automobiles; Cycles
17. Precision Instruments
18. Publishing; Paper Making; Graphic Arts
19. Arts and Luxuries
20. Finance and Commerce
21. Travel, Tourist, and Hotel Industries

Subsequently several changes in groupings were made, and several
new groups formed.[25]

[24] ILO, *Freedom of Association*, II, 104.
[25] In 1922, Group 22 (Railroads) and Group 23 (Insurance); in 1923, Group 24
(Foreign Trade) and Group 25 (Regional Associations); in 1926, Group 26 (Wood
Industry and Trade in Wood); in 1929, Group 27 (Internal Navigation) and Group
28 (Colonial Enterprises).

These Groups, remarkably similar to those captioned Economic Groups in the National Economic Chamber established under the Nazi regime in 1933, were designed to serve as coördinating bodies for a wide variety of subsidiary business organizations. These latter may be national, regional, or local; they may be concerned exclusively with business problems such as price and production control, or exclusively with employer issues, or with a wide variety of social and economic questions; they may represent but a single trade, or a federation of trades organizations of one sort or another; they may exercise coercion over members to compel conformity with group decisions (or with cartels or comptoirs), or may be extremely loose and weak. It may help somewhat to simplify the story in subsequent pages to arrange the leading types according to the following broad classification: [26]

NATIONAL ASSOCIATIONS

Classification	Examples
Comptoirs (or cartels): single-commodity contractual agreements (may also be regional, international and for groups of commodities	
Syndicats: trade associations of specialized trades	Iron-Works Committee (Comité des Forges)
Fédérations: grouped out of syndicate and trade associations	Union of Metal and Mining Industries
Confédérations: grouped out of closely allied Federations and/or syndicats	General Confederation of French Production

REGIONAL ASSOCIATIONS

Syndicats: single-trade associations	Calais Metal Industries Associations
intertrade associations	Groups for Paris and district, Nantes, Marseilles
Fédérations: single trade	Champagne Iron and Steel Committee

---

[26] ILO, *Freedom of Association*, II, 104. See also Archibald J. Wolfe, *Commercial Organizations in France* (Special Agents Series, No. 98, U.S. Dept. of Commerce, Washington, D.C., 1915), and "Employers' Organisations in France," *International Labour Review*, July, 1929.

Classification	Examples
intertrade	
(a) Regional federations of local associations in the region	Lyons Federation of Industrial Associations
(b) Regional federations of industrial and commercial unions in the region	Gironde Economic Federation of Employers' associations
Confédérations	Confederation of Commercial and Industrial Groups of France [27]

In addition to these there are several other groupings of specialized employer interests which are difficult to classify. Such for example are the regional organizations like the Industrial Societies of Amiens, Elbeuf, Lille, Nancy, Alsace, Reims, Mulhouse, Roubaix, whose "special aim . . . is to increase efficiency," and the "Regional Committees of the National Association for Economic Expansion." Analogous national organizations are the Union of Industrial Societies of France, which holds a biennial congress but has no permanent secretariat, and the National Association for Economic Expansion. There are also many different types of technical and semitechnical bodies centered around business interests which are too numerous and too difficult to classify for inclusion here.[28]

The term "Federation" is quite commonly used loosely to apply to all these groups except the Comptoirs and the national Confederations. They

are not all organized in the same way; their internal organization depends on and to some extent indicates their strength. But they all approximate more or less to the same type. In all cases there are the standard organs, a general meeting delegating very wide powers to a managing council. In the case of federations and in the larger associations, where the members belong to different specialized branches within a single manufacturing group, autonomous sections with their own officers and independent activities are formed within the federation or association in the general scheme of organization. Thus the

---

[27] This is the central headquarters of the industrial and commercial federations in existence since the war, while the Federation of Regional Associations "includes regional organizations of all kinds, but especially those of the type described as 'industrial, commercial, and agricultural associations.'" "Employers' Organisations in France."

[28] E. g., Central Interprofessional Committee of Apprenticeship, and the various committees concerned with technical and managerial problems of rationalization.

Union of Employers' Associations of the Textile Industries comprises cotton, linen, wool, silk, and jute sections; the General Association of Metal Founders comprises four sections for steel, copper and bronze, aluminium, and malleable iron; the Association of Engineering Industries is divided into 33 trade sections. In this case the groups tend to concern themselves only with technical and economic questions, while the federation attends to labor questions and social and financial problems.[29]

In addition, the leading federations are grouped in special committees for study of various questions such as apprenticeship, labor, tariffs, prices, and so forth. Continuity is secured by permanent secretariats, sometimes equipped with considerable staff assistance. In some cases a great deal of detailed information is collected and made available to members. The leading associations all have their own regular publications.[30]

Before returning to the Group arrangement under the CGPF, it may help to give some better idea of the scope and functioning of this elaborate meshwork of employer organizations to follow the International Labor Office's description of a prominent "specimen organization," the Iron Works Committee (Comité des Forges) and its creation, the Union of Metal and Mining Industries:

The committee has its headquarters in Paris at 7 Rue de Madrid; it is managed by a board of 23 active members consisting of a president, three vice-presidents, a treasurer, and 18 other members; there are also 6 honorary members. All manufacturers belonging to the industry may belong to the organization, and likewise establishments in foreign countries which have tariff agreements with France. Contributions are in proportion to gross tonnage or the number of workers employed. Each member has as many votes as the number of minimum contributions to which his contribution is equivalent up to a maximum of 20. The number of members was 281 in 1921; and is now 260 (149 employing less than 100 workers, 70 employing from 100 to 2,000, 41 employing a total of 280,000 workers).

. . . the Iron Works Committee . . . was largely instrumental in founding the Union of Metal and Mining Industries. The Union, which is higher up the scale than the Iron Works Committee in the general scheme of organizations, is composed, as often happens in em-

29 "Employers' Organisations in France."
30 "In 1920 there were, according to the Ministry of Labour, 303 publications issued by employers' associations and 45 by their federations." *Ibid.*

ployers' federations, of both national and regional associations. It includes 58 national associations for separate trades and 59 regional associations. As a union of National associations, its task is to co-ordinate their work in social and financial questions. As a union of regional associations, it endeavors to make sure that local solutions do not bring about conflicts between the interests of different areas.

Section 2 of the Rules of the Union defines its aims as follows:

The aims of the Union are:

(a) to study social, labor, and financial questions of general interest to the industries represented by the affiliated regional associations, and to follow the application of measures relating thereto;

(b) to determine the course of action to be followed in regard to these questions by the affiliated regional associations;

(c) to take part in the administration and management of social organizations to whose establishment it has contributed, and when they become autonomous, to offer them support.

(d) to represent the affiliated regional associations whenever combined action in these matters becomes necessary.

The Union may also, in accordance with the conditions laid down in section 11 below, examine questions of a technical, economic, or vocational nature over which divergences of interest might arise between affiliated regional associations, and endeavor to establish an agreement between them in this respect.

When an agreement has been reached, the Union may see that it is carried out, and, if necessary, may sustain its conclusions before the public authorities.

In addition to its year book, the Union publishes a monthly review dealing with social, labor, and financial questions, containing as a rule articles under the following headings: (1) social progress in France; (2) social progress abroad; (3) international labor legislation; (4) financial questions; (5) official documents; (6) Parliamentary business; (7) scientific management.

To this varied programme a task of conciliation is added by section 11 of the Rules. This interesting provision runs as follows:

The Board of Management of the Union . . . may, when it thinks necessary, appoint committees formed of persons belonging to the affiliated regional associations, and even of persons who do not belong to the Union but are well known to have special knowledge, to study these questions and report upon them.

It may also, either on its own initiative or on that of the regional associations affected, or of a group to represent them, take cognizance of all questions upon which it would seem desirable, from the point of view of the general interest, that an agreement should be reached between the industries belonging to the Union whose interests clash in respect of such questions. In these cases, the Board of Management shall use its best efforts to promote agreement, and may, if requested by the parties concerned, act as conciliator.

In 1926 the Union had about 7,000 members, employing 800,000 workers (6,000 with less than 100 workers, 1,000 with less than 2,000, 54 with more than 2,000).

Various social institutions have been founded under its auspices, such as the regional compensation funds for family allowances, the Building Credit Fund, the Cheap Housing Office, and the Anti-Tuberculosis Association. Few employers' federations in France have reached such a high degree of organization.[31]

Since the ILO Report was written, a considerable number of associations have approximated or exceeded the level of organization described in the above.

All these various associations were then brought together in the CGPF system of Groups. Membership in the groups, consequently, was made up entirely of associations, and not of firms or individuals. As constituted at the time of the Matignon agreement (1936), "each group is administered by a Committee of Direction, elected each year by the General Assembly of the Groups. . . . The Committee of Direction of each Group names each year its Bureau, composed, at the minimum, of a president, two vice-presidents, a treasurer and a secretary." [32] Except for the rule that each Group must have the appropriate machinery of the General Assembly meeting at least once a year, as well as a Committee of Direction charged with full authority to make decisions between Assembly dates, and a Central Office or Bureau, vested with duties of execution, the governing Statutes of the CGPF considered each Group as an entirely autonomous, self-sufficient, and self-governing body. It was free to admit any organization to membership it chose (provided it fell into the right category), study and deliberate on any subject or line of policy, and take any action it wished, which related to its own industry and trade and which did not contravene stated policies of the CGPF as a whole.

Each Committee of Direction elected its own officers. The presidents of the several committees (28 in number at the time of the Matignon agreement) then made up the Central Council of the Confédération générale de la Production Française. This Central

31 *Ibid.*
32 "Statuts Primitifs de la Confédération Générale de la Production Française," reproduced as an Appendix by Duchemin, *Organization syndicale,* pp. 279–84.

Council, the supreme governing and policy-forming body of the CGPF, in turn elected its own officers, consisting of a president, five vice-presidents, a treasurer and two secretaries. It is interesting to note that this election took place after the annual General Assembly of the CGPF, and that the resulting Bureau or Central Administration was then enabled to speak on behalf of the CGPF as a whole. When to this fact is added the additional rule that the General Assembly of the CGPF was made up of (1) four delegates (each with an alternate), elected by each Group one month prior to the General Assembly meeting, plus (2) the members of the existing Central Council—a total, for 28 Groups, of 140 persons, or, including "alternates," of 252 persons at the most—it can be seen how easily power could drift into the hands of a relatively small, compact group of determined men.

For all practical purposes, it appears that the Central Administration really was the CGPF. It drew up all the agendas, framed the subject matter for discussion and debate, managed its system of subcommittees, acted as go-between for all the various Groups, contracted agreements and alliances with other central associations and federations of employers with which the CGPF had mutual interests,[33] represented the CGPF before governmental committees either as lobbyists or appointed members, managed all CGPF finances, and submitted all proposals for change and reorganization. The composition of the Group representatives, and of the governing officers lends further support to this view. For the most part a single leading individual, his deputy, or a small coterie of closely related individuals with closely related corporate affiliations dominated the several Groups.[34] Such continuity of control in the

[33] E. g., Union des intérêts économiques and the Confédération des groupes commerciaux et industriels de France.

[34] Almost continuously from the beginning of the CGPF, M. Duchemin has represented the Chemical Industries, Group VIII, F. de Wendel, Group X, and Baron Petiet, Group XVI. Interests represented by Duchemin centered in the Etablissements Kuhlmann (capital stock of Fr. 316,500,000; assets, end of 1937, of Fr. 886,534,-853), which is the chemical trust (synthetic nitrates and other artificial fertilizers, sulphuric and nitric acids, artificial silk, coal-tar dyes, and pharmaceutical and photographic supplies), and the Compagnie des Mines d'Anzin (capital stock of Fr. 222,-500,000; assets, end of 1937, of Fr. 1,129,819,559), a coal and coke by-products firm. Assets of the Kuhlmann concern included Fr. 139 million in participations in more than twenty chemical and related firms. Duchemin held an official position in at least eight of these as well as in the Chemin de Fer du Nord, the Banque de Commerce Extérieur, Crédit Algérien, and the Union Industrielle de Crédit. De Wendel

Groups promoted similar continuity in the control of the Central Administration. Prior to 1936 the CGPF had but two presidents, M. Darcy from 1919 to 1925 and M. Duchemin from 1925 to 1936.

How much real power, however, did the pre-Matignon CGPF actually have? Opinions vary. The International Labor Office closes its sketch of the organization with the somewhat equivocal generalization, "In practice . . . the General Confederation of Production is, beyond doubt, only a permanent meeting place for the heads of different federations; its power is ephemeral, inasmuch as it depends on their consent, and yet considerable, if, by the exchange of views, it brings about unanimity between them." [35]

The latter object has dominated the CGPF from its beginning, as is well shown by that remarkable series of addresses given by M. Duchemin before its annual meetings from 1925 on. On the one hand, it was to bring about unity of points of view, unity of interests, unity of pressure, and unity of purposes amongst employer and business groups in the country in general. And on the other, it was to collaborate with the government in all things touching upon the vast medley of interests which its organizational dragnet covered.

How effectively the CGPF accomplished these objectives is extremely difficult to say. Its initial efforts in the promotion of employer unity led to the establishment of a series of more or less purely study and discussion groups such as the Economic Commission for the study of general economic questions, the Commission on Social Questions for the study of labor-employer relations, and the Commission for the Scientific Organization of Labor (primarily "scientific management").

---

interests spread out from the two iron and steel producing firms of Les Petits-Fils de F. de Wendel (capital stock of Fr. 117,180,000) and De Wendel et Cie (capital stock of Fr. 80,000,000). In 1938, Francois, Humbert and Maurice de Wendel held official positions in sixteen other companies, including the Banque de Union Parisienne, Suez, Peñarroya, the Union des Mines, several coal-mining companies, two tin companies, other iron and steel manufacturing companies, insurance companies, etc. Baron Petiet was president of the Union des Consummateurs de Produits Métallurgiques et Industriels (capital stock of Fr. 105,000,000) and of Equipment Electrique des Véhicules (capital stock of Fr. 13,000,000) and was vice-president of Société Métallurgique de la Bonneville (capital stock of Fr. 10,000,000). In each case the companies mentioned, or companies associated with them, dominate the more powerful trade associations, syndicats, comptoirs, federations, and confederations in the industry which, in turn, dominate the CGPF Group of which they are members.

[35] Wolfe, "Employers' Organisations in France."

Alongside these Commissions, it founded autonomous organizations with which it continued to work in intimate contact such as:

The Central Interprofessional Committee on Apprenticeship
The Industrial Hygiene Association
The Central Committee on Family Allowances
The Central Committee on Social Insurance
The Central Committee for Fiscal Study and Protection.[36]

The CGPF has sought to work with all special-interest or special-function business associations whose purposes dovetail at some point or other with its own objects. Thus it has coöperated with the National Association for Economic Expansion, "which gives as its object the increase of French export," and with the Association of Industry and Agriculture, which is especially interested "in problems of national tariff protection for industry and agriculture." It has established a special body called the Committee for Conciliation and Arbitration, charged with eliminating, wherever possible, conflicts between business interests, and with a view to forestalling intervention by public authorities.[37]

As for relations with the government, the CGPF from the outset followed a two-fold policy. On the one hand it asked for complete self-government, meaning by this a clear-cut circumscription of governmental and private business spheres of authority, with the government giving business any aid it might need, but, so far as control was concerned, following a policy of complete and unequivocal hands off. On the other hand, it wanted the right to participate directly in all governmental action affecting the interests of its members at any point, and freely importuned—*demanded* is perhaps the better word—governmental aid and assistance whenever such support could be turned to good business account.

A writer in the widely circulated *Revue des Deux Mondes* [38] speaks of "the participation of the professional groups [meaning trade and employers' associations] in the management of the state" in these words:

A remarkable characteristic of the professional groups is their tendency to intervene in the management of public affairs wherever social and

---

86 Duchemin, *op. cit.*, p. 8.   87 *Idem.*
38 Antoine de Tarle, "L'Organisation professionelle patronale en France," *Revue des Deux Mondes*, March, 1925, pp. 177–96.

economic questions are concerned. The employer justifies his social role: does not the responsibility of insuring the means of existence of the nation rest upon him? We have told in these pages [*Revue des Deux Mondes,* February 15, 1924] in what manner the great German associations insisted on terms which would bring about the decay of the State in Germany. It is not the same in France; the industrial groups are not looking for a substitute for public authority; they demand the right to collaborate on questions which are in their sphere. The principle has been granted. The constitutional bill on the Chambers of Commerce provides that they be consulted and that they give their advice on these questions. By a circular dated February 1, 1923, the Minister of Commerce confirmed the appeal which he had addressed to them in 1919, and invited them to get together with the Minister in order to facilitate the consultations which the Minister counted on having with them on economic questions.[39]

Thus organized, business was prepared to "intervene," in the words of M. Duchemin, in the affairs of government on a comprehensive scale.

Wherever a matter has come up dealing with legislation on social insurance, accidents in work or occupational diseases . . . of protection or the conservation of water resources . . . of proposed legislation dealing with patents and trade marks, of consular elections, the protection of savings, or the reform of the Law of 1867 dealing with Corporations, upon all these questions the Confederation of Employers has taken a position and has intervened with the proper public authorities and Ministerial Departments, or with Commissions of the two Chambers.[40]

Examples were offered of "intervention" dealing with tariff questions. It participated in all discussions of tariff truces, including, on one occasion the drafting of a "Memorandum to the French Government at the Second Conference for Concerted Economic Action." On another occasion it participated in the World Economic Conference at London. It collaborated with the government in negotiations dealing with and the organization of the Franco-German Economic Commission. Similarly the CGPF took active part in various committees, conventions, and negotiations

---

[39] Such "collaboration between the Government and industrialists and merchants," De Tarle continues, "is nothing new. . . . Louis XIV created the *Conseil du commerce* at the instigation of Colbert . . . in 1882, this Council having disappeared for almost a century, was re-established under the name of *Conseil superieur de l'industrie et du commerce.*"

[40] Duchemin, *op. cit.,* p. 6.

with the government dealing with import licensing, control of foreign exchange, fiscal and taxation problems, and the like.

On nearly all matters where the government has sought authoritative employer representation on governmental committees, the CGPF was designated as the proper agency. Examples are found in its participation in the work of such governmentally sponsored bodies as the following:

> The National Economic Council
> The National Council of Handicrafts
> The Higher Council on Educational Methods
> The Higher Commission on Occupational Diseases
> The Industrial Hygienic Commission
> The Commission on Engineering Awards.

In addition to these and other direct participation in governmental activities, the CGPF was the French employer representative at the International Labor Office, and it was spokesman for French industry at the International Economic Conference in 1927, the International Committee of Economic Experts in 1931, and the Lausanne Conference in 1932, and on other similar occasions. At all the meetings of the various national and regional Chambers of Commerce, the meetings of the International Chamber of Commerce, and meetings or conferences held by other collusively organized business groups the CGPF, its special delegates, or leading figures in its various Groups have actively participated.

Leading industrial personages, accustomed to thinking in terms of the power and achievements of the vast industrial properties at their immediate command, have spoken in glowing terms of these activities and of achievements wrought through them. Thus M. Duchemin, summarizing the evolution of the CGPF to its commanding position in 1936, quotes, in eulogy to his organization, the authoritative writer on French business and industrial life, M. de Lavergne:

In the strength of its 4000 syndicates, brought together in 27 Groups,[41] and spread over the whole of France, it coordinates and multiplies their efforts and can undertake, whenever it raises its voice, to formulate the viewpoint of the whole of the economic forces of the country. Confident

---

[41] Since 1929 one Group had, apparently, either been dropped or merged with some other Group.

in the energy of which the employers have always given proof and in the good sense of the workers of all classes and ranks, it throws its power, efficaciously, behind the individual efforts of all who are concerned to see France maintain the eminent place in the commercial and industrial activities which assures its position in the markets of the world. To the extent that it expands its efforts, in the measure that it promotes the material unity essential to its aims, it will render the greatest service to the industry and commerce of France and at the same time to the entire nation.[42]

But in the same year in which these expansive words were spoken, there occurred the threat of a general strike sweeping over the entire country, and the Popular Front, temporarily commanded by the poetic Premier Blum,[43] was enabled to inflict on the Confédération Générale de la Production Française its first serious setback, the famous Matignon Agreement—a setback so serious that it brought about the downfall of M. Duchemin, forced a complete reorganization of the Confederation, and realigned the configuration of inner command as it was to remain until internally disunited, republican France collapsed under the thunderous assault of the Nazi legions in the spring of 1940.

THE MATIGNON AGREEMENT AND ITS AFTERMATH

The Matignon Agreement was signed on June 7, 1936, between representatives of the Confédération Générale de la Production Française and the Confédération Générale du Travail (General Confederation of Labor—CGT).[44] Premier Léon Blum, as spokesman for the government and prime mover in the accord, added his signature to those affixed by the two parties to the compact.

There was nothing particularly striking in the specific provisions of the new agreement. These underwrote for "some millions of French workers the 40-hour working week, increases in pay ranging from 7 to 15 percent, the recognition of the trade unions, collective agreements, holidays with pay, and other social advantages." [45] While such gains were important, the principles underlying them

---

[42] Duchemin, op. cit., p. 11.

[43] Of course we do not mean to say that Blum's economic, political, and legal output are of no consequence.

[44] The CGT occupied in that year a position roughly analogous to the A.F. of L. in the United States, the General Federation of British Trade Unions in England, and the ADGB (Allgemeine Deutsche Gewerkschafts-Bund) in pre-Nazi Germany.

[45] International Labour Office, Yearbook, 1936–37, p. 11.

had long been accepted in many countries abroad, and in several French industries the specific changes involved but relatively slight departures from previous practices.

Of much greater importance is the fact that it was among the first [46] compacts signed in any major capitalistic (non-Fascist) country between representatives of employers and labor empowered to speak for their respective interests on a nation-wide basis. In concluding the agreement M. Duchemin and his associates [47] acted on behalf of French employers as a whole, and M. Jouhaux and his co-signers [48] served as *de facto* representatives of practically all French organized labor. No better demonstration than this could be given of the extent to which the CGPF had come to serve as supreme coördinator, synthesizer, and organizer of French business interests—a level fully equal to that of the Confédération Générale du Travail in the labor field.

But of principal importance in the present connection, is the fact that the Agreement, coming as it did in the heyday of the Popular Front movement and in the face of an unusually critical situation abroad, brought as an aftermath a complete shake-up in the CGPF. Forces, apparently led by the De Wendel [49] and Rothschild [50] interests, and long opposed to the policies of M. Duchemin in the labor relations fields, definitely gained the upper hand.[51] At an Extraordinary General Assembly, called on an emergency basis to meet in August, 1936, the association's name was changed from Confédération Générale de la Production Française to Confédération Générale du Patronat Français (General Confederation

[46] It was preceded in Germany by the Stinnes-Legier agreement (Zentralarbeitsgemeinschaft) of Nov. 15, 1918. The Confederation of Catholic Labor Unions endorsed the agreement enthusiastically.

[47] See pp. 145–49.

[48] While Jouhaux signed for the CGT, his signature was held by the Blum government generally valid for all French employees.

[49] See note 34 above.

[50] Railroads, insurance, and mining constituted the principal Rothschild holdings. Seven members of the family were on the board of directors of the Chemin de Fer du Nord (capital stock of Fr. 231,875,000; assets of Fr. 18,230,692,000) in 1937. Directorships in five other railroads, four insurance companies, and two mining concerns (one of the latter being the famous Spanish Peñarroya Company, in which the De Wendel, the Crédit Lyonnais, and the Kuhlmann interests were likewise represented) were also held within the family.

[51] It has been said that the shake-up in the CGPF was the consequence of the organization's failure to exert pressure on the Blum government in order to prevent the Matignon agreement and to achieve prosecution of the sit-down strikers.

of French Employers). A new constitution was drawn up, a new president elected, and a greatly increased range of influence made possible through extension of membership to include all fields of employer interests in trade, commerce, finance, and transport, as well as those of industry and manufacturing.

Various articles, discussions, resolutions, memorials, and books have fully set forth the position taken by the De Wendel-led groups. The demands of the CGT, they held, were clearly revolutionary and communistic. The concessions granted under the agreement were only taken by labor as evidence of employer weakness, and would necessarily give rise to even greater and more "exaggerated demands" on the part of the CGT. A militant employer body, the Committee of Foresight and Social Action (Comité de Prévoyance et d'Action Sociale), cited CGT sources of information as proof that the real objectives had not been stated in the Matignon Agreement at all.[52]

Marcel Roy was quoted from an article in *Syndicats*, the weekly publication of the CGT (edited by M. Belin, Secretary of the CGT and one of the CGT signers of the Matignon pact and subsequently Vichy minister of labor), as saying that since employer interests called for preservation of "the most despotic management of production" then "our interest demands that more and more the worker be called to take his place, which consists in guiding, and organizing production. . . . All good militant reasons favor worker control."[53] From the CGT "Guide for the Shop Delegate,"[54] it was found that the delegate had been advised "more and more to know the conditions of work and output so that workers' control in production might be really effective." Another

[52] *Le Rôle exact des délégués,* published by the Comité de Prévoyance et d'Action Sociale, Paris, 1937. In accounting for the evolution of French monopoly controls, and the attitude in social and political matters of organized French employer groups, I have purposely eliminated the Social Catholic Program, which has been briefly summarized in Chapter II. At certain stages this movement played a very important, perhaps even decisive role (as, e. g., in restraining French aid to the Spanish Loyalists—one of the most significant turning points in modern European history). But to go far into these antecedents would lead too far afield. See, however, Moon, *The Labor Problem and the Social Catholic Movement in France.*

[53] Quoted from *Syndicats,* April 15, 1937.

[54] Shop delegates function more or less as shop stewards in American trade unions —they are elected by and represent the men in the shop. But whether or not they were also representatives of the union has been a point of bitter dispute.

source was cited as saying that "worker control is the central point in the coming struggle."

This, the Comité found, came out to "bolshevism." Worker control in the factory, they said, would only be followed, as Lenin showed in 1917 when he "started the revolution," by "complete expropriation of industry for the profit of the state." The CGT was "becoming totalitarian under the influence of Communist elements." [55] Every single gain made by the CGT would serve only to add fuel to its revolutionary fires.[56]

The CGT, in short, was encroaching upon "liberty" and "freedom," and a situation had arisen in which "the employer, the ranks of authority, and the independent trade unions [57] must unite and fight against dictatorship, violence, attacks on the liberty of labor and thought, and injuries to the principle of ownership." And the first step towards a real "drawing together of employers and workers" was the "development and completion of employer organization." [58] The battle cry became, in the words of the new president, M. Gignoux, first, "employers be employers," and then "rally around your professional syndicate . . . there must be no more isolation." Consider, he argued, the crucial significance of the stakes: "Employers, you are not only responsible for your own concerns but for those of your colleagues and to those to whom you delegate a part of your authority. . . . You are the leaders: you have charge not only of men but of souls." [59]

The new point of departure, in other words, was to emphasize the totalitarian angle of social and economic issues. Fundamental interests were now clearly at stake. The object had now become fully to coördinate the whole of the French business system into a coherent, cohesive, and neatly integrated mechanism which might be centrally directed in defense of the underlying tenets and in protection of the institutional fabric of capitalism per se.

The first step was to expand the membership base so as to include

[55] *Syndicats*, April 15, 1937.

[56] *La Journée Industrielle*, April 2, 1937, complained that "Whereas when on June 7, increases of salary from 7 to 15 per cent had been considered, the new schedules of minimum salaries entered in the agreements have aggravated costs passing 25 per cent and even in certain cases reaching 50 per cent."

[57] "Independent trade unions" mean both non-CGT and company unions.

[58] C. J. Gignoux, *Patrons, soyez des patrons!* (Paris, 1937).

[59] *Ibid.* The situation, many felt, was practically identical with that which Italian industry faced in the early twenties at the time of Mussolini's march on Rome.

all branches and phases of French business, large or small, national or local, domestic or foreign. The new arrangement called for an enlarged series of thirty-five Groups, each in turn subdivided into a series of special industrial and trade categories. The grouping in the main follows vertical lines, that is, each group brings together all stages of production and distribution from raw materials and on through to the ultimate consumer.

Four types of organizations may belong to the Groups: (1) Professional (Branche professionelle),[60] (2) Interprofessional regional (Branche interprofessionelle régionale), (3) Technical (Organismes techniques), and (4) Miscellaneous (Associations adhérentes). The Professional organizations might include (a) "National professional Confederations which bring together by virtue of their close affinities Federations, Syndicates or Associations," (b) "National professional Federations which group together Associations or Syndicates, national or local, of a like professional nature," and (c) "National professional or regional syndicates." The Interprofessional regional type may be made up of Interregional Associations or Federations of such associations. It may also include any type of business organization found in any locality or region, and may even include isolated individual firms. The Technical bodies are those which are especially set up for purposes of study or promotion of any important topic of special group interest—"fiscal, social, economic, tariffs, foreign trade, and other questions." The Miscellaneous category is a catchall for every conceivable type of employer or business association not falling under any of the previous classifications.[61]

The CGPF was thus to determine the eligibility of each association to each group, reserving the right on the grant of admission to demand the submission of information, business, economic, or of any other kind, relevant to the purposes of the CGPF, and requiring of every single association that it agree "to pursue its activities according to directives laid down by the CGPF." [62]

---

[60] As previously indicated, the term "professional" means business grouping by industrial, trade, or occupational lines. It does not mean the "professions" in the English and American sense of the term.

[61] Duchemin, *op. cit.*, p. 297, "Statuts de la Confédération Générale du Patronat Français," adopted by the General Assembly, at meetings held on March 18 and April 26, 1938.

[62] *Idem.*

This latter clause appears only in the 1938 *Statuts,* and is in sharp contrast with the *Statuts* of the Confédération Générale de la Production Française. While heavy emphasis had been laid on the autonomous nature of each Group's activities, the new *Statuts* only at one place makes incidental reference to the old principle. With that minor concession,[63] the right and power of the central administration over member groups and their subsidiary bodies is emphasized at every turn and point.

The change represents a definite authoritarian trend, further reinforced by adjustments which must make possible a much greater centralization of power in the hands of organized business associations. Each Group now (prior to Nazi occupation) has its own permanent headquarters in Paris. Some of the Groups are equipped with large and efficient staffs. In a few cases headquarters appear to be identified with the offices of more powerful trade associations—a practice similar to that which became so widespread in America under the NRA Code procedure.

The Central Council under the new arrangement is made up primarily of delegates from the constituent associations,[64] not of the Groups as previously. The number of delegates each constituent body may designate is, in turn, determined by the Central Council. The Annual Assembly is chosen in the same way, the number of delegates sent by each association being four times the number allowed as members of the Council.

The Annual Assembly appears to be mainly a general forum for discussion, by Group delegates, for the giving of announcements by the CGPF administration, and for the ratification of budgets, policies, and plans laid down in the agenda. Real power resides in the hands of the Central Administration (*Bureau*) of the CGPF. This body is chosen from the members of the Council shortly after the adjournment of the Annual Assembly, and is made up of the president, one or more vice-presidents, a treasurer, two secretaries, honorary president, and delegates sent by the constituent associations of the several Groups.[65]

63 "Article 12. *Syndical Discipline:* The maximum autonomy is to be permitted to each constitutive organization." *Ibid.,* p. 302.

64 "Article 11, paragraph 2; Each group of the professional divisions sends to the Central Administration two delegates; whenever the branch of industry or commerce permits, one of the two delegates should be chosen from amongst the small or medium sized industrialists or traders." *Ibid.,* p. 300.

65 *Ibid.,* p. 302.

While this is a much larger body than under the previous arrangement, an unusual amount of power is vested in the president and the various special committees which he is authorized to appoint at will. In addition he has sole power to act in the name of the CGPF (except in money matters, where he shares the power with the treasurer). Upon joining the CGPF, all organizations must agree "to submit to the President of the CGPF, prior to the making of any definite decision, all questions which involve a fundamental principle relating to the economy as a whole." [66] The President and Council are granted authority to determine the terms and conditions under which such disputes or problems should be submitted, and are authorized to command at any time of any constituent association, or of any company or enterprise belonging to any member association, "all statistical information of a general nature, and, more particularly, so far as possible all round figures on invested capital, the volume of business turnover, and the number of paid employees." [67]

THE LOCATION OF POWER

Like most central organizations of its genre, the CGPF is a tissue of compromises yielded by conflicting groups. It will not do, however, to dismiss its activities as unimportant on that account. For despite the somewhat shadowy character of its substance, and the doubtful quality of its authority, there is clear evidence of growth in power and influence along lines similar to those outlined for like organizations in other major industrial countries.

1. At the bottom there has been steady and cumulative pressure to expand the organizational network so as to include all business interests in the whole of France, regardless of the scale on which the individual enterprise might operate, and irrespective of such things as legal status, trade or occupational lines, nature and location of markets, and so on. The 1936 reorganization of the CGPF and the outbreak of the Second World War lent increasing emphasis to this tendency towards universal, all-inclusive organization of French business enterprise.

2. Similarly, French business organization has shown a growing tendency to federate, coördinate, unify, simplify, eliminate duplication and overlapping, and to centralize direction in the determi-

[66] *Idem.*   [67] *Ibid.*, p. 300.

nation of leading policies in "roof" or "peak" associations or "confederations" of associations. The CGPF represents the most complete expression of this tendency to date. Its evolution has been paralleled by four complementary trends: (a) all local and regional trade or occupational ("professional") associations are brought into national federations; (b) in each locality, municipality, or other regional area, all local associations are brought together into local federations or confederations; (c) national associations or federations are brought together in technologically or organizationally interrelated "Groups"; and (d) each association, or federation, or "Group," or confederation tends to become vertical, that is, to include all associations from the production through the financing and distribution phases.

3. The policies upon which agreement is sought relate increasingly to issues having to do with the maintenance and defense of capitalistic institutions per se. In particular this means (a) a common front against organized labor, (b) promotion of a policy of "self-government in industry" [68] and (c) demands for the right actively to capture the power, to formally manipulate, and to interfere directly in the shaping up of governmental policy relating to every single phase of the economic, social, and political interests of organized business.

4. The looser and more "shadowy" associations shade imperceptibly into the more powerful, and these in turn into cartel, cartel-like, and quasi-cartel monopoly-oriented groupings. Practically all of the leading French Associations and Federations exercise to some extent or other one or all of the usual type of cartel functions.[69]

5. The guiding hands in this proliferating and power-congealing meshwork of French business organization seem to reach out from the heavy industries and finance. In the heavy industries the Comité des forges has played a dominating role, and in finance the giant banking house, Crédit Lyonnais. The policies which have in the end won out, and the position which has been finally taken on

---

[68] The spokesmen for the CGPF and similar groups constantly use this expression. See, e. g., the annual speeches of M. Duchemin, in his *Organisation syndicale.*

[69] See Jacques Lapergue, *Les Syndicats de producteurs en France* (Paris, 1925), and, especially, Pierre Bezard-Falgas, *Les Syndicats patronaux de l'industrie métallurgique en France* (Paris, 1922), particularly pp. 176–224 and 386–403.

the leading issues that have come to the fore with and following the Matigon Agreement, are those which these two groups—after many compromises—have favored.

Beyond this point it is extremely difficult to go, especially in the confused state of affairs one finds in contemporary France. It is, however, perhaps worth pointing out that behind the scenes in the evolution of the CGPF has gone on several long, and at times bitter, struggles, the two most important of which appear at present to have been resolved as follows:

Attitude toward labor.—As pointed out above, M. Duchemin represented interests which had long taken a more or less conciliatory attitude toward union labor. He appears, in this report, to have followed in the steps of M. Clémentel, Minister of Commerce, who called the CGPF into being in 1919. In this attitude he represented a policy for France quite similar to that adopted by Hugo Stinnes and Walther Rathenau in postwar Germany. Behind him one finds a vast and wide-ranging series of industrial, financial, transport, commercial, and miscellaneous enterprises. Most important of these were the Crédit Lyonnais,[70] the heavy chemicals Kuhlmann group,[71] the Gillet group,[72] the Lyon group,[73] and the Schneider group.[74]

Opposed to this vast assembly of gigantic business interests—sometimes referred to collectively as the "Gallican" group—were arrayed particularly the sprawling economic empires of the De Wendel [75] and Rothschild groups.[76] These had long been bitterly antiunion on all labor matters, and had consistently opposed Duchemin in his policy of reconciliation. Following Matignon, this

[70] Paid-in capital, Fr. 400 million; assets (1938) of Fr. 14,480 million; dividends, 1928–38 inclusive, 20 percent per annum.

[71] See footnote 34, above.

[72] Gillet-Thaon (laundry, dyeworks, rayon, mechanical construction, etc.). A holding company of Fr. 250 million capital stock.

[73] The Lyon group seems to have been a group of industrialists very closely related to and accepting the leadership of the Crédit Lyonnais.

[74] Schneider (Creusot), capital stock of Fr. 100 million; produces iron, steel and armaments.

[75] The De Wendel group, dominated by one of the oldest families in French industrial history (see Louis Launay, *De Wendel*, Vaucresson, 1938), is (was?) probably the most powerful single industrial aggregation in contemporary France. Control has been exercised mostly through two closely held holding companies. The Comité des Forges has been pretty much the mouthpiece of the De Wendel interests since its beginning.

[76] See footnote 47.

group definitely gained the upper hand, and down to the outbreak of the war appear to have won over the bulk of organized French business to their point of view.

Attitude toward rapprochement with Germany.—Conversely, the interests centered around Duchemin were in favor of close coöperation with Germany. The ramifications of the Crédit Lyonnais were scattered over the entire European continent.[77] But its most important tie with Germany was through the Kuhlmann and Gillet groups, which were, in turn, closely tied up with the huge German chemical trust, I.G. Farbenindustrie A.G. The Crédit Lyonnais was itself closely tied up with Swiss enterprises in turn largely dependent on, if not controlled by, the Deutsche Bank, and A.E.G. (Allgemeine Electrizitäts Gesellschaft—German General Electric Co.). Duchemin himself was a member of the Franco-German Committee—which seems to trace back to Hugo Stinnes—and in this capacity worked in close coöperation with Herr von Stauss of the Deutsche Bank. Schneider-Creusot was heavily interested in the Skoda works until shortly before the Munich affair, and as a heavy armament producer, seems to have worked in close coöperation with the Krupp interests.

The De Wendel and Rothschild interests, contrariwise, seem to have been closely tied up with British finance and heavy industry—notably Vickers (armaments). With Matignon and the outbreak of war, the De Wendel position seems to have gained ground. But it seems equally clear that with the recent military collapse, De Wendel interests have gone over wholesale to the Duchemin position. The Rothschild interests, on the other hand, being primarily Jewish controlled, have been largely liquidated.

The net result is that the De Wendel position on labor and the Duchemin-Crédit lyonnais position on coöperation with Germany have been fused. The final result, still in process of being worked out in detail, appears to be the equivalent of a transformation of the setup of the CGPF into the economic machinery for the French version of the corporate state.[78] But under the conditions of Ger-

[77] See Liefmann, *Beteiligunge und Finanzierungs Gesellschaften.*
[78] With the outbreak of the war M. Gignoux, who appears to have been valuable to De Wendel and the Comité des forges primarily as a journalist and promoter, was displaced, *de facto*, by Baron Petiet, an active member of the CGPF since its formation in 1919. Baron Petiet's principal private connection was with the Union

man conquest this means first that German industrial and business interests are to dictate (if not directly to control through stock ownership) [79] the terms of economic collaboration to their former French allies, and second, that France as a whole is to become a tributary (primarily agricultural) province in the German-controlled "New order in Europe."

On this showing French employers have cast off French political and French labor controls only to accept the much more rigorous and exacting German imperial domination.

---

des consommateurs de produits métallurgiques, a sort of half-cartel, half holding-company agglomeration of concerns producing airplanes, automobiles, trucks, and other types of machinery. There is some reason for believing that Baron Petiet was acceptable to both groups.

[79] It was been rumored that the daily occupation assessment of Fr. 400,000,000 (recently reported to have been reduced to Fr. 300,000,000) is in excess of German occupation requirements by somewhere between Fr. 275,000,000 and Fr. 300,000,000 (presumably reduced by the change referred to above), and that the balance is being invested by German authorities in the purchase of controlling shares in major French industrial, commercial, shipping, railroad and financial enterprises. These are then, apparently, being disposed of through sale to German concerns.

Part II

MANUFACTURING PEAK ASSOCIA-TIONS WITHIN THE LIBERAL-CAPITALIST SCHEME

Chapter V

BRITAIN'S "FEUDALISTIC SYSTEM OF CARTEL CONTROLS"

Even in England the first world war signalized a definite retreat from the theory and practice of classical norms. The peaceful interlude which followed consolidated the changed position. And the Second World War has turned retreat into rout. It is difficult to see in contemporary schemes of British war control—even after making due allowance for emergency factors—more than faint resemblance to the "simple and obvious system" of past times. But, more significant by far, one will scarcely find anything in developments leading up to the new controls which offer the slightest consolation to those who might hope for some future return to competitive and laissez faire "normalcy." For Britain, regardless of the outcome of the current struggle, the old order is doomed. As clearly as elsewhere, centralized policy controlling power in business is in the cards!

It may well be, as a writer in a recent issue of the London *Economist* gloomily suggests, that England is "slipping . . . into a feudalistic system of cartel control," but it can scarcely be claimed that she is or has been doing so "through inadvertence." [1] For, as Keynes, Lucas, Levy, the Liberal and Balfour Reports, and mounting data from other sources have shown, the controls set up under the cloak of wartime emergencies are built on foundations the genesis of which reaches back over many years. Moreover, from Left to Right, and regardless of the configuration of the issues at stake, there remains only a nostalgic hope for a return to the econ-

[1] "The Economic Front," *Economist*, Dec. 9, 1939. See also "The Cartelisation of England," *Economist*, March 18, 1939.

omy which so warmed the heart of John Stuart Mill.[2] Come what may, the old ideal as well as the actuality is "sick unto death." [3]

At the center of the multifarious control networks through which British economy has muddled so close to the brink of disaster, and closely interlinked with a confused jumble of governmental and quasi-governmental control boards, stands the Federation of British Industries. Its history is symptomatic of the forces making over the face of this schoolmistress of "free competition" and preceptress of laissez faire.

GENESIS: THE EBBTIDE OF ECONOMIC ORTHODOXY

The antecedents of the Federation of British Industries are found in concern over the rising power of the trade unions and over the decline of British dominance in overseas trade. The first of these two stimulants was uppermost when, following an informal meeting in London at the Westminster Palace Hotel, November 15, 1898, it was decided to set up the Employers' (or British) Parliamentary Council. The stated objectives were:

To take action with respect to any bills introduced in either house of Parliament, affecting the interests of trade, of free contract and of labor, or with respect to the action of imperial or local authorities affecting in any way the said interests.[4]

The immediate objectives soon became to defeat at all costs the Mines [eight-hour] Bill, which, it was feared, once passed would establish a precedent for extension of the eight-hour heresy to other trades and industries. Typical of the position of the Parliamentary Council for many years was the argument it brought to bear in this crucial struggle. It is noteworthy for its statement of underlying principles:

1. It is not, and ought not to be, the duty or business of Parliament to fix the hours during which adults may work.
2. Although the shortest hours of labor possible in each industry

---

[2] "Every restriction [of competition] is an evil, and every extension of it, even if for the time injuriously affecting some class of labourers, is always an ultimate good." John Stuart Mill, *Principles of Political Economy*, Ashley ed., p. 793.

[3] See the summary of contemporary British opinion given by A. F. Lucas, in his *Industrial Reconstruction and the Control of Competition* (London, 1937), in particular pp. 11–19.

[4] *American Industries*, Jan. 1, 1903.

should be sought by and are beneficial to the employed, such hours of daily labor should be the subject of separate negotiation and arrangement in each industry in each locality, and such arrangements should be arrived at by mutual discussion and understanding between employers and employed.

3. The system of inspectorship necessary for the enforcement of State regulation of labor would be vexatious and intolerable.

4. The function of the State is to protect, and not to restrain, the liberty of the subject, and a legal eight-hour day is an infringement of the liberty of an individual to make his own labor contract.

5. The growing tendency, as evidenced by the divisions on the Mines (eight hour) Bill, to look to the Legislature or Government to supply immediate remedies for all evils, however arising, in the struggle for existence, is of a most dangerous character and destructive of the spirit of sturdy independence which characterises the British nation.

6. Former Acts of Parliament, which were intended to regulate hours of labor, only provoked evasions and resistance on the part of employers and employed.

7. The present eight-hour day laws in thirteen of the United States are a dead letter; not one of them is enforced, or attempted to be enforced.

8. Well-organized workmen have but very rarely lost the gains really acquired by them in the way of reduction of hours of work, and the tendency to the reduction of the normal working day by voluntary effort and negotiations with employers does not appear to have exhausted itself.

9. A distinction must be drawn between an hour of work and an hour of duty.

10. Many workmen prefer longer hours five days of the week in order to obtain a weekly holiday.

11. When Parliament interfered to limit the hours of women and children in factories, both were being taxed beyond their strength, amid surroundings that were not generally as sanitary as they should have been. The hours of labor were much longer than they are now; the education of the children was being neglected; the health and maternity of the women were being injured; and other objectionable features were common. No one, however, can claim that nine or ten hours of work are unhealthful or oppressive.

12. Reductions of hours of labor bear heaviest, not on the employer, not on the man who has money to spend, but on those who cannot stand the increased speed, and are therefore forced to a choice between a lower standard of comfort or an intensity of strain which they cannot bear.

13. If the principle of State interference with working hours is con-

ceded, the Legislature may also seek to control the use of a man's leisure.

14. The logical sequence to State regulation of hours is State regulation of wages.[5]

Over a billion pounds of invested capital was said to be massed behind this denunciation of state interference in the labor contract. But, while it is true that, in the main, efforts of the Parliamentary Council did not go beyond organized lobbying to keep the state out of this field of regulation, it does not follow that its members rejected government aid to themselves on other scores. The famous "Germaniam esse delendam" article of the *Saturday Review*, written in 1897,[6] evoked a diapason of eulogy from organized trade and industrial circles from one end of the United Kingdom to the other. Over the intervening years the theme was to return more frequently and more insistently; the methods used by other countries to promote the economic interests of their nationals both at home and abroad—tariffs, subsidies, subventions, active military intervention in the outlying territories (as in Abyssinia)—must be copied and surpassed if British industry and trade were to survive.

Despite the tanfare of publicity which accompanied its first few meetings, the Parliamentary Council seems to have enjoyed relatively little success. As late as 1915 an American observer found that "A large section of the British industrial world, however, held aloof from the organization of the council and greatly diminished its chances for permanent existence." [7] A similar fate appears to have befallen a parallel attempt, inaugurated in 1905, "to federate manufacturers' organizations or firms in various industries into one association," [8] known as the Manufacturers' Association of Great Britain and established with the object "to stimulate and expand British trade in colonial and foreign markets." [9]

5 *Idem.*

6 Hoffman, *Great Britain and the German Trade Rivalry*, p. 281.

7 Archibald J. Wolfe, *Commercial Organizations in the United Kingdom* (Special Agents Series, No. 102, U.S. Dept. of Commerce, Washington, D.C., 1915), p. 39.

8 *Idem.*

9 The opening paragraph in the preliminary circular argued as follows: "By reason of her immense financial resources, her great shipping facilities, her social and political relations with so many British colonies and great barbaric and semi-barbaric states, Great Britain is, of all industrial lands, the best adapted for a world-wide export trade; while her unequalled power of cheap production and her great me-

Failure of these early efforts at centralization appear to be due, however, not to the belief that these methods were inappropriate to Britain, but simply to the fact that they were premature. The intervening years greatly expanded the local, national, and imperial networks of business organization which were so lacking in the late '90s. By the outbreak of the World War there were some 1,200 employers' associations in Great Britain, covering practically every leading district, every important trade and industry in the United Kingdom, and endowed with policies increasingly running the entire gamut of business interests. Together with the rapidly expanding Chambers of Commerce, already banded together in central organizations,[10] they were preparing the way for what must eventually give rise to demands for some degree or other of coördination and centralized direction.

It is true, furthermore, that relatively few observers saw in *these types* of business organization—rapid as their growth became during and following the decade of the '90s—serious compromise with the principles of free private enterprise. They were viewed in the main, by participants and observers alike, as primarily promotional, loosely "coöperative," or at best as defensive and temporary associations called into being to meet specific situations of mutual business interest. Only an occasional few saw in them the beginnings of politically potent and monopoly-oriented methods for

chanical ability mark her out as the world's workshop. All that is needed to extend her export trade, perhaps to double its present figures, is the co-ordination of her industrial forces, and the coöperation of her manufacturers, merchants, and traders." *American Industries*, Aug. 1, 1905, p. 12.

[10] The Association of Chambers of Commerce of the United Kingdom was formed in 1860; incorporated in 1875; by 1915 it was made up of 109 British Chambers of Commerce, having aggregate memberships of 28,000 concerns. Also important were The Chamber of Shipping of the United Kingdom, organized in 1887 and made up "of shipowners' associations of all the principal ports," and the British Imperial Council of Commerce. Inaugurated in 1911, the latter was designed to bring together "(a) The members of the Congress Organizing Committee of the London Chamber of Commerce as constituted on the date of the inauguration of the council; (b) representatives officially nominated by British chambers of commerce, boards of trade, or associations thereof throughout the world; (c) such members nominated by British chambers of commerce, boards of trade, or associations thereof from overseas as may be authorized to represent those bodies during a temporary residence in London; (d) such members, including those who have occupied distinguished positions in the British Imperial Service, whether associated with chambers of commerce, boards of trade, or associations thereof, or not, as the council may consider it desirable from time to time to choose." Wolfe, *Commercial Organizations in the United Kingdom*, p. 25.

the centralized manipulation of the business system as a whole.

This was partly true because a good many of the local and more loosely organized associations and chambers first appeared as counterweights to large concerns or cartels already exercising some degree or other of monopoly power. And of these latter there was a steady—in some cases spectacular—growth in the pre-war decades. Particularly noteworthy in this respect were the iron, steel, building materials, and engineering industries, certain of the light manufacturing industries (bedding, cotton textiles, boot and shoe, whisky, salt, thread, soap), and shipping and finance.[11] Relatively few fields of business were wholly untouched by some form of combination, though the peculiar nature of British economic organization made it difficult in many cases to recognize in these concretions significant foci for the exercise of nascent monopoly powers.

It required the experiences of wartime to bring these two trends in business organization to focus, and to show how far both the reality and belief in the principles of the classical order had been undermined within the nerve centers of the British business system.

BIRTH OF THE FBI: "LARGE, POWERFUL, WEALTHY"

In his speech as President of the first General Meeting of the Federation of British Industries (March 1917), Mr. Dudley Docker explained the aims which led him to take the initiative in forming the Federation.

We wanted [he said] to form an association sufficiently large, powerful and wealthy,

> to command the attention of the Government of this country when framing industrial legislation;
> to create an organization big enough to make terms with labour, terms by which we might succeed in bringing about understanding and cooperation;
> to bring about an organized effort for the furtherance of British trade interests generally.[12]

---

[11] See, in particular, Hermann Levy, *Monopolies, Cartels and Trusts in British Industry* (London, 1927), Parts II and III.

[12] From notes supplied by a prominent and authoritative business correspondent in London, who, on account of the contemporary posture of affairs, prefers to remain incognito. This authority, hereafter referred to as *Correspondent,* somewhat whimsically refers to the FBI as the "Federation for Burying Initiative," and its early parallel employers' organization, The National Confederation of Employers' Organizations, as the "Confederation of Embittered Obstructionists."

To this end he had arranged a preliminary meeting in January, 1916, at which the proposal was made that 100 firms be found willing to subscribe £1,000, each, to found such an association. On July 20, at a second preliminary meeting held at the Grand Hotel in London, firms representing an estimated £500,000,000 capital "decided to form the Federation of British Industries, with the object of promoting the coöperation of manufacturers with labor, with the government, and with each other in support of their common interests and for the general good of the country," as an enthusiastic reporter summarized the matter for the London *Times* Trade Supplement.[13] One hundred and twenty-four firms were found willing to guarantee £1,000 each to the needs of the new organization.

Sixty-two trade associations and 350 firms were thus banded together at the end of the first financial year (June 30, 1917). The blessing of the government was demonstrated when the Foreign Office "was kind enough to allow Mr. Roland Nugent [14] to come to us as Director and Secretary." [15] The Employers' Parliamentary Association was absorbed in the new Federation, and its branches became the District Branches of the FBI. The British Manufacturers' Association became a member, and took a place on the Executive Council. The British Empire Producers' Associations, another national, policy-forming body, coöperated in the establishment of a Joint Committee for Empire questions. Contacts were made with the British Commonwealth Union.

The National Association of Manufacturers in the United States had looked upon the FBI as a conversion to its objectives and organization principles. More important, particularly for Mr. Dudley Docker,[16] however, seems to have been the experience of the Swedish Federation of Industries, founded in 1910. But whatever the source or sources of inspiration, growth was rapid. At the end of the second financial year, June, 1918, membership had increased to include 129 trade associations, and 704 firms representative of

13 August, 1916.
14 Later Sir Roland Nugent: he was in the diplomatic service 1910–13; was transferred to the Foreign Office, 1913–17; and served FBI, 1916–17 and 1918–32.
15 *Correspondent.*
16 F. Dudley Docker of the Metropolitan Carriage, Wagon and Finance Company, now a Director of the Midland Bank and the Electric and Railway Finance Company. (Refused reëlection for a second term.)

practically every trade and industrial interest within the United Kingdom. By the middle thirties the Federation was proud to proclaim itself "the largest association of manufacturers in the world . . . accepted by Government, Press and Public as the authoritative voice of British Industry." [17]

ACTIVITIES AND POLICIES OF THE INDUSTRIAL "GENERAL STAFF" [18]

Viewing its task as that of coördinating the whole of the British industrial system before the public, labor, and (especially) the government, the FBI moved into the picture with dispatch and determination. Some idea of the scope and range of its activities at the outset can be given by listing the matters covered in its first annual report: [19]

Overseas Trade Committee set up to study the development of the Government service for the promotion of British trade in foreign countries.

Establishment of an Anglo-French Committee on Industry and Economics for joint discussion and solution of problems.

Framing of a Memorandum and Questionnaire to members in regard to the possible problems and developments in the industry of Great Britain after the war.

Supply of Federation representatives to the Departmental Committees
a) Colonial Office Committee on Blue Books
b) Foreign Office Committee on Commercial Attaches
c) Priority Advisory Committee.

Formal evidence submitted to Lord Balfour's Committee on industrial and commercial policy.

Joint deputation with the British Manufacturers Association (later National Union of Manufacturers) and the Association of Controlled Firms to the Ministry of Munitions and other Ministries drawing attention to the confusion and irritation caused in industry by Government orders and Departmental activities.

Establishment of a Committee on Patent Law on behalf of the Board of Trade.

Education Committee.

The President's address spoke of education as a "problem which lies

---

[17] Brochure of the FBI, entitled "Industry in Action."
[18] As characterized by *The Spectator*, Dec. 28, 1918, p. 754.
[19] Verbatim from *Correspondent*.

at the root of many of our difficulties" and "has particular relevance to the problem of industrial unrest." The Education Committee was very active for some four or five years and was particularly concerned with a) The Fisher Act of 1918 and the implications of compulsory continued education from an industrial standpoint; b) The proposal to raise the school-leaving age to fifteen.

Preliminary Committee set up to consider legislation affecting industrialists and manufacturers and to make such recommendations as appeared necessary from the point of view of the interests of industry.

Special Committee set up in connection with Excess Profits Duty.

Special Committee set up to examine the proposals and implications of the Reports of the Whitley Committee.[20]

Appointment of Legal Advisers, principally for the service of members conducting import and export trade.

But this was only the beginning. With each succeeding year the interests of the FBI have widened, and the range of its influence has spread, until today, "It is impossible to cover the whole range of the Federation's work . . . for practically no question which seems likely to affect the interests of its members is left untouched by its organization." [21] Since practically everything which goes on in the British Empire affects at some point the "interests of its members," the FBI is officially committed to a totalitarian coverage.

This point is borne out not only by many official declarations to such effect, but also by the manner in which problems put before the Federation have been shaped up for consideration. A single example will suffice. When in 1918 the Federation examined the question, "Is the existing organization of industry satisfactory for meeting present-day problems?" its Commercial Efficiency Committee indicated the following range of subjects "as a field for coöperation in the commercial and economic sphere through voluntary association: [22]

The avoidance of undue competition.

The regulation of prices—from the point of view of an economic price based on efficiency, and not from that of a monopoly price designed to exploit the consumer.

The general improvement and development of an industry by such means as:

---

20 See pp. 171–72, following.

21 Labour Research Department, *The Federation of British Industries* (Studies in Labour and Capital, No. 5, London, 1923), p. 6.

22 FBI, Committee on the Organisation of Industry, *Report* (June, 1935), pp. 4–5.

a) interchange of statistics;
b) standardisation of methods and details of costings and interchange of costings;
c) interchange of methods of working;
d) centralisation of research and experiment;
e) technical education and commercial training;
f) standardisations of plant, machinery and product;
g) specialisation;
h) joint publicity and propaganda;
i) regulation of the conditions and usages of training and their application to the various industries;
j) centralisation and control of sales;
k) demarcation of territory, to allow orders to be allotted to the works geographically best fitted to carry them out.

THE CONTROL OF SOURCES OF SUPPLY OF NECESSARY RAW MATERIALS

Readers familiar with the literature will recognize in the above the entire range of German and continental cartel controls, as well as an underwriting of a good many of those newer controls formally recognized only in overtly Fascist countries. "There is need," continues the above cited Report, "for the individual to subordinate his views to those of Industry for the achievement of a common policy, and for coöperation between Industries on a scale that pre-war conditions did not so insistently demand. *Public considerations* today place upon each industry a *collective responsibility* for efficient and economic production." (Italics mine.)

These "public considerations" and this "collective responsibility" justified, the FBI felt, extending the sphere of "coöperation" until the following could be achieved: (1) elimination of excess plant capacity, bringing about "coördination between supply and demand" and promotion of greater "concentration of output in efficient and up-to-date plants"; (2) limitation of "new entrants to an industry" in order better to relate productive capacity to market demands; (3) prevention of certain firms in some trades from gaining an "unfair advantage" without bearing their due proportion of development expenditure, such as centralised propaganda and research; (4) promotion of greater unity amongst British industries in negotiations with foreign competitors, and increased stability in world trade conditions; (5) expulsion from the conduct of business of firms "which can never hope to become profitable." [23]

It would be difficult to imagine a more comprehensive plan for the coördination of industry, which could still hope to stay within the framework of capitalistic institutions. The Federation of British Industries has stopped in principle at only one point: compulsion. Every time the issue has come up—and it tends to intrude itself more frequently and more insistently with the passage of time— of compelling all firms to belong to the appropriate subsidiary organization, and of laying out policies with which all members would be compelled to comply, the response has been negative.

The arguments against compulsion are of the usual order: It would tend towards rigidity and bureaucratization; it would curb initiative and slow down progress; it would result in a highly arbitrary classification of industry and would unduly circumvent the activities of many types of enterprises; it would enhance the power of the state, and thus serve to introduce at once the stultification of entrepreneurial action and the regimentation held characteristic of political administration. All these points are emphasized in the special Report of the Committee on the Organisation of Industry previously quoted, where it is held that the "special characteristics of our people and our system of government import a fundamental difference into the conditions which have to be met" from those obtaining in other countries where compulsion has been resorted to in these matters.

With that lack of candor characteristic of British business literature, the Federation of British Industries hesitates even to commit itself to "self-government in business." Yet the whole of the program which its deliberations, year after year, lay bare, are identical in tone, emphasis, and direction with what the Germans called *Selbstverwaltung* (literally "self-management") in business, and the Americans term "self-government" in business. It is even clear that many of its leading figures anticipate utilizing the formal powers of the state to enforce decisions rendered by the majority of an organized industry relative to interests affecting the industry or trade as a whole. To the contention of the committee majority in the Report cited, that "The procedure of putting into force by Order in Council the decisions of the majority of an industry, when

[23] *Ibid.*, pp. 6–7.

approved by an appointed Tribunal and by the President of the Board of Trade, would be an undesirable addition to bureaucratic powers," Lord Melchett, of the gigantic firm of Imperial Chemicals, gave the rejoinder that in his "opinion this method is the most convenient and would further protect industries against the danger of their affairs being made the subject of party controversy in Parliament. "Furthermore, procedure by Order in Council" does not, he said, involve "any extension of bureaucratic powers, since only an individual industry can frame or accept a scheme." [24]

There can be no doubt that Lord Melchett spoke at that time for large and growing sections of British industry. Subsequent developments have fully backed up the position he took, not by compromising the control of private enterprise over its leading policies, but by centralizing its direction.[25]

Before turning to consider somewhat more fully the way in which this has been accomplished, it will be well to obtain a clearer picture of how the FBI is organized to fulfill its stated functions.

ORGANIZATION AND PROCEDURE

By 1920 the organization of the FBI as it now stands was practically complete, only minor alterations having been introduced after that time. Membership may be either on a trade association or individual firm basis. This doubtless means a great deal of duplicate membership, inasmuch as the individual firm members are also in nearly all cases members of the constituent trade associations. Since in the main, only the large firms could afford to belong directly to the FBI, such dual membership put them into a position of commanding importance in the manipulation of significant policy issues.

To repeat, membership coverage has long been regarded as inclusive of practically all British industry. The 1925 "Yearbook and

24 It is interesting to note that Lord Melchett attributes his favorable attitude towards the Order in Council to practices inaugurated under the National Government: ". . . the extension of procedure by Order in Council on the advice of statutory committees, which we have witnessed since the National Government took office, has distinct advantages, both from the point of view of the relief of Parliamentary time, and further because, as in the case of the Tariff Advisory Committee, it enables highly specialized industrial and technical problems to be dealt with by impartial and experienced individuals." *Ibid.*, p. 15.
25 See pp. 181–88.

Register of British Manufactures," published by the FBI, pointed with pride to the fact that "In the eight years of its existence the Federation has succeeded in becoming almost completely representative of the industries of the country. It has enrolled as its members some 195 Trade Associations and 2,100 individual firms. Taking both classes of membership, it is in touch, directly or indirectly, with at least 20,000 manufacturing firms covering every industry in the country, with a capital of nearly £6,000,000,000 (roughly, $30,000,000,000) and giving employment to over 5,000,-000." Since that time coverage has been made even more complete for industry, and membership has been constructed so as to draw in allied fields of trade, banking, and insurance.[26]

Members are grouped in two ways, geographically and functionally (by trade and industry classifications). All the members who wish to do so may affiliate themselves directly with one of the twenty-three district offices. Each district office has a representative in the Grand Council. The districts are as follows (1937): [27]

London	Manchester
Birmingham	Northampton
Coventry	Nottingham
Stoke-on-Trent	Newcastle
Wolverhampton	Sheffield
and South Staffordshire	Wales (South)
Worcester	Home Counties (South)
Bradford	Home Counties (North)
Bristol	Scotland:
Hull	Glasgow and West of Scotland,
Leeds	Edinburgh, Forth and Border
Leicester	Ireland: Belfast
Liverpool	

Functionally, members are divided into Main Groups, and then into Sub-Groups or Sections (two cases only, Main Groups 5 and 9). There are twenty-four Main Groups, divided as follows:

1. Mining, Quarrying and Allied Trades
2. Mechanical Engineering
3. Shipbuilding, Marine Engi-

---

[26] Examples of the inclusion of nonindustrial interests are provided by the establishment of Main Groups of Agriculture, Banking and Insurance, and Public Utilities.

[27] Taken chiefly from the 19th (1935) and the 20th (1936) Annual Reports of the FBI.

neering, Constructional Steel-
work and Allied Trades
4. Electrical Engineering
5. Iron, Steel and Allied Trades
6. Chemicals, Fertilisers and Explosives
7. Foodstuffs and Tobacco
8. Agriculture
9. Building Trades
10. Rubber and Asbestos
11. Public Utility
12. Miscellaneous
13. Textiles
14. Glass and Clay Products
15. Printing, Printing Ink Manufacturers, Type Founders,
Process Workers and Allied
Trades

16. Paper Making, Manufacturing, Stationery, Envelope
Making, Paper Bag Making,
Box Making, and Allied
Trades
17. Banking and Insurance
18. Woodworking
19. Non-Ferrous Metals
20. Oils and Fats (including Soap,
Candles, and Margarine), Oil
Seed Crushing and by-products
21. Cutlery, Jewellery, Electro-
Plate and Allied Trades
22. Brewing, Distilling and Allied
Trades
23. Fisheries
24. Leather and Allied Trades

According to the by-laws, every member is allowed to join whatever Main or Sub-Group he chooses, provided his firm or trade
association falls into the proper classification. The governing body
is the Grand Council. Under grant of Charter, issued 1923, the
Grand Council consists of

the President, Past Presidents, Vice Presidents, Chairman and Vice
Chairman of the Federation, Representatives of Federation Districts
and Representatives of members who shall as far as possible be representatives of different industries. Until otherwise determined by the
Grand Council, such representatives will approximately consist of the
following:

(1) A representative of each Federation District.
(2) Representatives of Association Members on the basis of one representative for every 20,000 employers or part thereof engaged by
the Association Member of a Main Group or a Sub-Group.
(3) Representatives of Individual Members on the basis of one representative for every 40,000 employees or part thereof engaged by
the individual members in a Sub-Group provided that no representative is given if the part of 40,000 falls below 2,000.[28]

The Grand Council, which is the legally responsible governing
body of the FBI, is possessed of power "to act in all matters in the
name of the Federation," consisted at the beginning of the fiscal

[28] Royal Charter of Incorporation and Schedule of By-Laws, p. 16.

year 1937, of 380 members elected by some 155 [29] Main and Sub-Groups, 23 District Representatives, and 9 coöpted [30] members in addition to the President, Past Presidents and Vice Presidents. Most of its executive and administrative powers, however, are delegated to the Executive Committee.

This body is made up of FBI officials, serving *ex officio,* and elected representatives from the several Main Groups on the principle of one representative for every 100,000 employees of Associations and Individual Members, subject to the qualification that there should be a minimum of 2 allotted for each Main Group. Special appointments may be made from the districts, and a limited number of coöptations may be added at the discretion of the Grand Council. For the year beginning 1937 the Executive Committee was made up as follows: 5 ex officio; 112 elected; 7 district appointees; 13 coöpted—a total of 137 members.

The significance of this arrangement can be appreciated when it is realized that, as the inner controlling group in the Grand Council, the Executive Committee is in a position not only to control policy, but also to guide the detailed work of the Federation. Most of this latter work "is carried out by standing Sub-Committees, appointed by the Executive Committee. Each Sub-Committee consists as a rule of one representative of each Main Group, with the addition of a few specially qualified members. Each Sub-Committee controls its own sphere of activities, . . . subject to the general supervision and control of the Executive Committee." [31] Special *ad hoc* Sub-Committees may be appointed by either or both the Executive Committee and the Grand Council to examine into and report on particular problems.

The work of the Federation, detailed through these various committees, deals both "with subjects affecting industry as a whole or which affect more than one trade" and with "particular individual services for members, which are of a more private character." [32] How wide this dual coverage may be can be seen from a listing of

[29] The listing of Sub-Groups is not altogether consistent from one year to the next, so that it is impossible to determine from the Annual Reports either the precise number or the specific basis of Sub-Group classification.

[30] Members may be coöpted to a number not to exceed ten.

[31] Federation of British Industries, *Export Register* (London, 1920), p. 10.

[32] Letter to the author written, June 11, 1937, by J. Armitage of the Technical Department, FBI. (The list is incomplete.)

the main committees, and a brief resumé of the work undertaken in a few selected cases.

As of June, 1937, the following 14 standing committees were actively functioning: [33]

> Commercial and Company Law
> Contracts
> Coordinating of Statistics
> Empire
> Exhibitions and Fairs
> Exporters' Shipping
> Industrial Arts
> Overseas
> Production
> Rating and Valuation
> Riparian Owners
> Tariff and Commercial Treaties
> Taxation
> Transport

To select at random, the Overseas Committee established in 1920 an Overseas Department "under the control of two Assistant Directors, who are responsible to the Main Overseas Committee and its various Sub-Committees." [34]

The Overseas Department was then divided into nine sections:

General Section	Near East Section
American Section	Far East Section
Empire Section	East Indies Section
South European Section	Exhibition Section
North European Section	

The general section acts as a secretariat to the Directors and coordinates the works of the various geographical sections.

The geographical sections themselves are organized as intelligence centres for the various territories dealt with. They obtain information from the Commissioners and from other sources on all subjects which may interest Members, such as likely agents or customers, customs intricacies, local habits, trade movements, competition, local resources, etc.

The Exhibition Section deals with the technical work in connection with the organization of exhibitions abroad which the Federation of British Industries may desire to organise or participate in, such as the Athens Exhibition.

---

[33] *Idem.*   [34] Federation of British Industries, *Export Register*, p. 26.

A special department of the Federation, acting in conjunction both with the Overseas Department and the Industrial Grouping Department, carries out the selection and despatch of trade inquiries and similar particulars to those manufacturers likely to be interested. The system has been carefully evolved to avoid any possible delay, and also to ensure that every Member of the Federation who manufactures the goods referred to in the enquiry shall receive a notice of it. To make absolutely certain of this, details of all enquiries received during each week are printed in a confidential supplement to the official Bulletin of the Federation, which is sent out to Members every Monday. Neither in the circular letters nor in the Bulletin supplement are the names of enquirers given, and all Members interested communicate immediately with the Head Office. A similar procedure is adopted in cases when overseas firms apply to act as agents for particular classes of British goods.[35]

The system of Federation Commissioners, set up under this arrangement is equipped to do everything for the individual member but actually book orders. Located on the spot, and scattered throughout all the important commercial centers of the world, these Commissioners are required to establish centers for collecting and classifying information on movements and methods of trade, status of traders, local trade requirements, foreign competition; to recommend selling agents on request; to protect interests of Members and act for them in emergencies; to establish panels of legal advisers and interpreters; to build up libraries "containing translations of important documents, such as Customs regulations," and the like; assist in deposit and display of samples; coöperate with H. M. Government on behalf of Members; appoint advisory boards of prominent local business men sympathetic with British interests; display and distribute Members' catalogues; provide meeting places and Information Bureau for Members and their Agents; and to keep tab on all trade statistics relevant to Member interests.[36]

[35] Idem.

[36] Idem. See also a little pamphlet called "The Federation of British Industries, the Organization That Every Manufacturer Should Have at His Back," containing a list of "What the FBI Can Do" and a sampling of Members' Appreciations. FBI aid includes everything down to help with passports and rebates "on the charges at over 100 Continental hotels." Members express appreciation for aid on such problems as dealing with "Deduction of Tax at Source," "Difficulties with Foreign Customs Authorities," "Difficulties with Overseas Agents" (in this case the FBI representative supplied, it appears, espionage—"confidential information"—service), "Postal Regulations," and "Taxation" ("relief to the extent of approximately two-thirds of the amount of tax paid in Australia").

Any recent annual Report of the FBI will show how this type of work has been built up and elaborated over the intervening years. There is practically no phase of British industrial, commercial, and financial interests in any part of the world which is not touched upon by one or more of the services placed at the disposal of members through the FBI machinery. A special feature is the publication of the FBI Register of British Manufacturers, begun in 1920, and revised annually. Especially close relations are maintained throughout all these overseas activities with the International Chambers of Commerce, local British Chambers of Commerce established in foreign countries, and foreign departments of foreign chambers of commerce.

All this work overlaps, in many particulars that of other departments, committees, and subcommittees. An interesting example is provided in the 1936 Annual Report in representations made to the Board of Trade of H. M. Government regarding taxes in Rumania held to discriminate unduly against foreign concerns. Negotiations were in the same year carried on with local tax authorities in Australia, the United States, and France.

Another interesting example of how the FBI operates is found in the work of its Industrial Arts Committee. By 1935 some thirty industries were represented on this Committee. Activities reported on in 1936, included the following: coöperation with the Board of Education in the writing of a "Report on State Aided Art Education," incorporating the Federation's proposal that "the Royal College of Art should be reconstituted and that its primary purpose should be the study of applied art with particular reference to the requirements of industry and commerce"; participation of the Committee Chairman, Mr. Charles Tennyson on the Board of Trade Council for Art and Industry; [37] the establishment of a Scottish Sub-Committee for "securing and maintaining contacts between designers and industrialists" in that area; preparation of a memorandum on the request of the Board of Trade dealing with

[37] "The Council are taking steps to form a Register of qualified Industrial Designers, and invited the Federation to nominate three representatives of Industry to the Governing Body, which is to be responsible for the management of the Register. Three representatives from the textile, pottery and printing industries have accordingly been appointed, with alternatives to act in cases where the representatives come from the provinces. Mr. Tennyson is Chairman of the Governing Body of the Register." FBI, 20th Annual Report, p. 17.

training of Managers and other Executives in various manufacturing industries in an "understanding of the design of industrial products"; supplying evidence to the Board of Trade on contributions to industrial arts given by Museums; awarding prizes "to students of the Royal College of Art for industrial designers"; securing employment for art students.[38]

It is perhaps unnecessary to trace much further the detailed work of individual committees and their various subcommittees. What has been given is illustrative of the wide-ranging character of the work accomplished, and the totalitarian outlook of its guiding lights. The picture needs, however, to be extended slightly to show that the work of the Federation does not stop with the mere collection of information, and the giving of aid and advice to members. The Federation has, of course, done a great deal by these means to create a "climate of opinion" which is coherent and promotional not only of specific interests but also of the general social outlook of organized British industry. But within this atmosphere it has proceeded step by step to manipulate policy with a view to the consolidation of business stakes on issues that reach to the roots of the British political system.

Three examples will suffice to show the character of the objectives and the nature of the alignments sought, in carrying out those objectives: the attitude toward organized labor; relations with the government in peace times; and the quality of the "coöperation" with government in times of war emergency.

THE ATTITUDE TOWARD ORGANIZED LABOR

It was hoped by some in the formative days of the FBI that the new association might include "not merely the representatives of capital but those of labour." Under the stress of war conditions, trade union leaders had shown a conciliatory attitude. Why not hope, then, to bring about "something approaching a partnership between capital and labour in place of the armed neutrality, which is the best that can be hoped for under present circumstances." [39] To this end the FBI gave evidence before the government committee dealing with the Whitely Councils in 1917, and aided in the

---

[38] *Idem.*
[39] "Federation of British Industry," *Engineer* (London), Aug. 11, 1916.

formation of this wartime compromise with the "company-union" ideal.[40]

While there was little opposition amongst employer circles to the Whitely Committee idea as such, the trade unions appear to have been entirely too strong and too class conscious, even in war times, for the idea of "labor-capital partnership" to make much headway. At any rate, not much seems to have come out of the National Alliance of Employers and Employed; this was set up in 1917 and designed to have equal representation from both groups, in order to "come together in friendly consultations on labour problems." [41]

Failure to work harder along this line was due, however, to a decision to specialize the functions of the FBI on business, legislative, and trade matters, and to leave labor relations to the constituent trade associations and other central organizations which they might devise. In August, 1917, the Executive Council resolved: "In regard to labour matters, the FBI will not concern itself or interfere with any questions affecting working conditions or rates of pay, except at the request of the Employers' Associations or Federations established to deal with such questions. Any such request should, however, be addressed to the FBI through the medium of the Employers' Advisory Council, which should be invited to consider and advise the FBI on such matters." [42]

In 1919, members of the FBI participated in setting up its labor relations *alter ego,* the National Confederation of Employers' Organizations (subsequently renamed the British Employers' Confederation). Its purpose was to coördinate the parallel activities of employers' associations (made up of members who were also, for

[40] These were set up on a national, a district, and a works basis, with representation drawn equally from trade unions and employer associations. For a summary see *Characteristics of Company Unions* (Bulletin No. 364, Division of Industrial Relations, U.S. Dept. of Labor, Bureau of Labor Statistics, Washington, D.C., 1935). See also "Joint Industrial Councils in Great Britain," *International Labour Review,* Dec., 1921, pp. 563–78.

[41] ". . . the Federation has taken practical steps towards bringing about a real coöperation of Capital and Labour by assisting in the formation of the National Alliance of Employers and Employed. This body consists of representatives of employers' organizations and trade unions, and practically all the employers on the Executive Committee are Members of the Federation." Federation of British Industries, *Export Register,* p. 20.

[42] *Correspondent.*

the most part, members of the FBI) specifically concerned with negotiations with Trade Unions, and to treat "questions of wages and conditions of employment as settled through collective bargaining betwen employers and employed."[43] According to its 4th Annual Report (June, 1920), the FBI had established a working liaison with the NCEO concerned primarily with exchange of information. "A Joint Committee has been established and meets for regular discussions."

With the great general strike of 1926, and the formation of the National Government under the direction of Ramsay MacDonald, the British Employers' Confederation began to take on a more menacing tone. Much of the subsequent antilabor legislation was inspired directly by outstanding figures in the FBI machinery. Attempts at partial conciliation, such as those involved in the famous Mond-Turner Conversations on Industrial Relations running over 1928–29, had given way increasingly to attitudes bordering on open hostility.[44]

Members of the FBI have not relaxed their efforts with a mere negative attitude towards labor. Many of them feel called upon to take measures insuring an entirely different attitude in the future through apprenticeship training programs, a special propaganda funneled through the public school system,[45] and the use of various media for public-relations work. It is very difficult, in the face of typical British secretiveness, to learn much about these plans. But from such indications as can be gleaned here and there, the trend of thought and effort seems to be along the line of specialized train-

[43] *Idem.*

[44] Reporting to the 32d Annual Convention of the NAM, meeting at Chattanooga, Tenn., in 1927, the Secretary, George S. Boudinot, stated, "Your counsel observed a revolutionary change in the control of labor and employer combinations in England and Italy. A striking change, not confined to non-members of labor organizations, has taken place in British public opinion respecting trade union regulations. After deliberate consideration, powerful trade union organizations have abandoned the Labor Party because of the reaction within to the left wing of radicalism and the Soviet drive to capture the British trade union movement. Furthermore, the British Parliament, by its enactment of July 27, last, has severely limited the political and economic activities of trade unions."

[45] Another American observer, P. Harvey Middleton, writing in *American Industries*, Nov., 1924, on "Great Britain's Loud Speaker" (the FBI), listed among the FBI activities of merit, "meetings between the FBI Education Committee and the Association of Headmasters of Public and Secondary Schools to discuss suggestions for bringing the schools of the country into closer relation with industry."

ing of the young that they may in the future follow the business men as "their natural leaders," instead of their own Trade Union representatives.[46]

It is significant that this trend comes at a time when class-conscious employer organizations have been established with central headquarters, capable of both creating a climate of opinion amongst employers and of exercising some degree of united action in matters bearing on the combined interests of British employers as a whole. But it is of far greater import that these developments occur simultaneously with the cumulative dovetailing of organized business and the formal political machinery of the British imperial system.

RELATIONS WITH THE GOVERNMENT: IN TIMES OF PEACE

This is not the place to discuss in detail the extent to which Tory domination in England has woven the political and economic apparatus of class interests into a unified system of social control. The details are too numerous, in part too well concealed, and in part too difficult to trace for elaboration here. Moreover, portions of the story have been told adequately in a series of recent books.[47]

It will suffice here to summarize a few of the obvious trends in the British concentration movement, and to point out the role the FBI comes to assume as the political implications of these trends come ever more clearly to the fore.

1. The dominating concerns in the inner councils of the FBI are those organized on a monopoly or quasi-monopoly footing, or occupying leading positions in the rapidly spreading networks of cartel and cartel-like controls. This process was particularly rapid in the postwar years. "For the first time since the earlier days of capitalism," wrote Professor Levy in 1927, a "large section of English trade has become overrun with monopolist organisations. . . . The World War, its aftermath, and the world-wide economic crisis, lasting now for more than six years, have strengthened these tend-

---

[46] "For my part I cannot look upon the evil or foolish faces of some of the leaders of labour without a sense of deep humility. How greatly must we capitalist employers have neglected our duty, if the workers choose to follow, not us their natural leaders, but such men as these." Austin Hopkinson, *Religio Militis* (London, 1927), p. 113.

[47] See, in particular, Simon Haxey, *Tory M.P.* (London, 1939), and Ernest Davies, *National Capitalism* (London, 1939).

encies." [48] And since Levy wrote, as Lucas [49] and others have shown, these tendencies have been doubly accelerated by the events of the great depression and the outbreak of the Second World War.

Typical of the combines which operate monopolistically are such concerns as Imperial Chemicals (capitalized around £75,000,-000), Vickers in the iron and steel industry, Lever Brothers in the soap industry, J. and P. Coats in the thread industry, and the great banking systems with headquarters in London.

2. As Lucas has shown in his illuminating study, the trade association "is without question the most common medium of control in the present time" [50] in Great Britain. This is to say, the British trade association typically begins its existence by exercising the powers and seeking to gain the restrictive objectives which the American trade association was able to achieve only after NRA. Hence for all practical purposes, these price-fixing, output-restricting, market-area allocating bodies, operating with the use of such familiar devices as resale price maintenance, tying contracts, rebate systems, trade boycotts, and the like, are cartel-like bodies. Nothing basic in principle separates their forms of organization nor the methods of operation from the cartel. It is highly significant that the two terms, trade associations and cartels, are used more or less interchangeably in the general British literature devoted to discussing these trends.

3. The trade association device has been growing in Britain, as indicated above (p. 157) by leaps and bounds. Growth here, as elsewhere, is along three principal lines. Every industry and trade, both locally and nationally, acquires its appropriate association; the pressure on "outsiders" to join tends increasingly to expand the coverage of each appropriate association so as to include every single business concern falling in each separate classification or category; these tend increasingly to band together first locally or regionally, then nationally by industries, trades, and (cross-sectional) regions, in *peak* or *central* bodies, such as the FBI. Scattered, overlapping, confused as the organizational network is in many respects, still one finds in the literature clear indications that these three trends are everywhere convergent and unidirectional.

4. It is equally clear that the bulk of the larger and more power-

[48] Levy, *Monopolies, Cartels, and Trusts,* pp. 325–26.
[49] *Industrial Reconstruction.*   [50] *Ibid.,* p. 203.

ful trade associations are dominated as a rule by a few large inside concerns. The examples offered by Lucas of the methods by which Lever Brothers dominates the soap industry through the United Kingdom Soap Manufacturers' Association, the Salt Union its industry through the Salt Manufacturers' Association, and Imperial Chemicals the ammonia industry through the Sulphate of Ammonia Federation, Ltd., are merely spectacular instances of techniques which have become extremely widespread throughout the British Isles. So far as this is true—and the general trends seem to be in this direction—the trade association becomes in effect a cartel instrument to promote the monopoly policies of a single or a small group of giant concerns.

5. Somewhat the same thing can be said of the central and peak associations, such as the FBI. The large concern has an opportunity to make its weight felt first through a sort of triple membership: as individual corporate member, as member of constituent trade associations, and through membership in the regional bodies. Voting power, in the second place, for both the Grand Council and the Executive Committee, is on a basis proportional to number of workmen employed, a practice which inevitably throws the center of gravity in the hands of the large concerns. Further, analysis will show that the work undertaken by the various subcommittees has to do in large part with matters which can only be of advantage to the large concern equipped with great resources. Finally, the constitution and by-laws of the FBI are subject to change by the inside groups of the Grand Council and the Executive Committee, including extension of powers of appointment and (in particular) coöptation of members to key positions.

6. The influence of the FBI in governmental circles appears to have become exceedingly great. It is expressed directly via two routes. First, in the number of positions its members hold on governmental committees and the extent to which its representations before governmental bodies result in decisions and pursuit of policies favorable to its members and its general program; and second, the power possessed by its own officers, members of the Grand Council, Executive Committees, and various Subcommittees, on the one hand, and representatives of its leading companies and trade associations on the other, to influence governmental policies as Members of Parliament.

As for the first line of cross-fertilization, the FBI claims to be represented directly on the following governmental bodies: [51]

Board of Trade: Board of Trade Advisory Council
Board of Trade Council for Art and Industry
War Office: Technical co-ordinating Committee on General Stores
Motor Transport Co-ordinating Committee
Ministry of Health: Joint Advisory Committee on River Pollution
Town and Country Planning Advisory Committee
Mniistry of Agriculture: Standing Committee on River Pollution

Apparently representation is much wider than such a listing would appear to show. References are found scattered all through the literature, showing membership on *ad hoc* and smaller standing committees established not only by the national, but also by numerous county, municipal, and other local governing bodies. But of equal importance would appear to be the effect of its institutionalized pressure and lobby activities. A few examples taken from a single publication will suffice to show the general picture: [52]

Fiscal Policy: In 1930 the FBI secured an overwhelming mandate from its members to demand a change in our National Fiscal Policy. The publication early in 1931 of its proposals in "Industry and the Nation" was followed by an intensive campaign in Parliament and the Press, and in the Industrial districts. A special pamphlet "The Passing of Free Trade" was prepared to assist speakers on the subject. The National Government, returned to power in 1931, adopted the FBI's main recommendations, and Industry is now reaping substantial benefits from the protection of the Home market.
Imports: On the passing of the Import Duties Act 1932, the FBI set up a special department to assist members in preparing applications to the Import Duties Advisory Committee. . . . Concessions to the Dominions and foreign countries facilitating imports into Home markets are closely watched. The FBI has generally been successful in convincing the Government that no such agreement should be concluded before the industries affected have had an opportunity of producing information as to the effect of such imports upon British industry.
Foreign Countries: The FBI is the main channel of consultation with the Government in Commercial Treaty negotiations, and it also provides special facilities for international arrangements within particular industries.

---

[51] "Industry and Action," pamphlet of the FBI (undated), p. 11.
[52] *Ibid.*, pp. 4–5.

De-Rating of Machinery: The Rating and Valuation Act of 1925 records a notable achievement for Industry. The Bill introduced, after prolonged negotiations, by the Government contained a definition of the machinery to be included for Rating by the Local Authorities, which embodied the essentials of the FBI proposals.

Similar to these are the claim of successful coöperation with the government in matters dealing with exports, Empire problems, taxation, commercial law. Various annual reports elaborate and detail the picture at length. One writer summarizes FBI activities in a typical case as follows:

In the determination of the scope and nature of that policy [protection] the FBI has played a triumphant part. It has not hesitated to boast of its successful influence upon the Government. . . . By creation of the Tariff Advisory Committee with power to alter tariffs without reference to Parliament, the Government has in fact handed over to a body in close association with the owners of industry an important legislative function.[53]

The other side of this picture is the influence of organized business circles in the formation of governmental policy through membership in Parliament. A recent compilation from the Directory of Directors, the Stock Exchange Year-Book, and other sources shows that of 415 Parliamentary supporters of the National Government, some 181 possessed 775 corporate directorships.[54] These ranged over the entire business field, but appear to be largely concentrated in the big, national and Empire-wide trading, shipping, manufacturing, and financial enterprises. Through family and almost indefinitely ramifying intercorporate connections, corporate influence of these business M.P.'s likewise extends to the outer reaches of the entire British economic system. Thus in large—perhaps in decisive—part the influences, personalities, interests, and powers that go to shape up policies of individual business firms, the trade associations to which they belong, and the central policy-coördinating bodies, such as the FBI which they direct, go also to determine the objectives of governmental policies, and to guide and control the execution of those policies through the complex machinery of government administration and regulation.

7. Some conception of the long-run implications of this fusion of

53 H. R. Greaves, *Reactionary England* (London, 1936), p. 146.
54 Haxey, *op. cit.*, p. 37.

business and government may be had by looking over the various schemes for industrial reorganization that have come to the fore with increasing frequency in recent years. Such plans as embodied in the Coal Mines Acts, the Iron and Steel Reorganization Scheme, the "Reconstruction Levy" and various schemes proposed for reorganizing different industries by PEP (Political and Economic Planning) call for no less than extension of the principle of corporate organization to entire industries. It is worth while pointing out the following as typical of all such plans:

They are initially advocated, promoted, and lobbied for primarily (in some cases exclusively) by the larger, better organized and more powerful business interests. "Liberal" and labor groups have assented to such plans only tardily, only with many stipulated conditions (mostly ignored) or not at all.

They all visualize the establishment of a central governing body, capable in whole or in part of restricting competition, controlling capacity, regulating markets, prices and production.

They all wish for governmental sanctions in enforcing compliance with decisions arrived at, but wish freedom from "government coercion" in the process of exercising the decisions.

The central governing authorities projected are made up exclusively of business men, who govern the industry or trade as a unit. (The Board of Trade, or similar bodies are only to "regulate" in a general sense of the term.)

Central peak associations, such as the FBI and those with which it is affiliated, have not opposed any of these schemes on principle. On the contrary, except for specific features of specific programs, they have uniformly favored such plans, the moving figures in these schemes being simultaneously the leading lights in the central associations.

They do not, as a rule, oppose very considerable extension of governmental influence (so long as the government is "sympathetic") along what might be called "auxiliary lines." For example, they did not oppose:

a) The establishment of governmentally owned, or "mixed" (owned partly by government and partly by private interests) enterprises, such as The London Passenger Transport Board, The Central Electricity Board and The London Port Authority (mixed enterprises), The Post Office (which includes the telephone and telegraph systems of Great Britain. (Government ownership.)
b) Government aid in establishing monopolies in the home market (autarchy), and protection in Empire and foreign markets.
c) Provision of authority and machinery for punishment of "out-

siders" through regular legal channels, or provision by government with powers for eliminating the problem of the "outsider" entirely.

Somewhat different in origin were the Agricultural Marketing Acts [55] tracing back to 1931. Yet under the National Government, these Acts, which were intended to make possible organization of farmer-producers into coöperative or semicoöperative bodies, had come largely under the influence of packing houses, agricultural processors and distributors, and other allied interests.[56] Hence, even this application of the new type of "corporative" organization has come under the domination of groups whose first allegiance is to the interests and outlook represented by the Federation of British Industries.

8. There remains the fact to be mentioned, alluded to above, that opposition to this cumulative fusion of governmental and highly organized business systems seems almost completely to have dwindled away. Conservative and Tory elements want the new forms of corporate organization, and they desire the coöperation of the government in effecting the necessary changes against recalcitrant minority interests. And labor and liberal circles have apparently concurred in the movement, having asked—in the main—only for minor safeguards for their interests. The famous Liberal Report of 1926 recommended autonomous and "self-governing" bodies as one of the leading ways of solving Britain's industrial dilemma.[57] The first comprehensive plans for industrial reorganization along lines slowly evolved by monopoly-oriented business organization were laid down by the British Labour Party in 1931.

In a speech delivered, significantly enough, at the University of Berlin in 1926, the great British liberal and iconoclast J. M. Keynes held "that in many cases the ideal size for the unit of control

[55] Different only in the sense that the Agricultural Marketing Acts were promoted primarily by farming interests, while the industrial reorganization schemes were originally the Labour Government's answer to the various proposals which had been advanced by private industry. Needless to say, the form in which the Labour Government proposed industrial reorganization was not far removed from that proposed by a private enterprise, as may be shown by the nature and quality of the remarks and criticisms made at the time in business circles.

[56] See pp. 183–86.

[57] *Britain's Industrial Future* (London, 1938), the Report of the Liberal Industrial Inquiry; see in particular Books II and III. In its conclusions it refers to "the growth of coöperative self-government, which is the true aim of industrial policy" (p. 466).

and organisation lies somewhere between the individual and the modern State. I suggest, therefore, that progress lies in the growth and the recognition of semi-autonomous bodies within the State . . . a return, it may be said, towards medieval conceptions of separate autonomies." [58] Later he was to become even more explicit when, on the eve of the outbreak of the Second World War which he had forecast so many years before, he declared that an "amalgam of private capitalism and State Socialism . . . is the only practicable recipe for present conditions." [59]

Just how far State control was to reach in this British version of National Socialism it is hard to gather from the writings of Mr. Keynes or his contemporaries, but clearly self-government in business under the auspices of a regime determined "to make the private property system *work better*" [60] (italics in original) is en route to the goal. All of which does not prove, of course, that all British business is in favor either of the abandonment of "free competition" and "laissez faire" on the one hand, nor of the particular forms under which they cede control to central policy-controlling bodies on the other. An examination of any of the numerous proposals for control in any given industry will put the reader's mind at rest on that score.[61] But what is clear, is that the center of gravity has shifted in this direction, and that on the present showing there will shortly be no alternative to the British business man except to make the most of it.

RELATIONS TO THE GOVERNMENT: WAR TIMES

British war organization rests squarely on the associational machinery evolved over the peacetime interlude. A recent issue of the

[58] True, the "criterion of action" of each "is solely the public good as they understand it" but what public-relations counselor would offer any other explanation of any given act of any represented business? See J. M. Keynes, *The End of Laissez-Faire* (London, 1926), pp. 41–42.

[59] Debate between J. M. Keynes and Mr. Kingsley-Martin on "Democracy and Efficiency," *New Statesman and Nation,* Jan. 28, 1939. Mr Keynes hopes that this amalgam in defense of "private property and capitalism" will be "liberal," so that he may refer to it as "liberal socialism," and by "liberal" he means nonmonopolistically organized capitalism. Mr. Keynes has not been called a "semanticist."

[60] *Idem.*

[61] See discussions relating to the establishment of the Petroleum, Cotton, and Shipping Control Boards in recent issues of *The Economist,* and *New Statesman and Nation,* and similar sources.

Economist refers to this as the Conservative program which comes to rest in a

set of notions that sees its ideal of an economic system in an orderly organisation of industries, each ruled feudally from above by the business firms already established in it, linked in associations and confederations and, at the top, meeting on terms of sovereign equality such other Estates of the Realm as the Bank of England and the Government. Each British industry, faithful to the prescription, has spent the past decade in delimiting its fief, in organising its baronial courts, in securing and entrenching its holdings and in administering the legal powers of self-government conferred on it by a tolerant State. This is the order of ideas that has transformed the trade association from a body of doubtful legality, a conspiracy in restraint of trade, into a favoured instrumentality of the State, until membership in such a body has become as necessary to the business man who wishes to be successful as an old school tie has been to the ambitious Conservative politicians. It is the order of ideas that led to the Import Duties Act being drafted in such a way as to put a premium on self-seeking monopolies and a discount on the public interest; that turned "high profits and low turn-over" into the dominant slogan of British business; that raised the level of British costs to the highest in the world. It is a set of ideas that is admirable for obtaining security, "orderly development" and remunerative profits for those already established in the industry—at the cost of an irreducible body of general unemployment. It is emphatically not a set of ideas that can be expected to yield the maximum of production, or to give the country wealth in peace and strength in war.[62]

In an earlier issue [63] the *Economist* pointed out that this comes out simply to mean that

under the cover of wartime needs, the principle of Self-government of Industry has been given an official blessing. This is, in effect, merely the expansion and continuation of the Industrial policy that has been pursued by the Conservative Government for the past eight years, for in their hands control has nearly always meant the conferment of legal privileges on the organized producers already established in the industry . . . industries are being encouraged to control themselves.[64]

---

[62] "A Check on Production," *Economist*, June 15, 1940.

[63] "The Economic Front," *Economist*, Dec. 9, 1939.

[64] While government officials are thinking of post war planning, comments *New Statesman and Nation* (March 8, 1941), "the hard-faced men from the Midlands quietly get on with their job, Mr. Bevin and the other Socialist leaders utter blood-curdling threats, but the monopoly interests (just as in America under the NRA) are taking steps to safeguard their interests. We are to have planning—that is the present so-called controls, which are merely a glorified form of private monopolies

In contrast to the last war, when "the controllers were selected in the main from outside the industry to be controlled," in "this war industry is controlling itself." This "feudalistic system of cartel control" it illustrates with a list of controllers appointed by the two leading war-control ministries: [65]

MINISTRY OF SUPPLY

Commodity	Head Controller	Principal business interests or previous occupation
Aluminium	Hon. G. Cunliffe	Director, British Aluminium Company, Ltd.
Alcohol, molasses and solvents	Mr. A. V. Board	Chairman, British Industrial Solvents, Ltd.; Director, Distillers Co. Ltd., and International Sugar and Alcohol Co., Ltd.
Cotton	Sir Percy Ashley	Member of Import Duties Advisory Committee
Flax	Sir H. Lindsay	Director of the Imperial Institute
	Mr. J. S. Ferrier (Deputy)	Director, Wm. F. Malcolm & Co., Ltd. (flax, hemp and jute merchants)
Hemp	Mr. A. M. Landauer	Landauer & Co. (Hemp and fibre merchants)
Iron and Steel	Sir A. Duncan	Chairman, British Iron and Steel Federation; Member of Supply Council

run on a restrictive basis, are to be maintained. . . . What we shall get is a set of private monopolies fighting to win by State compulsion as big a share of the total real income for as little service as possible." Another writer in the same issue adds, "If this so-called self-government of industry is permitted to crystallize itself we shall be gravely prejudicing the problem of reconstruction. We shall find that we have lost our liberty to choose between a return to a competitive system and the establishment of a planned economic system. We shall be confronted with a strongly entrenched co-operative organization of industry on a restrictionist basis—not unlike the Italian fascist economy—impossible to unscramble. Unfortunately the influence of Trade Union leaders is exerted—unwittingly—in the same direction to the ultimate disadvantage of those whose interests they think they represent. But the record of the Duce's system surely does not invite imitation."

[65] "The Economic Front," *Economist*, Dec. 9, 1939.

Commodity	Head Controller	Principal business interests or previous occupation
Jute	Mr. G. Malcolm	Director, Ralli ·Bros., Ltd. (Merchant bankers)
Leather	Dr. E. C. Snow	United Tanners' Federation
Non-ferrous metals	Capt. O. Lyttelton	Chairman, Anglo-Oriental & General Investment Trust, Ltd.; chairman or director of various tin and other non-ferrous metal companies; managing director, British Metal Corporation, Ltd.
Paper	Mr. A. Ralph Reed	Chairman and managing director, Albert E. Reed & Co., Ltd. (paper manufacturers), and chairman of other paper companies
Silk and artificial silks	Mr. H. O. Hambleton	Wm. Frost and Co. (Silk throwsters)
Sulphuric acid fertilizers	Mr. F. C. O. Speyer	Director, Imperial Chemicals Industries, I.C.I. (Fertilizer and Synthetic Products) Ltd., (delegate), International Nitrogen Association, Ltd., Scottish Agricultural Industries, Ltd. (Subsidiary of Imperial Chemical Industries)
	Mr. N. Garrod Thomas	
	Mr. Howard Cunningham	Director, Scottish Agricultural Industries, Ltd.
Timber	Major A. I. Harris	Louis Bamberger & Sons (timber importers); Past-President, Timber Trade Association

Commodity	Head Controller	Principal business interests or previous occupation
Wool	Sir H. B. Schackleton	Taylor, Schackleton & Co. (weavers); Hon. President, Bradford Manufacturers' Federation; chairman, Wool Textile Delegation; president, Woolen & Worsted Trades Federation

MINISTRY OF FOODS

Butter	Mr. H. E. Davis	London Manager of Dominion of New Zealand Dairy Sales Division
Cereals and cereal products	Sir Alan Anderson	Chairman, Anderson, Green & Co. (shipbrokers and managers); member of Royal Commission on Wheat Supplies, 1914–19
Feeding stuffs	Sir Bruce Burt	Indian Agricultural Service
Tea	Sir Hubert Carr	Late managing director, Balmer, Lawrie and Co., Ltd., controlled by Lawrie (Alex.) & Co., Ltd., managing agents to tea estate companies
Canned fish	Mr. Dan Tobey	Chairman, companies controlled by Associated Canners, Ltd. (subsidiary, Lever Brothers & Unilever, Ltd.); director, Associated Canners, Ltd.
Meat and livestock	Sir Francis Boys	Vice-chairman, Livestock Commission; Member Bacon Development Board; Director and

Commodity	Head Controller	Principal business interests or previous occupation
Bacon and ham	Mr. J. F. Bodinnar	Vice-chairman, New Zealand Refrigerating Co., Ltd., 1923–33 Chairman, Bacon Marketing Board; Member, Bacon Development Board; Deputy-chairman, various bacon companies
Dried fruits	Mr. A. E. Gough (*Designate*)	Managing Director, Overseas Farmers Cooperative Federation, Ltd.
Sugar	Col. F. C. C. Balfour (*Chairman of Board*)	Chairman of Sugar Commission; formerly Sudan Political Service
Imported eggs	Mr. J. A. Peacock	Director and Secretary, Nurdin & Peacock, Ltd. (provision, egg and butter importers)
Potatoes	Capt. J. M. Mollett (*Designate*)	Chairman, Potato Marketing Board
Oils and fats	Mr. Herbert Davis	Director of Lever Bros. and Unilever, Ltd.
Condensed milk	Mr. E. W. Brown	Director of Napier, Brown & Co., Ltd. (sugar merchants)

The *Economist* finds [66] that for all practical purposes these Head Controllers can be said to be the direct representatives of the leading trade association or the allied nuclei of trade associations dominant in its field. Such an arrangement would seem, then, to be merely the wartime adaptation of a program [67] which calls for a

[66] "In this war-time organization of control the representative board of trade association is, it is true, replaced (usually) by the single controller. But the principle stands: industries are being encouraged to control themselves." *Ibid.*

[67] "This method of proceeding is . . . in line with the present Government's pre-war record. It is a continuation of the policy of handing over powers to such bodies as the colliery-owners, the Iron and Steel Federation, and the shipowners, and other capitalist groups which have been given authority to control production and prices, or to distribute public subsidies, or to impose levies for eliminating "redundant" plant, or what not. The present Government is pre-eminently a capitalist Govern-

centrally controlled "plutodemocracy," a sort of "new feudal system, with the British market, instead of the British land, parcelled out among the barons." [68]

Another example treated by the *Economist* (Feb. 15, 1941) as typical and symptomatic of the extent to which organized British business is taking advantage of the war situation to further consolidate monopolistic controls, is given by the development of the "Retailers' Front." It is worth quoting at length:

Associations of retail traders have grown very much in strength since the war started. Indeed, within their own ranks, it is often said that a few months of war have brought them nearer to their objectives than many years of hard work in peacetime. The reason is not far to seek. These associations aim to speak for entire trades with a single voice in accordance with a common policy; and the control of supplies and regulation of prices by the Government have brought home to "independent" retailers the need of some spokesman or intermediary between them and the authorities. Individual traders are in no position to make constant approaches to public departments and official committees for information or to bombard these bodies with complaints and suggestions. So in every branch of trade, they flock into associations in search of aid or shelter.

The tendency is natural and the result unexceptionable insofar as it makes wartime organization easier. In war economy cooperative groups can undoubtedly exercise useful functions. But some of the consequences must be suspect. The direction of these associations is always quasi-monopolistic domination of their trades, and in wartime this trend is encouraged in many ways. In every business scarcity and the limitations of supplies check newcomers. Prices tend to go up, and price cutters—hitherto the chief obstacles to the associations' policy of keeping prices up—fare badly. The associations wax while their rivals wane.

Moreover, the various associations work together. Representations on any question relating to, say, retail tobacconists will possibly be made, not only by their own associations, but also by the associations, unions and federations, local and national, of confectioners, newsagents, hotels and restaurants and off-license holders—perhaps even with the backing of that active general body, the Retail Distributors Association. Each trade is a hierarchy, beginning with the local or district organization and rising to a National Council or Federation, and as all these hierar-

---

ment, and almost its one idea in matters of economic policy has been to endow the big capitalist associations and combines with authority over the consumers." *New Statesman and Nation*, April 2, 1938.

[68] "The New Feudalism," *Economist*, April 2, 1938.

chies interlock in their activities, it means that horizontally, as well as vertically, over the whole field of retailing they exercise a nation-wide power in pursuit of aims which are often by no means national.[69]

As policy coördinator for this swiftly unfolding and cartel-like apparatus of trade associations, given an added fillip for more rapid extension of their powers and influence in the current national emergency, the Federation of British Industries takes on a new and far-reaching significance. Commanded at the top by a small coterie of officials who are drawn chiefly from large concerns or from concerns under the influence or control of the giants in their respective fields, and with both officials and controlling concerns bound together by an infinity of interconnections—personal, family, and institutional—into a tightly meshed business oligarchy vested with political powers of propaganda and coercion, this is the British pattern in the making; in trend, at least, it does not seem very different from that already dominant in states formally committed to the "corporate idea." The eventuality remains to be seen.

[69] "Retailers' Front," *Economist*, Feb. 15, 1941, pp. 206–7.

Chapter VI

THE AMERICAN WAY: "BUSINESS
SELF-REGIMENTATION"

THE ORIGIN of the National Association of Manufacturers stems from a decade of combinations par excellence. Between 1890 and 1900 more and larger combinations took place than in the entire preceding history of this country. This is true whether one directs attention to mere number of consolidations, number of workmen employed, or amount of capital involved. A speaker arguing for a federal law of incorporation before the National Association of Manufacturers in 1904 summarized the amazing record: [1]

Statistics show that in the decade between 1860 and 1870 only two industrial trusts, formed by the combination of formerly competing concerns, had been created, and that with a total capitalization of only thirteen millions of dollars. In the next decade between 1870 and 1880, four more were formed, with a capitalization of one hundred and thirty-five million dollars. Between 1880 and 1890 eighteen more were formed, with a capitalization of two hundred twenty-eight millions of dollars; while the last census shows one hundred eighty-three combinations with a capitalization of $3,619,039,200 . . . In 1902 it is claimed that there were 213 combinations, with a capitalization of seven billions of dollars; while now it is claimed that there are nearly 1,000 industrial combinations, not including railroads, with a nominal capitalization of $9,000,-000,000.[2]

[1] Alvin J. McCrary, "Another View of National Incorporation Needs," *American Industries*, Oct. 1, 1904, p. 13.

[2] ". . . by 1904 the trusts controlled fully two-fifths of the manufacturing capital of the country." Henry R. Seager and Charles A. Gulick, *Trust and Corporation Problems* (New York, 1929), p. 61. These authors define trusts somewhat more narrowly than the speaker before the NAM, their total estimated "trust" capitalization of 1904 being given as $5,000,000,000.

THE HISTORICAL SETTING: A TREND
TOWARDS MONOPOLY

Few fields of business activity escaped this flight from "free competition" entirely. In one form or another—corporate consolidations, pools, gentlemen's agreements, interlocking directorates—the larger movement affected the leading branches of industry, commerce, finance, and transportation. Though in line with trends reaching back through the preceding decades, the process was so swift and so far-reaching that it appeared to many that shortly it must engulf the whole of the American economic system. As the facts became generally known clamor against the trusts mounted, for it seemed that when, of the outstanding combinations, "26 controlled 80 per cent or more of the aggregate production in their fields; 57, 60 per cent or more; and 78, 50 per cent or more," [3] it was time that all classes sit up and take notice of the revolutionary changes being brought about in the American economic scene.

Smaller businessmen throughout the country concurred in the antitrust movement. But although then, as now,[4] the bulk of the complaints looking toward legislative and judicial action against the trusts emanated from affected business circles, businessmen showed little inclination to organize to such an end. Leaving these matters to the government, they chose, instead, to pool their resources so as to present a united front in promoting more extensive aid and grants of privilege from the political authorities which would prove of common value to them all. Thus arose, along with, and at first entirely independent of, the large combinations, the trade-association movement. The "trusts" had dramatized the advantages of massed and centrally directed economic power. The trade associations hoped not to level down the trusts, but to "democratize" analogous privileges for the business community as a whole.

---

[3] *Idem.*

[4] "It is business men and business men alone who file practically all the complaints with my division, and it is for business men that the anti-trust laws must be enforced." Thurman W. Arnold, Assistant Attorney General of the United States in an address before the American Bar Association, San Francisco, July 10, 1939. Release of the Temporary National Economic Committee (TNEC).

This covert and loose form of combination, commonly termed in American business circles "business coöperation" was entirely in keeping with the anticompetitive spirit of the times. It was further stimulated by the fact that the more open type of collusive action, the "pool," was quickly driven from the field as a result of federal antitrust prosecutions. Since the "pool" was the Americanized form of the cartel, this country was "saved . . . from the European cartel system," [5] the better to allow trade associations to grow more slowly into the exercise of powers and influence which in many respects now reach far beyond those of all except the more advanced cartels abroad.[6]

In this mushroom growth of new forms of business "self-regimentation," [7] the National Association of Manufacturers occupied from its inception in 1895 a central, and in some respects a commanding, position. It was by all odds the largest, most carefully laid out, and the most enduring of the looser forms of business organization established for the specific purpose of centralizing, unifying, coördinating, and more effectively focusing policies relating to the business system as a whole. Others had preceded it, but with typically much smaller industrial coverage and with much narrower range of interests.[8] It was the peculiar role of the NAM to undertake the coördination of the efforts of all business associations—existing, subsequently organized, and special-purpose—in the entirety of manufacturing industries of the whole United States.

THE CHANGING PROGRAM FOR INDUSTRIAL COÖRDINATION

The original statement of principles given out by the National Association of Manufacturers provided a précis for all that was to

[5] See Thurman Arnold, "The Anti-Trust Laws, Their Past and Future," address over the Columbia Broadcasting System, Aug. 19, 1939. Released by TNEC.

[6] As shown, for example, in Federal investigation of the National Electric Light Association (now the Edison Electrical Institute) and the National Lumber Manufacturers' Association. See also statements by Dr. Theodore J. Kreps, Economic Consultant of the TNEC (release of the TNEC, Jan. 15, 1940) and Professor Clair Wilcox (New York Times, Jan. 20, 1940) at the Cartel Hearings before the TNEC.

[7] This is the expression used by Thurman Arnold in his various speeches dealing with what is commonly called "coöperation" by businessmen.

[8] Such as the various associations established to fight organized labor, e. g., the Stove Founder's National Defense Association, an outgrowth of the National As-

follow: "The general objects and purposes for which the said corporation is formed are the promotion of the industrial interests of the United States, the betterment of the -relations between employer and employee, the education of the public in the principles of individual liberty and the ownership of property, the support of legislation in furtherance of those principles and opposition to legislation in derogation thereof." [9] According to later spokesmen, it has fulfilled this declaration of principles almost to the limits of desire. Speaking at the Thirty-Fourth Annual Meeting of the NAM, October, 1929, President Edgerton evaluated its achievements in colorful encomium:

> In eighteen hundred ninety-five near both the geographic and population centers of the United States, there occurred an event which though unheralded was even then generally recognized as of momentous importance to the nation. But its more complete significance required and has received the dispassionate testimony of history. At that auspicious time and appropriate place, the National Association of Manufacturers, fathered by necessity and summoned by conscious opportunity, sprang exultantly like Minerva from the forehead of Jove into immediately useful existence. Notice was thus given to the world for the first time that the American manufacturing industry had come of age, and that it could and thereafter would *speak with one voice on every occasion of common defense and on all occasions pertaining to its general welfare.*
>
> At our birth in 1895 there was scarcely a handful of industrial associations of any size or character in the United States. Those in existence were almost exclusively trade organizations formed primarily for defense against the rising cloud of labor trade unions. *Ours was the first and has continued to be the only general organization of manufacturers exclusively embracing all trades, conditions, sections, and sizes of industrial units.* We have witnessed and often assisted at birth of nearly every state association, of practically all the associations, and of many of the special organizations now serving particular trade, geographic, or other homogeneous groups.[10]

sociation of Stove Manufacturers, which was founded in 1886 as an antiunion employers' association. Similar were the American Newspaper Publishers' Association and the United Typothetae of America, both founded in 1887.

9 Constitution and By-Laws of the National Association of Manufacturers of the United States, Article II, Section I.

10 *Proceedings,* 34th Annual Meeting of the National Association of Manufacturers (Oct., 1929), pp. 14–15. Italics mine.

The age was one of organization, "an age," said President Kirby in 1911,[11] "when but little can be accomplished except through organization; an age when organization must cope with organization. . . ." All businessmen must join them, and join as many of them as they could. The NAM was to serve as the "mother of associations," that all American industry might be organized from center to circumference. But at the center was to stand the NAM, functioning as a central policy-pressure and policy-forming body for all organized activity, irrespective of the angle or the nature of the interest at stake. As a more recent brochure puts it, the NAM is dedicated to promotion of "Unit Thinking and Unit Acting on the Part of American Industry." [12] It represents "The Nation's Industry—Organized," [13] or "The Nation's Industry Synchronized," [14] the better to promote "the universalization of those saving principles of American Industry—the right of those who own property to control it." [15] Its spokesmen think of control of property as it relates to all things and with respect to all men, classes, interests, and principles.

The Association has accomplished its ends sometimes by direct pressure of organized lobbies, sometimes by the aid of propaganda, and sometimes by the further organization of business interests along special trade, regional, or industrial lines.[16] And its history traces the evolution of efforts to round out its program of centralizing common business policies to their full social, economic, and political implications.

In accordance with changes in the general economic and political scene, its major emphasis has shifted from time to time. Thus, at the beginning, the Association was primarily concerned with the dual objectives of tariff protection at home and promotion of favorable markets abroad. It held to this dominating interest until 1903, when, under the influence of a wave of strikes and trade-

---

[11] *Proceedings*, 16th Annual Convention (May, 1911), pp. 65–87.

[12] NAM, Pamphlet, 1935.   [13] NAM, Pamphlet, 1923.

[14] NAM, Pamphlet, "Being a Brief History of the National Association of Manufacturers," undated.

[15] Speech delivered by President John E. Edgerton, and published in the NAM *Proceedings*, Oct., 1929.

[16] For comprehensive discussion of these activities see LaFollette Committee Reports, Parts 17, 18, and 19, and Report No. 6, Part 6.

union activity, and through the direction of its new president David M. Parry, it shifted its efforts to combating trade unions and advancing the plan of the open shop. Although it did not abandon its original interest, but steadily increased its pressure for favorable tariff legislation, more active government aid in the expansion of foreign markets, and similar aims,[17] its activities were largely dominated by the problem of trade-union expansion until the United States entered the World War.

With the war and its aftermath, interests began to broaden out more nearly in line with the general agenda of the original statement of principles. The influence of the war on the NAM's conception of its role in the national economic picture was especially profound and far-reaching. As in all belligerent countries, war control in the United States was exercised primarily through the intermediation of businessmen and business organization. Businessmen held the principal control offices and made the key administrative decisions in economic affairs.[18] And in all their activities they naturally and habitually turned to their own organizations for the instrumentation of policies—policies which combined, so happily, patriotic performance of a critical "public duty" with lucrative gains to the trades and industries which the businessmen repre-

[17] Specifically, such as the following: "home markets should be retained" and "foreign relations . . . extended in every direction and manner not inconsistent therewith"; the "principle of reciprocity" should be applied wherever possible; there should be a "judicious system of subsidies of our merchant marine"; the Nicaraguan (and later the Panama) Canal should be constructed by the Federal Government; natural and artificial waterways "should be improved and extended." NAM pamphlet, "The Nation's Industry Synchronized."

[18] Aside from the regular governmental and war departments, the following were the principal war control agencies: Food Administration, presided over by Herbert Hoover, a mining industrialist; Fuel Administration, presided over by Harry A. Garfield, former President of the Cleveland Chamber of Commerce and Director of the Cleveland Trust Co.; War Industries Board, directed by Bernard Baruch, a Wall Street financier and stock-market operator; War Trade Board, directed by Vance McCormick, of the family associated with the International Harvester Co. In all these boards and committees, and throughout all leading offices in the regular federal machinery primarily concerned with the war and not filled by regular staff, businessmen predominated, made the decisions, gave the orders, set the prices, determined legitimate costs, and set allowable profit margins—in industries which they controlled or dominated in their private capacities, and out of which most of their concerns achieved large, and in a few cases, colossal earnings. See the summary report of the Nye Committee on the Munitions Industry, 74th Congress, 2d Session, Report No. 944, Part 4.

sented and which must now supply the necessary goods and services.[19]

During the war days two leading ideas struck root in the business community which were destined to exercise growing influence in the postwar years. The first of these was the conception of universal organization of all business enterprise into all-inclusive and appropriate trade and industrial associations. The War Emergency and Reconstruction Conference was held by the Chamber of Commerce of the United States [20] in December, 1918, and was participated in actively by representatives of the NAM. A "Resolution on trade associations" adopted by the conference summarized the point: "This conference heartily approves the plan of organizing each industry in the country in a representative national trade association and expresses the belief that every dealer, jobber, manufacturer, and producer of raw materials should be a member of the national organization in his trade and cordially support it in its work." [21]

The second, and related idea came subsequently to be known by the slogan "self-government in industry," meaning specifically that any such organization of trade, commerce, and industry should be autonomous, interdependent, self-regulating. The idea was discussed extensively in the literature of the day, and gave rise to a series of trade-practice agreements according to which the government was to turn over the governance of economic affairs, trade by trade, and industry by industry, to public-spirited business leaders.

[19] "The record of the war service committees," said Mr. Sibley, President of the Chamber of Commerce of the United States in an address before the Trade Association Executives in New York City, Jan. 28, 1936, "is one of lasting achievement." Business and government learned for the first time to work together "in time of emergency" and the businessman within his own industry "found himself in the position of working coöperatively." From pamphlet material published by the Chamber of Commerce of the United States.

An attempt was made at an Atlantic City convention, called shortly after the close of the war, to organize the various industry "war service committees," of which there were nearly 400, into a single organization to perpetuate in peace times the controls, and promote habits of "working together," etc., with which these organized business groups had become familiar in the emergency of war. The proposal contained most of the leading ideas subsequently incorporated into NRA.

[20] The National Association of Manufacturers participated actively in the organization of the Chamber of Commerce of the United States, though at times policies of the two central organizations seems to have been in rather serious conflict.

[21] Sibley, in his address of Jan. 28, 1936.

Though finally discouraged by an adverse judgment of the Attorney General that such "agreements" might be in violation of the Anti-Trust acts,[22] the idea persisted and, under the active support of the Department of Commerce and its vigorous secretary, Mr. Hoover, became a sort of theme-song of the "New Economic Era."

Correlative with these new interests, and largely under the stimulus of the labor difficulties and the "deportations delirium" of the immediate postwar period, many of the leading trade associations evolved a new labor program. Designed primarily to keep the "open shop"—sometimes known as the "American Plan," sometimes labeled "management relations," or "industrial relations," or "personnel relations"—the drive found its principal expression in active and widespread promotion of company unions. The leadership in this movement was quickly taken by the NAM.[23]

The idea underlying its "Open Shop Committee" was that the "American Plan" of no trade unions, and "free bargaining" between employer and employee (sometimes organized in company unions), would bring "industrial peace" throughout the nation. By these methods "harmony between labor and capital" was to be achieved "cooperatively," just as "self-government in industry" was to bring about uniformity in business practices while elevating these to a moral plane which would no longer require governmental regulation.

The great depression, which broke in the fall of 1929, brought this rosy-colored dream world of the New Economic Era to a rude close. In the midst of the ensuing confusion, the New Deal was born; offering, as many believed, a thoroughly rational set of compromises, it set grimly to the task of reconciling what soon proved to be at bottom irreconcilable conflicts of interest. NRA took over Mr. Hoover's revamped wartime idea of "self-government in industry" (a quasi-monopolistic notion) and tried to wed it to President Roosevelt's Jeffersonian conception of a felicitous economic paradise—an honest competitive system. It quickly appeared that

22 They were not, however, discontinued entirely. The FTC has continued down to the present time to organize "trade practice agreements," though under the guise of devices for eliminating "unfair" and "dishonest" trade practices. See TNEC Monograph No. 34.

23 See Albion Guilford Taylor, *Labor Policies of the National Association of Manufacturers* (University of Illinois Studies in the Social Sciences, Urbana, Ill., 1928).

the Codes served to transform the leading trade associations into cartel-like bodies endowed with extraordinary and far-reaching powers which came directly into conflict with previous antitrust legislation. And, at the same time that they appeared to offer a carte blanche to various forms of collusive action undertaken by these central agencies, Article 7a gave a tremendous stimulus to antipathetic labor organization. Once deflation had overtaken the flight of fancy which envisioned every man and all classes putting their shoulders to the wheel on behalf of a common aim (recovery and the general welfare) in an emergency of peace, disillusionment returned; it was accompanied by a new wave of strikes and lockouts and by a more virulent phase of both commercial and labor warfare.

The program and the mood of the National Association of Manufacturers shifted accordingly. If we properly interpret their literature, though happy about the adoption of their pet idea, "self-government in business," [24] they had smelled a rat in the New Deal program from the outset. Smelled it and pointed it out. But with the new formulation of the issues, symbolized in the mass expansion of the labor movement, all problems seemed transmuted into political and ideological terms.

The National Association of Manufacturers began to move into the picture with a new set of working objectives. Rather, one should say, with an old set of objectives seen in a quite new perspective.[25] This perspective called for a greatly expanded program of public relations. Beginning with a small allocation of some $36,500 in 1934, within four years the "public information program" had increased to $793,043 in 1937, or from 7.2 percent of the NAM's total budget to 55.1 percent.[26] Astonishing as this shift in emphasis may appear, the figures tell only a small part of the story. The totals here cited involve only out-of-pocket expenditures of the NAM; most of the "information" was disseminated through

[24] See the series of bulletins issued in 1934 by the NAM (jointly with the National Industrial Conference Board) and entitled "Industrial Self-Government."

[25] Referring to the labor program in a letter to Evart C. Stevens, President of the International Silver Company, on June 22, 1936, Colby M. Chester, President of the NAM said that "in 1903 the Association adopted a set of principles, which is still officially our 'Bible' in this field." The same is true of other declared principles.

[26] From the LaFollette Committee, Report No. 6, Part 6, *Labor Policies of Employers' Associations*, p. 168, "The National Association of Manufacturers."

space-and-time contributions of media or was paid for by other organizations.[27] If we may take at face value the testimony of William B. Warner, President of the NAM in 1937, that the total commercial value of the national public-information program "would be more like that amount [$793,043] for each state, instead of for the United States, if it were on a pay-as-you-go program," [28] then by 1937 the commercial value of this campaign was perhaps upwards of $36,000,000.

The central thesis of this outpouring of propaganda called for nothing short of conversion of the public at large to the economic objectives, the ideals, and the program of the business community as a whole. Its whole program for governmental aid, support, and coöperation, reaching back to the days of 1895, was now transformed into a campaign against "government interference in business." The only alternative offered by their programs was, by implication, full and complete government coördination with the needs, interests, and social outlook of organized business. And its whole anti-union drive, memorialized in thousands of articles, speeches, and brochures from 1903 on, was now to be transposed and fitted as a central foundation stone in the new and revitalized public-relations program. To overreach labor, to state the matter somewhat epigrammatically, it was first necessary to change the outlook of government; and to accomplish this purpose, it was first necessary to convert the general public. In this new propaganda offensive, nothing was to be left out which could influence in any decisive fashion the loyalty or social outlook of any member of the public, old or young, male or female, in the ranks of labor or the professional classes.

OUTWARD SPREAD OF THE ORGANIZATIONAL NETWORK

At first glance, the membership record of the National Association of Manufacturers is unimpressive. The initial gathering in 1895 included 583 manufacturing members. By 1901 membership had almost doubled, reaching in that year a total of 1,082. Yet, ac-

---

[27] Most of the radio, outdoor advertising, and newspaper space via which the propaganda was fed out was contributed space. To each of these in the year indicated was contributed a minimum of one million dollars. *Idem.*

[28] *Idem.*

cording to the 1900 Census, there were 296,440 manufacturing establishments in the United States.[29] On the surface such a coverage seems insignificant. Rapid as was the growth of membership in subsequent years,[30] the percentage of all manufacturing establishments brought into the organization has always been extremely small.

Inspection of the rather incomplete records, however, shows quite a different picture. Member concerns, if not always the largest in their fields, have typically been among the leaders. In a year (1915) when the membership fluctuated around 4,000, a spokesman for the association found that "The Members of our National Association of Manufacturers alone employ, in normal times, nearly six million workers, and the members of this association manufacture, in America, each year, more goods, measured by money values, than are produced by the entire population of any other nation of the world." [31] Ten years later another spokesman declared that members of the NAM represented an invested capital of something like four billion dollars.[32]

Impressive as such figures may be when taken by themselves—and the picture has not changed much with respect to coverage today [33]—it would still seem that on such a basis the NAM fell far short of its claim to represent the whole of industrial activity in America.[34] This defect has been remedied by the establishment of the National Industrial Council, organized and controlled by the NAM, and designed to include in its membership all associations, national and local, which represent all the industrial enterprises of America.

Originally known as the National Council for Industrial Defense, the National Industrial Council was founded in 1907 "as a

[29] This total did "not include 215,814 hand trades; 127,419 establishments with a product of less than $500; 138 governmental establishments and 383 educational, eleemosynary and penal institutions." Twentieth Century Fund, *Big Business, Its Growth and Its Place* (New York, 1937), p. 34.

[30] 2,707 in 1903; 4,000 in 1916; 4,500 in 1919; 6,000 in 1924. The most recent figure is given as 7,500. NAM brochure, "Women, Partners with Industry in the Economic and Social Advancement of the Nation."

[31] *American Industries*, May, 1915, p. 22.

[32] *Ibid.*, Nov., 1925, p. 5.   [33] See pp. 201–2.

[34] In a prepared statement before the LaFollette Committee, Mr. Walter B. Weisenburger of the NAM estimated that members of the NAM "employ between one-third and one-half of all workers in manufacturing industry." LaFollette Committee Reports, Part 18, pp. 7850–51.

joint legislative committee of the National Association of Manufacturers and the Citizens' Industrial Association of America." [35] Its membership is made up exclusively of associations, and its functions are controlled by the NAM through the devices of common officers, common headquarters, common research staff, and through a largely coöptative—in effect, largely self-elected and self-perpetuating—executive committee. By 1913 its membership included 253 national, state, and local organizations. By 1920, this number had grown to 300. Subsequently the Council has shown relatively slight increase in number of member associations, but the coverage of these associations has been enormously expanded.[36]

In fact, one of the purposes in establishing the NIC was to prevent undue multiplication, duplication, and overlapping of employer organizations. An NAM brochure of 1928 makes this clear. "While functioning as a national body, the leaders of the association realized the value of work on a decentralized basis and inaugurated campaigns for the organization of state manufacturers' associations. Their efforts were rewarded by the formation and development of many such organizations, and to coordinate their efforts, thus eliminating unnecessary duplication of effort, the National Industrial Council was organized by the Association." [37] This is a consistent following out of the original intentions of its founders, as is shown by the speech of President Van Cleave one year after the founding of the new body:

I called a meeting of representatives of a number of various organizations here at the Waldorf-Astoria, and after several meetings we finally succeeded in getting a simple working-plan. We realized the undesirability of multiplied associations, and we finally adopted the plan that, working under the auspices of the National Association of Manufacturers, we would ask of these various organizations, both national and state, and of the local boards of trade and associations of business men to authorize this council movement, which we designated the National Council for Industrial Defense, to authorize us to represent them. The

35 Clarence E. Bonnett, *Employers' Associations in the United States* (New York, 1922), p. 374.
36 In the statement of Mr. Weisenburger quoted in footnote 34, it is estimated that through the NIC the NAM "comes in contact with an additional 40,000 manufacturers."
37 NAM, "The Nation's Industry Synchronized," p. 14.

National Association of Manufacturers becomes primarily, but not fully the financial representative.[38]

Its purpose was and is to focus all manufacturing power, local and national, on behalf of mutual interests in general, but particularly with respect to legislation bearing upon the labor question. This is shown both by its declared objectives as stated in its constitution, and by general commentary in the trade press of the times. Among the stated objectives the following are particularly significant:

To establish and maintain a legislative reference bureau for the compilation, analysis and distribution of accurate and timely information respecting legislation affecting industrial relations.

To advise its members with respect to legislation proposed or enacted, affecting their business relations with the various departments of the national government and with state governments when deemed advisable.

To preserve and promote the principles of individual freedom for employers and employees in commerce and industry. To emphasize the essential worth of these, and to defend them against legislation calculated to impair or destroy them or the legal remedies by which they are efficiently protected. To appeal to public and legislative opinion respecting these matters through every medium through which it can be legitimately and effectively informed.

Vigorously to oppose class legislation in whatever form it proposes to make it lawful for one class of citizens to do that which remains unlawful for any other class to do. To encourage legislation tending to better the relations between employer and employee.[39]

In 1933 the NAM and in 1936 the NIC underwent general reorganization for the purpose of further centralizing control and tightening up the organizational structure. The changes brought about in the NAM, which we will discuss shortly, fall primarily under centralization of control—although a by-product of efforts along this line was to increase materially the badly impaired membership ranks.[40] The NIC, however, underwent a general overhauling, which transformed it from a loose federation of mis-

[38] NAM, *Proceedings* (1908), p. 295.
[39] Constitution, National Council for Industrial Defense.
[40] Members and noncontributing members had fallen, in 1933, to 1,469. Increase thereafter was as follows: 1934, 1,910; 1935, 2,490; 1936, 2,905; 1937, 3,008. In 1938 membership approached 4,000.

cellaneous trades organizations and employers associations into a compact and efficiently functioning affiliate of the NAM.

Prior to 1936, the NIC had been, in the words of William Frew Long, head of the Associated Industries of Cleveland, composed "almost entirely of State associations, and those of us in local associations rather resented that fact." [41] Furthermore, there had been thrown together under the old arrangement miscellaneous associations, large and small, special-purpose trade associations and general employer associations, without any clear grouping by interests, powers, or functions. This the reorganization was designed to correct, by setting up three distinct types of members. The first is made up of state industrial associations, some 35 [42] in number in 1940, which represent central coördinating associations similar on a state-wide basis to the NAM on a nation-wide basis. The second comprises industrial-employment-relations organizations, mostly on a city-wide basis, but including most of the central employers' associations in the leading manufacturing centers of America. There were 107 of these in 1940. The third group includes (1940) 92 national manufacturing associations, constituting the dominant large associations in both heavy and light manufacturing fields. There are also 14 "miscellaneous" association members.

To state the matter somewhat differently, the NIC is now made up of three functionally different types of associations whose membership is overlapping in part and whose interests are interlaced in an almost infinitely complex pattern. Most of the large manufacturing companies of America belong to the NAM in their corporate capacities. Most of them, likewise, are organized in manufacturing trade associations such as the Iron and Steel Institute, the Cotton Textile Institute, the National Electric Manufacturers Association, and the rest. Again, most of these concerns are located in or near large cities, and are members of employers' associations, such as the Associated Industries of Cleveland and the Industrial Association of San Francisco, primarily concerned with formulating and carrying through a common policy on all phases of labor relations. Finally, most of these manufacturers are to be found in the principal manufacturing states, and are members of state manu-

---

[41] Cited in La Follette Committee Reports, Part 6, No. 6, p. 61.

[42] From data given in a letter from Noel Sargent, Secretary of the NAM, dated Feb. 8, 1940.

facturers' associations interested in formulating common policies on a state-wide or regional basis. In part, consequently, individual membership is fourfold.

This holds almost exclusively, however, for members of the NAM, who, with very few exceptions, are members of the other three types of associations brought together in the NIC. But as one goes from the national manufacturing associations, to the more specifically employers' associations, and down to the state industrial associations, the coverage spreads, and the degree of duplication of membership declines. Under one or another form of representation, it seems probable that the NIC includes in its membership close to 80 percent of all manufacturing activity in the United States. The other 20 percent, with rare exceptions, is made up of small-scale and relatively unimportant concerns.

Thus the reorganization of the NIC has at once simplified, streamlined, and extended the reach of the NAM down through the entirety of the American industrial system. To employ the NAM's own term, the association has taken the step from the "nation's industry organized," to the "nation's industry synchronized."

Paralleling in part this elaborate policy-formulating meshwork is the National Industrial Conference Board. Originally established in 1916, as a by-product of experience in war-controls and war-time habits of "business cooperation," it was designed to serve a two-fold function. On the one hand it was to supply relevant information to the NAM and other sponsoring and member associations; on the other it was to provide the factual background for a convincing propaganda that has been adjusted, as it has evolved over the years, to meet all levels of intelligence and knowledge, and to affect professor, housewife, and day laborer.

It was, consequently, advertised as an "impartial, fact-finding body," whose object it would be to investigate all aspects of industrial life, and through its analyses and publications "promote good understanding and friendly relations between employees and employers for the benefit of both, and between those engaged in industry and the public, for the general good of the community." This was to be done in "cooperation with individuals, institutions, associations, and agencies of the Government," to the end that, by making its findings generally available to legislatures, scholars, labor and the general public, it might "encourage and promote the sound development of American industry by all proper and legitimate means." [43]

The NICB was a "war baby," and it participated actively in the promotions of coördination of the war effort. On the practical side, it assisted in, and by spokesman of the NAM has been given credit for, the formation of the War Labor Board. [44] On the ideological front it promoted "unit thinking." As Mr. L. W. O'Leary, President of the National Metal Trades Association expressed it in 1920, "The National Industrial Conference Board is of . . . great value in that it is bringing about uniformity of thought and action among employers, woefully lacking in the past. We are thinking together." [45]

The Board's research facilities are elaborate, expensive, and impressive. Occupying sumptuous quarters on lower Park Avenue, New York City, it is equipped with a large research staff, extensive library facilities, and a vast corps of domestic and foreign correspondents, who enable it to turn out research findings on a mass production basis. To give even an outline of its functions and product would require an extensive monograph. [46]

Its activities fall under three mains heads, Discussion, Research and Publication, and Service. The first includes four different types of special committee meetings: Private Meetings of the Conference Board (monthly), Advisory Committee Meetings (periodic), meetings of a Conference Board of Statisticians in Industry (monthly), and of the Conference of Corporate Statisticians (monthly). [47] Research and Publication include Books and Special Reports (comprising seven subdivisions), Periodical Publications (four subdivisions), and Confidential Memoranda (including key information sent on request to members, and also regular circulars). Service includes a Reference Library, Publicity, and Correspondence. Foreign correspondents, executive officials strategically located in the leading industrial centers of the world, keep the

---

43 Bonnett, *Employers' Associations*, p. 478.
44 *Ibid.*, p. 490.   45 *Ibid.*, p. 483.
46 A good general outline of the Conference Board's work, functions, and organization is given in its 23d Annual Report, revised to Jan. 1, 1940.
47 Additional conferences are held from time to time by business economists, personnel executives, and foreign trade executives.

Board in close and intimate contact with developments abroad. There is practically nothing the Board does not examine—local, national, or international—of interest to the economic, political, social and cultural interests of manufacturers' and allied associations.[48]

Having such an elaborate apparatus for soaking up, sifting, disseminating the raw materials for "thinking together" at their beck and call, the NAM and its numerous affiliates are "able to voice a united opinion on vital national questions," and to back up the NAM's claim that it "is the only organization exclusively representing the interests of American industry," [49] on all policies of mutual interest.

Consistent with the view that its central function is to coördinate the thought and action of all American industry, the NAM has promoted the extension of business organization, thus further expanding its own powers, and has at the same time discouraged any other type of organization that might split or divide those powers. A few examples will suffice to show the issues at stake.

It has actively promoted employers' associations (trade, regional, and local), which have become affiliated with it through the National Industrial Council, and it has also aided in the formation of many general- and special-purpose organizations. An example of the former activity is the participation in the organization of the U. S. Chamber of Commerce in 1912, which was established to promote all American business objectives similar to those championed by the NAM for industry. An example of the latter is found in the ill-fated Trades and Workers' Association, organized around 1910 by a Mr. Joseph W. Bryce, expatriate union leader, as an early effort to establish a nation-wide federation of company unions similar in membership and structure to the Labor Front of contemporary Germany.[50] This is illuminating not only for the anal-

---

[48] The "affiliated Organizations" include the Air Corps, the Military Intelligence Division, and the Ordnance Dept. of the U. S. Army, and the Bureau of Ordnance and the Intelligence Division of the U.S. Navy.

[49] NAM, Exhibit 3793, LaFollette Committee Reports, Part 17, pp. 7528–37.

[50] ". . . both employers and employees could become members of the Association." Branches were to be established in various cities, organized by "mixed" or "one trade" lines . . . such as carpenters' branch, a bricklayers' branch, etc., for each locality where there were NAM members. Employers were to lead and conduct all activities. Strikes, lockouts and boycotts were to be prohibited. This type of company-

ogies current times offer, but also because it anticipated issues which were subsequently to engage the NAM in a fundamental organizational problem.

It was not until after the World War that the NAM shifted its general position from violent opposition to unions as such to an attempt to control labor organization by the establishment of company-controlled unions. With the inauguration of the "Open-Shop" drive, according to plans and policy lines laid out by such organizations as the National Metal Trades Association, the Special Conference Committee,[51] and others,[52] members of the NAM had to face the question of setting up central associations especially to handle labor problems separate from other matters of common concern.

This issue came to a head in 1933 with the proposal of A. C. Rees, manager of the Associated Industries of Utah and chairman of the American Plan-Open Shop Conference, to establish a "Council of American Industry" which would parallel the NAM and the NIC in part, but would also "interest . . . large groups such as bankers, Mining Congress, utilities, railroads, telephone companies, shipping interests, oil, etc., . . ." not previously brought into the NAM controlled network.[53] Presented in this form, the issue took on a double meaning. In the first place, Rees was proposing a functional separation of employer-employee problems from the main concern of the NAM and its affiliate system. And, in the second place, this proposal was to unite all employers throughout the nation in all fields of business, whether industry, commerce, or finance.

William Frew Long, manager of the Associated Industries of

dominated labor union corresponds to the Social Catholic concept of "mixed syndicates" (Chapter II). The comparable idea of "parallel" or "collateral syndicates" has been advanced a number of times in the United States. One of the most recent of such proposals was to establish "A National Independent Labor Organization in the Steel Industry" in the late thirties, a plan backed by the NAM. See LaFollette Committee Reports, Part 17, p. 7451.

[51] A secret committee of ten large American corporations, organized in 1919 under the apparent leadership of the Standard Oil of New Jersey, for the purpose of evolving a common labor-relations program for American industry.

[52] Part 45 of the La Follette Commission Reports has material on the activities of the Special Conference Committee and refers to various organizations connected with the committee in one way or another. The committee is discussed further on pages 213–15 of this book.

[53] LaFollette Committee Reports, No. 6, Part 6, pp. 58–59.

Cleveland, succeeded in defeating the Rees plan on the first ground, but was faced with a curious difficulty in the second. If the NAM and its affiliated bodies were to expand their membership to include these additional business interests, how could it remain the exclusive representative of the manufacturing interests of America, as had always been its claim? And if it did not so expand, how could it defend its position as spokesman for the "business point of view as a whole," which it likewise claimed to be?

From the available literature we cannot infer precisely what stand the NAM will take on this issue; Long's reply argued, however, that the various affiliates of the NIC were established for just such purpose as Rees had in mind, and that they were sufficiently inclusive of various types of business interests to really speak for "the community as a whole" on local affairs. In support of this contention, an inspection of the available records, reveals membership and connections which include practically every local interest in the various affiliated employers' associations (organized on a city-wide basis), and in many of the state industrial associations. It does not apply, of course, to the third group made up of national, manufacturing trade associations.

The controversy settled one issue: there was to be no splitting up of the organization of industrial employers into functional groups such as obtains, for example, in England. Whether or not the NAM will attempt to expand its functions so as to represent all employers on a national basis, as its functional NIC affiliates do on a local basis, remains to be seen.[54]

Before leaving this description of the expansion of the NAM network, two other items should be mentioned. First, that its local and regional affiliates attempt to organize and attach to themselves the whole of their separate territories, just as the NAM attempts to do on a national basis. The state associations are particularly effective to this end, and in some areas they appear to have succeeded

[54] There is some evidence of willingness of the NAM to take in banking, financial, shipping, advertising, and similar interests. It is interesting in this connection to note that the proposal of Mr. Almon E. Roth, President of the San Francisco Employers' Council, for "one-big-Union-of-Employers" and "industry-wide collective bargaining," presented before the Industrial Relations Section of the Annual Meeting of the Chamber of Commerce of the United States, May 1, 1940 (mimeographed) inevitably leads to the industry-wide compacts which require that organized labor speaks for all labor as in the famous French "Matignon Agreement" (see pp. 139–45).

208 THE AMERICAN WAY

in making their associational dragnet almost 100 percent complete.[55]

And second, that the NAM has to date shown little disposition to surrender any of its power and influence to any superior body similarly designed to coördinate the activities of industry, trade, finance, and other fields, on behalf of business interests as a whole. At one time, apparently, it hoped for something of this nature from the organization of the Chamber of Commerce of the United States. Serious difficulties arose, attested by the withdrawal of the NAM from the Chamber in the early twenties. More recently, amicable relations have been established; but the Chamber is still far from serving the various associations of associations as a central, policy-coördinating body, in the manner of the NAM and the American Bankers' Association in their respective fields.

CENTRALIZING AND STRENGTHENING THE STRANDS
OF CONTROL WITHIN THE NAM

In estimating the degree of centralized power within the NAM to manipulate business policies, and the extent to which such policies may in effect be implemented, it is necessary to call to the mind of the reader certain familiar facts. These may be detailed seriatim:

1. With minor exceptions the NAM and its affiliates through the NIC are made up of corporations. Correlative with expansion of the NAM's influence throughout the manufacturing community has gone the cumulative transformation of business enterprise from a simple ownership to a corporate footing. Including all forms of American economic activity, business and nonbusiness alike, it has been estimated that the corporate share in 1929 was approximately 57 percent.[56] It is doubtless higher today. The very fact that change has been made from the simple individual business enterprise or partnership to the corporation represents in itself centralization of policy-determining power within the ranks of ownership. All property rights represented by bonds [57] and nonvoting

[55] See La Follette Committee Reports, Parts 20 and 21, for discussion of the organization of the Associated Industries of Cleveland.
[56] Twentieth Century Fund, *Big Business*, p. 16.
[57] I am ignoring the accounting distinction in this connection which excludes bonds from equity holdings. Suffice it to say that these constitute accumulated capital funds which are employed under this peculiar legal and accounting form, but are no less property, despite such identification.

shares are *ipso facto* separated from any voice in management and the determination of policy.

2. Within voting-share ranks, power to participate in the determination of policies is probably narrowed by as much again through the various devices analyzed in such studies as that of Berle and Means.[58] The "property atom" is further split through blocked voting interests, through devices like the holding company, and through the special influence of various interests operating through interlocking directorates, special trust funds, and financial circles. The result is to divide corporate property holders, so that progressively fewer of them participate in the formation of policies, and to concentrate in extremely small inside groups the policy-forming control.[59] The rest of the stockholders possessing voting rights fall into the same class as the nonvoting shareholders and bondholders, and go to make up a large and rapidly growing "rentier" [60] class. The larger the corporation, typically, the more significant this shift.

3. The swift growth in the relative importance of the corporate form and in the further "splitting of the property atom" is paralleled historically by continued extension of the combination movement noted at the beginning of this chapter. With the close of the World War, combination began on a new and higher scale than ever before. "During the ten years, 1919–1928, there were 1,268 combinations in manufacturing and mining," involving "the union of 4,135 separate concerns and the disappearance of 5,991"; and so on throughout practically every field of business enterprise. During the same period, 3,744 public-utility companies disappeared through consolidations.[61] Chain stores, chain-department and mail-order systems, chain and branch banking, and similar types of enterprises expanded with unprecedented speed.

[58] *The Modern Corporation.*

[59] For some rather spectacular examples of the power of small inside groups similar to those outlined by Berle and Means, in the hitherto quite unexplored field of life insurance, see the report of the TNEC *Investigation of Concentration of Economic Power*, Part 4, "Life Insurance."

[60] The term originated with the French government bond called the *rente*. The *rentier* class, made up of several million small bondholders who live largely by clipping coupons, and who, as bondholders, possess absolutely no rights over the source of their income, constitute a model which the holder of the American private corporate security is rapidly approaching. See p. 228.

[61] Twentieth Century Fund, *Big Business*, p. 32.

The results of this rather spectacular concentration of corporate holdings have been pretty well publicized. Speaking before the Temporary National Economic Committee, a representative of Dun and Bradstreet cited a few of the better-known examples. From various governmental sources he found that the output of automobiles was dominated to the extent of 86 percent by three companies; 47 percent of the beef products business by two companies; 20 percent of the bread and other bakery produced by three companies; 90 percent of the can output by three companies; 40 percent of cement by five; 80 percent of the cigarettes by three; 78 percent of the copper by four; 95 percent of the plate glass by two; 64 percent of the iron ore by four; 60.5 percent of the steel by three; and so on.[62] The National Resources Committee found that, using three criteria of size, the hundred largest companies under each respective heading "employed 20.7 per cent of all the manpower engaged in manufacturing, contributed 24.7 per cent of all the value added in manufacturing activity" and "accounted for 32.4 per cent of the value of products reported by all manufacturing plants."[63]

4. The real significance of such concentration is found less in the exercise of direct monopolistic powers[64] than in the position of leadership of these giant concerns in their respective fields. This leadership is applied in two principal ways. First, by such devices as "price leadership," "sharing the market," "price stabilization," "non-price competition," and the like;[65] these devices the smaller concerns are unable to oppose successfully, and must either "follow the leader" or face a variety of pressures which experience demonstrates they cannot possibly hope, in the normal course of affairs, to survive.

The second class of devices are those subsumed under the actions of the leading trade associations. As pointed out above, the effect of

[62] TNEC Hearings, *Investigation of Concentration of Economic Power*, Testimony of Willard Thorp, Part I, p. 137.

[63] National Resources Committee, *The Structure of the American Economy*, Part I (June, 1939), "Basic Characteristics," p. 102.

[64] "Monopolies in the crude sense of single sellers of products for which there are no nearby substitutes are extremely rare." A. R. Burns, *The Decline of Competition* (New York, 1936).

[65] For an elaborate, careful, and meticulously detailed discussion of these policies a reading of Burns, *op. cit.*, is indispensable.

NRA was to transform a large number of the leading trade associations into "cartels," possessing either *de facto* or *de jure* [66] powers along one or more lines similar to those of their European national and international prototypes. Many of the trade associations have advanced so far along this line as to approach in function the higher states of combined action which lead to the syndicates [67] and communities of interest.[68] Such leadership, possessing in many cases some degree of coercive power to compel conformity to policies laid down, is found more frequently in manufacturing fields than elsewhere. Hence the peculiar significance in this respect of the NAM, designed to serve as a policy coördinator for all industrial operations in America.

5. The leading concerns, in the principal trade associations appear simultaneously in the testimony of Thorp before the TNEC, in the investigations of Berle and Means and the National Resources Committee, and on the membership rolls of the NAM. Within the NAM this same small coterie of giant concerns are able to dominate, fairly completely, policies which affect to some extent all fields and functions of American industry. In evidence of this fact, the La Follette Committee findings disclosed that while the NAM claimed approximately 4,000 corporate members for the year 1938, all of its directorships together, for the period 1933–1937 inclusive, represented only 127 individuals from 89 firms. Adding to these figures some 118 additional concerns that contributed $2,000 or more in at least one of the five years, we obtain some 207 companies which "comprise approximately 5 per cent of the total estimated membership" and "whose contributions total $572,711 or 48.9 per cent of the total. It would . . . appear . . . from this analysis," said Mr. Robert Wohlforth, testifying before the Committee, "that about 207 companies, or approximately five

[66] *De jure* powers exist through the efforts of the lobby which succeeds in placing onto the statute books—federal, state, or local—laws under which recalcitrants may readily be forced into line. An example is the Robinson-Patman Act. The same holds true for most of the other federal and state "fair-trade practices" legislation.

[67] "Syndicates" are central selling agencies for cartels. Close American equivalent is the now widespread practice of central allocation of all sales through manipulation of bidding schedules.

[68] "Communities of interest" involve working arrangements so close as to constitute monopoly action. In Europe this is commonly regarded as an equivalent, and an immediate predecessor, to complete monopoly through formal combination.

per cent of the National Association of Manufacturers, are in a position to formulate the policies of the association." [69]

6. This small minority represents very largely giant concerns, as can be seen from a perusal of the lists of the boards of directors for different years, of the affiliations of the leading committee members, and of financial contributions.[70] Even within this small minority the machinery of organization provides for a still higher degree of centralized power. All policies are determined by the Board of Directors, elected by member bodies, but only after candidates are sifted through a nominating committee, which is, in turn, appointed by the president and approved of by the existing Board of Directors. Of the 66 members of the Board of Directors, nine are direct presidential appointees. The direction of the NAM is in the hands, consequently, of a group who are able to act in effect as a coöptative body, to perpetuate their influence indefinitely with the passage of time, and so to compel consistency of policy with a view to long-run interests.

7. The NAM in turn dominates the National Industrial Council. It is enabled cumulatively to strengthen its power to influence NIC membership, because of three cardinal facts. First, the associations belonging to the NIC are typically organized along lines similar to those outlined for the NAM. As indicated above, such organizations (a) permit a high degree of centralization in organizational control, (b) allow such centralized control to perpetuate itself coöptatively over time, and (c) provide a milieu in which the large concerns readily and typically rise to positions of commanding importance. Second, the leading firms in the associations affiliated with the NAM via the NIC are, with rare exceptions, members of the corporative "elite" who belong to the NAM. Thus

[69] LaFollette Committee Reports, Part 17, pp. 7385–87. Also Exhibit 3799, p. 7540. "Among the corporations that have retained directorships for 5 years are the American Rolling Mill Co., of Middletown, Ohio; the General Mills, Inc., of Minneapolis, Minn.; the International Business Machines Co., of New York; the Lambert Pharmacal Co., of St. Louis, Mo.; The Standard Oil Co., of Ohio; and the Eastman Kodak Co., of Rochester, New York." Among those which have had the same directors for four and three years continuously are to be found additional large-scale corporations.

[70] Among these for the five-year period are E. I. Dupont de Nemours and Co., $116,800; Standard Oil, $76,800; General Motors, $65,295; National Steel Corp., $42,050; Westinghouse Electric, $39,927.50; United States Steel, $37,500; Monsanto Chemical Co., of St. Louis, $36,775. Other contributors were the American Cyanamid Co., Chrysler Co., American Smelting and Refining, General Foods, Heinz, Pittsburgh Plate Glass.

instrumentation of NAM policies is facilitated through the central controls of the several associations indirectly subsidiary to it. And third, the NIC itself functions through an hierarchical series of policy controls which lead from the bottom to the top, through what are known as "pyramided conferences": Local and trade conferences lead to state and regional conferences and to industry conferences, and from thence on through to the national conferences held in conjunction with the officialdom of the NAM. These "pyramided conferences" do not constitute an expression of democratic sentiment within the business community; on the contrary, inspection of available records show that they provide means for (a) gaining information concerning movements, sentiments, and interests in the industrial world in order the better to (b) manipulate the "climate of opinion" and instrument policies emanating from on top.

8. By avoiding dual-functional organization throughout the complex machinery of the NAM and its affiliates, policies have been more highly centralized than they would otherwise have been. The group that directs business and political policies for the industrialists of America also manages social and labor problems.

9. The importance of these two points is heavily underlined when it is recalled that the history of the NAM has shown that, except for certain short intervals, its overshadowing interest has been in labor relations. A common interest in opposing organized labor has served to hold the membership together, to dominate the motives in organizing and perfecting the machinery of the NIC, and to provide a never-failing bond of opposition to liberal-social legislation of the New Deal variety.

It appears to be likewise true that the position taken by the NAM and its affiliates on labor matters has been formulated by an extremely small number of "inside firms" amongst the "insiders" who appear increasingly to dominate its policies. The Special Conference Committee, mentioned above, was organized in 1919 by ten giant concerns; [71] it has held monthly meetings since that

[71] The original corporations "coöperating" in this endeavor are Bethlehem Steel Co., E. I. DuPont de Nemours and Co., General Electric Co., General Motors Corp., Goodyear Tire and Rubber, International Harvester Co., Irving Trust Co., Standard Oil Co. (of New Jersey), United States Rubber Co., Westinghouse Mfg. Co. Subsequently two other concerns, the American Telephone and Telegraph Co. (1925) and

time [72] for the purpose of formulating common labor-relations programs for all American industry, and has led in systematizing the
promotion of policies consistently pursued by the NAM.

Not only are most of the member corporations of the Special
Conference Committee at once members of the inner controlling
group of the NAM and the leaders among American industrial
giants in their respective fields,[73] but also they represent a secret
coalition in direct furtherance of the specific forms of company
union fathered by the Colorado Fuel and Iron Company. Since
its inception, the Committee has met at the offices of the Standard
Oil of New Jersey, central unit of the gigantic Rockefeller oil,
mining, banking, real-estate empire. "Two members of the staff
of Industrial Relations Counselors, Inc., a firm which specializes
in advising corporations on problems of industrial relations, have
served individually as members of the committee." [74] From its

---

the United States Steel Corp. (1934) were added. LaFollette Committee Reports, Part
45, p. 16783.

[72] Personnel executives meet monthly, corporation executives semiannually.

[73] The Irving Trust Co. alone is not a member of the NAM. "The Committee considered the desirability of enlarging its membership through the inclusion of representatives from corporations in additional industries. However, investigation led to
the decision that this would be inadvisable because other corporations which were
outstanding leaders in their respective industries in the same degree as the sponsors
of the Special Conference Committee could not be found. Omitting the Irving Trust
Co., in 1937 the corporations represented on the Special Conference Committee employed more than 1,300,000 persons and paid total wages and salaries of more than
$2,400,000,000. At the end of 1937 these 11 corporations claimed total assets in excess
of $13,500,000,000. The American Telephone and Telegraph Co. has almost a com-
plete national coverage in the public utility field which it serves. The United States
Steel Corp. and the Bethlehem Steel Co. rank first and second, respectively, in the
steel industry—with Bethlehem, through its subsidiaries, also ranking first in shipbuilding. E. I. DuPont de Nemours and Co. is easily first in chemicals, and the
General Motors Corporation maintains an approximately similar position in the
motor car industry. The Goodyear Tire and Rubber Co. and the United States
Rubber Co. rank first and second, respectively, in their industry. The International
Harvester Co. is the outstanding manufacturer of farm equipment. The Standard
Oil Co. of New Jersey is not only the largest of the Standard Companies; it is also
regarded as the largest oil company in the world. The General Electric Co. is the
largest producer of electrical equipment, while the Westinghouse Electric and
Manufacturing Co. is next in rank . . . the United States Steel . . . through its
subsidiaries is the largest producer of coal in the country and also largest producers
of iron ore in the United States." La Follette Committee Reports, Part 45, pp. 16781,
16783–84.

[74] La Follette Commission Reports, Part 45, p. 16781. The two members were
A. H. Young, former representative of International Harvester, and C. H. Hicks,
former representative of Standard Oil Co. (New Jersey). Each was invited to remain
as a personal member of the committee, not as a representative of Industrial Relations

earliest days this same committee has been dominated in turn by Standard Oil, United States Steel, and the du Pont interests. Its secretary since 1923 has been E. S. Cowdrick, previously with the Colorado Fuel and Iron Company in an executive capacity.

The most important line of policies within the NAM, in short, seems to be traceable directly or indirectly to this inside clique within the inner councils of the organization [75]—a conclusion which is especially interesting when coupled to the fact that the original antilabor program was taken over from the heavy industries (National Metal Trades Association, in large part), and that that original program (Parryism) is still the "Bible" of the NAM.[76]

10. As the larger concerns which now constitute the central command of the NAM have come to the fore, the doctrinal position of its business leaders has been further coördinated in the elaboration of "public relations" propaganda. Nowhere else is shown so clearly the dominating position in the NAM of concerns such as those which are member to the Special Conference Committee. Public relations techniques were born,[77] nurtured, and brought to flower within these ranks. The specific purpose of the Committee is to coördinate all policy interests of the business community in order to "sell" to the public justification of the position taken by the configuration of those interests on any and all matters. Thus it brings together, into a single, central, and unified propaganda, "labor relations," "legislative relations," "agricul-

---

Counselors, Inc., an organization which was set up under the leadership of John D. Rockefeller, Jr., apparently to promote the "welfare capitalism" ideas expressed in speeches he made after "Bloody Ludlow" and elaborated in his book, *The Personal Relation in Industry* (New York, 1923). A. H. Young was director of Industrial Relations Counselors for some years. After leaving the organization in 1934 he was vice-president of United States Steel Corporation in charge of personnel relations.

[75] At any rate, the policies laid out by the Special Conference Committee are entirely coherent with those advocated by the NAM. It seems scarcely conceivable that the direction of influence could run the contrary direction, from the NAM to the members of the Special Conference Committee—particularly in view of the fact that these same members are the recognized leaders and pioneers in the policies adopted by the two interlaced groups. This holds for the policy of partial recognition of trade unions as bargaining agents, adopted subsequent to Supreme Court decisions upholding the NLRA.

[76] See footnote 26, above.

[77] Pioneer was Ivy Lee, the man who is given credit for transforming the elder John D. Rockefeller from the ogre of Ida M. Tarbell's *History of the Standard Oil Company* and "Bloody Ludlow" into the "seer of Pocantico Hills." Ivy Lee is still regarded as a sort of Solon of "public relations" technique.

tural trade relations," [78] and all other "relations" involving contacts with groups whose interests may at any point come in conflict with their own. Employing the techniques, the criteria, and in many ways the services of advertising agencies,[79] the NAM has moved into this field in a big way; this is evidenced by the phenomenal increase in public relations expenditures cited on p. 198, above.

THE "SCALAR PRINCIPLE"

The ten points outlined above do not by any means exhaust the list of ways of centralizing power within the structure of the American industrial system.[80] They do, however, show the principal lines of growth—lines which take on greater significance when it is realized that their effect is additive. These trends are unidirectional and convergent, and their result is to mobilize gradually American industry into a pattern of control adapted to the prototype of the corporation.

The principle underlying the organization of the prototype is called by Mooney and Reiley,[81] the "scalar principle." They define it as follows: "The scalar process is the same form in organization which is sometimes called hierarchical . . . a scale means a series of steps; hence, something graduated. In organization it means the graduation of duties, not according to differentiated functions, for this involves another and distinct principle of organization,[82] but simply according to degrees of authority and corresponding responsibility. For convenience we shall hereafter call this phenomenon of organization the scalar chain."

The "scalar chain" is given effect through "1. *Leadership, 2. Delegation, 3. Functional Definition.*" The first defines the line of direction, as running from the top down, along any given line of policy. The second describes the principles of delegating power

[78] Separate bureaus and departments have been set up within the NAM for each of these divisional interests.

[79] Young and Rubicam, one of the largest advertising agencies in the world, handle public relations for the NAM.

[80] A particularly important omission is the influence exerted on the educational system of the country through the activities of such an organization as the American Management Association.

[81] J. D. Mooney and A. C. Reiley, *Onward Industry!* Mooney is an outstanding executive of the General Motors Corp.

[82] "Functional organization" as used here refers to division of authority from executive headquarters down.

down through the hierarchy of command and subordination. The third traces the lines by way of which leadership circumscribes fields of specialized authority through the pyramid of control.

Within the corporation, all policies emanate from the control above. In the union of this power to determine policy with the execution thereof, all authority necessarily proceeds from the top to the bottom and all responsibility from the bottom to the top. This is, of course, the inverse of "democratic" control; it follows the structural conditions of dictatorial power. In so far as the lines of control native to the private business corporation have been kept unsullied by important compromise of principle, they approximate those long familiar in the structure of modern military formations. Here, what in political circles would be called legislative, executive, and judicial functions are gathered together in the same hands. And these controlling hands, so far as policy formulation and execution are concerned, are found at the peak of the pyramid and are manipulated without significant check from its base.

So far as it is possible to trace trends within the organization of the NAM, they all appear to converge, in order to compress the general policy formulation of American business into the molds evolved by the corporation. Which is to say that just as the giant corporation takes on as an incident to its growth a definite political significance as a wielder of power over increasing numbers of people and their interests, so it is inevitable that the NAM should in its much larger sphere be transformed, as it grows and expands, into a community force ever more politically potent and politically conscious. On the evidence it would appear that three things then begin to happen to the propaganda program. All economic issues are transmuted into terms of social and cultural issues, increasingly, as the political implications and the military possibilities of cumulated economic power are realized. Propaganda then becomes a matter of converting the public, or all special divisions of the public—small businessmen, consumers, labor, farmers, housewives —to the point of view of the control pyramid. This accounts for the vast outpouring of so-called "educational" literature of the NAM, now designed to enter into every nook and cranny of American life, economic, political, social, and cultural.[83] It is a propa-

---

[83] See in particular the NAM "You and Industry" series, eight in number. These are, seriatim, "The American Way," "Men and Machines," "Taxes and You," "The

ganda reaching to the roots of the principles which underlie contemporary capitalistic civilization—that is to say, the propaganda
is an ideological outpouring.[84]

Second, the combination of monopoly powers and competitive
privileges (so far as the state is concerned) leads all discussion regarding undesirable regulation [85] by the government to proposals
for "self-management" or "self-government" in business. For the
gigantic aggregations of economic power and the centrally manipulated, policy-forming pyramids, "self-government in business" represent precisely what laissez faire does for competitive (that is,
"unorganized") economics. It became the theme song of NRA: it
is the perfect adaptation to the elaborate system of business advisory boards originally set up by leading trade associations under
the auspices of the Chamber of Commerce of the United States, in
connection with the War Industries Board.[86] It visualizes all economic activity organized in a system of eventually all-inclusive
trade, industrial, and occupational categories, each of which will,
through its governing hierarchy, establish and administer the policies governing the behavior of its members in all important respects. "If business is to rule itself . . . it will be through trade
associations," a circular of the American Trade Association Executives announces. Can it be that full national expansion of this idea

---

American Standard of Living," "The Future of America," "Pattern of Progress,"
"What is Industry?" "Yardsticks of American Progress." These are masterpieces of
statistical, descriptive, and argumentative exegesis, designed to *convert* to a *point of
view.* "A united front in presenting the case of industry to federal, state, and local
governments and to the general public" is the objective, says a folder of the National
Industrial Council (undated), and the techniques are those of the lobby and of advertising applied to the "sale of ideas." Concerning advertising, see the program of
Battan, Barton, Durstine, and Osborn for the du Pont "Cavalcade of America" radio
series and the McDonald Cook poster series for the NAM, "Prosperity Dwells Where
Harmony Reigns."

[84] "The employer organizes the forces of production. He is the *natural leader of
his workmen,* and is able by instruction, example and fair dealing to bring to bear
constantly upon them influences for *right thinking* and action for *loyalty* to the
common *enterprise.*" Open Shop Report, *Proceedings* of the 28th Annual Meeting
of the NAM (May, 1923), pp. 156–59. (Italics mine.) According to the New York
Times (Dec. 11, 1940) report of the NAM textbook survey, the NAM found "faith
building . . . lacks" in American public schools. These statements are typical of
the more recent literature (compare with Italian, German, and Japanese material
above).

[85] "Undesirable" in terms of the needs, interests, and aspirations of the dominating
elements in the business world.

[86] See Mary van Kleeck, *Creative America* (New York, 1936).

will lead here, as it surely has abroad, directly, to employ the medieval expression, into a "corporatively organized society?" [87]

In the third place, the obverse face of "self-government" in business appears clearly to seek for coördination of political policies to the requirements of monopoly-oriented business. Internally the NAM program favors maintenance of all domestic markets free from foreign competition. Externally it has always sought the maximum of aid from government in the promotion of interests abroad. Rationalization of the internal emphasis would seem on all the evidence, to date, to lead directly to autarchy [88] and the companion use of the government for the purpose of suppressing antagonistic social elements.[89] Externally it has already led to the business variant of "Hemisphere Unity," a blocking out of the world into what the Germans call *Grossraumwirtschaften* (and the Japanese, "Co-Prosperity Sphere")—literally, "great-space economics" for imperial expansion.[90] Both these programs have evolved naturally

[87] The pressures can lead directly to the type of proposal recently elaborated (Feb. 9, 1940) by sixteen Catholic prelates meeting in Washington, D.C., in which they proposed a "Guild or Corporative System" for America. (a) At no point is this proposal at odds with the propaganda of NAM; (b) the proposal is practically identical with that of the papal encyclical *Quadragesimo Anno* (1931), which formed the basis of Chancellor Schuschnigg's Austrian variant of "Clerical Fascism."

[88] "Autarchy" is commonly applied as a term of derision to the "self-sufficiency" program of the Third Reich. But an examination of the elements of this "autarchic" program will merely show that some bad calculations have been made in regard to self-sufficiency as an argument for promoting higher tariffs, monetary and exchange controls, systems of subsidies and subventions, etc., which are in no sense of the term new. Since the end of the *Blütezeit* of laissez faire with the introduction of the Bismarck tariff of 1879, programs along all these lines have been adopted by all the major industrial countries of the world. And, once these programs get well under way, there has been a long-run increase in their range of application, the severity of their controls, and the political implications of their continued pursuit. "Buy British" or "Buy American" are just as clearly "autarchic" sentiments as anything the Nazis have devised. See also pp. 252–53.

[89] See the "Labor Program of the NAM," formulated in 1903, and the speech of President David M. Parry in support thereof. See also a novel written by David M. Parry, called "The Scarlet Empire," which ran serially in *American Industries* in 1913—the story of how society goes to pieces through failure to suppress ideas and programs which run counter to the interests of the business public. See, further, "Industrial Strife and the Third Party," a special pamphlet of the NAM which states its whole doctrinal position on labor; and see also the NAM's more recent "Sentinels of America" campaign "on behalf of the private enterprise system," a program that calls for a modern private system for reporting "misstatements"—somewhat reminiscent of the system of "delation" evolved by the Roman Emperor Tiberius, and copied so frequently in recent times by organized private espionage agencies of one sort or another.

[90] These are seen in the future to be, respectively, Great Britain and the British

out of the lines of emphasis laid down in the original program of the NAM. Since then there has been no fundamental departure at any time from the tenets those proposals are based upon. Government, in this view, becomes an aid, an ally, a means for the instrumentation of the interests of this transformed system of interlocking business-control pyramids,[91] and the indispensable means for dissolution of the national and ideological forms of its detractors.

Empire, France and her African and overseas possessions, Japan and hegemony of the Chinese, Siberian and Korean mainland, Italy and hegemony of the Mediterranean, and Germany with hegemony of Mittel-europa. More recently, the British have been talking of a "greater Turkey," to include parts of Iran, all of Turkestan, Azerbaijan, and other Turkish-speaking peoples of the Near and Central East.

[91] See the discussions in the NAM publications centering around such topics as its interest and participation in the formation of the Department of Commerce and Labor; the Panama Canal; the formation of the War Industries Board; the informational and promotion services of the Department of Commerce; tariff policies; NRA; the participation of its leading members in the Industrial Mobilization Plan; and the constitution of the new higher command of "National Defense" headed up by Mr. Knudsen. Whatever else may be the outcome of the current struggle, it is probably safe to say that American efforts will eventually mean the complete displacement by American interests of German, Italian, Japanese, and possibly the winning of British holdings throughout the two Americas.

Part III

COMPARISON AND CONTRAST OF TRENDS IN BUSINESS POLICY FORMATIONS

Chapter VII

ECONOMIC POLICIES: MONOPOLY, PROTECTION, PRIVILEGE

THE LEADING economic resultant of the evolution of centralized policy-forming power in business might simply be termed: Promotion of Monopoly.[1] Interpreted broadly, such an identification would be consistent with the records, yet it also greatly oversimplifies the picture. For present purposes, the better to show the changed sources, nature, and interconnections among the principal carriers of monopoly powers, analysis may be broken down to deal with the collusive practices of:

the industrial, commercial, and financial giants in the corporate world;
cartels, rings, pools, syndicates, and trade associations which may have taken on one or more of the several cartel functions; and
trade associations, cartels, and similar federations of business interests when grouped or banded together into confederational, central, or "peak" associations (*Spitzenverbände*).

Most analyses of monopoly trends deal primarily or exclusively with the first of these three. The more theoretical treatments center around problems in the mechanics of price manipulation under circumstances showing some determinate departure from perfectly or purely competitive norms.[2] Other writers confine themselves to

---

[1] Compare pp. 7–10, above.

[2] The Federal Trade Commission, in its Report to the Temporary National Economic Committee, ". . . Re Monopolistic Practices in Industries" (TNEC Hearings, Part 5-A, p. 2305) summarized under this head all cases centered around "acts and practices [which] are . . . calculated and tend to interfere with the *natural play* of *normal competitive forces,* with a resultant increased concentration of private economic power in the hands of private and limited groups, and in the imposition of *unnatural limitations and restrictions* on trade with consequent injury to the public." I have italicized the obvious jokers, but more questionable still is the identification: decline of competition = corresponding rise of monopoly powers. Strictly

"trust," combination, and "conspiracy policies" of the corporate giants as these "affect the public interest," or as they constitute objects of legislative and regulatory control by the government. The former consider monopoly problems solely within the economic frame of reference; the latter typically ignore both the economic and political frames of reference.

In the present connection, we wish to present a third—and partially overlapping—set of issues relating to the monopolistic policies of organized business in which political and economic facets are inextricably interwoven. First, what are the long-run changes in the structure, functioning, and "balance-of-power" relationships within and amongst the great combinations which at once narrow and concentrate leadership within their own immediate corporate frontiers, while enhancing further their power to shape the larger destinies of the looser forms of business organization which are subsumed under the other two headings above? How far and how generally are the "trusts" enabled to pose the issues for these other federations of business interests, and what is the nature and "direction" of the issues they pose? In what manner and by what means are they enabled to implement policies advocated for the trade, the industry, and the economic system as a whole? And in what respects do the nature of the policies advocated on the one hand, and the means for partial or full instrumentation outside of their own immediate corporate frontiers on the other, become altered as interests broaden to the wider horizons?

It will not be possible to offer here more than a rough classification of the reasons for such a relative increase in the manipulative

---

speaking, of course, "imperfect competition" and the exercise of monopoly powers through "monopolistic competition" cannot be used as though the terms are interchangeable, as implied in the above FTC statement; see J. M. Clark, "Towards a Concept of Workable Competition," *American Economic Review*, XXX (June, 1940), especially pp. 244–45). But it is only in an abstract, classificatory sense of the terms that competition and monopoly can be kept antiseptic to each other (cf. Robinson, Introduction) under the best of circumstances—perhaps not even then; and in general it is true that historically the decline of competition is practically coterminous and coextensive with the advance of some one or more collusive controls— which controls, to be true, may actually heighten the level and sharpen the edge of competition. But the new competition is cumulatively of a different type; it complies with different procedural rules, and pursues greatly altered ends, as compared with the old type, the cogent and witty Mrs. Robinson to the contrary notwith·standing.

powers of big business.[3] Nor is there need in the present connection for much more. The chief interest centers in the bearing such power has on the policies of looser types of business organization— now growing with such amazing speed in numbers, influence, and range of interests throughout the capitalistic world. Similarly, present attention focuses on the activities of what might be called intermediate, or perhaps better, transitional, forms of collusion commonly known as cartels, rings, pools, syndicates, and the like. Some writers, notably Germans following in the path blazed by Liefmann, have devoted a great deal of attention to the monopoly features, trends, or results of these contractual and semicontractual devices for exercising controls similar to those long employed by several of the corporate giants. This latter interest is growing rapidly, particularly in America, under the stimulus of a vigorous revival of antitrust prosecutions inaugurated by Jackson and Arnold. But here again we shall be concerned less with the techniques employed or the precise results of market, price, and production manipulation and more with the changes that have taken place in the structure, functioning, and effective powers of these bodies, changes which enable them to be used for effectuating some degree of uniform and monopoly-oriented policies throughout the economic system as a whole.

All of which is to say that our attention must here be focused primarily on the confederations and *Spitzenverbände*. It is now an indisputable fact that centralized business policies are directed by corporate giants which supply the *Spitzenverbände* with effective leadership. Increasingly, these policies cluster around and bear upon the fundamental sanctions in which are enmeshed the institutional taproots for the capitalistic system as a whole; and, increasingly, monopoly-oriented pressures applied by the combines and cartels take on meaning as they are analyzed in this context, and lose significance—if they do not, in fact, become at times wholly inexplicable—when taken separately and in isolation therefrom. "People of the same trade seldom meet together, even for merriment and diversion, but the conversation ends in a conspiracy against the public, or in some contrivance to raise prices." Thus

[3] In this chapter, consequently, direct relationships between big business and various types of government regulatory, investigational, and taxing authorities are being deliberately ignored. They will be taken up in the following chapter.

observed the wily Adam Smith, and the observation is as true today as when first uttered. But what happens to the quality and the objectives of such conspiracies when they are not only actively encouraged by the trend of leading opinion throughout both business and governmental circles, but also when they are centrally directed by huge combines which Smith would have assumed, out of hand, to be monsters of willful, capricious, and dangerous power?

In other words, the crux of the matter lies not in the absolute number, nor in the underlying structure, nor even in the rate of growth in these several nuclei of collusive practices, as such; rather the problem is how far these are more or less consciously being arranged by experienced and compactly organized groups in patterns designed to promote the continued functioning of this cumulatively anticompetitive type of business system as a whole. It is not true, to repeat familiar warnings, that there are no important counter- or cross-currents working against the spread of collusive practices; but we shall deal in the following pages with the dominant not the recessive characteristics, with those which are convergent, mutually reinforcing and additive, not with those which cancel each other or which are absorbed in rear guard action.

Not, again, that the pattern is uniform in all respects, from one industry, or industrial area, or country, to another. Even the scattered and unsatisfactory data available to the interested reader should quickly put that question to rest. But just as when, despite infinite variations in individual members, the biologist recognizes that the species, *sui generis,* still exists with wholly distinctive structural and pathological characteristics which are determinate for the life cycles of every single member, so here there is a basic sameness in purpose, a general uniformity of direction-impulse, an archetypal pattern of actual or projected controls which underlie the manifolds of variation in every major and minor country organized on a capitalistic footing.

With attention focused, then, on policies, let us consider the more significant changes that bear most directly upon the nature, blending, configuration, and quality of the programs of the leading confederational groupings.

CHANGES UNDERLYING POLICY-FORMULATION
OF THE CORPORATE GIANTS

In the first place, the more recent history of each major capitalistic country shows clearly that there is no tendency for the combination movement as such to disappear, or perhaps even to slow down. No doubts on this score are permitted by a careful or even a casual examination of the data from the famous Pujo Investigation down through the numerous chronicles of great American fortunes; of the records of the merger and combination movement during the World War and after; of the material published by Attorney General Robert Jackson when Commissioner of the Bureau of Internal Revenue; or of the data submitted by Thorp of Dun and Bradstreet before the opening meetings of the Temporary National Economic Committee; and of the Anti-Trust Division of the Department of Justice thereafter. A like story comes out of the investigations of the Balfour Committee, and the studies of Levy, Lucas, and others for England. Similarly for pre-Nazi Germany, as shown by the voluminous reports of the *Enqueteausschuss*,[4] and for post-Nazi Germany by the extraordinarily compact but exhaustive summary of Dr. Keiser.[5] Carl Schmidt has recently summarized the record of concentration in Fascist Italy, confirming thereby statements repeatedly made in the official Italian literature.[6] The same picture holds for France, and in an even more pronounced fashion for Japan, as set forth in the official published data.

[4] As shown particularly in the reports dealing with the coal, iron and steel, heavy chemicals, and machine industries. See also various issues of *Die Wirtschaftskurve* through the twenties.

[5] Dr. Keiser thinks there may be some tendency in the future for combination to slow down, though such a forecast cannot be read directly from the record to date.

[6] Carl T. Schmidt, "Joint-Stock Enterprises in Italy," *American Economic Review*, XXX (March, 1940), pp. 82–86; see also various annual reports of the Confederation of Fascist Industrialists. At the 1928 meeting of the National Association of Manufacturers, Miss Elizabeth Humes, Assistant Trade Commissioner in Rome of the United States Department of Commerce, reported that "Following in the footsteps of Germany, Mussolini's government is encouraging industrial amalgamations. To this end, taxation on industrial mergers has been abolished. The outstanding industries of the country, including the automobile, the rayon, the cotton, the chemical, the iron and steel industries are all in process of absorbing the smaller concerns and concentrating the buying, manufacturing and distributing branches in the hands of a few powerful corporations." *Proceedings* of the 34th Annual Meeting (Oct., 1929), pp. 381–84.

These records of concentration do not necessarily show increased social concentration of either wealth or income. Such may very well be taking place, but they relate primarily to three phenomena: (a) growth in the relative importance of the corporate form of organization (this differs from the case in Germany, as indicated on p. 40); (b) increase in the relative size of the larger concerns; and (c) a continuation of the process of absorption of, or morganatic alliance with, smaller and competing enterprises through merger, branch and affiliate status, minority shareholdings, and so forth.

In the second place, there is to be found within all these countries the process termed by Berle and Means as the "splitting of the property atom." Ownership is cumulatively being separated from management and control, just as previously the laborer was separated from ownership. But the matter does not come to rest there. Although the owners of corporate securities are steadily drifting into the status of a *rentier* class [7]—formally, in the totalitarian

[7] A number of writers (e. g., Joan Robinson, *Essays in the Theory of Employment*, New York, 1937) habitually refer to holders of corporate securities as a "rentier class." In testimony given by representatives of the big corporations of the German heavy industries before the *Enquete Ausschuss*, bitter complaint against the demands of stockholders for higher and higher dividends was frequently followed by proposals for fixing maximum and minimum dividend disbursements (commonly called "stabilization of dividends") which could be required of management in exchange for non-interference by management in the flow when earned. Numerous American companies have advocated, and a few have experimented with, schemes of this sort. Of perhaps even greater significance is the growing importance in the investment markets of insurance companies, investment trusts, estates handled in trust, university and other special endowments for research, charitable, or other purposes (hospitals, clinics, etc.)—all of which have a much greater interest in regularity and reliability of return, than in the making of speculative gains. The pressures they exert, the influences they represent, and the policies they favor all restrict interest in management to—the while heavily emphasizing—safe, regular, conservative return. We have here a certain institutionalization of the rentier-ownership-status and its appropriate mentality which, operating directly within the inner circles of private ownership, promises to become the rule and not the exception. In Japan a similar effect is achieved by the common practice of the general investing public of putting their money in savings accounts, and not in industrial securities. The banks then invest the funds in industrial, or commercial enterprises affiliated—more often than not—directly with them. Much the same appears to be the case in Italy.

Thus the suggestion made by J. M. Keynes, *The General Theory of Employment, Interest and Money* (London, 1936), p. 221, that the rentier class will, or should be allowed to, disappear as interest rates decline to zero, is bound to run into cumulatively more determined opposition. As with Richard Jones's noted reply to Ricardo's theory of no rent land, given these powerfully organized groups with so definite and critical an interest, a regular surplus will be had whether it is earned or not! See TNEC Monograph No. 29, *The Distribution of Ownership in the 200 Largest Non-Financial Corporations*, particularly the detailed analysis of the twenty largest holdings in each corporation in Appendix X, pp. 623-1439.

countries [8] and *de facto* in the liberal-capitalistic—the changed status is no longer traceable entirely either to reduction of equity rights through stock and debenture reclassifications or to mere blocked holdings strategically placed at the head of a control pyramid such as the holding company. In the huge corporate complexes of all major capitalistic countries there are growing up inner blocs of bureaucratically self-perpetuating interests; these blocs may have next to no ownership stakes in the vast properties, which nevertheless they are able to manipulate, through the exigencies of special knowledge, outside contacts, inside personal or committee compacts, or other methods of acquiring strategic position.[9] The influence of the purse (banking and finance) has long been recognized in the management of corporate affairs. But in recent years the powers of strategically interlocking legal, accounting, management engineering,[10] and other special "competence" and contact groups have grown step by step with—and sometimes follow more or less closely the lines of—increasing functionalization of duties and offices. This is, in turn, a by-product of increase in the size, complexity, and range of corporate interests.[11]

The net effect is not only that the "atom of property" is split, but also that ownership is, in a sense, being "set aside." The limits of property holdings, as determined by the fictions of legally circumscribed, corporate and quasi-corporate ownership rights, no longer define the membership of, nor restrain closely the strategic massing of power by, closely coöperating inter- and intra-corporate

[8] Most clearly in Germany where disbursements have been limited to 6%—in a few cases to 8%—irrespective of amounts earned. Simultaneously stock- and bondholders have lost practically all ownership or contingent property rights.

[9] Interesting in this connection are the data tabulated by Robert A. Gordon, showing the remarkably low percentage stockholdings of management in a sample of 155 large corporations. "Ownership by Management and Control Groups in the Large Corporations," *Quarterly Journal of Economics* (May, 1938), pp. 371, 378, 381. Most recent and most reliable are the data of the TNEC Monograph, No. 29, *The Distribution of Ownership*, p. 104.

[10] An interesting example is offered by Thurman Arnold of how a group of efficiency engineers, having practically no ownership rights in the properties in question, managed to obtain control of almost the whole of the paper-box industry. *The Bottlenecks of Business*, pp. 181–82. See also TNEC Monograph No. 29, Appendices VI and VII, pp. 357–558.

[11] See, in particular, the data on concentration in the National Resources Committee, *The Structure of the American Economy*; see also TNEC Monographs No. 11, *Bureaucracy and Trusteeship in Large Corporations*, Chapter VI, and No. 27, *The Structure of Industry*, Parts V and VI.

cliques. There has grown up a sort of inner-council *condottiere*, whose members are no longer constrained by the changing location of their own property holdings or those of others within or without the expanding corporate frontiers. So far as these inner governing cliques are concerned, one by one all the old ownership frontiers are being abandoned, and power flows out from the inner sancta like water through a shattered system of dykes. The corporation, as Sombart has pointed out at great length, is enabled to amass and extend holdings without limit; but in pursuit of effective power the *Realpolitik* of corporate direction, having once sprung the old restraints of ownership, now enables management to stride afield in a handsome pair of Seven-League Boots.

No better evidence of how this change takes place can be submitted, in the third place, than is to be found in examination of the bewildering array of devices, some already in use and others newly forged, for creating effective strategic alliances amongst the major corporate groups. A useful illustration is the growing monopoly of patents.[12] This is employed as a springboard for enhancing market, price, production, capacity, and numerous other controls which greatly transcend the normal limits and cut in a thousand ways athwart the lines of ordinary corporate power. Such controls may be effected in a number of ways. One method results in drawing the giants closer together at the top of the corporate

---

[12] The American Telephone and Telegraph Co. controls 15,000 patents; the General Electric Co. between 8,000 and 9,000. See, Arnold, *Bottlenecks of Business*, p. 27. A report of the Patent Office notes an increase in the number of patents granted a small percentage of concerns from 1900 on: "The greatest number of patents received by any corporation in 1936, was by the General Electric Company, with 476. It also received the greatest number in 1935, with 521, and even in 1900, it was then at the top of the list of recipients of U.S. patents, having received in that year, 100 patents. Corporations that received more than 100 patents in 1936, are: General Electric Co., 476; Radio Corporation of America, 364; DuPont Company, 346; General Motors Corp., 263; Westinghouse Electric and Mfg. Co., 248; Bell Telephone Laboratories, Inc., 236; United Shoe Machinery Corp., 189; General Aniline Works, Inc., 152; Westinghouse Air Brake Co., 136; I. G. Farbenindustrie Aktiengesellschaft, 132; American Telephone and Telegraph Co., 110; Celanese Corp. of America, 102." In the same year, "15 corporations received from 50 to 100 patents each; 50 corporations received from 25 to 50 patents each; and 132 corporations received 10 to 25 patents each [the number of patents granted in 1900 was 60% of the number granted in 1936] . . . and these constituted only 2% of the total number of patents granted that year." John Boyle, Jr., "Corporation Patent Holdings," *Journal of the Patent Office Society*, XIX (Sept., 1937), No. 9, pp. 698–99. See also TNEC Monograph No. 31, *Patents and Free Enterprise*.

pyramids. Thus the establishment of the Ethyl Corporation brought together certain special interests of Standard Oil of New Jersey, General Motors, and Du Pont. The patents underlying RCA came largely from Westinghouse, General Electric, and Bell Telephone, and the subsequent segregation was more a matter of convenience than of separation through incompatibility. The Carboloy Company, manufacturing hard-metal compounds for cutting dies in machine-tool construction, brought together Krupp and General Electric into a close price-fixing and market-allocation agreement. The two huge German electric-manufacturing concerns, the Siemens and A.E.G. groups, pooled their incandescent lamp patents to form Osram, as did General Electric and Westinghouse in the United States to establish Mazda. Zeiss and Bausch and Lomb; the great German dye trust, I. G. Farbenindustrie A.G., and Standard Oil of New Jersey; the armaments producers of Germany, Italy, France, England, and the United States; these and many others have been similarly brought together in close working agreements resulting in price, market, production, and other controls.[13]

A number of other well-known factors contribute to this result, among them control over technical innovations due to ownership of large research facilities,[14] interlocking directorates, "communities of interest," common dependence upon the same financial interests. But coincident with the processes of drawing together at the top is the spread downward and outward of power and influence to reach the small concerns—a process which springs from the same ability to manipulate resources and controls by inner cliques operating amongst the giants. The licensing agreement of the

[13] A particularly interesting example of how research and patent exchange has brought industries together is shown on an "Electronic's Chart of the Sound Picture Industry of the World," reproduced as a frontispiece by Toulmin, *Trade Agreements and the Anti-Trust Laws*, which shows how Westinghouse, General Electric, and the American Telephone and Telegraph Co. via RCA have been brought into close working arrangements with British, French, German, and Dutch producers of film apparatus on the one hand, and systems of movie distribution on the other. See also TNEC Monograph No. 21, *Competition and Monopoly in American Industry*.

[14] In some cases—the great German dye trust is an outstanding example—pooling of research facilities played a major role in the grouping of the chemical industry first into a series of interlocking cartels, then into a "community of interests," and finally into formal corporate consolidation. Arnold, *Bottlenecks of Business*, cites a number of examples where through leverages of a similar character large concerns have been able to absorb the small.

Hartford-Empire, Owens-Illinois group in the glass-container industry is symptomatic. Here the group was able to decide who should produce what types of glass containers, in what amounts, and also in what territories they might sell, and at what prices.[15] Similar controls are exercised by the Ethyl Corporation, the large movie-producing companies (block-booking), Osram, Montecatini, Schneider-Creusot, Krupp, Vickers, Imperial Chemicals, and many others. The net effect of such controls is to place the small, so-called "independent" producer or distributor [16] in a position of permanent vassalage to the giants. The various reports of the Temporary National Economic Committee, the Senate Committee on Patent Pooling, and the Nye Munitions Committee show how far and how exacting this type of control over the small businessman is becoming. The field of distribution offers many similar examples.[17] In Japan the small are likened to "sub-contractors" to the large. But the picture is reproduced wherever the giant enterprises have struck root, and wherever the forms and fictions of law [18] make possible establishment of such coercive controls by the large over the small.

A fourth development is the rise to dominating positions within the larger corporate complexes of closely interlinked families and blocked familial and interfamilial interests. "America's 60 Fami-

[15] See TNEC Hearings, Part 2, "Patents, Automobile Industry, Glass Container Industry."

[16] An excellent example is provided by the case of the McKesson-Robbins fiasco, in which it developed that through a system of job-lot selling on long-run contracts the firm had been able to force increasing numbers of retail drug outlets into a position of almost complete financial dependence on it. It has been estimated that, in the city of San Francisco, calling in of outstanding obligations to the defunct concern would immediately have bankrupted about 40% of all the retail drug outlets in the city.

[17] See, in particular, the Hearings on the Robinson-Patman Act, the recommendations of the TNEC for repeal of the Miller-Tydings Act in their final Report and Recommendations, and the Anti-Trust indictments of the Department of Justice against the Borden and National Dairies Companies; also literature on the agitation in Germany against the department store combines of Wertheim, Leonard Tiets, Karstadt's, Bata (stores serving as outlet for the manufacturing plants of Bata).

[18] Thurman Arnold has intimated in a number of speeches that the net effect of attempts to enforce the Sherman Anti-Trust Act has been only to streamline, and, in some respects, render more circuitous—but not seriously to inhibit the growth of—"combinations in restraint of trade." A like fate seems to have befallen the famous "law against the abuse of economic power" passed in Germany in 1923. See Neumann, *Behemoth*, pp. 16, 238, 261–63.

lies [19] are paralleled by the French "200," [20] the aristocracy of British "Cousinhood," [21] the Junker-Industrial baronry of Nazi Germany,[22] the *Zaibatsu* of Japan, and the aristocratic latifondi-industrial princelings of the Rome-Milan-Turin "Axis." The family pattern of the *Zaibatsu*, outlined in the chapter on Japan is merely the simplest and most obvious of these family complexes. But like the House of Mitsui, the group de Wendel,[23] the spreading empires of the DuPonts and the Rockefellers, the ramifications of the houses of Buccleuch and Beaufort, or that of Krupp, Flick, Röchling, Quandt in Germany,[24] these other ownership complexes are being built up and consolidated by intermarriage, trust segregations and administrations, club, fraternal, clique, and "group" (De Wendel, Gillet, Krupp, DuPont, etc.) interlinkages which cumulatively take on a consanguinous, familial, patriarchal, "dynastic" character, and which show next to no "areal" identification with properties bounded by formal corporate holdings, or with national or even the usual types of business frontiers. "Influence," "alliances," "mutual interests," "nepotism," "sinecure," "pull" and the like move into the center of the picture.

[19] See in particular, Ferdinand Lundberg, *America's 60 Families* (New York, 1937). Large family-controlled corporations in America, cited in a recent study of the nation's 200 largest non-financial corporations made by the Federal Income Tax Division, included the Ford family with $624,975,000 in the Ford Co., the DuPont family with $573,690,000 holdings in E. I. DuPont and the U.S. Rubber Co., The Rockefeller family with $396,583,000 in the Standard Oil Cos. of New Jersey, Indiana, and California and Socony Vacuum Oil Co., the Mellon family with $390,000,000 in Gulf Oil, Alcoa and Koppers, the McCormick family with $111,102,000 in the International Harvester Co., the Hartford family with $105,702,000 in the A. and P. Co., the Harkness family with $104,891,000 in the Standard Oil Cos. of New Jersey, Indiana and California and Socony Vacuum Oil Co., the Duke family with $89,455,000 in Duke Power, Alcoa, and Liggett and Myers, the Pew family with $76,628,000 in Sun Oil, the Pitcairn family with $65,576,000 in Pittsburgh Glass, the Clark family with $57,215,000 in Singers, the Reynolds family with $54,766,000 in Reynolds Tobacco, and the Kress family with $50,044,000 in Kress. New York *Times*, Oct. 16, 1940. See also TNEC Monograph No. 29, pp. 1505–28.

[20] See "Blum Grapples with the 200 Families" by P. J. Philip, New York *Times*, June 14, 1936.

[21] Haxey. *Tory M.P.*

[22] See Brandt, *op. cit.;* Kolnai, *The War against the West*, pp. 322–93. An interesting example of family influence in a single industry, the German machine making industry. is provided bv a recent article by Dr. Otto Suhr, "Familientradition im Machinenbau," *Zeitschrift für Betriebswirtschaft*, Feb., 1939.

[23] See Louis R. Launay. *De Wendel* (Vaucresson, 1938).

[24] See Neumann, *op. cit.*, pp. 288–96.

A fifth factor is found in the fact that leadership within the circle of the giants seems to be shifting steadily towards the heavy and the "laboratory-baby" industries. The heavy industries occupied a key position in the producers'-goods industries during the period of rapid expansion of industrial apparatus in the North Atlantic industrial nucleus before 1914, and were intimately connected with war and armaments programs from that time on; for these reasons they have long occupied positions of commanding importance in the field of corporate concentration. The "laboratory babies" include electric manufactures and power, rubber, automobiles, airplanes, radio, aluminum, petroleum, movie production, telephone and telegraph, rayon, plastics, heavy chemicals, and so on. These industries have either been launched on a large-scale basis or have quickly and by forced-draft growth become gigantic manufacturing and marketing systems early in their careers; [25] most of them are less than fifty years old; all are dominated by huge, closely interlocking corporate complexes. The significance of this leadership lies in the following facts.

1. Metals, fuels, and heavy chemicals have, since 1914, been increasingly dependent (secularly) upon war and armaments preparations for full prosperity. The principal exceptions are to be found in the United States during the middle and late twenties, and in the Ruhr and Rhine during the rehabilitation and "rationalization" period (1924–29). After 1914 elsewhere, and in the United States after 1939, war and armaments programs have comprised so large a part of total demand that once the adjustments in capacity have been made to meet these markets permanently, the failure of the demand looms as a major and irreparable catastrophe not only to individual industries, but also to the entirety of the industrial complexes of which they are the gravitational centers.

2. The heavy and armaments industries have, with the advance of science and technology, largely grown together "organically" at the manufacturing base. So close have become the materials,

[25] Many older, empirically grounded industries have long since become dependent upon laboratory research. Steel-making is itself a conspicuous example: continuous heat-processing, vertical integration from the ores and fuels on through to the finished plates or tubes, etc., by-product utilization (ammonia, tars, and allied distillates from by-product coke ovens), increasing use of alloys such as molybdenum, magnesium, nickel,—all these require heavier and more consistent reliance on laboratory experimentation and control.

processing, and in part, the product interdependencies among certain industries—coal, coal by-products, heavy industrial chemicals, war munitions, steel, steel-alloy, light metals (in particular aluminum and magnesium), armaments, shipbuilding, machine and machine-tool building, and numerous others that are closely allied—that these industries form a series of complexes wherein only the fictions of corporate groupings survive (as in the railroad systems of the United States and England) to confute the impression that one is dealing here with a single technological network.

3. No clear line separates these heavy-armament industries from the other "laboratory babies." Neither technologically nor in terms of the configuration of corporate interests can a sharp line of demarcation be drawn in any major industrial country between heavy and light chemicals; between machine industries manufacturing for peace and for war; between explosives and gas manufacture and the making of rayon, nylon, and plastics; between the manufacture of electrical apparatus and the alloy and light metals manufactures on the one hand and the automobile, rubber, airplane, engineering, and similar industries on the other. If space were available, illustrations both from the technological and the corporate sides could be multiplied almost endlessly from the different countries we have cited. And the over-all movement through modern industry in general is clearly in this direction.

Firms working in these fields are thus drawn together by common problems of scientific research, of manufacturing, and of management and control.[26] Access to the field is increasingly shut off by monopoly rights over laboratories, by exclusive and patent-controlled processes and products, by systems of pooling of patents within narrower and narrower circles, by high costs of initial capital requirements, the inability to command a market without grant of special privileges by concerns already existing in the industry, but above all, by the nature of the industrial complex the newcomer must be adjusted to at the outset. In short, all the necessary conditions exist for expansion of supermonopoly powers throughout these complexes as well as throughout the individual corpora-

[26] Factors of a management and service character have played a very important role in the combination movement in public utilities in general. See James C. Bonbright and Gardiner C. Means, *The Holding Company* (New York, 1932), pp. 176-87, 312-15.

tions comprising them. On the other hand, in so far as they are dependent upon war or upon public-works programs, they are faced with the further monopoly-encouraging conditions of "monopsony"—single buyers. Probably half the demand of Kuhlmann, Schneider-Creusot, Montecatini, Vickers, Krupp, Skoda, specialized branches of Bethlehem, DuPont, the *Zaibatsu*, and of the various aircraft companies falls into this class, whether war is being waged or not. In wartime, some such proportion (or a higher one) becomes valid for the bulk of other companies falling into the same classifications. As will be shown later, war or a status of suspended belligerency is swiftly becoming the normal, not the exceptional state of contemporary affairs. And the existence of a single buyer almost invariably promotes combination against sellers—in wartime the rule almost becomes a maxim.[27]

Two other factors deserve mention in this catalogue of forces which cumulatively enhance the relative importance of the giants in the larger coördination movement. They need not detain us long, since both are obvious and well known. The first is the fact that the interlinkages between the great industrial combines and the central financial and banking institutions have generally become so close that the division between them is functional rather than corporate. The greatest industrial concerns in Japan and Germany are the principal bankers. The Crédit Lyonnais is probably the most powerful single force in French industry. Equally close are the tie-ups between the great central banks and the huge industrial and transport combines in Italy, England, and the United States.[28] The finance committee with its various banking and other financial connections tends to come to the fore within the industrial

[27] Once capacity has been adjusted to war demands, the conditions of peace mean excess capacity and unemployment; if the war realignment is structurally far-reaching, this excess can probably only be taken up by huge public-works programs —thus perpetuating into peacetimes, in proportion to the excess, the monopoly-promoting conditions of monopsony. All intercartel agreements, of course, have a like effect, and war tends greatly to accelerate such compacts.

[28] See Bonbright and Means, *op. cit.*, for a description of how the three great investment banking houses of Morgan, Drexel, and Bonbright were enabled by a combination of well-placed minority holdings (in companies whose stocks were widely held by the general public), financial power, and their enormous influence and prestige, to control almost the whole of the American electric utility industry. For comparable data, see Liefmann, *Beteiligungs- und Finanzierungsgesellschaften*, covering English, French, German, American, Swiss, Belgian, and other financing holding-company, trust, investment trust, and similar forms of business organization.

control pyramids; simultaneously blocks of special industrial interests tend to dominate the policies of the great banking houses at the center of the financial webs of control upon which the entire business community is dependent.[29]

There can be no question but that such interconnections and interdependencies in the more important capitalistic countries enable the giant concerns to exercise undue leverage over the small businessman. The attempt by various national governments to provide special banking facilities for easy and cheap credit to little business shows how acute the problem has become.[30]

But there is one final sphere in which the power of the giants over smaller concerns is practically without recourse from any angle—that of international trade. The foreign banking, industrial, and commercial systems of concessions, branches, affiliates, minority holdings, communities of interest, interlocking directorates, compacts and agreements of the several great national combines are too well known to require elaboration here.[31] It only needs to be pointed out that, in the principal lines of manufacture and sale, no small enterprise or grouping of small enterprises has any chance of breaking into foreign markets against the opposition of the giants acting in concert, without allying themselves with or selling through one of these or a group of them.

And on this score, there is much less of a tendency for the giants

---

[29] Particularly true in Germany where a number of the leading industrial giants have established their own so-called "House banks." Somewhat similar is the case of the Rockefeller, DuPont, and Mellon controlled banks in the United States.

[30] This subject largely dominated the hearings, plans, and negotiations of Secretary Roper, inaugurated in 1937 to solve the problems of the "little business man," and became a theme song for the crop of little businessmen's associations which sprang up shortly thereafter. See, e. g., the platforms of the Smaller Business Association and the American Federation of Little Business. The various governmentally controlled banks working with the Japanese National Planning Council and the Capital Adjustment Commission appear to have had the little businessman in mind for special attention. Similar agencies have been proposed or established in both Italy and Germany, though results in salvage of the little businessman's fortunes do not seem very striking in such quarters.

[31] Two very interesting recent examples are provided by exposés of the armament industry's ramifications and the international network of the Aluminum Company of America. See H. C. Engelbrecht and F. C. Hanighen, *Merchants of Death* (New York, 1934), largely based on data from the Nye Investigation of the munitions industry; and see also proceedings in equity in the District Court of the United States for the Southern District of New York, Brief for the United States in Support of a Preliminary Finding of Conspiracy among Alcoa, Aluminum Limited and the Foreign Aluminum Companies (June 1, 1939).

to help their own small competing nationals in foreign markets than for them to divide by special agreement domestic and foreign markets amongst the huge combines dominant in the several national territories.[32] Thus Krupp, Vickers and Schneider-Creusot got together to divide and allocate markets for arms and munitions. General Electric and Krupp divide the markets for bar-metal compounds, the German Dye Trust and Standard Oil markets for hydrogenated oil products, and so ad infinitum. In these agreements markets are increasingly divided along the following lines: (a) the domestic market is reserved for each, or some specific portion of it is allotted to domestic manufacture (e. g., the Bausch and Lomb-Zeiss agreements on optical glass; General Electric and foreign producers on incandescent lamps); (b) the adjoining space or continental area is reserved for each or a combination of each concept of *Grossraumwirtschaft* (e. g., agreements of DuPont and Imperial Chemicals on munitions; Alcoa and the Aluminum Cartel); and (c) "competing" territories are handled increasingly in such a fashion that either the price structures agreed upon will not be disturbed through "open competition," or dumping is resorted to on a bitterly cutthroat basis. If the former, it is usually because patents are so pooled or agreements so drawn that "outsiders" cannot possibly break in; and if the latter, then because no small concern unaided and by itself can possibly meet the pace once the struggle reaches a sanguinary stage.[33]

[32] "One case concerns an American optical company, which, during the last 5 years, has manufactured, distributed, and sold approximately 50% of all U.S. military optical instruments. These have included periscopes, range finders, altimeters, bomb sights, torpedo directors, etc. This corporation arranged with a leading German corporation, operating in the same field, to divide the world market; to limit sales to allotted territory; and to fix and maintain prices and terms of sale. The German and American corporations agreed to conceal the existence of the contract from third parties, and the latter corporation agreed to pay to the other a royalty equal to a percentage of the gross sales price of each military optical instrument sold, including equipment sold to the United States Government." Resolution by Senator Wheeler calling for an Investigation of Interstate Commerce Conditions Affecting National Defense, Sept. 18, 1940.

[33] It is noteworthy that none of the small American business groups has been able to see any other solution to its problems except to pool resources and behave—in imitation of those against whom they are organizing—collusively with respect not to the large concerns or trade associations of the large, but with respect to that portion of the public which it may be able to call its own. Conversely, one will search through the records of monopolistic practices of the large combines in vain for instances where the little businessman was left unscathed, even when he was not the direct object of attack.

Such a classification of the reasons for the growing relative importance of the giants in the formulation of business policies does not by any manner of means exhaust the possible listing. But it may possibly cover the most important cases. A little careful inspection of the voluminous records on which these generalizations are based will show convincing evidence not only that these trends are contemporaneous and mutually reinforcing, but also that no competitive restraints or combination of competitive restraints can any longer be expected to stop or seriously to inhibit the vaulting powers of these great interlinked aggregations of large-scale corporate enterprise. Government may be able to do so if, when, and where it is able to shake itself free from direct or indirect manipulation by the powers it seeks to control. But so far as it fails to do so, by so much the mantle of political authority is simply shifted *de facto* from its former popular, or constitutional, base to another which stems from the inner councils of these huge corporate complexes.[34] But of that, more later.

CHANGES UNDERLYING POLICY-FORMULATION
WITHIN THE CARTELS

The term "cartel" has lost its old precision. Once it stood simply for a contractual relationship, usually enforceable at law, between a number of enterprises which had banded themselves together for a fixed period of time in order the better to regulate prices, or production, or marketing terms, conditions and areas, or some other feature of business relating to a single or a closely related group of commodities produced by its members. Now that the term has come into general circulation, it has come to mean any sort of compact—whether recognized and enforceable by law or not—between two or more concerns for the purpose of manipulating one or more of the elements of conducting business to the advantage of the participating parties. Even in the classical home of the cartel, Germany, it has long been difficult to distinguish be-

[34] The comment of the *Wall Street Journal*, April 28, 1941, on recent developments in Japanese "Co-prosperity sphere" plans is illuminating: "Recent strengthening of the power of business circles in the Konoye Cabinet will not mean abandonment of Japan's plans for economic regimentation and southward expansion. A good many leading 'liberal' businessmen, including the newly-appointed economic coördinator, Masatsune Ogura, whom some industrialists refer to as Japan's Göring, are toying with the idea of totalitarianism in Japan, only a totalitarianism run by businessmen."

tween the practices of cartels and those of many of the more power-ful trade associations such as the Federation of German Machine Building Associations (VDMA) or the Association of German Iron and Steel Industrialists. British writers use the terms "trade as-sociations" and "cartels" more or less interchangeably. In France the members of the Comité des Forges have entered into many dif-ferent "comptoirs," but what of the Comité des Forges itself? Many of its activities have long been of a distinctly cartel-like character.[35] Thurman Arnold of the Anti-Trust Division uses the term to apply to any American trade association pursuing policies which bind its members to behave non-competitively.[36]

More than mere loose thinking is involved here. Actually, a vast and complicated system of collusive practices has come into being since the First World War having the effect of cartel agreements; it appears under a multiplicity of guises and is given effect through a wide variety of associational forms. To the economist the realities of practice, not the fictions of law or the accidents of terminology, must occupy the center of the stage. And from this point of view, it is probably not too far from the truth to say that practically all of the swiftly proliferating meshwork of trade associations found in all capitalistic countries of the world perform one or more func-tions of a distinctly cartel-like character. Adam Smith's dictum ap-plies to the usual, not the exceptional case. And even those which are economically functionless seem on investigation to be going through motions, like the wind-up of the pitcher before delivery of the ball, prefatory to more forceful and purposive action.

A couple of examples will serve to show how pervasive cartel-like policies have become. In Germany, none of the laws commonly called "Cartel Laws" apply singly and solely to collusive groups formally recognized in law as Cartels. For example, the famous "Law Against the Abuse of Economic Power" ("Verordnung gegen Missbrauch wirtschaftlicher Machtstellungen"), passed in 1923, ap-plied to "Syndicates, Cartels, Conventions and Similar Agree-

---

[35] See, in particular, Bezard-Faglas, Les Syndicats patronaux de l'industrie métal-lurgique en France.

[36] Compare Arnold, op. cit. with the report on cartels prepared by Theodore J. Kreps and presented before the Temporary National Economic Committee. The Kreps view, which seems to have shared in the thinking of Mr. Leon Henderson of the TNEC, inclines quite favorably towards good cartels, while frowning—not very severely—at the bad.

ments." The text of the law (as of those which followed in July, 1930, August, 1930, August, 1931, December, 1931, and July, 1933) refers but incidentally to those combinations as "Cartels." The last-named law (1933), "Concerning the Forming of Compulsory Cartels," places the cartel at the center of the discussion only because it refers to all agreements entered into under authority of pre-existing laws by the generic term "cartel." [37] The Cartel Bureau (Kartellstelle) of the old National Federation of German Industry (Reichsverband der deutschen Industrie) handled cartel problems as specialized activities of its members, separately grouped in the Federation by industry and trade categories and organized as trade associations. The left hand took care of cartel problems; the right hand managed the larger interests into which cartel practices were dovetailed.[38]

There can be no question but that the National Federation of German Industry and all of its member bodies were engaged directly or indirectly in the exercise of cartel controls. And, as has been pointed out elsewhere,[39] the organizational network of pre-Nazi Germany, brought together and centralized in the *Spitzenverbände*, was well-nigh all-inclusive by the time the new regime took over. Not far behind Germany of that date stand England, France,[40] and the United States of the present. Fascist Italy and post-Nazi Germany [41] have seen the web of cartel-like controls still further extended.

[37] For texts of these laws, and an exhaustive commentary on the history of cartel policy in post-war Germany, see Callman, *op. cit.*

[38] See Max Metzner, *Kartelle und Kartellpolitik* (Berlin, 1926), and Wagenführ, *Kartelle in Deutschland*.

[39] See Brady, *The Rationalization Movement in German Industry* (Berkeley, Calif., 1933), Chapter V, and *The Spirit and Structure of German Fascism* (New York, 1937), Chapter IX; also, W. F. Bruck, *Social and Economic History of Germany from Wilhelm II to Hitler, 1888–1938* and Franz Neumann, *Behemoth*.

[40] The "new" corporative order recently announced in conquered France seems much less revolutionary when viewed in light of the reorganization of the Confédération Générale du Patronat Français, following conclusion of the Matignon Agreement in 1936, with the Confédération Générale du Travail. The new groupings, the new tone, and the new policies which followed the Agreement were entirely in keeping with Nazi and Fascist patterns.

[41] "Only transitorily and superficially did the beginnings of the new relationship between the state and the economy appear hostile to cartels. The development of National Socialist cartel policies during the last year shows a replacement of rigorous cartel supervision by policies designed to guide the economy and regularize markets with and through the cartels. This is readily shown in the law and in legal inter-

A second example may be taken from the building industry in the United States. According to Assistant Attorney General Arnold: [42]

Producers of building materials have fixed prices either by private arrangements or as the principal activity of trade associations. Owners of patents on building materials have used them to establish restrictive structures of price control, control of sales methods, and limits upon the quantities sold. . . . Some of these patent holders have taken advantage of their control over patented products to require their licensees to give them control of unpatented products also. By the use of basing point systems and zone price systems, various building materials industries have established by formula a rigid structure of uniform prices throughout the country; and in some of these industries such price formulas have encouraged the wasteful shipment of products to great distances. The use of joint selling agencies has been another means by which some of these groups have undertaken to maintain their prices. In some groups the various producers have subscribed to the theory that every member of the industry should have a definite share of whatever business there is to be done, and that no concern should try to get more than its share by price competition.

Supplementing these various devices for keeping the prices of building materials high have been a series of other devices used to discipline competitors who are unwilling to play ball. In one industry the means is cutting off the supply of raw materials. In another it is starting a series of harassing lawsuits. In a third it is the harassment of distributors by selling through the seller's own factory branches at prices lower than those at which the distributor is permitted to resell. In a fourth it is the maintenance of orthodox channels of distribution by concerted refusal to sell to groups representing new methods of sale or new price policies.

But this is only the beginning. In addition, "there is a growing concentration of control in many of these industries" through combination, merger, communities of interest, and the like. This holds for the distribution of building materials, and down through all the various systems of contracting and subcontracting characteristics of the industry.[43] Nor are the data local; the situation is ap-

pretation of the law." Fritz Ruhle, "Kartellpolitik und Weltbewerbeordnung," *Zeitschrift für Betriebswirtschaft,* 1938, pp. 337–49. See also Bruck, *op. cit.,* pp. 222–26 and, particularly, Neumann, *op. cit.,* pp. 261–73.

[42] In an address before the National Association of Purchasing Agents at the Fairmont Hotel, San Francisco, California, May 22, 1939. Department of Justice news release.

[43] In some of these efforts the trade unions are alleged to have coöperated freely.

parently typical of the building industry throughout the entire country.[44] Yet the situation within this industry is in no wise unique. In approaching the problem of cartel-like controls within the California food industries, for example, the Anti-Trust Division is faced with a situation so far advanced along the road of what the London *Economist* calls "feudalistic cartel controls" [45] that prosecution is faced with only one alternative to passing up the whole matter as beyond redemption, and that is to issue a blanket indictment against the entire industry.[46] Similarly with the petroleum, movie-production, electric household-appliance, and milk industries,[47] and many if not almost all of the other important industrial groupings of America.

See, e. g., Civil Action No. 698 in the District Court of the United States for the Western District of Pennsylvania, the United States *vs.* the Voluntary Code of he Heating, Piping and Air-Conditioning Industry for Allegheny County, Pennsylvania, *et al.*, Dec. 8, 1939.

[44] As shown by the effort of building materials dealers in "41 federated units located in approximately 32 states throughout the United States" (FTC Docket No. 2191, Dec. 30, 1937) the local, regional, and in some respects the national markets for building materials are governed by cartel agreements affecting the bulk of the industry. Though enjoined from further such practices by the FTC in 1937, it would not appear from the statement by Mr. Arnold, nor from the numerous indictments handed down by the Anti-Trust Division in 1939 and 1940 against the building industry, that monopolistic practices were checked nor even seriously impeded by the FTC action. "The housing investigation [conducted by Mr. Arnold] resulted in the indictment of 1,358 defendants" (New York *Times,* November 25, 1940), and the evidence adduced was such as to encourage belief that Mr. Arnold had even then but barely scratched the surface. In fact his economic advisor, Corwin D. Edwards, has clearly so stated in his illuminating discussion, "The New Anti-Trust Procedure as Illustrated in the Construction Industry," *Public Policy,* II (1941), 321–40.

[45] "The Economic Front," *Economist,* Dec. 9, 1939. See also the article "The Cartellisation of England," in the *Economist,* March 18, 1940.

[46] Under the California Pro-Rate Act, for example, 65 percent of the producers by number and product may cause a state of "emergency" to be declared by the State Agricultural Commissioner, after which a Pro-Rate Commission can be established possessed of power to establish crop quotas, crop surpluses, length of the canning season (14 to 16 days for peaches, for example), grades, grades that are marketable, etc. Costs of administration, such as advertising, are collectable through the state tax machinery, and failure to pay is regarded as the equivalent of tax delinquency. Numbers of farmers are not accurately known in most crop districts, and in many cases the farmers are either tenants of processors and distributors or of banks, or in debt to concerns such as American Can and Continental Can; for all practical purposes the agreements are completely controlled by nonfarmer interests.

[47] See, in particular, the indictments by the Anti-Trust Division of the Borden Company, *et al.,* in the Chicago and Detroit districts. Much the same picture as

Speaking very broadly, it seems possible to summarize the general lines of development in this expansion and permeation of cartel policies throughout the national systems of the various capitalistic countries under the following five points.

1. The line between combinations, mergers, communities of interest, intercompany compacts on the one extreme and large national trade associations on the other is, of course, structurally pretty clear. But between the two poles there is an almost infinite gradation of constantly changing forms, techniques, practices and policies. In general, trade associations throughout the world are taking on cartel functions so rapidly that the distinction between different types of cartels and these associations is badly blurred, and in many respects all essential differences are lacking. This is recognized as true by leading authorities in England, France, pre-Nazi Germany, the United States, and Japan. In Fascist Italy and Nazi Germany differences are in part technical and in part functional, but in the main cartel-type controls have been accepted as normal and natural for all trades and industries, and the attitude, if not necessarily the detailed forms of their respective "corporate economies," appears to be prototypal for developments in other countries of comparison.

2. It is a characteristic common to practically all leading trade associations and cartels that they seek to eliminate "outsiders" or "free-riders." The compulsory cartel has achieved this objective in Germany. It is the aim of some of the more closely held British and French cartels, of the various agricultural marketing agreements set up in the United States, Germany, England, and Japan, and of all the trade associations which have succeeded in preserving the leading controls envisaged in NRA, and it is also a motive underlying the new arrangement of Groups under the Confédération Générale du Patronat Français, and, of course, in general, for the economies of the directly corporate systems. Elsewhere there is a general tendency either to eliminate "outsiders" entirely, or to bring together in the collusive group such an overwhelming majority of the industry that "free-riders" would be either of only local

given in these indictments evidently holds for most other large milk-marketing areas. See also Corwin D. Edwards, "Trade Barriers Created by Business," *Indiana Law Journal*, Dec., 1940, pp. 169–90.

significance,[48] or so small and scattered that they might be forced into line at will upon pain of total extinction.

3. There is a clear and wholly unmistakable tendency for the large concerns to dominate more and more completely all forms of cartels and trade associations. This was clearly shown in the bulk of the leading NRA codes, is evident in most of the national and regional trade associations in America, and appears to be true of all the leading German, French, and British cartels and trade associations. Frequently, cartel activities have paved the way for combination of the horizontal type, as for example in the German and British heavy chemicals industries. Sometimes the way was prepared by cartels for vertical integration, with the result that independent enterprises tended to disappear entirely.[49] Frequently, as in the British salt, thread, chemicals, and armaments industries, trade associations were organized as adjuncts for further extending the monopolistic controls of large combines.[50] The existence of cartel controls not uncommonly enhances the superior bargaining power of large concerns producing goods or using materials not included within the cartel bailiwick, as in the case of the vertically organized German steel combine contrasted with the "pure" collieries. The combine, when producing for "self-consumption," was not required to charge profit margins at different stages of production, with the result that the combine possessed a considerable—at times well-nigh decisive—advantage over nonintegrated competitors.[51] But in nearly all cases, both within the totalitarian countries and without, the lead in the organization and direction of both cartels and trade associations is typically and increasingly being taken by the corporate giants. The policies of these organizations, that is to say, are being molded to the interests, the outlooks, and the programs of the great monopoly-minded corporate groupings.

[48] Even here there is a tendency to force recalcitrants into line on many issues—such as labor policies, taxation measures, price maintenance, etc.

[49] See Herbert von Beckerath, *Modern Industrial Organization* (New York, 1933), in particular Chapters II and VIII.

[50] There are many American examples, e. g., the National Glass Distributor's Association, organized by the Pittsburgh Plate Glass Company; the New York Sheet Metal Roofing and Air-Conditioning Contractor's Association, dominated by the Fox Furnace Company; the Associated Milk Dealers of Chicago, dominated by Borden's.

[51] Particularly interesting in this connection is the evidence submitted to the *Enqueteausschuss*, by various industrialists connected with the iron, steel, coal and heavy chemicals industries.

4. That is why the following trends, clearly discernible within both cartels and trade associations in general, take on such great significance; these organizations are (a) becoming more permanent, less easily broken up by the changing fortunes of business cycles, and their contractual or semicontractual obligations are entered into with an eye to longer-run objectives. Simultaneously, (b) interests are spreading out from a single line of control (such as prices, or production, or marketing areas, or conditions and terms of delivery, or patent pooling) to take on other functions, and, in some cases (notably the "compulsory cartels"), the whole range of cartel functions. With this go (c) tendencies for the cartel to resort to some degree of central management of supplies or sales ("syndicates"), or labor, or engineering and accounting. This is, in turn, (d) paralleled by a general and well-nigh universal tendency for all these associations—in "proportion" as they take on a more cartel-like character—to band or group together into regional, commodity, and industrial central or peak associations (*Spitzenverbände*). Finally, (e) there is an almost universal tendency, once this level of development has been reached, for members increasingly to try to limit business transactions to members, and for trade associations and cartels to deal with each other as exclusive agents for their respective memberships. The governance of the resulting system of intertrade compacts, agreements, negotiations and relationships then comes to be one of the principal activities of the *Spitzenverbände*.[52]

5. The relationship between the foregoing tendencies and the correlative rise and universalization of "mercantilistic" practices— wherein the normal course of business as usual leans ever more heavily upon a generalized system of state aid—within the several national states, becomes clearly one of mutuality, interaction, and interdependence. The two lines of change have a common histori-

[52] See, Bruck, *op. cit.* and Neumann, *op. cit.*, pp. 263-65, for a more recent discussion of National Socialism. In the 1925 *Yearbook and Register of British Manufacturers*, published by the Federation of British Industries, mention is made of ". . . a strong feeling . . . that so far as possible, members should give each other preference in placing orders, and the system of inter-trading is now rapidly gaining ground amongst members" (p. 23). The Nazis and the Fascists, with their widespread systems of inter-trade compacts, appear as the culmination and logical fulfillment of a process which becomes more and more formal and general as the networks of business spread out, lines of influence are transmuted into frames of control, and powers are gathered up and centralized in peak associations.

cal origin, and they run their parallel courses over the same span of time. In a multitude of ways advance in one leads to advance in the other.

Neither cartels nor trade associations, of course, can any longer be called "children of necessity." But tariffs, subsidies, subventions, government loans without interest, laws allowing resale price maintenance, can, however, be regarded as successful products of the mounting demand of massed special interest groups of businessmen, and their direct, coördinated, and organized efforts to see that governments stand perpetually prepared to grant whatever aid their several plans and programs require. Without important exception in any of the major capitalistic countries, the necessary enabling laws have been lobbied through by business interests. The *Spitzenverbände* endeavor to see only that the basic laws and the mass of administrative decisions flowing from them generalize the gains and even cut the losses. The rule, as in early mercantilistic times, becomes one of concession, grant, honoraria, "special privilege." Fully rationalized and centrally governed via the *Spitzenverbände,* organized to the outer limits of trade and industry, the logical result of such generalized *Priviligierung* is cumulative approximation to the generic conditions of the corporate or "guild" state.[53]

THE ECONOMIC POLICIES OF THE
SPITZENVERBÄNDE

This means a great deal more than that the business life of the major capitalistic countries is being organized in ever more closely coöperating, bureaucratically directed, and monopolistic federations of business interests. It means that direction throughout all this vast proliferating machinery is ever more clearly and insistently being centered in the hands of the corporate giants. It is not only their interests that dominate in the larger sphere of action, but their manners of procedure, their organizational patterns, their points of view, and their conceptions of the larger objectives of economic policy as a whole. The shape of things present and to

[53] This is the term employed by the official Italian propaganda agency in America, the Italian Library of Information, to characterize for American readers the leading features of Fascist social-economic organization. See *The Organization of Production and the Syndical Corporative System, an Outline Study.*

come in this universe of motion are, to be true, by no means free of confusion, but the general lines of force are ribbed boldly in view.

The "Industrial Complex."—The case is more easily made before the law or to the general public for treating an entire industry, or a series of closely related industries, as a single managerial entity where the integrative pressures of technology have led directly to the concept of a single, all-inclusive engineering system—local, regional, national, or continental wide, a system which can only be broken up by going to more primitive methods of production.[54] Falling into this class are the systems of transportation and communication: railroad, highway, inland-river and coastwise shipping, airplane, bus, truck, telephone, telegraph, cable, postal service, radio, gas, water, pipeline, and power grid (inclusive of production, transmission, and distribution). In all these cases engineering, cost accounting, and management factors all conspire to favor for each appropriate territory a single, unified, and all-inclusive network under a single management charged with the task of organizing the whole with the minimum of duplication and overlapping. In some cases, such as the transportation and the communication groups, similar factors create conditions favorable to mono-management on an interindustrial and interservice basis; thus the railroads are technologically integrated systems, and other industries in these groups are bound together into actual or potential one-management systems.

This general category of industries is commonly said to be made up of "natural monopolies," and its members are thought to be peculiarly "affected with a public interest." But whether so considered or not, and whether owned and operated as governmental,

---

[54] Developments of this character, combined with the increasing freedom of managerial circles from direct responsibility to the rank and file of property owners, have excited James Burnham to prophesy, in his *Managerial Revolution* (New York, 1941), that managers will become the new "ruling class" in the place of the capitalists. The whole argument is based on a misunderstanding of the location and source of power of existing managements both here and abroad, and confuses machinery of execution with structures of domination; in the same way, Paul Einzig ("Hitler's 'New Order' in Theory and Practice," *Economic Journal*, Vol. LI, No. 201, April, 1941) confuses planning and central management with antidemocratic and regional exploitation. But "planning" is a "tool" and "structure" is a "device" and nothing more. The question is not "management" and "planning," but who manages what, by what means, and to what ends.

private, or "mixed" enterprises, these industries are all characterized by the case they present for being organized as single, central
managerial systems.[55] Throughout there is a clear and unmistakable long-run tendency for corporate groupings to be reshuffled so as
to correspond to management imperatives—for, in other words,
corporate holdings or management controls to become coterminous with industrial, engineering frontiers.[56] Most backward in
these respects are the railroad systems of the United States,[57] England [58] and France; the telegraph and radio systems of the United
States; [59] the power systems of Germany,[60] the United States, and

[55] Which does not, of course, preclude a high degree of regional or functional decentralization of a system functioning as a single managerial entity. The A. T. and T.,
perhaps the best example outside of the postal services in the United States where
corporate and network frontiers are almost entirely identical, has also been the leader
in the development of methods of managerial decentralization.

[56] How important these factors may become in future governmental policies toward
"trust" developments is shown by Mr. Arnold's dictum, speaking on behalf of the
Anti-Trust Division of the Department of Justice, that "the rule of reason is the
recognition of the necessities of organization in a machine age." This he interprets
to mean specifically that the government will not proceed against, (1) "combinations
which actually contribute to the efficiency of mass production," (2) "concerted action
which goes no further than to insure orderly marketing conditions," and (3) those
"monopolistic restraints" which, if proceeded against, would involve "economic dislocation in great industries." Speech before the National Association of Purchasing
Agents, San Francisco, California, May 22, 1939 (Department of Justice news release).
It is not hard to see how a good combination of ambidextrous legal talent, gifted
cost accounting, and clever management engineering might bring almost any combination out of the antitrust shoals under shelter of these wide-ranging criteria.

[57] It is significant, however, that the ICC has long been committed to the principle
of regional amalgamation, fusion of terminal facilities, etc. See in particular, the
various reports of Commissioner Eastman during his incumbency as Coördinator of
Transportation.

[58] The English railroads, over fifty major and several minor lines, were brought
together into four major systems in the early twenties. Measures are now being taken
to fuse these four into a single rail network.

[59] There is not the slightest justification from a competitive or a general economic
point of view for the duplicate systems of Western Union and Postal Telegraph. No
parallel to this duplication is to be found in any other major industrial country in
the world. The American radio system is somewhat more complex, but it is equally
out of date.

[60] See, however, the plan of Oskar von Miller, *Ausführungen des Sachverständigen
Dr. Oskar von Miller über die derzeit wichtigsten Fragen der Elektrizitätswirtschaft*,
and *Gutachten über die Reichselektrizitätsversorgung* (Berlin, 1930). Much of this
plan has actually been carried into effect. Under stimulus, however, of a developing
war psychology, accompanied by military plans for industrial decentralization of industry, there has more recently developed considerable opposition to a central German power grid. See, various issues of *ETZ* from 1932 to 1936, the *Archiv für Wärme-
wirtschaft*, and *Elektrizitätswirtschaft*, German journals devoted to the electric power
industry; and see also F. Lawaczek, *Technik und Wirtschaft im Dritten Reich* (Mu

France; and the bus, truck, and internal waterways systems of all countries except Germany.[61] Intertransport systems have been worked out comprehensively only in Germany,[62] and intercommunications systems only in Germany, Italy, and England.[63]

A situation somewhat similar to that of the public utilities is found with all those industries which have (a) been growing together, quasi-organically, at the manufacturing base, and to which (b) entrance is controlled through closely guarded engineering and research factors. In the first case there is a tendency for a complex of industries (the Russians use the term "Combinat") and in the second case for entire single industries to be fused together, so that in analysis one is compelled more and more to proceed as though one were dealing with single managerial units instead of collectivities of separate enterprises. Either or both tendencies appear to be pronounced with all those types of enterprises termed "laboratory babies" above (heavy chemicals, plastics, electrical apparatus, pulp and paper, armaments). These industries may possess a common source or series of sources of raw materials, or a series of dovetailed "flow-type" processes, or monopoly of the necessary initial knowledge obtainable only from secret sources of information, or basic and indispensable patents on machinery, processes, or products. Such possession enables a single concern or a group of closely cooperating concerns to force entire industries into line, with the effect that one or more of the conditions and terms of conducting

---

nich, 1932). Plans of the Belgian engineer Oliven for an European-wide superpower grid have fallen afoul of analogous misfortunes.

[61] A fair degree of unification has been achieved in the United States in the bus systems operating between major traffic terminals, and in some cases between railroad and bus transport. Steps have been taken by a number of railroads, led by the Pennsylvania, to dovetail rail and local freight trucking facilities.

[62] The German intertransport network is not altogether complete, but it has become very nearly so with simultaneous over-all organization of each of the separate types, and then interlinkage step by step amongst them as fast as plans could be worked out. Model systems, in this respect, are the long-distance rail, short-distance bus, the rail, airplane, and postal bus passenger service, the Rhine water and rail freight traffic, and the rail and truck pick-up and delivery system in Berlin. The initial efforts of the giant Hermann Göring Works to unify the Danubian water transport system foreshadow extension of the networks for the whole of the European mainland. See Lachman, op. cit.

[63] Most complete are those of Germany and England, where all communication services are centered in the post office. The Italian and Japanese are not far removed from a like level of development.

business are centrally managed and controlled throughout the entire industry.[64]

Certain of the conditions peculiar to the "laboratory babies," of course, are rapidly coming to govern the vast majority of the leading industries throughout the world. But in the absence of such pressures, the effect of partial managerial control may be had through the pooling of resources by the establishment of central coöperative facilities, such as laboratories, market information services, and joint management committees of one sort or another dealing with standards, grades, advertising, apprenticeship, foremanship, public relations.[65] Individual firms may seek to depart from this coöperative set-up; but if the information is of critical importance, or if the standards are fundamental to the evolution of a system of interchangeable parts, or if the failure to adhere to the advertising schedule thereby causes a dangerous pyramiding of competitive costs, then firms may be compelled to hew pretty close to the line fixed, and will rarely be able to go far beyond the techniques and practices agreed upon in conference.[66] The environment, that is to say, becomes favorable for acting as though the association of cartel had become, through close and long collaboration on vital issues, to some degree or other a single-management enterprise, and as though the member concerns were branch

[64] Perhaps the best examples are to be found in the interests grouped around Standard Oil and DuPont in the United States, Imperial Chemicals in England, and the I. G. Farbenindustrie, Krupp, and possibly the Hermann Göring Works in Germany.

[65] There are several dozen trade-association laboratories in the United States (e. g., the Electrical Testing Laboratories of the Edison Electrical Institute and the National Electric Manufacturers Association, and the American Gas Association's laboratories in Cleveland), in England (e. g., the British Cotton Industry Research Association and the Research Association of the British Rubber and Tire Manufacturers), and in Germany. A particularly interesting development in the latter country is the evolution of a chain of industry-government supported industrial laboratories known as the Kaiser Wilhelm Gesellschaft, covering nearly every branch of industry in every field. Also of particular interest is the Reichskuratorium für Wirtschaftlichkeit, a central "rationalization" coördinating body. (See Brady, *The Rationalization Movement in German Industry*.) A similar body has been set up in Japan but appears to have met with indifferent success. Standards bodies, to be found in every manufacturing country, provide also a very interesting method of bringing industrial establishments together. (See *Industrial Standardization*, National Industrial Conference Board, New York, 1929); but the methods here are legion.

[66] Such is the case in all "simplification," "typification," fits and gauges, dimensional standards for interchangeable parts, methods of testing and rating, standards for control instruments, etc. See TNEC Monograph No. 24, *Consumer Standards*.

or regional offices rather than independent business units—for be-
having, in short, as though central direction had been given over to
a "syndicate" or a "community of interests," or a formal combination (as in the case of the great German dye trust).

Here again, the position of the *Spitzenverbände* has been uniformly to foster, promote, and encourage. This is shown not only
by the detail of the activities on which they center their attention,
but also by the industrial groupings of their membership. The
Grand Council of the Federation of British Industries bears more
than a superficial likeness to the National Council of Confederations of the Italian Corporate State and the *Gruppen* arrangement
under the Chamber of Commerce and Industry in Nazi Germany.
The grouping of the Confédération Générale du Patronat Français appears to be a compromise between the German and Italian
models, and the new plans for France's industrial reorganization
under the Vichy regime appear to require but relatively small
changes in that pattern. In all cases and with increasing clarity, the
industry is the unit and associational forms are expected more and
more to adjust their activities to these frontiers.

Privilege and protection.—Paging through the literature of the
several central manufacturing associations of the various major
capitalistic countries, the patterns of privilege and protection,
varying greatly in detail, appear to be cut from the same cloth.
They do not require great elaboration here, for already a vast
literature has been written around them. However, in juxtaposition with the foregoing discussion and each other, they help to
show how strongly and deeply the current is running towards what
the Germans call *Ordnungswirtschaft* (ordered, bound up, organized, directed). The elements that make up the pattern are as follows.

1. A trend toward protection against foreign competition reaches
back to the Bismarck tariff of 1879. Definitely protectionist and
"autarchic" in all countries, its basis of autarchy is not the nation,
but the maximum area of empire or sphere of influence. Protective
tariffs are to autarchic programs as youth is to age; autarchy might
be regarded as generalized and rationalized protection, and the
basis is imperial, or continental (*Grossraumwirtschaft*) self-sufficient systems. All nations now have systems of "imperial prefer-

ence," of which the British scheme worked out at Ottawa is only the better known and more spectacular. The long-run changes over time are the following: (a) tariff walls have been heightened and generalized to meet the needs of every organized interest grouping; (b) the forms of protection and aid have been multiplied to meet every peculiar need; (c) the whole of the network of national protection and aid has gradually been articulated into a more or less rationalized system of economic-political aggrandizement; (d) administration has been placed in the hands of administrative bodies given wide latitude in the use of the tools for the advance of national economic interests both at home and abroad— *Machtpolitik;* [67] (e) these administrative bodies may be publicly owned, privately owned (as with British industrial reorganization schemes for coal, shipping, retail trade and textiles), or "mixed" (as in the case of the Hermann Göringwerke, the British Central Electricity Board, the leading Japanese "development companies" in Manchuria, North China and the South Seas). But in any case, they tend to become all-inclusive monopolies in a sense analogous to the early mercantilistic trading companies.

2. The second element is protection against competition at home. Appearing under the common euphemism, "fair trade practice," laws cumulatively circumscribing and hedging competition about with a multitude of controls and administrative rules are now to be found in every major capitalistic country. Promoted by business pressure-groups, and growing in number and range of importance with amazing speed, these laws all tend to promote—after the models of the exclusive monopoly and cartel—some degree of price fixation, systems of discount, brokerage fee allowances, circumscription of marketing areas, conditions and terms of delivery and sale, and the like. The Programs of the Robinson-Patman Act, the Miller-Tydings Bill, the Agricultural Marketing Act, the Capper-Volstead Act, the 45 or more state price-maintenance laws, and a vast supporting, corollary, supplementary, and elaborating outpouring of federal, state and local legislation and administrative

---

[67] This interest—protection from foreign competition—was the major force behind the organization of the National Association of Manufacturers, one of the predecessor bodies of the Reichsverband der deutschen Industrie, the Confédération Générale de la Production Française (predecessor body to the Confédération Genérale du Patronat Français, and the Federation of British Industries.

rulings can be duplicated now in every country of the world.[68] The differences here between policies advocated by the *Spitzenverbände* and their supplementary pressure groups in the United States on the one hand, and in the totalitarian countries on the other is one of degree, not of kind or method.[69] The Nazis, for example, understood NRA at its inception to be in keeping with the corporate ideas of "stabilized business" advocated by the Nazi state.[70] War has a tendency to accelerate the pace, not to alter the lines of growth.[71]

[68] It should be noticed, however, that the growth of internal trade barriers is not necessarily in harmony with these other trends—may, in fact, break down efforts to block out different types of special trade or interest controls. Cf., the equivocal position of the Automobile Manufacturers' Association to state resale price-maintenance, antidiscrimination, antitrust, below-cost and motor-vehicle dealer licensing laws (outlined in a series of charts, 1937).

[69] "Under the guise of establishing standards of 'fair trade practice,' competition was sublimated to the extent of virtual extinction. In many industries it forthwith became 'unfair' to utilize existing productive capacity even to the extent that actual orders for goods indicated to be profitable from the standpoint of particular management and warrantable from the standpoint of the social economy. 'Spread out the business!' It became 'unfair' to underbid other producers—witness the numerous code provisions requiring the maintenance of fixed margins and the recovery of standardized, indeed arbitrary, 'average costs.' " Myron Watkins, "The Economic Implications of Unfair Competition," *Iowa Law Review*, Jan., 1936, p. 269. Since the demise of NRA all these practices have become more or less common throughout American economic life. For Germany, see especially Heinz Mullensiefen, *Das neue Kartell-, Zwangskartell- und Preisüberwachungsrecht* (1934), and *Freiheit und Bindung in der geordneten Wirtschaft* (1939). For Italy, any issue of the voluminous and complete, *Sindicate e Corporazione*, and Helmut Vollweiler, *Der Staats- und Wirtschaftsaufbau im Faschistischen Italien* (Wurzburg-Aumühle, 1939). For England, Lucas, *Industrial Reconstruction;* Levy, *Monopolies, Cartels, and Trusts,* current issues of the London *Economist,* and various plans for industrial reorganization of PEP (Political and Economic Planning). For the United States, Burns, *The Decline of Competition;* Ewald T. Grether, *Price Control under Fair Trade Legislation* (New York, 1939).

[70] They based this judgment, as the author can testify from numerous personal interviews with leading German businessmen during 1935, upon such as the following: "The 'Key' factor in the NRA program is America's 3,500 larger (State and National) trade associations—and the over 10,000 local Trade Associations, Chambers of Commerce, etc. The whole fabric of business organizations is inter-twined and ready to coöperate with the some 500 industries now under approved Codes and with the National Recovery Administration in all sound 'Business-Government Partnership' plans." Statement of the American Trade Association Executives, prepared by the Trade Association Section of the Marketing Research and Service Division of the Bureau of Foreign and Domestic Commerce, U.S. Dept. of Commerce, and issued as "High Lights of the NRA, Chart No. 3," July 10, 1934.

[71] Practically all the important British food industries, for example, now brought into control boards under Britain's "feudalistic system of cartel control," have behind them "marketing" agreements quite similar to those worked out by the AAA in the United States, and which now govern, under one authority or another, almost the entirety of the highly specialized fruit and vegetable crops of California. A reading

3. The third, protection against dissolution and from becoming extra-marginal, takes many different forms—the limitation of capacity, capacity factors, incoming concerns, and provision of public funds for "bailing out" otherwise bankrupt firms.[72] The fringes of high-cost concerns are lopped-off and at the same time innovations are controlled. In an "emergency," government regulates, "protects," and supplies generous aid. What was once defined as an "emergency" then tends to become a permanent condition, reinforced, maintained and "stabilized" as a part of business-as-usual (relief disbursements, programs of public works, military expenditures, credit controls, government credit, price regulation). In general the effect is that prices are lowered or costs are adjusted so that the least efficient concern is brought into the organized system of protection.[73] In the patois, average revenues of the firm closest to the margin are "pegged" above average costs.[74] But costs are construed not as sums which add but as categories whose dimensions are a function of policies centered in and controlled through the new systems of protection.

4. The fourth element is protection against the business cycle and analogous hazards. The attitude of business is slowly changing from hostility toward programs of armaments (wartime) and

---

of the "Statutory Rules and Orders" for the potato-marketing agreement, or for pigs, bacon, milk, etc., based upon the British Agricultural Marketing Act of 1931, will show that the English intended that these boards should be possessed of powers which might readily be expanded to control the several food industries lock, stock and barrel, and with reference to all problems of production and distribution, and for all persons or parties involved therein. In many respects they are scarcely to be distinguished from the Nazi *Marktordnungsgrundsätze* for German agriculture.

[72] See, in particular, the summary of Code provisions given in *The National Recovery Administration*, by Leverett Lyon and others (Washington, D.C., 1935), which details at great length Code devices for achieving "protection" against all the usual hazards of competitive business. For the period since the demise of NRA, perhaps the best source of information is the various reports of the Institute of Distribution.

[73] It was accepted as a ruling principle in the regulated economies of both World Wars that profits should be guaranteed every enterprise participating in war production. Since all enterprises are thus subject to—and actually have become involved in—war control, this system of *compulsory profits* has come out to mean as many or almost as many price schedules as there are cost schedules. The NRA codes and the corporate systems of Italy and Germany have applied these wartime principles to many of the processes of peace. But they are applied neither in the totalitarian nor in the "liberal-capitalistic" countries to the tolerated, profitless, outsider fringe. The fringe, however, is not extra-marginal; it is *outside the pale of granted privilege.*

[74] With the tendency, as shown in the NRA Codes, for example, to include a "normal return on investment" over and above interest payments, not as revenue but as cost! See Watkins, "The Economic Implications of Unfair Competition."

public-works (peacetime) in times of depression, to one of acceptance and—particularly so far as armaments are concerned—enthusiastic support.[75] Surpluses of manpower (unemployment), of goods (met by the equivalent of "valorization," market surplus, "ever-normal granary" methods) and of capacity are becoming natural, normal, chronic features of highly developed capitalist civilization. It is only a question of time until methods applied partially or sporadically in the field of agriculture will be generalized over the entire economic system. All the *Spitzenverbände* seem to agree that these methods can only be administered by central public authority, by the aid of war, public works and other supporting programs, and under the administration of businessmen who will see to it that the results of such policies, intended to "help business," are not such as to hurt business as a result of "mistaken idealism," "reformism," or "socialistic" ideas. And all such policies call for protection against the demands of competing interests (that is, little-business and nonbusiness interests).[76]

Centralized Control.—Without exception—in England, France, Germany, Japan, Italy, and the United States, Belgium, Holland, Czecho-Slovakia, Poland, Sweden, and in all other countries still existing or now submerged, which have central, national *Spitzenverbände*—all inclusive plans and programs for industry, trade, and interindustry organization are referred to as "self-government in business." [77] So far as one may generalize from past trends and present incomplete records of experimentation,[78] the concept of "self-government in business" means something like this: in a fashion somewhat similar to, and possibly patterned in some re-

[75] The monthly letters of the National City Bank during 1938 and 1939, make extremely interesting reading in this connection. Government spending for relief, public works, etc., was regarded as the balance wheel of the economic system, and the arguments employed by the National City Bank are almost identical with those running through German business periodicals and expressed directly to the author by leading German businessmen who dwelt most enthusiastically on the public-work and armaments programs of the Third Reich.

[76] These will be dealt with in the following chapter.

[77] The German expression alone means "self-management" (*Selbstverwaltung*). But this is in keeping with German tradition, which always admits at every stage of the game, tighter, more inclusive, and more rigid central control.

[78] See, in this connection, the various efforts by NRA to evolve "master plans," "blanket codes," and "blue eagle" dicta; see also the various German and Italian laws (of which the current French "corporate" pattern appears to be a blend) relating to cartels, price control and price supervision.

spects directly after, the systems of managerial decentralization by regions and functions evolved by concerns such as General Motors, the A. T. and T., Imperial Chemicals, I. G. Farben, and Vereinigte Stahlwerke, trade associations wish to administer or "govern" each and every industry as semi- or wholly autonomous groups within a framework of control laid down by the central authorities. It is a concept not unlike that of corporate guild economy in the medieval period, except that here leadership is taken by a coöptative elite dominated by the huge corporate combines and communities of interest.[79] The authority carries with it legal or quasi-legal power to enforce compliance upon the totality of the industry and, furthermore, compliance practices are governed by codified rules of the general order of codes of "fair-trade practices," [80] which assume a set of directives of an ultimately social and political character. This is the capitalistic equivalent to agrarian states' rights doctrines as viewed by a champion of planter aristocracy such as John Calhoun.

Compliance by the entire industry with the dicta of the coöpted "self-governing" cliques involves a rationalization and systematization of cartel-like pattern of control for all industry. So far as the economic side is concerned this means that business feels that provisions must be made to (1) prevent "cutthroat competition" within the industry,[81] (2) keep "monopolistic competition" within industries whose products may be partially or wholly substitutable for each other from taking on a similar cutthroat character [82]—a sort of domestication of competition within the central control network which shifts a problem of economic warfare into one of intrigue, cabal, and junta—and (3) require of each industry (as of each member concern within each industry) rigid adherence to the decisions of the central authorities, so far as these decisions touch

---

[79] See the following chapter for an elaboration of the "coöperative" principle.

[80] The Group *Industrie* of the Reichswirtschaftskammer has made an attempt to codify "fair-trade practices" for all German industry. Something of the sort has been attempted by most national and regional chambers of commerce, and by most *Spitzenverbände* in every major industrial country.

[81] "Cutthroat competition" is, of course, the obverse of "fair-trade practices." "Fair-trade practices" equal, in the main, cartel controls; in practice "cutthroat competition" comes to mean loss to those who, unlike Eugene O'Neill's "Hairy Ape," *belong*.

[82] As when Alcoa attempts to control magnesium (a competitive light metal), or rayon, silk; or butter, margerine; etc.

upon issues which bind them all together into a coherent system of national business administration.

This latter requirement, centering as it does on the issues and the structures of domination, necessarily reaches far beyond the economic issues of a system of self-regulated capitalism. Far more than "free competition" and laissez faire go out the window with the shift from "monopoly competition" to "self-regulated monopoly." With this shift goes a gradual taking over of the offices and prerogatives of government. If the *Spitzenverbände* continue to travel along the same paths, government by the business system will find their members pulling together on social and political issues, however restive they may become under controls which they impose upon themselves [83] by their own developing monopoly practices of "self-regimentation."

[83] "We are faced," Mr. Arnold holds, "with a choice of either enforcing the anti-trust laws or drifting in the direction of the self-regimentation of business." Again, "Since the war a weak government permitted the whole German production and distributing system to be organized from top to bottom by trade associations and cartels. Sporadic attempts prior to 1930 to allow new and independent enterprise a chance were stifled. Industrial Germany became so self-regimented that there was a place for everyone and everyone had to keep his place. The cartel system led only to higher prices. Here was regimentation without leadership and arbitrary power without control. Germany became organized to such an extent that a Fuehrer was inevitable; had it not been Hitler it would have been someone else." Speech before the Cleveland Bar Association, March 7, 1939 (Dept. of Justice News Release). The implication that the advance of monopoly controls leads to Fascist-type systems corresponds entirely with the facts. See also Bruck, *Social and Economic History of Germany*, and the various articles of the London *Economist* cited above. But there is likewise a dangerous over-simplification in so stating the matter, as will be pointed out in the following chapter.

Chapter VIII

SOCIAL POLICIES: STATUS, TRUSTEESHIP, HARMONY

AS MONOPOLY STANDS at the center of the new economics, so status is the heart of its appropriate social outlook. The two are complementary products of that modernized system of "granted privilege," "special concession," "neo-mercantilism," "generalized protection," and "feudalistic capitalism" [1] being brought about by the growing centralization of policy-forming power which is so common a feature of all major capitalistic economies. What private monopoly is to the economic side, the structure and ideology of status is to the social. Given the one, the other follows.

A perhaps somewhat more acceptable and comforting, though obviously less straightforward, way of expressing the same notion would be to speak of the apotheosis of trusteeship (stewardship).[2] Certainly this term, the precise equivalent of authoritative leadership, enjoys a steadily widening popularity as a mode of justifying both the growing concentration of power within the several forms of pyramidal authority, and the specific use of this power as it is brought to bear upon the interests of different classes of the population. It appears commonly in a context devoted to such companion ideas as "self-government in business," "service in busi-

---

[1] See Werner Sombart's discussion of guild and mercantilistic systems of *Privilegierung* in his *Moderne Kapitalismus* (Leipzig, 1924), I, Part I, 375 ff., and Part II, 614–15, for purposes of contrast with points made in articles appearing in the London *Economist*, "The Economic Front," Dec. 9, 1939, and "The Cartelisation of England," March 18, 1939.

[2] "Stewardship" is the term preferred by "Tie-Wig" exponents of New England Calvinist theocracy as championed by Fisher Ames and Robert Treat Paine in the early nineteenth century; cf., J. Parrington, *Main Currents in American Thought* (New York, 1939), II, 275–95. But the underlying ideological content of Brahmin Whiggery and big business public relations is cut of much the same doctrinal cloth.

ness," and "profits through service." [3] It has become a favorite expression amongst the more successful public-relations counselors not only in the United States, but also abroad. The Japanese *Zaibatsu* think of themselves as trustees much as did the younger Rockefeller who, in his "Industrial Creed," stated the case for "Welfare Capitalism" so convincingly that he was able to set the new tone for American business.[4] In Nazi Germany it has become the custom to refer to the businessman as "trustee of the community's welfare."

There are those who fear that one or more public interests may be imperiled by the great powers thus "entrusted" to business "leaders," and yet wish not to be severely critical of what appears to them here to stay so long as the capitalistic system survives; they therefore lean heavily on the staff of the "trustee relation." A spirit of mutual regard, hold the authors of a remarkable little government document of recent vintage, will do much to render happy and profitable this relation between the "trustee" and those dependent upon the quality of the passions governing his behavior: "A widespread, favorable attitude of mind is a first essential to effective trusteeship in big business. People must expect and assume that managers will look out for interests other than their own. Managers in turn will then attempt to live up to expectations." [5]

It will do no great harm to the better understanding of the hard realities which stand behind this engaging language to point out that the concept of trusteeship has always suffused the thinking of all proponents of and apologists for those systems of evolving status which have been compelled, for one reason or another, to take

[3] "The objectives of industrial organization have . . . been defined as profit through service, profit in this sense meaning the compensatory material gain or reward obtained through service." Mooney and Reiley, *Onward Industry!*, p. 342. A similar expression of this idea appears in TNEC Monograph No. 7, *Measurement of the Social Performance of Business*, p. 1: "Business is not merely nor even in the first instance a struggle of individuals for wealth. It is a way of life, a system of providing goods and services. It is not a segment of the community, coöperating or warring with other segments, such as labor, consumers, or farmers. It is not superior nor inferior to the community. It is the community engaged in getting its daily bread. Its goals, its ethics, its welfare are inseparable from the goals and aspirations and welfare of the community. No matter how much or how often the business phases of social or community activity may be abstracted, analyzed, and separately discussed the fundamental and organic unity between business and the community is indissoluble."

[4] *The Personal Relation in Industry.*

[5] TNEC, Monograph No. 11, *Bureaucracy and Trusteeship in Large Corporations*, p. 130.

steps to create a favorable public opinion. The differences here between the language of a patriarchal imperialist such as the divine Augustus of early imperial Rome or of the Benevolent Despots of eighteenth-century Europe on the one hand, and that of an Ivy Lee or a Robert Ley on the other, is one not of content, nor even of felicity of phrase and refinement of expression, but of the times and the fields of application.

That greatest of all Benevolent Despots, Frederick the Great, played the role of thoughtful but stern *paterfamilias* to his people in much the same spirit as the Emperor of contemporary Japan, moved by the silken etiquette of *Bushido,* does to his. Thomas Aquinas, the great Church logician, spoke for the "trustee" relation of superior to inferior in the tight hierarchy of graduated medieval infeudation. Robert Ley, Leader of the Nazi Labor Front, employs a similar language on behalf of his colleague Darré's "New Nobility of Blood and Soil," wrought out of Prussian Junkers, industrial baronry, and military warlords. And a leading American industrialist, James D. Mooney, with no less gravity, reiterates a like argument in defense of the "leader-led" hierarchies of command and subordination which govern the vast sprawling economic empires of American private enterprise.

The ideology of trusteeship, as Max Weber has shown at length in his great sociological study,[6] is and always has been a characteristic feature of all patriarchal, patrimonial, and "charismatic" forms of despotic authority. The "master set," which wishes to "lead" as though through a "calling," has always looked upon itself as "steward" or "trustee" to the people which it governs. Of such is the age-old language of ruling class paternalism. But, of course, fine benevolence of phrase or action caters no less to a system of *status* for that. On the contrary both historically and sociologically, such conceptions are unthinkable in the absence of it.

Returning then to our original characterization, what social policies advocated by and through the *Spitzenverbände* are so sufficiently common and uniform throughout the vast and highly centralized business machinery of every major capitalistic country

6 *Grundriss der Sozialökonomik,* Part III; in particular Chapters III ("Die Typen der Herrschaft"), VII ("Patrimonialismus"), VIII ("Wirkung des Patriarchalismus und des Feudalismus"), and XI ("Staat und Hierokratie"). See also Thorstein Veblen, *The Theory of the Leisure Class* (New York, 1899), and *Absentee Ownership and Business Enterprise in Recent Times* (New York, 1923).

that they may be regarded as an integral part of the new business outlook?

ATTITUDE OF MANAGERIAL AND DIRECTORIAL [7] RANKS TOWARDS THEMSELVES

The Hammonds, in their penetrating studies of early English factory conditions,[8] found that the typical capitalist of the age of the Combination Acts thought of himself ". . . as the great benefactor . . . who incidentally receives income in the form of profits." [9] And so likewise in our times. "The purpose of business," one of our definitely more democratically minded businessmen, Mr. Filene, once wrote, "is to produce and to distribute to all humanity the things which humanity, with its new-found power, can now be organized to make only if it can be organized to buy and use them." But in the words of what Virgil Jordan, President of the National Industrial Conference Board, once referred to as the professional "Troubadours of Trade," the doctrine is subtly transformed. The businessman now "leads," not because he is selfish and greedy, but because his unusual abilities burden him with the care for the fortunes of less gifted mankind, argues Mr. Link, successful counselor to the great in American business circles.

The employer who assumes the responsibility of giving work to other people, of providing the necessary weekly payroll, of entrusting larger responsibilities to his subordinates as the business grows, of meeting the risks of competition, labor problems, manufacturing difficulties, and the thousand and one griefs that go with almost every business, manifests daily a high order of unselfishness. Through his energy and leadership, he improves the lot of his employees far beyond the point which their personal efforts would have made possible. The fact that he may benefit, materially, more than any other one individual, is inevitable in the situation and not an indictment of his character.[10]

This statement can be taken as fully representative of the run of the more astute and farsighted, reactionary, employer opinion throughout all the business literature of the *Spitzenverbände*. But

[7] The "directorial" ranks may not, in fact, have much real power. See the TNEC Monograph, No. 11.
[8] *The Town Labourer.*
[9] "Confessions of an Economist," *New Republic*, Dec. 29, 1926.
[10] *The Return to Religion* (The Macmillan Company, New York, 1936).

more, that benevolently postured attitude is carried by such employers not only into labor, but also into all social relations between themselves and the general public. A leading spokesman for American public-relations counselors has deftly used the career of John D. Rockefeller, Jr., as a basis for a sermon in eulogy of the paternal outlook: [11] "He (Mr. Rockefeller) has given complete expression to Mr. Vail's dictum that 'the rights of private property are not, and cannot be, superior to public welfare.' Conscientiously he has developed and maintained the principle of stewardship and of what amounts to a virtual accounting to the public in the administration of a fortune—viewed not so much as personal wealth but as a public trust." In another passage Mr. Batchelor refers to "diversification of industrial ownership" as a factor compelling businessmen to "thoroughly subordinate their personal interests—security trading, for example—in a new sense of genuine trusteeship."

Speaking on behalf of the industrial giants in the German business community at a Nürnberg conference, Dr. Schacht [12] held that "the time is past when the notion of economic self-seeking and unrestricted use of profits made can be allowed to dominate. To be sure, no individual enterprise, no less the national economy, can exist without making a surplus, but the gains must once again be applied in the sense of and in service to the total community." In a remarkably militant book, penned on the eve of the second World War, the new leader of the Confédération Générale du Patronat Français, M. Gignoux, stated the position of French militant employers vis-à-vis the Popular Front in almost precisely the same terms.[13] Other quotations by the hundred might be cited from British, Italian and similar sources.

The natural role of the self-appointed trustee is universally held to be, throughout this same literature, that of community "leader." In Germany and Italy he is officially assigned this honored position in all economic affairs. In the American literature attempts are being made to have the term gradually supplant that of "employer" in the latter's relationships with labor, of "big business" or "trust"

[11] Bronson Batchelor, *Profitable Public Relations* (New York, 1938), pp. 40, 76.
[12] Cited by A. B. Krause, *Organisation von Arbeit und Wirtschaft* (Berlin, 1935), p. 75.
[13] Gignoux, *Patrons, soyez des patrons!*

in its relationships with small business, and of "business men" in their relationships with the general public. The term "capitalist" has largely disappeared from such business literature, and organizations like the National Association of Manufacturers and the Federation of British Industries, not to mention the academically highly reputable National Bureau of Economic Research, no longer use it at all. Mr. Virgil Jordan, head of the National Industrial Conference Board, has repeatedly argued in a series of widely quoted speeches that businessmen lead through the "enterprise system" as the "only trustworthy custodian[s] of the sole basis of prosperity and security of the American public, which is their capital resources and their working capacity." [14]

This leadership of militant big business is most commonly and easily justified as a "technical" necessity. It is held, that is to say, to be a system of guidance by the intellectually equipped and socially able—a society run for the good of all by an elite caste of experts. This theme appears over and over again, and with increasing frequency in the literature of the *Spitzenverbände*. Practically all leading big-business spokesmen are agreed on the underlying argument. One runs, not infrequently, into direct analogies to Plato's system of government by "experts" (argued, needless to say, without benefit of Plato's propertyless communism of the leader guardians).[15] Sometimes, and this is particularly true of the Italian and American business literature, "leader" ranks are held to be continuously renewed and invigorated by a process of selec-

[14] Virgil Jordan, "The Economic Outlook" (American Management Association, Personnel Series, No. 29, 1937), pp. 20-21.

[15] The idea of a society run by experts is, of course, quite old. Plato was the first scientific millennialist, but the *Republic* was largely the Periclean aristocrat's version of the "saturn legend," in itself as old as all prehistoric and primitive myths of a "golden age" of past or future. Following Plato, one finds the scientific utopias of Leibnitz, Campanella, Andrea, Granvil, Bacon, Hooke, the Encyclopedists in general, the naive positivism of Comte (and the somewhat more skeptical positivism of Hume and Bayle), Bellamy, Kropotkin, Veblen (*Engineers and the Price System*), and many others—not to mention the "Technocrats" and Mr. H. G. Wells. But Plato's system was not merely a harking back to the days of agricultural aristocracy, reformed under the guidance of "experts" as the ideal "Republic." The new system was a regimented slavocracy and it was launched as a criticism of the leveling tendencies of his time. Democracy was the real enemy in this *demos*. See the article by Gregory Vlastos in *Philosophical Review*, May, 1941. The same holds for Mr. Lawrence Dennis' system of rule by the "elite" and Mr. James Burnham's "manager-rulers." See also the rather savagely whimsical caricature of such regimentation by Aldous Huxley in his *Brave New World* (New York, 1932).

tive coöptation, or a sort of institutionalized adoption of the able from below. The Japanese have formalized such a system in selecting their plant and enterprise managers (*Banto*) is a fashion quite reminiscent of the Undershaft foundlings in Bernard Shaw's brilliant dramatic production, *Major Barbara*. This practice of absorbing the able from the socially inferior ranks, first advocated by Plato in his famous metals analogy, is in line with Pareto's concept of the "circulating elite," which now plays such an important part in the Biblical literature of Italian Fascism. The idea has been reproduced in the writings of numerous spokesmen for the Nazis,[16] in various books by Lawrence Dennis in America, and in one form or another by Link, Carrel, Pitkin, and others. It has appeared on many occasions in the *Proceedings* of the National Association of Manufacturers as proof of the existence of "democracy in business."[17]

Outside of the United States—but, more recently, here also—the notion of the technical superiority of the upper managerial layers has, as indicated in the literature and programs of many militant business spokesmen, been giving way to the idea that through long but cumulative processes of biosocial selection these same layers are coming to represent a self-evident and scientifically demonstrable elite of innate, hereditary, biomental superiority. The transi-

---

[16] Especially interesting in this connection are the Nazi "Junker" schools, a sort of party-ideological, graduate seminar system, modeled, apparently, somewhat after a combination of Plato's recommendations for the training of future Guardians, and the Janissaries recruited by the Turks from the select amongst the conquered Christian youth. But the future "Junkers"—they graduate with this honored title—appear to be selected almost exclusively from the upper social layers of landed nobility, industrial baronry, military hierarchy, and party functionaries.

[17] See NAM pamphlets and other literature on "Industry and You," "The American Way," etc. Selection in such a manner, of course, has nothing whatever to do with "democracy." "Equality of opportunity," so long as it means an equal chance of being selected for advancement by the governing hierarchy—in itself apparently becoming more difficult within the higher business ranks of the liberal-capitalistic countries (see p. 273)—has no more to do with "democracy" than had the recruiting of the Janissaries by the Turks, or the advancement procedures of an officer-caste army or the Catholic hierarchy. "Democracy" is a political concept that has to do with the *location of power to formulate policies, determine objectives, and check administration under policy directives;* it implies nothing directly regarding the mechanics of recruitment, and it is wholly alien to systems of graduated subservience. The correlation between "ability" and position may under certain circumstances appear to be the same under democracy and under "leader" hierarchies answerable only to themselves, but the location of power and the objectives pursued necessarily place them poles apart.

tion from the one to the other position is taken by easy stages. From the belief that, left to themselves and undisturbed by "blind leaders of the blind" (as Virgil Jordan likes to characterize militant labor leaders and liberal champions of popular causes), "the common . . . and . . . working people of this country follow their natural leaders, the owners and managers of industry," [18] it requires no great stretch of the imagination to argue that selective breeding of the able will ultimately develop a real aristocracy of brains and culture. It is then simple to conclude, conversely, that the lower orders of society will inevitably settle to those several social-occupational levels which their relative inheritance factors in glands, genes, chromosomes and cortical layers select for them.

One of the earliest American expressions [19] of this attitude associated with the rise of monopoly-capitalism was *The Passing of the Great Race* (1916), written by a prominent New York corporation attorney, Madison Grant, largely out of a book which was for a long time unknown except by scholars—Houston Stewart Chamberlain's [20] *Foundations of the Nineteenth Century*. Chamberlain's book, based upon a thesis advanced by a French nobleman, de Gobineau, has been resurrected by Alfred Rosenberg as the foundation for his "Myth of the Twentieth Century," the central thesis of which is the racial superiority of the Germanic or "Nordic" stock. Madison Grant was a trustee of the American Museum of Natural History in New York; his book has a Preface by Henry Fairfield Osborn.[21] The book states a number of theses which, in a somewhat altered form, have since secured such wide and tacit—if not always explicit—acceptance in upper business circles, that they are worth quoting at some length:

Modern anthropology has demonstrated that racial lines are not only absolutely independent of both national and linguistic groupings, but that in many cases these racial lines cut through them at sharp angles

[18] Report of the Committee on Employment Relations of the NAM, 1926.
[19] Ignoring, of course, the leaders of early (pre-business monopoly) American Tory opinion such as Alexander Hamilton, John Marshall, and Daniel Webster.
[20] Chamberlain was a hyphenate German of English parentage, having moved to Germany at an early age.
[21] Curator of the Natural History Museum. He wrote, "If I were asked: What is the greatest danger which threatens the American republic today? I would certainly reply: The gradual dying out among our people of those hereditary traits through which the principles of our religious, political, and social foundations were laid

and correspond closely with the divisions of social cleavage. The great lesson of the science of race is the immutability of somatological or bodily characters, with which is closely associated the immutability of psychical predispositions and impulses. This continuity of inheritance has a most important bearing on the theory of democracy and still more upon that of socialism, and those engaged in social uplift and in revolutionary movements are consequently usually very intolerant of the limitations imposed by heredity.

Democratic theories of government in their modern form are based on dogmas of equality formulated some hundred and fifty years ago, and rest upon the assumption that environment and not heredity is the controlling factor in human development. Philanthropy and noble purpose dictated the doctrine expressed in the Declaration of Independence, the document which today constitutes the actual basis of American institutions. The men who wrote the words, "we hold these truths to be self-evident, that all men are created equal," were themselves the owners of slaves, and despised the Indians as something less than human.

. . . In America we have nearly succeeded in destroying the privilege of birth; that is, the intellectual and moral advantage a man of good stock brings into the world with him. We are now engaged in destroying the privilege of wealth; that is, the reward of successful intelligence and industry, and in some quarters there is developing a tendency to attack the privilege of intellect and to deprive a man of the advantages of an early and thorough education. . . . True aristocracy is a government by the wisest and best, always a small minority in any population. Human society is like a serpent dragging its long body on the ground, but with the head always thrust a little in advance and a little elevated above the earth. The serpent's tail, in human society represented by the anti-social forces, was in the past dragged by sheer force along the path of progress.[22]

The dogmatic racism of this statement has largely lost caste outside of Germany and Japan.[23] But overlooking this element, we find here a four-fold correlation that is rapidly gaining favor among the social theorists who serve the reactionary leader ranks of highly organized business: (1) physiological characteristics are identified with (2) psychomental capacities, which combination is held to

down, and their insidious replacement by traits of less noble character." Osborn was particularly worried about the colored races, and the influx of immigrants from south-eastern Europe.

[22] *Passing of the Great Race* (New York, 1916), pp. xv–xvi, 6, 7. At the time he wrote the book Grant was Chairman of the New York Zoölogical Society, Trustee of the American Museum of Natural History, and Councilor of the American Geographical Society.

[23] Leading exceptions are books by Lothrop Stoddard and Albert Edward Wiggin.

(3) circumscribe and limit the social-occupational status of the major wealth and income brackets, for each of which there is supposed to be (4) an appropriate social doctrine of greatest appeal. According to this thesis the "elite" think aristocratically while the "morons, culls, perverts," upon whom Mr. Pitkin pours the vials of his wrath, are needlessly deluded by the "white lie" of democracy and come to think socialistically or "bolshevistically." [24] The latter cannot produce the necessary genius to command, argues Mr. Carrel,[25] and a "democracy" which offers them such participation is a will-o'-the-wisp they may follow only into the abysmal swamps of hopeless failure. Thus one comes to the painful conclusion that any social order shaped to meet the vain hopes of the undisciplined "rabble" can only be the "irreconcilable foe of freedom, the inevitable oppressor of talent and distinction." [26]

No one any longer questions that ideas such as these dominate the social thinking of the upper business circles of Germany, Italy, and

---

[24] ". . . most well-mannered debaters carry on with the White Lie of Democracy; and thus reach worthless conclusions. A land swarming with tens of millions of morons, perverts, culls, outcasts, criminals, and lesser breeds of low-grade humans cannot escape the evils all such cause. . . . So long as we have an underworld of 4,000,000 or more scoundrels willing to do anything for a price. and a twilight world of fully 40,000,000 people of profound stupidity or ignorance, or indifference, and a population of nearly 70,000,000 who cannot support themselves entirely and hence must think first of cost, whenever they buy things, we shall have a nasty mess on our hands." Walter B. Pitkin, Let's Get What We Want (New York, 1935), pp. 72, 283. This book has had an extraordinarily wide sale amongst militant business circles.

[25] ". . . most of the members of the proletarian class owe their situation to the hereditary weakness of their organs and their mind. . . . Today, the weak should not be artificially maintained in wealth and power. It is imperative that social classes should be synonymous with biological classes. Each individual must rise or sink to the level for which he is fitted by the quality of his tissues and of his soul. The social ascension of those who possess the best organs and the best minds should be aided. Each one must have his natural place. Modern nations will save themselves by developing the strong. Not by protecting the weak." Alexis Carrel, Man the Unknown (New York, 1935), p. 298. This book, likewise, enjoyed a phenomenal sale throughout the business world, and reviews in business journals were uniformly laudatory in the highest degree. The head of one of the largest advertising companies in America was so impressed with its "social doctrine" that he at one time proposed that Mr. Henry Ford be asked to subsidize a cheap printing so that the book might be read by every businessman in America.

[26] "Is democracy the left hand of freedom—or is it a moist gorilla paw that grasps free manhood by the gorge? Democracy is the irreconcilable foe of freedom, the inevitable oppressor of talent and distinction." John Corbin, The Return of the Middle Classes (New York, 1922). A similar idea runs through many of Mr. Bruce Barton's speeches (see, e. g., his parable of the "golf handicap").

Japan.[27] Nor is there much doubt that the caste-like sentiments of the same circles in Tory England and Bourbon France are stamped with a similar die. But readers unfamiliar with the records might well be surprised to discover for how long, and how generally like ideas have run through certain American business literature. Three samples, fairly representative of the run of the mill, may be cited, two directly from National Association of Manufacturers sources, and the third from a theoretical summary of vocational selection experts.

In a novel published serially (1913) in *American Industries*, official publication of the NAM, Mr. David M. Parry, long president of the Association and formulator in 1903 of its bitterly antilabor code—from which the NAM has never retreated [28]—has a character assail "this cursed Democracy—this damnable Democracy which like an octopus with a million tentacles is throttling the manhood of our entire race." [29] The story is confessedly of the order of parable, being the tale of a fabled "Atlantis" in which are highlighted what Mr. Parry feels to be the evils of his own America. He ends his allegory with the comment that his fanciful narrative, though "crudely told . . . has the merit of veracity." Through it, he wrote, he feels "right glad" that "I have done my duty according to my light in preserving for mankind an account of the nation that through its worship of Social Equality went down to destruction."

Parry's homily appeared in the midst of a great deal of speculation about rising social unrest. One of the great correctives hoped for by himself and his colleagues was that the educational system might be so reorganized and reshaped that each class would—much as the Alphas, Betas, Gammas, and Epsilons in Aldous Huxley's phantom *Brave New World*—be properly routed to those occupational tasks for which its members were bio-mentally most adapted. Thus has arisen special interest, for example, in certain uses which can be made by company-controlled apprentice-training plans. Running throughout the literature of the NAM and foreign parallel bodies from their very earliest days has been this special emphasis. Typical in the American literature is the following analysis:

[27] See, in particular, Kolnai, *The War against the West.*
[28] See Chapter VI, footnote 77, above.   [29] "The Scarlet Empire."

according to an official spokesman for the NAM, there are "Three Kinds of Children," for whom there must be "Three Kinds of Schools": [30]

The abstract-minded and imaginative children . . . learn readily from the printed page. Most of the children *whose ancestors* were in the professions and the higher occupations, so-called, are of this class, as well as many from the humbler callings [concept of the "circulating elite"].

The concrete, or hand-minded children . . . those who can only with extreme difficulty, and then imperfectly, learn from the abstractions of the printed page. These children constitute at least half of all the child life of the nation, being that half who leave our schools by the end of the sixth grade, with substantially no education beyond the imperfect command of reading, writing, and arithmetic, and a bit of domestic geography; that is, of the three R's, which, in themselves, are not education in any sense, but only the tools whereby education may be attained in the seventh, eighth and later grades, if at all—*all those studies which develop judgment, citizenship and efficiency coming in these higher grades.*

The great intermediate class, comprising all degrees of efficiency from those who by the narrowest margin fall short of the requirements of the first class to those *whose capabilities just save them from the third class.*

For each of these bio-mentally delineated groups there was to be an appropriate type of schooling: one type would keep the "abstract-minded and imaginative" from becoming "impractical, overzealous, unbalanced theorists, often referred to in reproach as the educated class," [31] while the other would place the "hand-minded" in vocational schools under the guidance of social-elite businessmen. "It is inevitable," argued another leading spokesman for the NAM, "that a great responsibility for the real education of the mass of people in this country lies with the business corporation." [32]

The third example of this attitude is taken from two specialists in vocational guidance who have expressed, in a remarkable chart, conclusions regarding the correlation between "intelligence" and "occupational fitness." This chart drawn by Fryer and Sparling, called "Corresponding Intelligence-Achievement Values," defines the "intelligence test," upon which the occupational classifications

---

[30] *Proceedings* of the 17th Annual Convention (1912), pp. 149–77. (Italics mine.)
[31] *Idem.* [32] *Proceedings* of the 28th Annual Meeting of the NAM, 1923.

reproduced in the chart are based, as "a measure of what the individual has learned, from which can be predicted his capacity to learn in the future." [33] It is impossible to avoid the implication that the correlations established between occupation and "intelligence" are understood to rest upon assumptions of innate qualitative differences.[34]

The most interesting feature of this belief is the service it performs for the larger idea, that if each person in each class can be trained and fitted for that particular occupation for which he is innately adapted, then a "natural harmony" of graduated leader-led interests arises. By a further easy transition it appears to follow that organic relationships of a bio-functional character bind the different classes of society into the "scalar chain" in such a way that failure to perform properly at any one point throws the whole social metabolism out of gear. The final result amounts to this: led by the superior classes—more or less constantly renewed in strength and numbers by coöptation from the "sport" elite selectively bred from below—all social ranks team together to advance the good of all (as interpreted by the leaders) by enhancing the specific and unique good of each individual. And the specific and unique good of the individual is determined by his foreordained functional position in the organic body politic.

The underlying idea here is, in some respects at least, a curious combination of Smithian liberties, Benthamite hedonism, and Hobbesian social philosophy; this combination long served as the leading theoretical foundation for a lofty justification of the Nassau Senior version of socially irresponsible capitalistic activities moving within the orbital systems of "free competition" and "laissez faire." In the blending, an underlying harmony was freely mixed with generalized contempt for the popular ranks. Bentham, like Hobbes before him and from whom he took many of his leading ideas, despised the lower orders. Unlike Hobbes, however, he

---

[33] Douglas Fryer and E. J. Sparling, "Intelligence and Occupational Adjustment," *Occupations—The Vocational Guidance Magazine*, June, 1934, pp. 55–63. Businessmen are found in the upper "intelligence" ratings, but musicians and chemists, for example, do not do so well.

[34] Just what does such a statement mean. Since what has been learned is considered solely in terms of achievement and without regard to the presence or absence of opportunities or environmental factors, the presumption is that one reads backwards from achievements to innate capacities.

believed that "free choice" would elevate the superior and lower the dregs to their natural position. But in an hierarchically organized society (such as Hobbes desired and whose formal authoritarianism Bentham rejected), where advancement from below becomes increasingly a matter of coöptation from above and where the wished-for pattern of social authority is coherent with the prototypal leader-led systems of the spreading business corporation, military service, or clerical bureaucracy, it is not difficult to see how what was once recognized as a system of desirable "freedom" may be readily transmuted into a set of prescriptive dogmas in support of authoritative regimentation.

Three critical questions need to be answered at this point: (1) Is advancement into the upper social reaches of the several capitalistic countries becoming in fact more difficult? (2) Whether or no, and so far as the guiding business heads are concerned, is "leadership" in business circles interpreted by its spokesmen to mean rightful power to fix and determine the content of social economic policies uninhibited by independent "democratic" check from the ranks below? (3) Do these same circles believe that benevolent paternalism is freed of the taint of despotism merely because the basic issues may be so authoritatively and dexterously interpreted, the relevant facts so presented, and the symbols most deeply rooted in popular systems of value so manipulated that the general populace can be made to "want" or appear to "want" to do whatever the self-perpetuating elite require of them?

The answer to the first question has largely been given. Within the totalitarian countries, not wholly excluding even the new layers of the party hierarchies, the upper social ranks are and have long been for all practical purposes closed to those below. To a lesser extent, but increasingly with the passage of time, the same seems to be true of the nontotalitarian countries. Studies by Sorokin and others in the United States seem to indicate clearly that arteries of vertical advancement are becoming fewer and more pinched as one approaches the top-flight business ranks.[35] Somewhat the same thing appears to be true of many of the leading professions [36] and

[35] See, in particular, Maurice Dobb, *Capitalist Enterprise and Social Progress* (London, 1925), particularly Chapter IX, "Advantage and Class."

[36] The periods of training are becoming longer for doctors, lawyers, teachers and many others, and at the same time the living expenses are rising, tuition and labora-

of most political careers.[37] But wherever vertical advancement is still common it comes more and more by the process of coöpting from below, by circles which acknowledge no right of the populace to demand a direct accounting of either policies or execution of policies which affect its fortunes.

The answers to the second and third questions are clearly, and without important exception anywhere in the reactionary ranks of the capitalistic world, in the affirmative. "Democratic" check on all issues that reach to the roots of domination appears within these circles to be not only not the fulfillment, but the direct antagonist of genuine social "harmony." Conversely, when freed from such restraints, the resultant appears to the "circulating elite" as the only satisfactory environment in which the life cycles of individuals and groups may work themselves out, as in short, the only real world of "freedom"—or even, "democracy." As pointed out above, an official Italian propaganda publication of the Fascist Confederation of Industrialists characteristically feels free to speak of Fascism as "authoritarian democracy." A like theme of "responsibility to the public" runs through the Nazi literature. It is practically certain that if a coup d'état ever comes in America from the right it will be advertised as a defense of democratic freedoms and a blow at Fascism.[38]

This "new democracy," however, is as strictly antiegalitarian as its "freedoms" are antilibertarian and its "liberties" authoritatively circumscribed. It is, in other words, the ideal of the old Platonic state dressed in somewhat new clothes and adapted to modern times. Under it policy decisions are made exclusively by the self-appointed "leader" ranks, and the lower social classes would be authoritatively directed on behalf of the "general welfare." Many leading Nazi and Fascist writers have willingly acknowledged the old Greek master, though they usually prefer for obvious reasons to

tory fees are higher, the period of "starvation" after admittance to the prerogatives "of the cloth" longer, the dangers of unemployment greater.

[37] Only a powerful political machine or a man of "independent" or more than average income can any longer afford to run for or hold the bulk of our current political offices. Long accepted as a principle abroad, we face the actuality in a more acute form with each passing decade here.

[38] See the very interesting book by Harnett T. Kane, *Louisiana Hayride* (New York, 1941), dealing with the totalitarian regime of the late Huey Long, which he describes as an American "rehearsal for dictatorship."

avoid the term "Republic." American readers are familiar with the concept in the writings of the preindustrial Federalist proponents of New England commercial and trading capitalism, and in the literature of the Calhoun school, which spoke for the planter aristocracy of the old South. It is a tribute to the astuteness of certain antidemocratic public-relations counselors that the contemporary literature of "welfare capitalism" has not been commonly recognized as cast from the same mold.

In this version, when all the classes of the projected social order have been properly educated, trained, and ideologically grounded, so that each learns to do his "bit" and perform his natural function, then, to employ the contemporary jargon, "harmony reigns." There is no point upon which the business literature of all the *Spitzenverbände* agree so completely as this. Without exception, social "harmony" between capital and labor is the leading theme song. And "harmony" is interpreted to mean "coöperation" and "unity" between business and the public, merchant and the farmer, big and little businesses, and between all other interests on the one hand, and the directors of big business and their organizations on the other. When implemented with an adequate propaganda, appropriately directed to meet the "needs" and peculiarities of each special interest, the new paternal society becomes to its proponents not despotism but the Hobbesian natural order.

Plainly this "harmony" propaganda looks forward to a system of status, as may readily be seen by a brief résumé of the evolving attitude of big business towards the problems of organized labor.

THE CONTENT OF "HARMONY" IN LABOR RELATIONS

"Prosperity Dwells Where Harmony Reigns" runs the caption of a series of outdoor posters addressed to public partisans of the militant employer cause and scattered by the National Association of Manufacturers from one end of the United States to another. The kernel of the Nazi concept of *Gemeinschaft* or "community feeling" in labor relations is one of "harmony" between the *Führer* (employer-"leader") and his *Gefolgschaft* or "followers." The essence of the relationship is said to be "harmony," "goodwill," "mutual duties and responsibilities," and these express an "organic" interdependence which requires absence of difference of opinion, conflicting organizations, and competing interests. The "National Harmonizing Society" of Japan views these matters in a similar light.

Gignoux, the militant author of *Patrons, soyez des Patrons!* (Employers, Be Employers!), and president of the violently anti-labor Confédération Générale du Patronat Français (General Confederation of French Employers), told his employer-following in 1937, that "you are not only responsible for your own concerns but for those of your colleagues and to those to whom you delegate a part of your authority. . . . You are the heads; you not only have charge of men but souls." [39] The reorganizers of the new "corporate order" in Pétain's decapitated empire looked first to "union" in the form of "loyal coöperation" between employer and employee, and then, without change of pace, to "collaboration" between conquering Germany and conquered France. A speaker before the National Association of Manufacturers in 1923 referred to Mussolini as "without question of doubt one of the big men of Europe today" for his vigorous action in discharging workmen who were not reconciled to the harmony between capital and labor provided under decree by the new Fascist government [40]—a harmony founded, as an official eulogist in a widely circulated pamphlet [41] has floridly expressed the matter, on the principle of the "illuminated and disinterested control of capital and labor by means of the coöperative-corporative binomial destined to produce a stable and constructive social equilibrium." The employer, in the words

[39] Gignoux, *op. cit.*

[40] Remarks by Mr. Adolph Mueller, Proceedings of the 28th Annual Meeting of the NAM, May, 1923.

[41] *La crisi sociale da Cristo a Mussolini*, by Gaetano Lisanti (undated); see also the two famous papal encyclicals on the "Social Question," *Rerum Novarum* (1891) and *Quadragesimo anno* (1931), outlined in Chapter II above. The former (as indicated above, in Chapter IV) called for "social harmony" and "class collaboration" along lines of *integral syndicalism (mixed or collateral)*; the second formally accepted the (Fascist) "special syndical and corporative organization . . . inaugurated . . . within recent times," becoming thereby not only in effect a collaborator with the Fascist system of Mussolini, but also the inspirer of the ill-fated Clerical Fascism of Dollfuss and Schuschnigg in Austria and the Falangist system of Franco in Spain. Its program was also officially recommended to the United States by sixteen Catholic prelates on Feb. 9, 1940, speaking for the National Catholic Welfare Conference, in the form of a proposal for a "Guild or Corporative System." The same propaganda in South America (see Harold Callender in the New York *Times*, (April 28, 1941) is advanced through clerical circles; it is pro-Nazi and anti-American.

of "Open Shop Committee" of the NAM, "is the natural leader of his workmen." [42] "The real and ideal union is the one between employer and employee" as a recent bulletin of the NAM has announced.

The obverse of this felicitous state is held to arise the instant trade unions appear on the scene. If one traces back through the literature of the *Spitzenverbände*, one finds the language of invective heaped on trade unions and trade union-leaders so uniformly the same that all of it might well have been issued from a single headquarters. Many of the *Spitzenverbände* have originated out of a desire to organize all employers along class lines, [43] or have shortly made this one of their principal interests. [44]

The attitude of employers in Germany and Italy under totalitarian colors is too well known to require elaboration here. There trade unions, strikes, boycotts, and even the more familiar methods of employee retaliation have been formally outlawed. In England, France, and the United States the position is much the same, but no power has yet made such drastic action on behalf of the *Spitzenverbände* possible. The program of the NAM, known for years by the term Parryism—after its author, David M. Parry (see p. 194, above)—was launched in 1903 and is still held as the official position; it may be taken as typical of the attitude of all the *Spitzenverbände*.

According to Parry,

organized labor knows but one law and that is the law of physical force —the law of the Huns and Vandals, the law of the savage. All its purposes are accomplished either by actual force or by the threat of force. It does not place its·reliance upon reason and justice, but in strikes, boycotts and coercion. It is, in all essential features, a mob power knowing

---

[42] "He is the natural leader of his workmen, and is able by instruction, example and fair dealing to bring to bear constantly upon them influences for right-thinking and action and for loyalty to the common enterprise." *Proceedings* of the 28th Annual Meeting of the NAM, May, 1923.

[43] As, e. g., for all those employers' organizations with which labor problems are the primary concern such as the Norwegian Employers' Association, founded in 1900, the Swedish Employers' Federation, organized in 1902, and the Confederation of British Employers' Organizations, organized in 1919. As in Germany, Holland, Japan and a number of other countries, employer organizations were set up as parallel and coöperating bodies along with the industrial *Spitzenverbände*, which included much the same membership.

[44] As with the NAM from 1903 to the present, and the Confédération Générale du Patronat Français after reorganization following the Matignon Agreement in 1936.

no master except its own will. Its history is stained with blood and ruin. It extends its tactics of coercion and intimation over all classes, dictating to the press and to the politicians and strangling independence of thought and American manhood.[45]

There is no evil for which organized labor could not be held accountable by Mr. Parry. It "denies to those outside its ranks the individual right to dispose of their labor as it sees fit" (denies "freedom of labor"), and asserts that each workman is "his own judge of the length of time he shall work" and how much he shall do on the job. It takes no account of the "varying degrees of natural aptitude and powers of endurance" of different individuals, and places, through restrictions on output, a premium on "indolence and incompetency" and thereby reduces all labor to one "dead level." Its "leaders are found to be agitators and demagogues, men who appeal to prejudice and envy, who are constantly instilling a hatred of wealth and ability, and who, in incendiary speeches, attempt to stir up men to seize by physical force that which their merit cannot obtain for them." [46]

This phraseology could be duplicated in the language of anti-labor organizations in every major capitalistic country in the world. The position of the NAM has not changed on the major issue, as the La Follette Committee reports on labor espionage, employer strike-breaking tactics,[47] and so forth, have shown at great length, or as may be read from reports to the National Labor Relations Board on the cases of Little Steel and Remington Rand.[48] Following the Matignon Agreement in 1936 between the CGT, representing the bulk of French Organized labor, and the CGPF, representing organized French business, French employers not only reorganized their central association on a militant basis similar

[45] Report of President David M. Parry, *Proceedings* of the 8th Annual Convention of the NAM, April 14–16, 1903.

[46] *Ibid.*

[47] See the various sections of Report 6, Part 6 of the La Follette Committee Reports.

[48] In its Labor Relations Bulletin, July 20, 1936, the NAM referred to the "Mohawk Valley Formula," by way of which Remington-Rand broke the strike at its plants as "constructive" and "a real contribution to civic dignity.".The National Labor Relations Board summary of the case found that the Formula called for "employment of strike-breaking agencies . . . use of spies, 'missionaries' and armed guards . . . attempts to turn civil authorities and business and other interests in the various cities against the union . . . intensive publicity and propaganda . . . based upon deliberate falsehoods and exaggerations," and so on.

throughout to that of the NAM, but also established a special watchtower Committee of Foresight and Social Action (Comité de Prévoyance et d'Action Sociale), which set as its goal the complete and final overcoming of the much feared trend towards "the dictatorship of the proletariat," the "crumbling of authority," [49] the establishment of worker soviets" in the factories through the "sit-down strike" and the "occupation of factories," [50] which they professed to see threatening all French industry.

But how achieve the objective? The Committee on Resolutions of the NAM once declared [51] that "fair dealing" between employer and employee is centered not on the existence of "organizations of labor as such," but is conditioned upon the complete abolition of "boycotts, blacklists and other *illegal acts of interference with the personal liberty of employer and employee*" (italics mine). To this end it affirmed the complete freedom of the employer to hire and fire at will, and of the employee to work or quit irrespective of "membership or non-membership in any labor organizations." Such membership was not to constitute a basis for discrimination, but neither must employers be interfered with in the "management of their business, in determining the amount and quality of their products, and in the use of any methods, or systems of pay which are just and equitable." Mutually satisfactory wages and working conditions could only be worked out individually between employer and employee, and at no time should the employer be intimidated by threat of strikes, nor should he be required to resort to the lockout. These principles, the Association announced again in 1907 are matters not of "capital against labor, nor employers against employees, but . . . of good citizenship against bad citizenship . . . of Americanism and patriotism against demagogism and socialism." [52]

---

49 See, e. g., Gignoux, *op. cit.*: M. Duchemin, "Sur l'Accord Matignon," *Revue de Paris*, Feb. 1, 1937; and various issues of *La Journée Industrielle*, official publication of the Confédération Générale du Patronat Français.

50 Particularly interesting are some of the publications of the Comité de Prévoyance et d'Action Sociale, such as the following: *Les Dangers economiques et sociaux du controls de l'embauchage; L'exposition a-t-elle été sabotée?* [by the CGT]; and *La Réglémentation de l'embauchage et du licenciément en Allemagne* (similar articles for the United States and Italy).

51 *Proceedings* of the 8th Annual Convention.

52 *Proceedings* of the 12th Annual Convention, Committee on Resolutions reporting on "Industrial Peace."

The employers' case as stated here remains unaltered to this day. The argument rests on three closely related theses: (1) strikes, boycotts, blacklists, are or ought to be declared illegal; that is, they are blows directed not only against the employer, but also against the laws of the land (the American form of government). These are methods of intimidation which are not and cannot be sanctioned by law, and even the lockout employed in retaliation is a defensive weapon which employers should not be forced to utilize in a society governed by the rule of law. (2) Complete freedom of the employer can only be effected by keeping unabridged his right to hire, fire, and control the conditions and terms of employment, and complete freedom of the employee can only be maintained by keeping free access to all jobs and the terms on which employment is taken without the interference at any point by the collective will of his fellows. (3) Collective antiemployer trade-union action emanates from insincere labor leadership (demagogues; racketeers) whose objectives are to undermine the institutions of the country (Americanism and patriotism) on behalf of "alien" and "socialistic" doctrines.

This position of the National Association of Manufacturers is a *précis* not only for their own subsequent history, but also for the social policies of all the other *Spitzenverbände*. The language has changed from time to time and from country to country, but upon this doctrinal tripod rests the whole superstructure of antilabor policies of employer organizations throughout the world. By the same token, the social programs of the *Spitzenverbände,* both within and without totalitarian countries, are directed along three main lines: (1) render militant labor action impossible or at least severely actionable by law; (2) control the conditions and terms of the wage contract; and (3) "re-educate" and reorient the social ideology of the previously "misled" labor masses.

Space is not available for detailed review of the history of these efforts. It is noteworthy, however, that the first action taken within the Fascist and Nazi systems was the complete abolition of all trade unions. The Konoye-Matsuoka regime in Japan had by the end of 1940 practically completed a similar task. The Pétain government in France moved to destroy all trade unions, and particularly the militant CGT, as the first step in its program of "collaboration" with the triumphant Nazis. Along with abolition of trade unions, strikes, lockouts, boycotts, blacklists and all similar tools of social warfare have been declared illegal in that rump state. Much the same effect was for a period of time achieved in England as a result of the Trades Disputes Act and other legislation following the great coal strike in 1926. It seems probable on the evidence of emphatic and oft-repeated declarations by accredited spokesmen, that if either the labor-relations alter ego of the Federation of British Industries—the Confederation of Employers' Organizations—or the National Association of Manufacturers were given a carte blanche to write onto the statute books what they felt to be the most desirable legislation, the law in both England and the United States would promptly come clearly into line with the antilabor prohibitive ordinances of the Axis states.

Further proof than is provided by the many express statements of the two latter associations (in condemnation of the weapons of militant labor action) that such action would ensue is provided by comparison of the internal programs of the alternative or substitute types of labor organization devised by capitalistic interests within and without totalitarian circles. Salvemini has referred to the Fascist "Workers Confederations" as a system of nation-wide "Company Unions." [53] The same may be said of the Nazi "Labor Front" (*Arbeitsfront*).[54] Yet, as pointed out above, the former is entirely in line with the preëxisting Catholic program of "integral syndicalism" first clearly formulated by church spokesmen in the 1850s [55] and popular with the great corporate interests of the Po industrial complex on the eve of the Fascist coup d'état, while the latter is a readaptation of the underlying ideas which dominated the establishment of the "Works Committee of the Industrial Employers and Employees of Germany" (Arbeitsausschuss der gewerblichen Arbeitgeber und Arbeitnehmer Deutschlands); the last-named group was formed during the revolutionary interlude fol-

---

[53] Salvemini, *Under the Axe of Fascism;* see, particularly, Chapter VII, "Company Unions, Nazi Unions, and Fascist Unions."

[54] See Brady, *The Spirit and Structure of German Fascism,* Chapter IV, "Labor Must Follow Where Capital Leads."

[55] See Gide and Rist, *History of Economic Doctrines,* particularly the section entitled, "Doctrines That Owe Their Inspiration to Christianity," pp. 483–517; the papal encyclicals *Rerum Novarum* and *Quadragesimo Anno,* and Moon, *The Labor Problem.*

lowing the war, on the initiative of the Federation of German Employers' Associations (Vereinigung der deutschen Arbeitgeber-verbände), alter ego of the Federation of German Industries (Reichs-verband der deutschen Industrie).[56]

Now an examination of either of these predecessor bodies, or of those which followed with the triumph of corporate principles, will show that they all had in common plans for a systematic application throughout their entire economic systems of what has long been known in the United States as "company unionism." Neither, that is to say, the specific programs, nor the idea of expanding and fed-erating nation-wide networks of such employer-controlled labor associations is confined to countries now in the Axis block. Some-thing of the nature of Italian collateral syndicalism seems to have been envisaged by the Federation of British Industries with its "National Alliance of Employers and Employed" set up in 1920.[57] Since the triumph of the Tories in 1926 this rather mild attempt to adapt to peacetime conditions the principles of a but partially employer-controlled wartime Whitleyism has been kept from crys-tallizing along Labor Front lines. The primary reason for this has been internal factionalism amongst the "Confederation of Embit-tered Obstructionists"—as a friendly critic refers to the Confed-eration of Employers' Organizations—and not to any significant differences of opinion as to the desirable objectives.

The first pioneering effort to set up a nation-wide federation of company unions—equivalent to the Labor Front—was, in fact, American. In 1912, an expatriate union leader named Joseph W. Bryce presented a plan before the Annual Convention of the NAM which called for a nation-wide organization to be known as the Trades and Workers Association; this was to be made up jointly of employers and employees, organized along occupational lines in city and regional confederations, which were in turn federated into the central association. Employers were to assume the position

[56] In turn a member of the Zentralverband der deutschen Arbeitgeberverbände.

[57] In the formative days of the Federation of British Industries it had been hoped by some that the Federation itself might include "not merely the representatives of capital but those of labour . . . something approaching a partnership between capital and labour in place of the armed neutrality, which is the best that can be hoped for under present circumstances." The Whitley councils were regarded as a temporary method of coping with mounting wartime dissatisfaction of British labor over rising costs of living in face of war profiteering.

throughout of leaders to the employee ranks.[58] Employers and employees, when joining the organization were both to sign a like obligation, "on the word of honor of a man" to promote "industrial peace . . . by organizing branch associations all over this land which shall teach, preach and practice this doctrine, not by erecting an army of strike breakers, but by creating an association of men and women who shall gain fair treatment by giving fair treatment and will not strike." [59]

Bryce was warmly applauded, but interest was lukewarm. By that time the danger of unionism seemed to the members of the NAM not so imminent as it had in 1903. But this attitude of complacency was rudely shaken a year later with the bombshell of "Bloody Ludlow." Thereafter the Rockefeller type of "Company Union" [60] gained great popularity. During the twenties this company unionism became the Siamese twin to the NAM's Open Shop or "American Plan." With the coming of the great depression, the program was widened out, the better to cope first with the rising labor unrest which accompanied mounting unemployment, and then successively with the pro-labor "Article 7a" of the NRA and the National Labor Relations Board. The rise of the CIO brought this phase of the antiunion drive to a rather disastrous close.

[58] *Proceedings* of the 17th Annual Convention of the NAM, 1912.

[59] The plan was "to establish branches of our Association in the various cities. Those branches may be what we term mixed branches of the various trades, or where there are sufficient numbers of any one trade they may form a branch of their own, such as a carpenters' branch, a bricklayers' branch, etc." When this had been done in each locality where the NAM had members, "Our next move is to establish a labor bureau" to find employment for members by making special "arrangements with the various industries to supply them with efficient men, organized upon the peace principles." These arrangements provided for preferential employment of Trades and Workers Association members. Then, "when we obtain work for our members, we say to them, 'Now it is up to you to make good. If you are an efficient loyal employee, good wages, good working conditions and steady employment will be furnished you in so far as it is possible.' " This, said Mr. Bryce, should insure to employers "interested and peaceful employees . . . who want to remain at work without interference from agitators and bulldozers" with their "rights by continuing at work." *Ibid.*

[60] There are two basic American types, the "committee" type, which stems from the more benevolent "welfare capitalism" schemes and traces its origin to the Filene Coöperative Association established in 1898. The second, known as the "joint committee" type, was devised for the purpose of preventing unions by direct control over substitute union organization, and made its appearance first under the auspices of Rockefeller interests following "Bloody Ludlow" in 1913. It was described by Vice-President Hayes as "pure paternalism" and "benevolent feudalism." See *Characteristics of Company Unions* (U.S. Dept. of Labor, Bulletin No. 634, 1935).

In its wake has come a threefold shift of emphasis focused on the conquest of the "workers' soul" or general social point of view. In the first place there appears a new and pronounced emphasis upon vocational education, apprenticeship training, and foremanship conferences. So far as may be read from the available records, the last of these three is more or less uniquely American, although it appears to have been elaborated as one of the principal means for "re-educating" workmen by personnel experts committed to company-union techniques.[61] The other two, very important in the early stages of industrial evolution, have in recent years been paid a great and growing attention. They list high in the annals of all the leading *Spitzenverbände*, and may be considered merely as two phases of a single program having the dual objectives of (1) attaching to each separate plant a compact corps of especially selected and trained workmen chosen in advance for subsequent advancement through the managerial ranks, and (2) attaching to the interests of management, via a special ideological training supported by an appropriately graduated incentive system, the ambitious youth who would otherwise be apt to become future labor leaders.

In many places the success of this program from the employer's point of view has been rather astonishing. Especially noteworthy was the pre-Nazi system of *Dinta* (Deutsches Institut für Technische Arbeitsschulung), founded in 1926 and established by the beginning of 1933 in somewhere between 350 and 500 of the largest industrial plants in Germany.[62] Its director, Arnhold, was subsequently made director of vocational education for all Nazi Germany—a fact which takes on added significance when it is realized

[61] E. S. Cowdrick, for example, has taken a very prominent position in the discussion and plans for foremanship training, and Cowdrick was for years closely associated with the company union program of the Colorado Fuel and Mine Co. Later he became administrative head of the Special Conference Committee, established in 1919 by a group of large American corporations for the purpose of holding monthly meetings on the premises of the Standard Oil Co. of New Jersey dedicated to the elaboration of a mutually satisfactory and uniform approach on corporate labor problems.

[62] See Brady, *The Spirit and Structure of German Fascism*, pp. 161–70. "The problem," said Arnhold in 1927 (*Dinta* was organized in the Stahlhaus in 1926 under the sponsorship of Voegler, chairman of the big steel trust Vereinigte Stahlwerke), "is to take in hand leadership of all from earliest childhood to the oldest man, not—and I must emphasize this once more—for social purposes but from the point of view of productivity. I consider men the most important factor which industry must nourish and lead."

that under the principles of the "caste state" (*Ständesstaat*) all education is thought to be directly or indirectly vocational. The *Dinta* unit has many interesting parallels in France, England and the United States, not to mention the other Axis powers. The Ford vocational schools are an outstanding American example.[63]

A second and correlative shift of emphasis looks towards the further conquest of the worker point of view through gradual but cumulative supersession of noncommercial over commercial incentive systems. The pioneering work here in the United States was done by the A. T. and T. in its now famous "Hawthorne Experiments," wherein it was shown that after-work and social group, interest-in-the-job, job competitions, and similar interests could be made to yield worker output far in excess of those induced by the more usual "commercial incentives" of reduced hours and higher wages.[64] Those experiments have had an extraordinary influence in American personnel literature, and largely underlie the work of the British Institute for Industrial Psychology.[65] They follow lines very close to those promoted in Germany by a number of large corporations before the coming of the Nazi regime. The central idea of the Labor Front under the new regime has for its stated objective the effort to "suppress the materialism" and "instead divert the gaze of the workers to the spiritual values of the nation." [66]

[63] The Ford schools—as also the Ford conception of scattered and ruralized industrial communities—may be taken as prototypal of these efforts in America. The reader will find the literature of personnel agencies, such as the Personnel Research Federation and the National Occupational Conference, replete with plans, programs, and propaganda for these schools. A good many of the larger American corporations have carried schooling on through to the university level, though the more or less vocational aspect tends to be minimized as one proceeds up through facilities provided for office and upper managerial ranks.

[64] For a description and favorable comment on the Hawthorne Experiments, see F. J. Roethlisberger and W. J. Dickson, *Management and the Worker* (Boston, 1934); L. J. Henderson, T. N. Whitehead, and Elton Mayo, "The Effects of Social Environment," in *Papers on the Science of Administration,* ed. Luther Gulick and L. Urwick (New York, 1937); and Elton Mayo, *The Human Problems of an Industrial Civilization* (New York, 1933).

[65] A publication of the British Institute for Industrial Psychology, written by G. H. Miles (London, 1932) is prefaced by an advertisement which states that the author "discusses the root problem of industry—how to supply adequate incentives so that the maximum energy of each worker, from the managing director to the office boy, may be *aroused and directed in the best interests of the firm.*" Commercial incentives throughout are played down; noncommercial incentives heavily emphasized.

[66] Robert Ley, Fuehrer of the *Arbeitsfront,* in "New Forms of Community Work"

Trades unions, all spokesmen for the *Spitzenverbände* agree, thrive on "materialism"—the interest drives for higher wages, shorter hours, better working conditions, job security, and the like. Employer specialists in the causes of industrial unrest have felt that if employer-controlled substitutes could be found for these labor objectives it would be possible to bring the labor movement under control. Thus has arisen the general series of company social programs known by the common designation of "welfare capitalism." They are to be found in every major capitalist country in the world, some of them dating their programs back beyond the turn of the century.[67] Outstanding examples are Krupp, Siemens and Halske, I. G. Farbenindustrie and Zeiss in Germany, Imperial Chemicals in England, the Harmel works at Val-de-Bois and the various properties with which Henri Fayol was associated in France, Mitsui in Japan, and Ford, General Motors, Standard Oil of New Jersey, Procter and Gamble, Goodyear Tire and Rubber Co. and the A. T. and T. in the United States.[68] These schemes run all the way from free lunches at noon to provision of recreational grounds and parks, retirement and other types of social insurance, club facilities, house journals and newspapers.[69]

The Italian "After-Work" (*Dopolavoro*) and the Nazi "Strength through Joy" (*Kraft durch Freude*) movements, supported by various affiliated and auxiliary services, represent a sort of generalizing and nationalizing of this type of labor neutralizing company activity. Sports, hiking clubs, playing fields, and clubrooms are designed

---

(in English), *Herausgegeben vom Reichsarbeits- und Reichswirtschaftsrat* (Berlin, 1935).

[67] Notably, Krupp. A special guide book (*Führer durch die Essener Wohnsiedlungen der Firma Krupp*, 1930, published by the Krupp Company), quoted from the biography of the elder Krupp, written in defense of his settlements and general welfare program for Krupp employees inaugurated in the early 1860s, the following: "I am firmly convinced," Krupp said, "that everything I have recommended is necessary, and that the results will more than pay for themselves. We have much to gain thereby. Who knows but that when, after years and days, a general revolt will go through the land, when there will be a general uprising of all laborers against their employers, but that we shall be the only ones passed by if we are able to do what is required in time? . . . The command of the establishment shall not be lost, the sympathy of the people shall not be forfeited, there shall be no strikes called. . . . In the foreground of general objectives [stands] increasing the attachment to the plant, the working place, the profession."

[68] For exhaustive data, favorable to such plans, consult particularly the several reports of the Goodyear and, the Procter and Gamble companies.

[69] See various reports of the National Industrial Conference Board summarizing employer welfare plans.

mostly to appeal to the youth. In the more fully developed programs, special activities and facilities are provided likewise for the older employees, male and female, and for sweethearts, wives, mothers, and dependents. The coverage here is all-inclusive, and the range of interests brought into these systems of ideological regimentation soon becomes logically "totalitarian"—that is, it attempts to control both form and content of the *totality* of worker ideas and activities. The attitude of the big and dominating companies which have become interested in such programs within the various capitalistic countries is for all practical purposes uniform and highly enthusiastic.[70]

With but minor exceptions, the variety of motives underlying these various programs from company unionism on through to the more engaging forms of "welfare capitalism" all have as a common denominator the objective of neutralizing militant labor organization. In the course of time—most fully realized in the totalitarian countries—these programs have been knit into coherent and balanced systems for waging "total war" on the common ideological front. More than that, in the hands of personnel experts, trained in various scientific management schools, the aim of these programs has changed from the desire to prevent antiemployer organization to an intention to control—on behalf of determinate employer social interests as well as of employee interests—the underlying values and thinking processes of all employees. As the Japanese have so quaintly put the matter, extirpation of "dangerous thoughts" is giving way to "ideological reconstruction" of "thought offenders," who need to "liquidate their dangerous and contagious thoughts." [71]

Thus it may be said the general objective of all "harmony" programs is to transfigure the employers into the roles of instructors,

[70] Particularly interesting in this connection is a book written by Dr. Rexford B. Hersey, of the Wharton School at the University of Pennsylvania, called *Seele und Gefühl des Arbeiter, Psychologie des Menschenführung*. Hersey, a leading figure in American scientific management circles and an advisor to the Pennsylvania Railroad on personnel problems, was so impressed with what he saw in Germany under Reichsbahn and Labor Front auspices that he wrote this very laudatory book; Nazi leaders were so impressed with the book that a German edition was published with a foreword by Dr. Robert Ley, Leader of the Labor Front. Both Dr. Hersey and Dr. Ley, apparently, see quite eye to eye.

[71] "Japan to Keep Thought Offenders Locked up so Duty of Conversion Can Be Carried Out," Otto D. Tolischus, New York *Times*, May 16, 1941.

guides, and "leaders" of their men. Conversely, labor is to look to the employers for leadership and guidance—literally, to "entrust" the employer with their individual and collective welfare while conforming their innermost thoughts with the requirements of his ideas and the configuration of his interests. The accepted large-scale employer version of "harmony" in labor relations, in other words, could lead only to "the servile state."

THE CONTENT OF "HARMONY" IN PUBLIC RELATIONS

"By following the dictates of their own interests landowners and farmers become, in the natural order of things, the best trustees and guardians for the public." Thus spoke the official representatives of England's pre- and early industrial Squirearchy.[72] But in order to find the precise equivalent for contemporary times, one has only to page through the voluminous literature of official business propaganda in any major capitalist country. Almost without exception the big businessman is coming to think of himself as the person who guides, "educates," and "leads" the general public on behalf of the common or "community" good, with the result, that although he is typically the possessor of vast wealth and prepotent political and social authority, spokesmen for his interests yet seek to remold the businessman in the public eye as the least selfish of all.[73] In this redaction, not profits but "service" becomes his leading aim; he, and all too often he alone, thinks of the sacrifices of the public when strikes occur and of the benefactions that flow to the public when "progress" under his benign guidance takes another momentous step forward.

American readers are now, thanks to the labors of public-relations counselors over the last decade or so, thoroughly familiar with this picture of the domestic business tycoon. They are apt, however, to misunderstand a like picture of businessmen abroad, where social backgrounds are quite different from those at home. Broadly speaking the importance of public relations—whose pri-

---

[72] See J. L. and Barbara Hammond, *The Town Labourer, 1760–1832* (London, 1917).
[73] "Indeed, the very essence of business success lies in the degree to which the employer, in competition with others, can benefit both his employees and his customers. . . . The employer . . . manifests daily a high order of unselfishness." Link, TNEC Monograph No. 11, pp. 80, 81.

mary purpose is to paint just such a picture—decreases as one moves away from countries with long and deep-seated liberal, democratic, and parliamentary institutions. In those countries, such as Japan, Italy, and Germany, where forces behind the transition from feudal and despotic authorities were either but short lived or unable, for one reason or another, to prevail for long against a more tenacious past, public-relations activity as we know it is almost nonexistent. The benevolent or "patronal" position of the businessman is there largely taken care of by the surviving etiquettes and the formal compulsion of invidious social status, and is quickly reinforced in the event of emergency by official government propaganda.

Even here there is a great difference between a country such as Germany, where liberal education and some popular familiarity with democratic institutions had taken more than superficial root, and countries like Italy and Japan where the reverse was the case. For these reasons National Socialist propaganda was necessarily, and by all means, better organized, more distinctly employer conscious, more vociferous, and more versatile than the propaganda of either Italy or Japan. And at the other end of the scale, public-relations propaganda of the corporate growth in the United States —where social station, the insignia of rank and power, and day-to-day contacts with the claims of squirearchy, royalty and empire are much less striking or almost nonexistent—is more highly colored and ambidextrous than it has ever become even in England.

In countries within the totalitarian bloc all this is commonly, and as a matter of course, taken for granted. So, likewise, is the specific purpose and the general content of the official propaganda. The specific purpose is always and universally that of consolidating the economic and political power of the upper social layers. And the content is designed to inculcate public loyalty to the same social layers whenever their authority or rights of leadership are seriously questioned. Just what symbolism it uses, and by what methods or routes popular acceptance of the dictates of the upper social layers is achieved, will depend upon times, circumstances, and historical antecedents. But the purpose is always the same, and the central theme is always that felicitous relation between the rulers and the ruled, between master and man which is said to represent "social harmony."

Most public relations as we know it in America, to make a long story short, not only strives to "sell the public" on the "enterprise system," but also makes its appeal primarily to the symbolism and myths of "social harmony" and "class collaboration," as these have been transmuted to fit into the ideological framework of the "middle class" outlook.

That "social harmony," with its implied—when not directly insisted upon—blind acceptance of the "leadership" of compactly organized business, is the object of American public relations is so well known that it no longer requires proof. The series of advertisements by the NAM captioned "Prosperity Dwells Where Harmony Reigns," is typical of the central strain running through all big-business controlled propaganda here and abroad. In a society where the burgherdom has played such an important role throughout its history as it has in the United States, this really means "middle class relations."

That the central appeal in American public-relations literature is directed largely, if not exclusively, to the middle class can easily be demonstrated. Aside from early sporadic efforts, the first clear appeal made in peacetimes for public support of the business system as such came during the postwar years, when middle-class "unions" of one sort or another were organized in the various formerly belligerent countries as an offset to resurgence of popular demands and threatened civil strife. In one form or another they were established by militant business interests in the United States, England, France, Italy and Germany.[74] With the return to "pros-

[74] In England the Middle Classes Union, organized in 1919 to defend the "people with the middle interests" claimed that it was able to destroy successively a railroad strike, a coal strike, and a dock strike. In France a "confederation of Intellectual Workers" was formed about the same time. It claimed 120,000 members in 1921 dedicated to the position that demands of intellectuals "had nothing in common with those of the manual laborers." New York *Times*, May 22, 1921. In Italy "a number of organizations comparable to what may be called a vast middle-class union" were "formed throughout the various cities and towns" during 1920 which brought together "the gentlemen of assured income" in forces sufficiently powerful to "break the back" of a strike of postal clerks and railroad employees. New York *Times*, May 23, 1920. In Germany a similar union made up primarily of professional people had doctors and hospital help who refused during the period of the Spartacist revolts

perity," and the subsidence of popular discontent, middle-class unions everywhere went on the rocks.

But with the beginning of the great depression of the early thirties, the leading business concerns made new and much more effective efforts to mobilize sentiments along these lines. By this time, however, a number of factors conspired to alter greatly the type of appeal within the United States. The factors, outlined in this study, include the growth in the relative importance of the *Spitzenverbände* and the dominant position of the giant corporations within these newer networks, together with an increasing concentration of control over the media for the dissemination of information on the one hand, and the critical character of American relations with countries which had formally gone over to a totalitarian basis on the other. The change in appeal was twofold. One emphasis led to the organization of various types of semi- or openly vigilante Citizens' Committees and Citizens' Forums. The other led to the rise of public-relations counselors, frequently in connection with organized advertising agencies, but everywhere openly and frankly employing the techniques and the approach of high-pressure advertising. Fusion of these two in the middle thirties, with advertising steadily gaining the guiding power, had led by the latter part of the decade to the swift articulation of an organized nation-wide business propaganda for the "sale of ideas" to the American people dealing with promotion of the values and merits of "the enterprise system."

Just what this means can be seen when it is realized that advertising in America, contrary to the common impression, had come by the early thirties to direct its appeals not to the broad masses but primarily to the middle-income layers. The expression long employed in these circles to describe the shift of the basis of the

---

to serve "sick Proletarians" in a "counter strike," with the result that these same "sick proletarians could thenceforth obtain neither drugs nor medical attention, while proletarian patients were left unattended in their beds." The result was a breaking of the strike. Lothrop Stoddard, "The Common People's Union," *World's Work* XXXIX (Nov., 1919), No. 1, pp. 102–4. And in 1920, on the suggestion of Chauncey Depew of the New York Central Railroad, a People's Union was established with headquarters at the New York Press Club. It announced in its first official statement that "The breath of our life is public opinion. This movement is answer to a demand by the country's press for protection of the organized public from the terrible consequences of general strikes." New York *Times*, July 22, 1920. See also, Corbin, *The Return of the Middle Class.*

appeal from mass markets to the middle class has been, "the market is a diamond." The phrase means simply that, when incomes are aggregated by layers horizontally across the typical income pyramid, purchasing power by income layers takes on the shape of a diamond, not a triangle. Advertising copy is then written to a mass market, rated in terms of purchasing power, across the center of a diamond and not the base of a pyramid. Sales above or below whatever may be determined as the two limiting bands of profitable appeal are then regarded as of the order of "windfall gains." Only to the income territory within the two bands, however, does "it pay to advertise." [75]

The market for every commodity has been shown to have some variation on the general diamond shape, including even the cheapest and most widely sold foodstuffs. Likewise the market for consumer goods as a whole shows the diamond pattern. But it is interesting to note that the companies which advertise, the agencies which write the advertising copy, and the media through which advertising appeals are made are not only typically large-scale, exclusive, and closely controlled by the upper social strata, whose incomes are above the upper band, but also that the lower band, depending upon the commodity, excludes from between 20 and 60 percent or more of the entire population of the United States. This only means, of course, that the upper social layers purchase but small quantities of mass produced goods and services from which they draw their incomes, and that the lower income layers have insufficient purchasing power to be worth the cost of the appeal.

Consequently, when militant interests within the advertising industry begin to take over the "sale of ideas," its copy is written primarily as appeal to the middle-income layers. Such a fusion of advertising and public relations not only directs attention to the values, institutions, and symbolisms of the middle layers, but also does so at a time when the income, occupation, and social security status of these same ranks is becoming peculiarly and increasingly unstable. The "average citizen," for example, is gradually losing his property stakes. The little businessman is in a more precarious position than at any time since the very beginning of the capitalis-

[75] See W. H. Mullen, "Diamond as Market Pattern," *Printers' Ink*, Feb. 6, 1936, pp. 66–70.

tic system. The farmer-operator is in the process of being transferred from an independent owner to a dependent tenant. It is becoming more expensive to acquire education for, and proficiency
in, the learned professions, with the result that the professions are
becoming more exclusive and opportunities for jobs more restricted. A large and increasing range of skilled crafts and white-
collar workers are being proletarized. And so on, ad infinitum. Yet
the very multiplicity of variables in the picture, the varied social
antecedents of these ranks, and the general confusion wrought by
the swiftness of some of the changes, when coupled to the momentous social and political issues at stake, makes these people while in
the very process of being declassed still peculiarly susceptible to a
"middle class" appeal directed by the upper social stratum.

The content of the appeal made to these ranks by such advertising is not only geared to "middle class" ideologies, but also, so to
speak, to its modes of speech and manners of thought. Historically
the "middle classes" took root as rising trading, commercial, and
industrial classes, deeply imbued with what Sombart has called the
ideologies of "holy economy" as practiced by an Alberti, a Jacob
Fugger or such a shrewd and calculating Yankee *Bonhomme* as
Benjamin Franklin. The characteristic gospel of Franklin's "get
ahead," altered and transmuted by the evolving techniques of
"high pressure," has led directly to the ripened techniques of much
contemporary advertising.

These can be said to center around such generally accepted, if
not almost hallowed ideas as *caeterus paribus,* "all the traffic will
bear," "repetition is reputation," and "truth is believability."
When these techniques and ideas are focused on the "sale of ideas,"
the net result may be summarized as forceful persuasion, via calculating doctrinal exegesis, of those potentially convertible social
layers who are most apt to be won over to the rules of status at the
lowest per capita cost, by articulate and ideologically ambidextrous
spokesmen for those who have a special vested interest in the maintenance of the status quo. And the content of this propaganda is the
notion of "social harmony."

It would be extremely interesting to compare the forms, ideas,
appeals, and symbolisms employed by this American propaganda
with those being evolved abroad—particularly within the totali-

tarian countries. The American techniques are, of course, characteristically of native vintage, yet the care of the central "harmony" argument on the one hand, and the cavalier disregard of the usual canons of scientific truth on the other, amount to much the same thing both in this country and abroad. When such a blending is fully centralized and carefully rationalized, the logical result can only be a "ministry of propaganda" directed towards the defense and maintenance of whatever slowly consolidating hierarchy of policy-making power its characteristic ideology was devised to promote.

It is, then, perhaps unnecessary to remark that public relations in America are thus increasingly designed as means for coördinating (1) labor or "industrial" relations activity, (2) advertising or "consumer relations," (3) small business or "trade relations," and (4) farmer or "agricultural relations." Which is to say that while public relations directs its programs primarily at the conquest of the "soul" of the middle classes, its officers are attempting to make this appeal the center around which to group all other propaganda efforts directed to the coördination of all groups and interests to the evolving ideologies of status.

And from all our historical evidence it is entirely obvious that, in a regime of benevolent status, "social harmony" calls for the "leadership" of the "trustee" in all things and with respect to all people. Otherwise it becomes unalloyed despotism.

But under neither circumstance, of course, is the result reconcilable with democratic institutions—except in the propaganda.

Chapter IX

POLITICAL POLICIES: BUREAUCRACY, HIERARCHY, TOTALITARIANISM

"THE ANIMOSITY of German capitalism against the state," wrote Professor Bonn on the eve of the Nazi coup d'état, "does not rest upon fundamental theoretical foundations, but upon purely opportunistic considerations. It is opposed to the state when state control is in the hands of a political majority whose permanent good will it doubts. German capitalism, which would like to be freed of the power of the state, and which seeks to push back state intervention as far as possible, is constructed exclusively upon the most thorough intervention of the state." [1] A correct generalization this, but one which might have been as readily applied to monopolistically-oriented business in any other major or minor capitalistic country. For the confessed objectives of German business which filled Bonn with gloomy foreboding—the drive for a well-nigh all-inclusive system of tariff protection, ever more elaborate subsidies and subventions, more and more governmental aid in the control over competition—were at that same time coming swiftly to dominate the programs of organized business all over the world.

German levels of organization were at that time doubtless somewhat higher than those obtaining abroad, the clarity of her business leaders less confused by serious factional cross-currents, and the attitude of the government in general was far more lenient. But the patterns of thought, the modes of procedure, the forms of organization, and the principles at stake were shared by companion interests in England, France, the United States and elsewhere. There was nothing in principle to distinguish the programs of the Reichsverband der deutschen Industrie from that of the National Asso-

[1] M. J. Bonn, *Das Schicksal des deutschen Kapitalismus*, (1931), pp. 95–96, 98.

ciation of Manufacturers in the United States or the Confédération Générale de la Production Française, nor of the immense and rapidly proliferating meshwork of trade-associations, cartels, syndicates, chambers, and business institutes brought together in these general purpose peak associations, or *Spitzenverbände*. Nor, least of all, was there anything to distinguish the trend of economic thinking, social outlook, and political interests of the huge combinations which had come increasingly to dominate the inner councils of their respective central associations in the capitalistic countries.

Since the time Bonn wrote his study, this dual process of expanding business organization and business-government interpenetration has been greatly speeded up. Within three major capitalistic countries the fusion between private enterprise and political authority has been extended far enough for the habit of regarding politics and economics as but two facets of a single thing to become the rule and not the exception. Fascist Italy has greatly expanded the power and influence of the "Corporate System." Germany has become National Socialist, and the whole of her elaborate economic machinery has been given some degree of official political status. Japan has followed suit, and from latest reports France under the occupation is treading the same path. NRA within the United States pointed in the same general direction, and the more recent developments of the National Defense program appear to be picking up where that ill-fated experiment left off. British war controls, as the London *Economist* has pointed out in a series of caustic articles, have vested in private hands political authorities which sanctify *de jure* what was rapidly becoming *de facto* a "feudalistic system of cartel control."

Now, in appraising the significance of this morganatic alliance of private economic power and government it is important to remember, that the former derives from a system of monopoly, or of interlocking monopoly-minded groups, and that the institutional umbilicus of this monopoly-orientation feeds upon the sanctions of private property. It is, of course, a truism that even in its germinal form private property is far more than a mere economic category; that it is equally a "political" institution. Through ownership of productive means, the individual is, under capitalism, vested with a bundle of definitive rights and prerogatives. Under these sanctions he is granted narrowly defined but inherently exclusive power to manipulate people in an environment of rigorously interdependent human relations. Whether, as Spencer once wrote in a scorching passage, "the original deeds were written with the sword," it is nevertheless true that with and through such possessions one can coerce, bend others to one's will, withhold, restrain, settle the fate and alter the fortunes of growing numbers of non-owners without, and increasingly against, their consent. The natural frame of reference of ownership is, and has been from the beginning, as clearly political as economic, as obviously "Machiavellian" as "Ricardian."

Fee simple is related to private monopoly as youth is to age, as acorn to oak. It is the minuscular shape, the germinal form, the archetypal pattern for the proliferating giants which have sprung from its institutional loins. If private ownership of the means of production prevails throughout an economic system and is largely unimpaired by hostile countervailing forces, then, sooner or later monopoly in all its manifold expressions must appear on the scene. For property is power, and collusion is as "natural" as competition—a fact which the great Adam Smith was quick to recognize.[2] Because this is true, growth of such possessions expresses power cumulatively; left to itself this power is additive, unidirectional, without internal restraints and external limits. Its higher economic form of expression is monopoly, and monopoly prerogatives are to power as fulcrum is to lever.

[2] The passages are well known: "Masters are always and everywhere in a sort of tacit, but constant and uniform combination, not to raise the wages of labour above their actual rate. To violate this combination is everywhere a most unpopular action [today it would be known as an "unfair trade practice"!], and a sort of reproach to a master among his neighbors and equals. We seldom, indeed, hear of this combination because it is the usual, and one may say, the natural state of things which nobody ever hears of." Again, "People of the same trade seldom meet together, even for merriment and diversion, but the conversation ends in a conspiracy against the public, or in some contrivance to raise prices. It is impossible indeed to prevent such meetings, by any law which either could be executed, or would be consistent with liberty and justice. *But though the law cannot hinder people of the same trade from sometimes assembling together, it ought to do nothing to facilitate such assemblies; much less to render them necessary.*" Adam Smith, *The Wealth of Nations,* Cannan ed., pp. 66–67, 128. Italics mine. This latter, of course, is exactly what is done by NRA, price maintenance, "unfair trade practice," marketing control and other recent types of legislation, which are to be found in similar form in practically all other countries, totalitarian and non-totalitarian alike; except for the word "necessary" one must now substitute the word "compulsory" in about half the cases!

Power is compulsive, and when distributed unequally between bargaining groups is irreconcilable with "free contract." Fee simple distributes power unevenly between the "haves" and the "have-nots"; monopoly heightens and complicates the disproportionalities in the graduated ranks of both. Law and the courts as frequently underline as correct the resultant distortion. It is this configuration of coercive forces, disproportionately matched, which accounts for the usual and inherently lop-sided "contract," and not the nature of the "rights" of bargaining groups. Power, in private hands, comes up against such claims as water comes to a wall, taking advantage of every crevice, depression, resource, or structural weakness. The proper expression is not "expansion of power" from these property nuclei, but cumulative permeation of power, as the history of the unfolding controls of all the great combines, cartels, trade associations, and *Spitzenverbände* abundantly shows.

Now it is a common characteristic of all monopoly-oriented groupings, major and minor, that each newly acquired leverage is typically employed for further collusive, rather than for competitive, efforts. Not "monopolistic competition" but "monopolistic collusion" paces the gathering up and centralization of power to determine business policies over ever widening areas.[3] In plans lying behind the strategies of price fixation such things as production control, market allocations, and similar economic programs become increasingly the vehicles for strengthening tactical position in the pressure politics of collusive *Realpolitik;* they are not ends in themselves as so many recent economic theorists have mistakenly assumed.[4] But more than that, as struggle for strategic position

[3] See Callman, *Das deutsche Kartellrecht* and *Unlautere Wettbewerb;* Lucas, *Industrial Reconstruction,* for the British story; and the various reports of the LaFollette Committee, the Temporary National Economic Committee, and the indictments of the Anti-Trust Division of the Department of Justice and the Federal Trade Commission.

[4] E. g., and most notoriously, Edward Chamberlain, *The Theory of Monopolistic Competition,* and Joan Robinson, *The Economics of Imperfect Competition.* (Not, however, J. M. Keynes, though many of his proposals in this connection appear as the product of "split-personality.") Chamberlain by implication (Appendix E, "Some Arguments in Favor of Trade-Mark Infringement and 'Unfair Trading'") and Mrs. Robinson explicitly recognize as much when they admit that their examination of monopolistic practices assume the absence of collusive intent or strategies reaching beyond the end of maximum gains. But it will no longer do to insist that an economist qua economist can only remain true to himself when he acts naïvely towards half to two-thirds of his problem, or, becoming sophisticated, insists on

broadens out over wider and wider areas, both ends and means become increasingly enmeshed in more or less distinctly and canonically social and political issues—issues which, to employ the language of Karl Mannheim, reach to the "roots of domination" and thus become "vested with a public interest" in a new and revolutionary sense of the term.

Why this is so may be read directly from the record by the more astute who have steeped themselves in the raw materials of the combination and business organization movements. But there is a certain "internal logic" to these transmutations of monopoly-minded policy which may be thrown into fluoroscopic relief by a less direct and time-consuming method. Consider first the nature of the new business self-bureaucratization.

THE NATURE OF BUSINESS BUREAUCRATIZATION

To say that business enterprise in all major capitalistic countries is becoming bureaucratic is to add nothing new. It is so well accepted in the technical literature as to no longer require proof.[5] Obviously the vast control apparatus and the elaborate organizational machinery of large-scale enterprises, of cartels and trade associations, and of their various peak associations call for functional division of duties, for circumscription of tasks and fixation of special responsibilities, for hierarchies of command and subordination, for special systems of recruitment and training of personnel at different levels of competence. Obviously the growth in size and complexity of the individual business enterprise, the spread of ever more inclusive cartel and trade association networks, the gathering up and centralizing of policies in series of

throwing the baby out with the bathwater simply because in his family tree such a baby must surely be illegitimate. The earlier economists, as well as the earlier political theorists (e. g., Machiavelli, Bodin, Hobbes, Filmer, Locke, Bentham, Burke) made no such mistake. For the orthodox tradition, after the lame synthesis of John Stuart Mill, the separation of economics and politics became an issue as important as the separation of church and state, but at a time when, in contrast with the latter, the real historical interdependence between the two was growing ever closer and more rigorous with the passage of time.

[5] See, in particular, Mooney and Reiley, *Onward Industry!* on "The Principles of Organization and Their Significance to Modern Industry"; Marshall Dimock and Howard K. Hyde, in TNEC Monograph No. 11, *Bureaucracy and Trusteeship,* and the various summary volumes of the huge German *Enqueteausschuss,* in particular the *Gesamtbericht.* See also, Louis D. Brandeis' provocative volume, *The Curse of Bigness* (New York, 1936).

interlocking *Spitzenverbände*, the formalization of relationships not only amongst these various business groupings but vis-à-vis the ever widening system of governmental regulation (whether friendly or hostile to business) and the ever greater attention paid to expert staff counsel, not to mention the science of management and administration itself—obviously these mean steady and cumulative bureaucratization of business. On present showing it is possible to predict that in the normal course of events the time will shortly arrive when all business activity, big and little, and from center to circumference, will be enmeshed in bureaucratic machinery, will conduct its activities in terms of bureaucratic dicta, following bureaucratic procedures, and complying with bureaucratic criteria.

Business, that is to say, is becoming organized; that organization is becoming large scale, highly centralized, and complex; and such centralization and complexity define the area of bureaucratic control. But there are many types of bureaucracies, good and bad. The question is not, "Is business being bureaucratized?" but rather, "What type of bureaucracy is coming to dominate in business circles?"

There are three clues which merit especially close and careful inspection. First is the system of recruitment and training. The more one pages through the literature and publicity of the giant corporations and the networks of business and employer organization brought together under the central policy direction of the *Spitzenverbände* the more one is struck by the increasing attention devoted to this subject. A variety of motives dominate. A common incentive is specialized training for specialized jobs. Uppermost in many cases is the desire to take control over jobs away from the trade unions.[6] In many cases this objective appears to be more narrowly conceived as the recruitment of an absolutely loyal corps of workers from which the future managerial forces will be selected.[7]

[6] See Sidney and Beatrice Webb, *The History of Trade Unionism* (New York, 1920). In the early days employers fought apprenticeship programs, since these were employed by unions for the purpose of restricting labor supply. Now the roles are in many cases reversed, unions opposing apprenticeship plans designed to break down their own monopoly controls over labor supply on the one hand, and their partial control over the attitude of the lower managerial corps recruited directly from union ranks. This was particularly clear in the case of *Dinta*. See p. 283.

[7] This seems to have been the original purpose of *Dinta* when it was organized in

Quite generally the purpose is to attach managerial—and sometimes even nonmanagerial—ranks directly to the individual company or trade so as to cut down the high expense associated with turnover of an executive and staff personnel which it is becoming increasingly costly to "break in." [8] Again, and perhaps more commonly in recent years, the device provides an extremely effective method for the spread of antitrade union propaganda.

Trends here move on three closely related levels. Most common and perhaps best known are apprenticeship programs. One line of emphasis in these programs calls for systematic and far-reaching attempts to overhaul public-school educational programs on more purely vocational lines. This feature has been particularly marked in England and Germany. Under the Nazis, and to a lesser extent in Italy and Japan, the program of *Dinta* and other closely allied groups has been extended to cover all educational training in the country. The second line of emphasis calls for greatly extending formal company-controlled apprenticeship training systems throughout industry in general. More recently in the United States, governmentally sponsored, but privately directed, local, state and national apprenticeship training programs have been worked out on a basis sufficiently comprehensive to forecast the time when they will include all jobs requiring some degree of skill. The various *Spitzenverbände* have without exception shown a lively and sustained interest in these systems for sifting, shaping, guiding, and controlling the lower levels of future labor ranks.

A parallel interest has led in the United States to "foremanship training." Both the National Association of Manufacturers and the United States Chamber of Commerce and their various subsidiary and member bodies have paid much attention to this feature of recruitment, since it is recognized that the foreman is the "front line representative of management." Ideally, "foremanship training" performs somewhat the same functions for the nonexecutive

---

1926, and of the National Association of Manufacturers when it first began to show an active interest—c. 1910–12—in apprenticeship programs.

[8] A particularly important problem where automatic machinery has been developed to the point where staff is largely of an engineering or semi-engineering supervisory character, and in cases where processes have become so highly specialized—machine tool production, airplane manufacture and repair—that the costs of spoilage, quite aside from the direct costs of training, from faulty workmanship are high and may ramify, bottle-neckwise, far beyond the individual operation or process.

managerial ranks that apprenticeship and vocational education do for those who habitually handle the machines.

Within these two levels, training is in many instances almost entirely technical. But increasingly—notoriously in such cases as Ford, General Motors, Standard Oil of New Jersey, Mitsui, I. G. Farbenindustrie, Siemens and Halske, and particularly *Dinta*—there has been added schooling in economics, sociology, history, and other subjects which may be manipulated to support the general social and philosophical point of view of management. It is probably safe to say that no large company, trade association, *Spitzenverband,* or governmental employee-training program is now entirely free of this ideological coloring. In many cases, company propaganda plays a role as important or even more important than the formal technical training itself. This is particularly apt to be the case in company "colleges," such as that of the Standard Oil Company of New Jersey.[9]

Through these methods business is attempting to create its own "officialdom" [10] and its own "civil service," [11] dedicated to business ends and loyal to business philosophies. However much the content of specific programs may vary in detail, the general tendency here is to evolve specialized training for specialized jobs, to delimit, define, and circumscribe each and every specialized task, to define responsibilities and duties within each bracket of competence, to arrange these competencies in a rationally articulated hierarchy of command and subordination in which vertical movement is lim-

[9] See also literature of the Goodyear Tire and Rubber Co. on the "Goodyear Industrial Union," which offers, amongst other courses, one on "Business Science" dealing with "The individual in self-analysis, his relation to others, his attitude towards his job and his understanding of the proper approach to the job." (Circular of the Goodyear Tire and Rubber Co.) How many of these "schools" and "colleges" there may be, what ground they cover, what differences they show from one country to another, and to what uses they are being put nobody knows. A careful and critical study is much needed.

[10] A particularly penetrating book was written by Kurt Wiedenfeld (one of the more acute German economists subsequently to enlist in the Nazi services), called *Kapitalismus und Beamtentum: Produzententum und Konsumententum in der Weltmarkt-Wirtschaft* (1932). See also, TNEC Monograph No. 11.

[11] One of the common shortcomings of the more recent books on wage theory, as, e. g., J. R. Hicks, *The Theory of Wages,* (London, 1932), is that employers are assumed to take a purely passive role vis-à-vis labor in that he is treated as a bargainer who does not really bargain since he is interested only in the wage-cost: labor-efficiency calculus, and whose only choices are (a) the sea in which he fishes, and (b) the bait he will use (bait is all of one sort; it varies only by more-or-less).

ited and defined by "seniority," formal rules, and other formally graduated systems of employer-controlled rewards and punishments, and to direct the whole of these efforts along a more or less common ideological front.

Above foreman ranks, the story is somewhat different. A line somewhat similar to that found in governmental circles between "civil service" and "political appointees" seems to run between the two lower levels of business staff on the one hand and the directorial and upper managerial ranks on the other. Here, as has been pointed out, the evidence seems to show that "position," "pull," "family," "contacts," "family wealth," "nepotism," "sinecure," "indulgences," and the like are, becoming increasingly important. These upper layers seem to be "inbreeding" in business, just as the leading families of the upper wealth brackets from which they are mostly drawn intermarry within the charmed circles of the Social Register. There can be no question but that coöptation is the rule and not the exception throughout all business large and small, and that the practice holds as generally for the trade associations and their various *Spitzenverbände* as it does in principle for the more compact corporate set up.[12] But more, that within the upper executive and directorial layers, coöptation is increasingly from socially acceptable ranks, and that the rules that guide selection come more and more to be woven of the same cloth as those which define the limits, the attitudes, the codes, and the social and political philosophies of self-conscious ruling-class status.

Before pursuing the implications of these developments a bit further, it will be useful to consider briefly the two other "clues" to the nature of business bureaucracy hinted at above. The first of these relates to the fact that all attempts to rationalize business organization lead, under liberal-capitalistic political conditions, to dual, overlapping, and, in part, "competing," managements which become increasingly costly, inefficient, cumbersome, and confusing with the passage of time, and which sooner or later require, by more or less common agreement, surgical treatment. It is a well-known fact that few efforts to coördinate, for example, private natural monopolies over territories coextensive with their natural potentialities have been successfully carried through without ac-

12 See pp. 259-65, above.

tive governmental aid. The American Telephone and Telegraph Company is a partial exception, as are a few local tram and electric power systems. Railway unification, however, has nowhere been carried through except by government fiat. The Interstate Commerce Commission has striven for railway unification for years. The railway unification which led to the British "Big 4" in the early twenties and the development of the unified rail networks of Germany and Japan were forced through on the initiative of their respective governments. The same holds for most electric power "grid" schemes, unification of postal and telegraph systems, and most local and metropolitan transit networks.

The monopoly urge, in other words, seems to be typically stopped before monopoly has been really achieved. The results—the reasons why need not detain us at this point, for they require independent analysis, case by case and industry by industry [13]—however, belie at least in part the superficial impression. They seem to be about as follows: (1) monopoly efforts are funneled increasingly through the machinery of trade association, Chamber of Commerce, and *Spitzenverband;* (2) within these councils a broad line separates the inner governing cliques made up of the corporate giants and their medium and smaller satellite concerns; (3) the former divide markets, manipulate prices and production, and in general so direct affairs that, the total possible "take" being treated as given, each of the former receives his due allotment where the gains are relatively speaking assured, and the latter are granted the more or less unprofitable fringes; (4) there is a cumulative pressure to "settle into the allotted groove," and not to encroach upon "most-favored company" territory, nor to push entirely out those whose existence on sufferance is deemed a continuous advantage for propaganda and other reasons; (5) disputes concerning position are increasingly handled by the equivalent of negotiation, arbitration, "treaty-making," special grant and privilege, etc.; (6) enterprise management is kept in a largely fractionalized state within each industry or trade, more or less irrespective of geographic, technological, and other features; [14] (7) increasingly,

[13] Further combination may be stopped by fear of Anti-Trust prosecution, as in the United States.

[14] Patent pooling, standard grades and labels, simplification of types and varieties, cartel and syndicate practices, and the like, do not militate against this generaliza-

the leading functions of the trade association or *Spitzenverband* becomes the guidance and leadership on all social and political issues. Finally, so long as either the internal coördinative functions or the external representative tasks of the central associations are pursued in the face of partially or largely antagonistic political authorities, the two facets will be dovetailed into a single program known as "self-government in business." [15]

Consequently, the more "self-government in business" there is, the more governmental regulation there must be. And the more governmental regulatory machinery expands, the more complete and thorough becomes the duplication of managerial and administrative hierarchies between government and private enterprise. Governmental regulatory agencies have shown a more or less common pattern of development: (1) they tend to become permanent bodies well staffed with expert panels; (2) they find that regulation which has been instituted at any point—price, market allocation, or the like—leads them step by step to cover the whole range of business policies of regulated concerns; (3) regulation gradually comes to embrace the entire trade or industry; (4) it gathers into its hands increasingly legislative and judicial as well as administrative authority. Under pressure to expand functions along these lines, regulatory authorities gradually begin to compile information which runs the gamut of business and industry interests; to organize information, prosecution, negotiation, and its own internal administration along functional lines characteristic of the industry as a whole; to build up staffs until they come to approximate the business administration which they face constantly across the conference table or the courtroom; and to acquire powers— sometimes negative and more frequently positive—which involve *de facto* participation in the management of the enterprises falling into the authority's bailiwick.[16]

---

tion, for these represent cost cutting, orgnization simplifying, and strategic manipulation factors. There is little or no evidence that they tend to "rationalize" the industry either to the public good, or to cut down the plethora of separate managements. So far as the public good is concerned, these devices usually appear in combinations which retard the pace of change; they tend to slow down the weeding out which would occur under either "normal" competitive or monopoly conditions.

[15] See pp. 227-39, above.

[16] It would be possible to show this in great detail by dissecting any of a large number of governmental regulatory authorities in the United States or abroad. The

There are some reasons for regarding the typical governmental regulatory body as organizationally superior to those evolved by the businesses they regulate,[17] but that is quite another matter. Of key importance in the present connection are two by-products of the developments traced above. First, as pointed out above, there tends to be duplication all the way up and down the line between government and business administrative machines. And second, a large and increasing percentage of staff, and of the necessary facilities in terms of office space, office personnel, files, and the paraphernalia for grinding out countless memoranda is taken up with the tactics of manoeuvre, concealment and uncovering of key information, legalistic haggling, enforcement and evasion, and so on, ad infinitum, brought about and dependent upon the conflicting interests expressed in such dual administrative control.

Facing this situation, what do the *Spitzenverbände* propose to do? First, they tend to duplicate in their own central headquarters

chairman of one of the largest Federal regulatory agencies—perhaps the best known —hazarded the guess in private conversation with the author some four years ago that his Commission would ultimately be compelled to duplicate every scrap of information, every leading staff officer and specialist, concerning companies and trade associations they were charged to regulate in the public interest. Perhaps not in absolute numbers, he thought, since they might never be under compulsion to become as inefficiently organized as the industry, taken as a whole, patently was. But certainly on a scale capable ultimately of taking over the entire industry without serious hitch should business management and staffs be suddenly stricken, let us say, by a highly selective desire for permanent vacations. A similar judgment was given by equally highly placed German and British regulatory authorities with respect to their own administrative machineries.

[17] Partly because they have come into the picture later than the companies and administrative bodies which they seek to regulate; partly because they tend to be manned by experts and not by business "politicos"—civil service requirements for staff, bad as they may be in many instances, are obviously superior to the staffs they face in training, in singleness of purpose, and in the quality of their loyalty; partly because they bear responsibilities which are matters of public record wherein their actions and decisions are constantly subject to either legislative or judicial review; and partly because they have arisen in most countries after the trend towards centralization of governmental regulatory authority in the hands of the federal—as against local, state, and provincial—has asserted itself. To an increasing extent, there is less duplication here than division of authority so that local bodies take over primarily the residue functions which relate to purely local matters. There is, however, a contrary tendency to set up governmental regulatory bodies which have to do not with a single industry or set of narrowly related industries, but with business functions (e. g., securities and trading, surplus commodities, pure food and drug). This means that each business must face not one but a series of regulatory bodies. And at many points the functions and prerogatives of these latter are bound to duplicate and overlap each other.

the regulatory set-up [18]—thereby tending in many respects to further duplicate functions, staff, and facilities—of their own membership. Not uncommonly, as an interesting by-play, they, or their member associations, or the strategically placed corporations which shape their leading policies attempt to entice governmental staff to join their own payrolls at higher salaries.[19] But most significantly, they seek direct representation on committees, commissions, advisory bodies, and other governmental agencies which were either established at the outset for the specific purpose (or subsequently acquired the power) of determining in whole or in part the very policies which guide the administrative bodies themselves.

Thus the Federation of British Industries claimed before the outbreak of war to be directly represented on the Board of Trade Advisory Council and Council for Art and Industry, the War Office Technical Coördinating Committee on General Stores and Motor Transport Coördinating Committee, the Ministry of Health Joint Advisory Committee on River Pollution and the Town and Country Planning Advisory Committee, and the Ministry of Agriculture's Standing Committee on River Pollution. But this is only the beginning. It claimed that its representations before governmental bodies have resulted in adoption of its own plans for fiscal policy, tariff policy, imperial trade, commercial treaties.[20] There is scarcely a governmental committee or commission which affects its

[18] This is most readily shown in the departmentalization of the various *Spitzenverbände*, the range of the expanding committee and staff functions, the nature of the regional and functional groupings of membership, the content of regular reports to members in their official publications and annual congresses, etc. The same holds for many of their own member associations and certain of their larger member corporations. See the annual reports of the National Association of Manufacturers; the *Yearbook and Register of British Manufacturers*, put out by the Federation of British Industries; the speeches, and especially the organizational data given in the appendices, collected in the book of M. Rene P. Duchemin (President d'honneur de la Confédération Générale du Patronat Français), *Organisation syndicale Patronale en France;* and see also *Fascist Era*, the yearbook of the Fascist Confederation of Industrialists; and sketches by Dr. Horst Wagenführ of the Reichsverband der deutschen Industrie and the Verein Deutscher Maschinenbau Anstalten in his *Kartelle in Deutschland.*

[19] Probably one-half of the leading figures amongst the directorial, executive, and staff ranks of the leading *Spitzenverbände* have gone directly from governmental regulatory bodies to the firms and associations which they formerly regulated. Higher salaries are the common reason given. A careful study might reveal many others.

[20] See, in particular, the NAM pamphlet "Industry and Action."

Members' interests at any given point upon which it did not claim membership or influence of decisive importance. Since the outbreak of hostilities, under the system of war control bodies, this fusion has been rendered almost complete.

The British picture is not unusual but is typical for the liberal-capitalistic countries as a group.[21] But it becomes quickly altered—in some respects drastically—the instant monopoly and business coördinative drives move from a "liberal" to an "authoritarian" environment. As evidenced in Germany and Italy, though by somewhat different routes, the inauguration of totalitarianism results in a general overhauling of business machinery along the following lines: (1) "streamlining," that is, a considerable mass of overlapping and duplicate trade association, regional and national, and peak association machinery is cut away.[22] (2) Correlatively, the combination and cartel movement is greatly strengthened; large and increasing numbers of small concerns are eliminated; compulsory association membership becomes the rule. (3) The relationships between governmental committees and commissions are altered in several ways, but in general these relationships become functional instead of "fighting," coördinative instead of duplicating and overlapping, and "self-government" follows lines of managerial decentralization rather than principles of checks and balances between governmental and private authorities. The basis of the "efficiency" claims of all totalitarian systems is the cutting thorough and setting aside of conflicting machinery which has arisen (paradoxically, as a result of governmental "interference") to coördinate and simplify business itself, or to prevent the inefficient disposal of social resources according to the common formulae of "business as usual," or both. Finally, (4) the former "self-governing" bodies are more or less formally vested with legal or quasi-legal powers to formulate policy within the larger "totalitarian" directives, and to implement decisions with powers of enforcement.

[21] See the sources cited in footnote 18 above.

[22] This could readily be shown by following through in detail the change in any given line of industry or trade. But such "streamlining," coupled with other changes indicated above, may well mean in many cases quite new and greatly elaborated machinery. For example, unorganized trades will now be organized; unfederated will now be federated; relationships between and amongst central associations and their various functional and regional divsions will be handled by various combinations of compacts, *ad hoc* and permanent committees, and so on.

Great and far-reaching as many of these changes may be in detail, they are, however, fully and without important exception in line with preceding trends. This could be shown in great detail by tracing through the successive changes, for example, which led to the formation in 1917 of the Reichsverband der deutschen Industrie out of two bodies representing respectively the heavy and light manufacturing industries, and the steps taken to transform the resultant body in 1933 into the Reichsgruppe Industrie. Or, again, by those whereby the former General Confederation of Italian Industry was made over into the Fascist Confederation of Industrialists. Another example is offered in the changes which signalized the pretty complete overhauling of the Confédération Générale de la Production Française, following the famous Matignon Agreement in 1936, into the Confédération Générale du Patronat Français. The formal dissolution in late 1940 of this latter body, which was modeled more or less directly after the Fascist pattern in Italy, seems to have been preparatory to remodeling along more distinctly Nazi lines.

Whether traced along lines of structure, function, or authority, these changes would be found consistent with past trends. They represent a very considerable "tightening" up, to be sure, but even the more rigorous and authoritarian controls are consistent with past lines of growth. Still another check is provided by noting the nature of the changes these various associations and their *Spitzenverbände* undergo between so-called "emergency" and "normal" periods. Quite aside from the fact that it has now become customary to justify all "tightening" up by appeal to "emergency" conditions,[23] and that we have at least two major attempts to carry through far-reaching reorganization of business-governmental relationships in peacetimes—those of the NRA and the various British industrial reorganization schemes [24]—the ease with which

23 This is the case with all the various British industrial reorganization schemes such as those for railroads, cotton textiles, coal and steel, and with controls established under such laws as the Miller-Tydings, the Robinson-Patman, and the various state marketing and resale price maintenance laws. Much the same, of course, was true of the whole of the NRA and the AAA.

24 Not to mention a series of attempts made in practically every country in the world immediately following the great war to carry over wartime controls into

these transitions have been made between peace and war and back again to peace fully bears out the above contention, the main difference being that the binding sanctions are qualitatively quite different. In these respects, the Second World War has differed from the First in that the transition from peace to war is greatly facilitated by the much higher level of business organization, in which authorities, controls, and group objectives are more completely worked out along lines required for ready adaptation to war conditions. That this is so largely arises from the fact that peacetime endeavors in the major capitalistic countries to extend the network and expand the controls of business organization were almost without exception based upon former wartime experience.[25] Thus it comes about that it is precisely in war and emergency times that the dominance of big business in the councils of state comes most clearly to the fore. What was true of the United States in 1917–18, in the depression and the period of NRA, and in the National Defense efforts of 1940–41 can be duplicated in all other major capitalist countries. Mr. Knudsen, Edward Stettinius, and Bernard Baruch are paralleled by Mr. Ogura in Japan, Lord Beaverbrook in England, and Hermann Göring (himself a leading industrialist), Friedrich Flick, and their group in Germany.

Now the essence of the newer strategies of wartime controls—where the military arm is, in effect, regarded as merely the "cutting edge" of a belligerently mobilized industrial system taken as a whole—is authoritarian hierarchy with totalitarian coverage. Thus, since war controls represent an ever simpler transmutation from normal peacetime conditions, our third clue to the nature of evolving business bureaucracy lies in these factors. Let us examine them a bit more carefully.

---

peacetime conditions—one of the by-products of which was the formation of many of the *Spitzenverbände* themselves. Particularly interesting in this connection are the attempts made in the United States to formulate a national council out of the various "war advisory committees" established by leading trade associations during the war to represent business interests in the various war-control boards. An attempt to bring all these together into a single national organization, made at an Atlantic City convention in 1919, broke down. The plan, it seemed, was premature!

[25] This was especially true of NRA, largely an adaptation of Mr. Hoover's Trade Practice conventions, in turn based directly on war control ideas.

THE "SLANT" OF THE HIERARCHICAL OR "SCALAR" PRINCIPLE

So far as structure and control factors are concerned, trade associations and their *Spitzenverbände* tend to be modeled after the pattern of the typical large-scale corporation. The managerial hierarchy of command and subordination follows typically the "line" or "military" form of organization: any necessary breakdown in function and staff is so dovetailed into the "line" of authority as to take maximum advantage of expert counsel and whatever principles of decentralization of management may be appropriate in each separate case. Policy-making power lies typically in the directorial and managerial ranks, and is not subject to check from below. So far as concerns the lower reaches of the hierarchy of command and the labor that performs the functions which management directs, the system is completely authoritarian (antidemocratic); all duties and responsibilities are fixed from above except when counter-organization of labor or other organized special interest groups may be able to force concessions via governmental or direct-action pressure.

More recently, as has been outlined in numerous places,[26] management has succeeded in largely freeing itself from owner or investor control. Conversely, labor is increasingly able to make its voice heard and its power felt only so far as it operates under the protection of government. The trade union may be the power.that forces the government to act, but without government intervention the trade union finds itself increasingly unable effectively to make its influences felt or even to recruit its members. A first condition to trade-union bargaining power is favorable law. That is to say, even in labor relations organized business finds itself facing the government.

Free in large part of direct investor control,[27] managements which for one reason or another are primarily interested in executive and not in larger policy matters, may be able greatly to ration-

[26] See the works of such authors as Berle, Means, Bonbright, Gordon, and others, referred to in Chapter VII.

[27] Here again government takes the place of the disenfranchised. Something the equivalent of the Securities and Exchange Commission is now to be found in most capitalist countries.

alize productive operations where formerly such changes were in-
hibited by investor interest in higher returns.[28] But even where
this proves both possible and, from the point of view of management, desirable, management now largely swings free from all
direct controls other than those which may be imposed upon it by
governmental authority; this fact will and apparently does mean
that the executive and managerial end will be handled by paid
functionaries, the better to allow the leading figures within these
ranks to focus the massed power of their pendulous corporations
upon larger issues of policy. Business leadership not only acquires
political interests, but it turns to the political arena already backed
by enormous, fully mobilized, and easily focused power. There are
but few good modern parallels for this situation in the field of in-
ternal-pressure politics. For most apt comparison one must turn to
the massed and personally manipulable powers of ancient and
tribal armies of legionaries and retainers, or to the medieval baronry of the crusading knights.

So far as this picture holds, the appropriate medium for expressing, and the machinery for canalizing and focusing, the social and
political power of management is the trade association and its
Spitzenverbände. To the extent that paid functionaries in the hierarchy of management are enabled to handle matters on an authoritative but expert or "civil service" basis (because they have been
recruited from an especially trained and ideologically precondi-
tioned corps), to that extent will policy matters be the more completely funneled through supra-managerial apparatus organized
for this specific purpose. Such rationalization, simplification, and
centralization as may on occasion be attempted within these latter
bodies become, thus, merely problems of efficient organization [29]
of largely, if not primarily, political bodies.

[28] A number of railroad reorganizations (e. g., the New York, New Haven and
Hartford) have greatly improved operations, road, rolling stock, and service facilities which cannot possibly—except perhaps in the very long run—benefit stockholders. For all practical purposes the roads are run expertly, the compromise now being
not between owner-income interests and public service/demands—the ICC keeping
an ever watchful eye on affairs—but between career-management and public service,
the ICC now regarding prospective changes with a friendlier attitude.

[29] In many cases, perhaps making the rule and not the exceptions, career men run
associations, and much association activity seems a by-product of expansion of point-
less tasks and "services," bureaucratically overstaffed and incompetently run by

But the question of how far and in what ways rational organization of the productive properties underlying management, or the manipulative machinery lying over these directorial levels, may be affected by the new functional segregation is somewhat beside the point at present. It is doubtful if the run of recent improvements below the upper layers is as great as one might be led to suspect at first.[30] But the significant point is that trade associations and their *Spitzenverbände* are largely, if not in many cases exclusively, political-pressure bodies. This remains true even in those cases where trade associations act as coördinating bodies for cartels, or where they themselves have taken on cartel functions. The records are, of course, unsatisfactory, since here as elsewhere they leave next to no traces, such collusive practices as they may resort to proceeding by rules known from times immemorial within inner political party circles, and not by the etiquette of written statements and formal contracts.[31] Secrecy, long the essence of national diplomacy, becomes entirely natural and normal, as the *Spitzenverband* becomes a politically potent pressure group.

But the main concern of the supra-managerial business organizations is not, strictly speaking, economic. Even where it is so, the issues at stake are increasingly burdened with social, philosophical, and political problems. That this is true can readily be substantiated by any reader who will take the trouble to leaf through a few thousand pages of trade-association literature, or who can find time to sit in on a few hundred of their congresses and conventions. What he will find is that the issues relate predominately, at some remove or other, to known, felt, or feared challenges by labor or

---

functionaries whose main efforts are devoted to proving to a gullible membership that the completely or primarily useless is of overwhelming importance.

[30] See the records of plant reorganizations reproduced in the pages of the *Bulletin* of the International Management Institute (now defunct).

[31] Thus, when the author of the TNEC Monograph No. 18, *Trade Association Survey*, dealing with trade associations in the United States, finds little ground for the belief that trade associations have "engaged in collusive restraints of trade," he cites as proof not evidence, but the lack of it! Which is only to say that he has confused not only the nature of trade-association activity, but also the nature of such collusion and of its characteristic proofs. The evidence of NRA might have disabused the author, who was familiar with its practices, of this naïve interpretation. But if nothing else, he might have turned to a brief review of the last year's crop of antitrust indictments for proof that the very reverse was true. Political machines rarely keep vouchers or reduce understandings to the written form, as Lincoln Steffens was not the first to discover, nor Clarence Darrow (cf. his review of NRA) the last.

other groups—operating independently or through regular political channels—to the tenets underlying the capitalistic system as a whole.

As political-pressure bodies, the trade associations and their *Spitzenverbände* will be found responsible to their membership on the principle of representation, *de jure* or *de facto* according to property holdings and clique groupings. In practice, except perhaps for some of the associations representing smaller businesses,[32] clearly most of them are as closely controlled by a few of the business giants as the bulk of their underlying corporate properties are controlled by a minor fraction of the managerial and directorial personnel. That is to say, where the structure of organization and methods of control recognized in constitution and by-laws do not permit—which typically they do—centralized, self-perpetuating control, the *Realpolitik* of power and clique effects a like result. This picture is so well accepted in association circles throughout the world and is so typical and general as to seem clearly beyond dispute in point of fact.

Both above and below the level of corporate managerial circles, the "scalar chain" or principle of graduated hierarchical controls obtains. Leadership, so far as the respective underlying hierarchy of command and subordination is concerned, is typically self-appointed, self-perpetuating, and autocratic. In the submanagerial zones, this leadership impinges on the nonproperty interests of labor and the general public. But in the supra-managerial zones it bears largely, and in some respects exclusively, on business interests in general. Authority in both ranges from the top down, and responsibility from the bottom up. Below, authority coördinates the non- or but partially-property minded in an operative complex— policy being predetermined and given. Above, authority coördinates big and little business in a policy complex forged as a by-product of the *Realpolitik* practiced by their own self-appointed general staffs. The same individuals, the same groups and cliques, the same interests dominate in each sphere; in each the principle of

---

[32] Although the evidence seems to indicate clearly that many of the leading small businessmen's associations have been formed on the initiative of the large. This is the case with many of the British associations, and with the vast network of trade or "guild" associations which have sprung into existence in Japan over the past five years.

organization, relating as it does to policy issues, is that of an inherently undemocratic, authoritarian hierarchy. And in neither is it the property interest of the bulk of the corporate property holders which dominates the stage. Yet the issues are increasingly of a "system-defending" or ideological character which reach to the "roots of domination" in a capitalistically organized world.

THE CONTENT OF THE NEW OUTLOOK

Contrary to certain implications of current usage, "totalitarianism," like "bureaucracy," is not necessarily undesirable if it is taken to mean a social-psychological outlook possessing at once a coherent unifying philosophy and a general program of action which comprehend the totality of organized social life. In this sense, even democracy, as a theoretically coherent web of postulates, freedoms, and qualified restraints, is "totalitarian." But the question naturally arises as to what the aim and content of a general doctrinal and programmatic position may be, when it appears that its formulators are responsible neither to the general public nor even to the property interests upon whose sanctions their authoritative powers rest. And how understand—how, indeed, even begin to formulate—a program when it seems impossible to define the interests to be promoted?

The difficulty, however, is more apparent than real. The leading managerial and directorial figures within the inner business sancta are real, not fictitious people, and they are drawn from, or have been absorbed into, the upper layers of wealth and income whose stakes it is their function to defend.[33] Under current conditions, they are called upon to defend these general interests in an environment wherein the issues are increasingly so drawn as to appear in some sense or other to jeopardize the whole system of evolving status and special-class privilege whose mobilized resources they have acquired "emergency powers" to command. And for the opening struggle they have largely fought themselves free of the procedural and other forms of red tape imposed upon them by law— under the general business rule of "live and let live"—in a vast

[33] It is at this point that Burnham's *Managerial Revolution* flies off at a dangerous tangent and leads him to an analysis as misleading as it is superficially plausible.

political environment hostile to undue centralization of naked economic power. It cannot be forgotten that the world of relatively small-scale middle-class business of the not distant past, out of whose rich gleanings the great monopoly-oriented economic empires of the present gathered their first strengths, feared arbitrary political authority above all else. In limiting the state to laissez faire, they were careful to see that its functions were so defined as to make the state the specialized guardian of its own duty not to interfere as the tool of any hostile interest.

The history of government regulation of business has been primarily the history of attempts of small business to employ government to defend their interests against the encroachments of business monopolies,[34] and of the latter to wrest the initiative from the small.[35] The business giants, operating to an increasing extent in these matters through trade associations and their *Spitzenverbände,* seem to have found an effective means for neutralizing this opposition, and to be in a fair way to the achievement of a "unified" and "harmonious" outlook of the business world vis-a-vis labor and any other challenging interest.

Real conflicts of interests within the business world have not been eliminated by these means, but to some degree they have been coördinated. Such successes as the various *Spitzenverbände* seem to have achieved in their legislative and allied efforts in the several capitalistic countries seem to stem in large part from the fact that they have been able to act as though business were united in bringing their collective pressures to bear upon government. It holds as a corollary to this that the bitterest and most ruthless attacks will be made upon those businesses large or small which refuse to play the game according to the new rules. The more "self-government in business," the more quickly the "price cutter," the business "alien," or any other footloose tycoon will be brought to

[34] The vast and overwhelming bulk of complaints against the exercise of monopoly controls coming into the United States Department of Justice's Anti-Trust Division come, as Mr. Arnold has frequently pointed out, from business circles. The pressure for enactment of state and federal antitrust controls, as—for that matter—the bulk of the business regulatory machinery, emanates from similar circles.

[35] As, for example, in the bulk of the resale price maintenance laws, agricultural marketing-agreement enabling acts, etc., now to be found on the statute books of most capitalistic countries.

heel by any means at the disposal of the central direction. The more complete the authority and the more centralized the power to act, the more quickly and drastically such action will be taken.[36]

Thus, there slowly emerges an apparent single view, a seeming common cause, and appearance of a general business "harmony," the semblance of a certain common business social philosophy which takes on form and content step by step with the growth and expansion of the centralized influence of the great peak associations.[37] And in proportion as this seeming internal unification takes place in organized business, one finds slowly being evolved parallel ideas vis-à-vis all other interests which, however and by whichever route they may come in conflict with any given business or aspect of business control, have no alternative but to appear to challenge the business world as a whole. Given comprehensive organization —the common ideal of the trade association all over the world— this posture of affairs appears inevitable in the very nature of the case. If conflicting interests, as, for example, in the case of labor, are organized on an equally comprehensive basis, the effect will be thrown in much sharper relief. And it is an effect that has gradually become universally evident throughout the capitalistic world of the last half century.

How do the trade, employer, and business *Spitzenverbände* then proceed to meet challenges which they are led to interpret as in conflict with the tenets underlying the capitalistic world as such? By somewhat varying routes, organized business amongst the several capitalistic countries has arrived at pretty much a common set of solutions. For the sake of brevity, and because they recapitulate a part of what has been said above, these may be summarized as follows:

[36] Consequently, the ejection or strategic demotion from the central councils of a Hjalmar Schacht, a Herr Thyssen or a Robert Stewart, not to mention the Jews when the opportune moment comes, becomes thoroughly understandable and a matter of course. Whoever does not play according to the accepted rules will be thrown out, just as whoever is weak will be absorbed in the strategies that lead to business mergers, and their expulsion or absorption is proof not of the weakness but of the strength of organized business.

[37] Which does not mean, of course, that the old conflicts do not exist, but that in a certain sense they have been "domesticated." It is noteworthy that in the United States the growth of centralized business organization has been paralleled by both increasing concern over the fate of small business, and by its increased mortality (see the Prologue of the TNEC reports). In both Germany and Italy, the plight of little business, long before the outbreak of war, was becoming steadily worse.

1. *Control over popular organizations:* the company union is father to the idea of universal, comprehensive, all-inclusive business-controlled joint labor-employer membership federations, of which the German Labor Front and the Italian General Confederation of Labor [38] are the highest development to date. Similar ideas have run through the literature of American, French, and British business. An attempt was made to set up such a body in the United States in 1912; the Federation of British Industries was originally intended to include both labor and employers. The programs of De Mun, Harmel, and the French Social Catholic movement evolved similar ideas before the turn of the twentieth century [39]; the new French industrial reorganization plans follow similar lines. The ideas and patterns of the company union are applied wherever any other form of popular organization—of farmers, consumers, little businessmen, professionals, women—has struck root. The idea is everywhere and in all countries the same: mass organization centered around the ideologies of the upper business and social hierarchies and controlled by the self-appointed and self-perpetuating "natural" leaders from those ranks.

2. *The militarization of employer-employee relations:* by a reassertion of authority in the hands of the employer similar to that which obtains in the army. This can be read from all complaints in the literature of the *Spitzenverbände* and their subsidiary bodies when faced with effective labor protest, as in the events centered around the British General Strike in 1926, the movements of the French Popular Front centered in the Matignon Agreement of June, 1936, the rise of the CIO in the United States and complaints demanding modification of the National Labor Relations Board, and in the successes of German, Italian, and Japanese employers, scored on the initiation of Fascist-type systems. A corollary is the militarization of legislative (substitution of the "edict" for statute law) and judicial (through the procedures of martial law) powers, with the consequent disappearance of the line between civil and military, the discipline of war and peace. The regimen of the "unorganized" industrial plant such as that of Ford is here prototypal of objectives seen as desirable by spokesmen who may have power to suggest or act in the larger sphere.

3. *The evolution of a "harmony-of-all-interests" propaganda in which the employer appears as benevolent pater familias:* such was the blending which underlay the social legislation of Bismarck, the programs of De Mun and Du Pin in the French Social Catholic movement, the Papal Encyclicals of *Rerum Novarum* in 1891 and *Quadragesimo Anno* in 1931, the "Clerical Fascism" of Dollfuss and Schuschnigg in Austria and of Franco in Spain, the NRA and some

---

[38] Salvemini, *Under the Axe of Fascism,* Chapter VII.
[39] See above, pp. 58–66.

of the American New Deal Legislation, the Japanese National Harmonizing Movement, and, of course, the whole of "welfare capitalism." The employer as "patron" or "trustee" becomes the *beau idéal* of the business world. Correlatively the trustee concept still is applied in all other relationships of real or potential conflict between organized business and the general public. The parallel to "industrial relations" is "public relations," and this latter is growing by every known criterion of relative importance in a sort of geometric ratio to all other corporate publicity interests, both in the United States and abroad.[40] "Public relations" advances the concept of a natural "harmony" of interest between business and the public, business and the consumer, business and social and economic progress. The relationship is that of "trustee of the people's property and welfare." [41]

4. *The "educational emphasis" looks two ways:* towards "neutralizing" the hostile amongst adults, while engraining "loyal" staff and especially the younger generation "through the doctrine of the organization itself." "Neutralization" involves recognition, wherever the *Realpolitik* of strategy may determine, of trade unions and similar organizations; emphasis upon "cooperation" by promotion of labor-employer community activities; regional decentralization of plants; legal restraints upon the "abuse" of labor power; use of police power, strike breakers, espionage at need; the mobilization of the middle and professional classes into patriotic and other federations; [42] attacks on opposition leadership under the guise of attacking "racketeering"; encouragement of fear of "aliens," "fifth-columnists," and other menaces which encourage in turn emphasis upon group loyalties, patriotic sentiments; especial types of interest programs and propaganda for women, children, and the aged, etc. Conversely, education of the young calls for control over apprenticeship training; purge of school textbooks; vocational emphasis with belief in an eventual occupational stratification in which there is a one-to-one correspondence between economic station and presumptive I.Q.; [43] evolution of a system of rewards and punishments which

---

40 For example, the NAM public-relations program was first granted a small sum of money in 1934. By 1937 public-relations expenditures were larger than those for all purposes combined before 1934—a sum which was estimated, at commercial rates, to equal in that year around $36,000,000 for the whole United States. Since that year these expenditures have been probably doubled.

41 See Batchelor, *Profitable Public Relations. Bureaucracy and Trusteeship.* The Nazi motto, *Gemeinnutz geht vor Eigennutz,* carries the precise equivalent for German businessmen for the dictum, "A widespread, favorable attitude of mind is a first essential to effective trusteeship in big business. People must expect and assume that managers will look out for interests other than their own. Managers in turn will then attempt to live up to expectations." TNEC Monograph No. 11, p. 130.

42 See pp. 287–90.   43 See pp. 280–86.

turn on the axis of loyalty to the concern; the substitution of non-commercial for commercial incentives; of group and "social" for individual and personal incentives.

5. *The key to control is political:* executive authority and policy-forming power are concentrated in the same coöptatively renewed ranks, and these recognize that the key to power is twofold; (1) consolidation of all the "ins" in a solid, interest-conscious bloc; (2) a popular following, the key to which is alliance with any faction, movement, or party which has or may acquire popular following without disturbing the general social structure of command and subordination. This means compromise with the *nouveau puissant* as they are co-opted into the movement on all matters relating to "the take"—an old practice in relationships between political rings and powerful vested interests all over the world, but now generalized to entire national economics, and rationalized with an eye to sterilization of "take" knowledge and demand for participation below the upper ranks. And for these lower reaches, the evolving programs of the organized business world look to well-ordered, and especially trained and loyal cadres of hierarchically controlled employees over whom as "leaders" they have complete charge—as Gignoux of the Confédération Générale du Patronat Français expressed the matter— "not only of men but of souls."

6. *The new power complexes are inherently expansive:* two things are united in this reaching for political power. One is the tendency of all democratically irresponsible power aggregations to expand without limit. And the other is the fact that the "life styles" of the units which form the cells of the new power pyramids have each and all been dominated by a tendency to expand without limit—a fact with which all great business leaders have been thoroughly familiar and which has been traced at great length by Sombart and others. Given control or power decisively to influence the national state, imperial expansion is inevitable. The more or less rational combination of fully articulated systems of protection and privilege combined with imperial expansion, on the one hand, and the integrative pressures of a rationally articulated industrial technology, on the other, lead logically to the concept of the next largest politically omnicompetent and coherently organized imperial area, "great-space economics" (*Grossraumwirtschaften*).[44]

---

[44] All through the Godesberg and Munich discussions the Federation of British Industries was carrying on negotiations with the Reichsgruppe Industrie. "On March 16, the day after the fall of Prague, the Düsseldorf discussions culminated in the signature in London of an agreement between agents of the Federation of British Industries and the Reichsgruppe Industrie to 'replace destructive competition by constructive coöperation.' It contemplated the creation of a series of Anglo-German cartels." Frederick L. Schuman, *Night Over Europe*, p. 107. Similar conversations

"The soul of Amenhotep is higher than Orion, and it is united with the underworld"—so runs a melancholy passage from the ancient Egyptian "Book of the Dead." The roots of power of the several *Spitzenverbände* are intertwined in the sanctions of evolving imperial class status, but monopoly-oriented business which attempts to evade effective democratic restraints can dominate government only through control over the thinking processes of the mass of the people who dwell at the base of the social pyramid. "Dangerous thoughts," as the Japanese are so acutely aware, breed democratic heresies. Antidemocratic "totalitarianism" can triumph only through ultimate consolidation of its "authoritarianism" by the seizure of political controls. Every single step in the path which leads in our times to use of the expedients which spell ultimate resort to the coup d'état are now sufficiently well known to be recognizable at a glance. And nothing fundamental in history, program, structure of organization, or social outlook divides clearly the policies of the *Spitzenverbände* within the "totalitarian" countries from those of the liberal-capitalist states. Within Germany, Italy, Japan, and France these bodies made the critical decisions without which the final destruction of democracy could not have taken place.

Is it possible that the lesson will be learned elsewhere before it is too late?

---

were carried on between Japanese interests and the Federation of British Industries through a good deal of the crisis period when the Japanese took over Manchukuo. Nothing is to be found in the literature of the National Association of Manufacturers to indicate disapproval of the structure of controls effected through the machinery of German and Italian *Spitzenverbände*, though considerable sympathy is frequently expressed that these latter should be so closely controlled by the government—a sentiment, incidentally, which the leading figures on the inner business circles in the totalitarian countries rarely reciprocate. Yet the Germans thought of NRA in 1935 as the equivalent of what they had brought on themselves, and wondered not a little that there should be so much complaint among American businessmen against their own program of "self-government in business" (The Germans use the same term), which they themselves had clearly helped to shape and guide from its initial stages on—and which must, so these same persons argued, be surely seen as the inevitable pattern of the future if business and the capitalistic system are to survive in America as elsewhere.

BIBLIOGRAPHY

OFFICIAL AND SEMIOFFICIAL SOURCES

Annuario Statistico Italiano, Series 2, Vol. VII (1917–18).

Commerce, U.S. Dept. of. Special Agents Series: No. 98, "Commercial Organizations in France"; No. 102, "Commercial Organizations in the United Kingdom." Washington, D.C., 1915.

—— Bureau of Foreign and Domestic Commerce. Commercial and Industrial Organizations of the United States. Washington, D.C., 1931.

—— Bureau of Foreign and Domestic Commerce, Trade Association Section of the Marketing and Research Division. "High Lights of the NRA, Chart 3." Washington, D.C., July 10, 1934.

Congress of the United States, 75th Congress, 3d Session. Senate Document 173, "Message from the President of the United States, Transmitting Recommendations Relative to the Strengthening and Enforcement of Anti-Trust Laws."

Enqueteausschuss. Ausschuss zur Untersuchung der Erzeugungs- und Absatzbedingungen der deutschen Wirtschaft. 1926–31.

Fascist Confederation of Industrialists. *Fascist Era, Year XVII.*

Federal Trade Commission. Docket No. 2191, Dec. 30, 1937.

Federation of British Industries. Export Register. London, 1920.

—— "Industry and Action." Pamphlet, undated.

—— Committee on the Organisation of Industry. *Report,* June, 1935.

International Labor Office. Series A, No. 31, Freedom of Association. Geneva, 1927. Vols. II, IV.

—— Yearbook, 1936–37.

Jahrbuch der Berufsverbände im deutschen Reich. 1930.

Japan Year Book, 1938–39, 1939–40.

Labor, U.S. Dept. of. Bureau of Labor Statistics, Division of Industrial Relations. Bulletin, No. 364, "Characteristics of Company Unions." Washington, D.C., 1935.

Labour Research Dept. Studies in Labour and Capital, No. 5: "The Federation of British Industries." London, 1923.

La Follette Committee Reports. Parts 17, 18, 19, 20, 21, 45. Officially: U.S. Congress, Senate, Committee on Education and Labor, Violations of Free Speech and Assembly and Interference with Rights of Labor; Hearings before a Subcommittee on . . . S. Res. 266.

Liberal Industrial Inquiry. "Britain's Industrial Future." London, 1938.

Mitsubishi Economic Research Bureau. *Monthly Circular,* Dec., 1937.

National Association of Manufacturers. Annual Conventions, *Proceedings* (1903–29).

National Association of Manufacturers. "Industrial Self-Government." Series of bulletins, 1934.
—— "Industry and Action." Pamphlets.
—— Labor Relations Bulletin, July 20, 1936.
—— "The Nation's Industry Synchronized." Pamphlet, undated.
—— "The Nation's Industry—Organized." Pamphlet, 1923.
—— "Unit Thinking and Unit Acting on the Part of American Industry." Pamphlet, 1935.
—— "Women, Partners with Industry in the Economic and Social Advancement of the Nation." Brochure.
—— "You and Industry."
—— Committee on Employment Relations. Report, 1926.
National Economic and Social Planning Association, Planning Pamphlet No. 4, "Germany's Challenge to America's Defense." Washington, D.C., 1941.
National Industrial Conference Board. Industrial Standardization. New York, 1929.
—— 23d Annual Report, revised to Jan. 1, 1940.
National Resources Committee. The Structure of the American Economy. Washington, D.C., 1939.
Nye Committee on the Munitions Industry. 74th Congress, 2d Session, Report No. 944, Part 4.
Quadragesimo Anno. Papal Encyclical, 1931.
Resumé statistique de l'empire du Japon. Tokyo, 1912, 1924, 1930, 1934, 1936.
Temporary National Economic Committee. Hearings: Part 2, "Patents, Automobile Industry, Glass Container Industry"; Part 5-A.
—— "Investigation of Concentration of Economic Power." Pursuant to Public Resolution, No. 113, 75th Congress.
—— Monographs: No. 7, Measurement of the Social Performance of Business; No. 9, Taxation of Corporate Enterprise; No. 11, Bureaucracy and Trusteeship in Large Corporations; No. 17, Problems of Small Business; No. 18, Trade Association Survey; No. 21, Competition and Monopoly in American Industry; No. 24, Consumer Standards; No. 26, Economic Power and Political Pressures; No. 27, The Structure of Industry; No. 29, The Distribution of Ownership in the 200 Largest Non-Financial Corporations; No. 31, Patents and Free Enterprise; No. 34, Control of Unfair Competitive Trade Practices through Trade Practice Conference Procedure of the Federal Trade Commission; No. 35, Large Scale Organization in the Food Industries; No. 36, Reports of the Federal Trade Commission on the Natural Gas, Gas Pipe, Agricultural Implement, Machinery, and Motor Vehicle Industries; No. 39, Control of the Petroleum Industry by Major Oil Companies; No. 43, The Motion Picture Industry.

GENERAL WORKS

Allen, George C. "The Concentration of Economic Control in Japan." *Economic Journal*, XLVII (June, 1937), 271–86.
—— Japan; the Hungry Guest. London, 1938.
—— Modern Japan and Its Problems. London, 1928.
Arnold, Thurman W. Address before the Denver Bar Association, May 15, 1939. Mimeographed release, U.S. Dept. of Justice.
—— Address before the National Association of Purchasing Agents, May 22, 1939.
—— "The Anti-Trust Laws, Their Past and Future." Address over the Columbia Broadcasting System, Aug. 19, 1939. Released by the Temporary National Economic Committee.
—— Bottlenecks of Business. New York, 1940.
Asahi, Isoshi. The Economic Strength of Japan. Tokyo, 1939.
Batchelor, Bronson. Profitable Public Relations. New York, 1938.
Beckerath, Herbert von. Modern Industrial Organization. Trans. R. Newcomb and F. Krebs; Introduction by F. W. Taussig. New York, 1933.
Berle, Adolph A., Jr., and Gardiner C. Means. The Modern Corporation and Private Property. New York, 1933.
Bezard-Falgas, Pierre. Les Syndicats patronaux de l'industrie métallurgique en France. Paris, 1922.
Bonbright, James C., and Gardiner C. Means. The Holding Company, Its Public Significance and Its Regulation. New York, 1932.
Bonn, M. J. Das Schicksal des deutschen Kapitalismus. 1931.
Bonnett, Clarence E. Employers' Associations in the United States. New York, 1922.
Boyle, John, Jr. "Corporation Patent Holdings." *Journal of the Patent Office Society*, XIX (Sept., 1937), No. 9.
Brady, Robert A. The Rationalization Movement in German Industry. Berkeley, Calif., 1933.
—— The Spirit and Structure of German Fascism. New York, 1937.
Brandeis, Louis D. The Curse of Bigness. New York, 1934.
Brandt, Karl. "Junkers to the Fore Again." *Foreign Affairs*, XIV (Oct., 1935), 120–34.
Bratter, Herbert M. "The Role of Subsidies in Japan's Economic Development." *Pacific Affairs*, IV (May, 1931), 377–93.
Bruck, W. F. Social and Economic History of Germany from Wilhelm II to Hitler, 1888–1938. Oxford and New York, 1938.
Buchez, Philip. Essai d'un traité complet de philosophie du point de vue du catholicisme et du progrès. Paris, 1838–40.
Burnham, James. The Managerial Revolution. New York, 1941.
Burns, Arthur R. The Decline of Competition. New York, 1936.

Byas, Hugh. The Japanese Enemy, His Power and His Vulnerability. New York, 1942.
—— "Japan's Censors Aspire to 'Thought Control.'" New York Times, April 18, 1937.
—— "Japan's Fascist March." New York Times, Dec. 15, 1940.
Callman, Rudolf. Das deutsche Kartellrecht. Berlin, 1934.
Carrel, Alexis. Man the Unknown. New York, 1935.
"Cartelisation of England, The." Economist (London), March 18, 1939.
Chamberlain, Houston Stewart. Foundations of the Nineteenth Century. New York, 1911.
Chamberlin, Edward H. The Theory of Monopolistic Competition. Cambridge, Mass., 1933.
Chamberlin, William H. Japan over Asia. Boston, 1937.
"Check on Production, A." Economist (London), June 15, 1940.
Clark, J. M. "Towards a Concept of Workable Competition." American Economic Review, XXX (June, 1940).
Comité de Prévoyance et d'Action Sociale. Le Rôle exact des délégués. Paris, 1937.
Corbin, John. The Return of the Middle Classes. New York, 1922.
Corradini, E. Il volere d'Italia. Naples, 1911.
Crosser, Paul K. Ideologies and American Labor. New York, 1941.
Darré, R. W. Neuadel aus Blut und Boden. Munich, 1939.
Davies, Ernest. National Capitalism. London, 1939.
Dobb, Maurice. Capitalist Enterprise and Social Progress. London, 1925.
Duchemin, René P. Organisation syndicale patronale en France. Paris, 1940.
—— "Sur l'Accord Matignon." Revue de Paris, Feb. 1, 1937.
Dutt, Palme. Fascism and Social Revolution. London, 1934.
Ebenstein, William. Fascist Italy. New York, 1939.
"Economic Front, The." Economist (London), Dec. 9, 1939.
Edwards, Corwin D. "The New Anti-Trust Procedure as Illustrated in the Construction Industry." Public Policy, II (1941), 321–40.
—— "Trade Barriers Created by Business." Indiana Law Journal, Dec., 1940, pp. 169–91.
Einzig, Paul. "Hitler's 'New Order' in Theory and Practice." Economic Journal, LI, No. 201, April, 1941.
"Employers' Organisations in France." International Labour Review, July, 1927, pp. 50–77.
Engelbrecht, Helmuth C., and F. C. Hanighen. Merchants of Death. New York, 1934.
Fascist Confederation of Industrialists. Fascist Era, Year XVII.
"Federation of British Industry." Engineer (London), Aug. 11, 1916.
Felt, D. E. In American Industries, June, 1916, p. 15.

Florinsky, Michael T. Fascism and National Socialism. New York, 1936.

Fortune. Special Japan Issue, Sept., 1936.

Franck, Louis R. Les Etapes de l'économie fasciste italienne. Paris, 1939.

Frankfurter Zeitung. Monthly Supplement, "Die Wirtschaftkurve."

Fryer, Douglas, and E. J. Sparling. "Intelligence and Occupational Adjustment." *Occupations—the Vocational Guidance Magazine,* June, 1934, pp. 55–63.

Fujihara, Ginjiro. The Spirit of Japanese Industry. Tokyo, 1936.

George, Henry. The Condition of Labor, an Open Letter to Pope Leo XIII. New York, 1891.

Gide, Charles, and Charles Rist. History of Economic Doctrines from the Time of the Physiocrats to the Present Day. Boston, 1915.

Gignoux, C. J. Patrons, soyez des patrons! Paris, 1937.

Gordon, Robert A. "Ownership by Management and Control Groups in the Large Corporation." *Quarterly Journal of Economics,* May, 1938.

Gorgolini, Pietro. The Fascist Movement in Italian Life. Boston and London, 1923.

Gorman, George. "Japan's Three Principles." *Oriental Economist,* March, 1940.

Grant, Madison. The Passing of the Great Race. New York, 1916.

Greaves, Harold R. Reactionary England. London, 1936.

Grether, Ewald T. Price Control under Fair Trade Legislation. New York, 1939.

Guérin, Daniel. Fascism and Big Business. New York, 1939.

Hahn, Karl. Die Industrielisierung Japans. Giessen, 1932.

Hammond, John L., and Barbara Hammond. The Town Labourer, 1760–1832. London, 1917; reissue, New York and London, 1933.

Handwörterbuch der Staatswissenschaft. Jena, 1928.

Haxey, Simon. Tory M. P. London, 1939. (Also published as England's Money Lords: Tory M. P. New York, 1939.)

Heckscher, Eli F. Mercantilism. New York and London, 1935.

Henderson, Leon J., and others. "The Effects of Social Environment." In Papers on the Science of Administration, ed. Gulick and Urwick. New York, 1937.

Hersey, Rexford B. Seele und Gefühl des Arbeiter, Psychologie des Menschenführung. Leipzig, 1935.

Hicks, John R. The Theory of Wages. London, 1932.

Higuchi, Hirose. In *Japan Times Weekly and Trans-Pacific,* March 27, 1941.

Hoffman, Ross J. S. Great Britain and the German Trade Rivalry, 1875–1914. Philadelphia, 1933.

Hopkinson, Austin. Religio Militis. London, 1927.

Huxley, Aldous. Brave New World. New York, 1932.
Italian Library of Information. The Organization of Production and the Syndical Corporative System. New York, 1941.
Iwasaki, Uichi. The Working Forces in Japanese Politics. New York, 1921.
Japan Economic Federation. *East Asia Economic News* (monthly).
"Joint Industrial Councils in Great Britain." *International Labour Review,* Dec., 1921, pp. 563–78.
Jordan, Virgil. "The Economic Outlook." American Management Association, Personnel Series, No. 29. 1937.
Kane, Harnett T. Louisiana Hayride; the American Rehearsal for Dictatorship, 1928–1940. New York, 1941.
Kawai, Eijiro. "Neue politische Kräfte des wirtschaftlichen Aufbaues." *Weltwirtschaftliches Archiv,* XLVI (July, 1937).
Keiser, Günter. "Der jungste Konzentrations prozess." *Die Wirtschafts-Kurve,* II (1939), 135–56, 214–34.
Keynes, John M. The End of Laissez-Faire. London, 1926.
—— The General Theory of Employment, Interest and Money. New York and London, 1936.
—— and Kingsley-Martin. "Democracy and Efficiency." *New Statesman and Nation,* Jan. 28, 1939.
Kolnai, Aurel. The War against the West. New York, 1938.
Kraus, Johannes B. "Wirtschaftsgesinnung und völkisch-politische Grundbedingungen als Voraussetzungen des japanischen Industrielisierungsprozessen." *Weltwirtschaftliches Archiv,* XLVI (July, 1937), 45–61.
Krause, A. B. Organisation von Arbeit und Wirtschaft. Berlin, 1935.
"Kriegswirtschaftslehre und Kriegswirtschaftspolitik." Handwörterbuch der Staatswissenschaft. 4th ed. (Jena, 1928), V, 984–1022.
Krupp Company, Essen, Germany. Führer durch die Essener Wohnsiedlungen der Firma Krupp. 1930.
Lamennais, Abbé de. La Question du travail. 1848.
Langsam, Walter C., and J. M. Eagan. Documents and Readings in the History of Europe since 1918. Chicago, 1939.
Lapergue, Jacques. Les Syndicats de producteurs en France. Paris, 1925.
Launay, Louis. De Wendel. Vaucresson, 1938.
Lawaczek, F. Technik und Wirtschaft im Dritten Reich. Munich, 1932.
Lederer, Emil, and Emy Lederer-Seidler. Japan in Transition. New Haven, Conn., 1938.
Levy, Hermann. Industrial Germany, a Study of Its Monopoly Organisations and Their Control by the State. Cambridge, England, 1935.
—— Monopolies, Cartels and Trusts in British Industry. 2d ed., New York and London, 1927.
Ley, Robert. "New Forms of Community Work." Herausgegeben vom

Reichsarteits- und Reichswirtschaftsrat. Berlin, 1935.

Liefmann, Robert. Beteiligunge und finanzierungs Gesellschaften. Jena, 1921.

Lisani, Gaetano. La crisi sociale da Cristo a Mussolini. Undated.

Loewenstein, Karl. "Law in the Third Reich." *Yale Law Journal*, XLV (March, 1936), 779–815.

Lucas, Arthur F. Industrial Reconstruction and the Control of Competition. New York and London, 1937.

Lundberg, Ferdinand. America's 60 Families. New York, 1937.

Lyon, Leverett S., and others. The National Recovery Administration. Washington, D.C., 1935.

McCrary, Alvin J. "Another View of National Incorporation Needs." *American Industries*, Oct. 1, 1904.

Marktordnungsgrundsätze der Reichsgruppe Industrie. Undated.

Mayo, Elton. The Human Problems of an Industrial Civilization. New York, 1933.

Metzner, Max. Kartelle und Kartellpolitik. Berlin, 1926.

Michels, Robert. Italien von Heute. Leipzig, 1930.

Middleton, P. Harvey. "Great Britain's Loud Speaker." *American Industries*, Nov., 1924.

Miles, George H. Problem of Incentives in Industry. London, 1932.

Mill, John Stuart. Principles of Political Economy. Ashley ed., 1909.

Miller, Oskar von. Ausführungen des Sachverständigen Dr. Oskar von Miller über die derzeit wichtigsten Fragen der Elektrizitätwirtschaft.

—— Gutachten uber die Reichselektrizitätsversorgung. Berlin, 1930.

Moon, Parker Thomas. The Labor Problem and the Social Catholic Movement in France. New York, 1921.

Mooney, James D., and Alan C. Reiley. Onward Industry! the Principles of Organization and Their Significance to Modern Industry. New York, 1931.

Moulton, Harold G., and J. Ko. Japan, an Economic and Financial Appraisal. Washington, D.C., 1931.

Mullen, W. H. "Diamond as Market Pattern." *Printer's Ink*, Feb. 6, 1936, pp. 66–70.

Mullensiefen, Heinz. Freiheit und Bindung in der geordneten Wirtschaft. 1939.

—— Das neue Kartell-, Zwangskartell- und Preisüberwachungsrecht. 1934.

—— Von der Kartellpolitik zur Marktordnung und Preisüberwachung. Berlin, 1935.

Mussolini, Benito. The Corporate State. Florence, 1936. (Also available as Four Speeches on the Corporate State. New York, 1935.)

Narasaki, Toshio. "Oriental Great Economic Circle and Transportation Policy." *East Asia Economic News*, Jan., 1941.

Nasu, Shiroshi. "Ziele und Ausrichtung der japanischen Agrarpolitik in der Gegenwart." *Weltwirtschaftliches Archiv*, XLVI (July, 1937), 157–84.

Neumann, Franz. Behemoth: the Structure and Practice of National Socialism. New York, 1942.

"New Feudalism, The." *Economist* (London), April 2, 1938.

Newman, Joseph. Goodbye Japan. New York, 1942.

Nitobe, Inazo. Bushido, the Soul of Japan. Philadelphia, 1900.

O'Conroy, Taid. The Menace of Japan. New York, 1934.

Ogburn, William F., and William Jaffé. The Economic Development of Post-War France. New York, 1929.

Orchard, John E., and Dorothy Orchard. Japan's Economic Position; the Progress of Industrialization. New York, 1930.

"Organ for Spiritual Drive Favored." *Japan Times and Mail*, Aug. 3, 1938.

Otsuka, I. "Characteristic Features of Japanese Small Industries and Policies for Their Development." *Kyoto University Economic Review*, Oct. 1939.

Parrington, Vernon L. Main Currents in American Thought. New York, 1939.

Parry, David M. "The Scarlet Empire." Serialized in *American Industries*, 1913.

Pfennig, Andreas. "Das Eliten-Problem in seiner Bedeutung für den Kulturbereich der Wirtschaft." *Zeitschrift für die gesamte Staatswissenschaft*, Vol. 99 (1939).

Philip, P. J. "Blum Grapples with the 200 Families." New York *Times*, June 14, 1936.

Pitigliani, Fausto. The Italian Corporative State. London, 1933.

Pitkin, Walter B. Let's Get What We Want. New York, 1935.

Pribram, Karl. Cartel Problems. Washington, D.C., 1935.

"Retailers' Front." *Economist* (London), Feb. 15, 1941, pp. 206–7.

Robinson, Joan. The Economics of Imperfect Competition. New York and London, 1933.

—— Essays in the Theory of Employment. New York and London, 1937.

Rockefeller, John D., Jr. The Personal Relation in Industry. New York, 1923.

Roethlisberger, F. J., and W. J. Dickson. Management and the Worker; Technical vs. Social Organization in an Industrial Plant. Boston, 1934.

Rossi, Angelo. The Rise of Italian Fascism, 1918–1922. London, 1938.

Royama, Masamachi. "Die wirtschaftsrechtliche Struktur als Grundlage des japanische Wirtschaftsaufschwungs." *Weltwirtschaftliches Archiv*, XLVI (July, 1937), 79–92.

Ruhle, Fritz. "Kartellpolitik und Weltbewerbeordnung." *Zeitschrift für Betriebswirtschaft* (1938), pp. 337–49.

Russell, Oland D. The House of Mitsui. Boston, 1939.

Salvemini, Gaetano. Under the Axe of Fascism. New York, 1936.

Schalldach, Elisabeth. Rationalisierungsmassnahmen der Nachinflationszeit im Urteil der deutschen freien Gewerkschaften. Jena, 1930.

Schmidt, Carl T. The Corporate State in Action. New York, 1939.

—— "Joint-Stock Enterprises in Italy." *American Economic Review*, XXX (March, 1940).

—— The Plough and the Sword. New York, 1938.

Schuman, Frederick L. Night over Europe; the Diplomacy of Nemesis, 1939–40. New York, 1941.

Schumpeter, Joseph. Business Cycles. New York, 1939.

Seager, Henry R., and Charles A. Gulick. Trust and Corporation Problems. New York, 1929.

Seldes, George. Sawdust Caesar; the Untold History of Mussolini and Fascism. New York, 1935.

Smith, Neil Skene. "Japan's Business Families." *Economist* (London), June 18, 1938, pp. 651–56.

Sombart, Werner. Der moderne Kapitalismus. 2 vols., Leipzig, 1902; 4th ed., 3 vols., Munich, 1921–27.

Sprague, Jesse R. High Pressure. New York, 1938.

Stoddard, Lothrop. "The Common People's Union." *World's Work*, XXXIX (Nov., 1919), No. 1.

Sturgess, Kenneth. American Chambers of Commerce. New York, 1915.

Suhr, Otto. "Familientradition im Maschinenbau." *Zeitschrift fur Betriebswirtschaft*, Feb., 1939.

Sweezy, Maxine Yaple. "Distribution of Wealth and Income under the Nazis." *Review of Economic Statistics*, XXI (Nov., 1939), 178–84.

Takata, Yasuma. "Kulturelle und geistige Voraussetzungen fur Japans Aufstieg." *Weltwirtschaftliches Archiv*, XLVI (July, 1937), 1–13.

Takeichiro, Moriyama. "Rescuing Radicals by Law." *Contemporary Japan*, Sept., 1937.

Tanin, O., and E. Yohan. Militarism and Fascism in Japan. London, 1934.

Tarbell, Ida M. History of the Standard Oil Company. New York, 1904.

Tarle, Antoine de. L'Organisation professionelle patronale en France." *Revue des Deux Mondes*, March, 1925, pp. 177–96.

Tarnow, Fritz. Warum arm sein? Berlin, 1929.

Taylor, Albion Guilford. Labor Policies of the National Association of Manufacturers. University of Illinois Studies in the Social Sciences. Urbana, Ill., 1928.

Thresher, M. B. In *Oriental Affairs*, July, 1940.

Tolischus, Otto. "Japan to Keep Thought Offenders Locked Up so Duty of Conversion Can Be Carried Out." New York *Times*, May 16, 1941.

Toulmin, H. A. Trade Agreements and the Anti-Trust Laws; Including Forms and an Analysis of the Robinson-Patman Act. Cincinnati, 1937.

Twentieth Century Fund. Big Business, Its Growth and Its Place. New York, 1937.

Van Kleeck, Mary. Creative America. New York, 1936.

Varga, E., and L. Mendelsohn, eds. New Data for V. I. Lenin's "Imperialism: the Highest Stage of Capitalism." New York, 1938.

Veblen, Thorstein. Absentee Ownership and Business Enterprise in Recent Times. New York, 1923.

—— Engineers and the Price System. New York, 1921.

—— Essays in Our Changing Order. New York, 1934.

—— Imperial Germany and the Industrial Revolution. New York, 1915.

—— The Theory of the Leisure Class. New York, 1899.

Villey, Etienne. L'Organisation professionelle des employeurs dans l'industrie française. Paris, 1923.

Vlastos, Gregory. In *Philosophical Review*, May, 1941.

Vollweiler, Helmut. Der Staats- und Wirtschaftsaufbau im Faschistischen Italien. Wurzburg-Aumühle, 1939.

Wagenführ, Horst. Kartelle in Deutschland. Nürnberg, 1931.

Watkins, Myron. "The Economic Implications of Unfair Competition." *Iowa Law Review*, Jan., 1936.

Webb, Sidney, and Beatrice Webb. The History of Trade Unionism. Rev. ed., New York, 1920.

Weber, Max. Grundriss der Sozialökonomik. 1925.

Wiedenfeld, Kurt. Kapitalismus und Beamtentum: Produzententum und Konsumententum in der Weltmarkt-Wirtschaft. 1932.

Wolfe, Archibald J. Commercial Organizations in France. U.S. Dept. of Commerce, Special Agents Series, No. 98. Washington, D.C. 1915.

—— Commercial Organizations in the United Kingdom. U.S. Dept. of Commerce, Special Agents Series, No. 108. Washington, D.C., 1915.

—— "Employers' Organisations in France." *International Labour Review*, July, 1929.

Woytinsky, Wladimir. Die Welt in Zahlen. Berlin, 1926.

Yanaga, Chitoshi. In *Pacific Affairs*, June, 1940.

INDEX